49.9 S
75 I

Object-Oriented Simulation with Hierarchical, Modular Models
Intelligent Agents and Endomorphic Systems

Object-Oriented Simulation with Hierarchical, Modular Models
Intelligent Agents and Endomorphic Systems

Bernard P. Zeigler

Artificial Intelligence and Simulation Group
Department of Electrical and Computer Engineering
University of Arizona
Tucson, Arizona

ACADEMIC PRESS, INC.
Harcourt Brace Jovanovich, Publishers

Boston   San Diego   New York
London   Sydney   Tokyo   Toronto

This book is printed on acid-free paper. ∞

Copyright © 1990 by Academic Press, Inc.
All rights reserved.
No part of this publication may be reproduced or
transmitted in any form or by any means, electronic
or mechanical, including photocopy, recording, or
any information storage and retrieval system, without
permission in writing from the publisher.

ACADEMIC PRESS, INC.
1250 Sixth Avenue, San Diego, CA 92101

United Kingdom Edition published by
ACADEMIC PRESS LIMITED
24–28 Oval Road, London NW1 7DX

Library of Congress Cataloging-in-Publication Data

Zeigler, Bernard P.
  Object-oriented simulation with hierarchical, modular models:
intelligent agents and endomorphic systems / Bernard P. Zeigler.
     p.   cm.
  Includes bibliographical references (p.).
  ISBN 0-12-778452-7 (alk. paper)
    1. Digital computer simulation.   2. Artificial intelligence.
3. Object-oriented programming.   I. Title.
QA76.9.C65Z435   1990
003.3—dc20   89-18569
                                                                             CIP

Printed in the United States of America

    91 92 93 9 8 7 6 5 4 3 2

Contents

Preface   xiii

1 DIMENSIONS OF KNOWLEDGE REPRESENTATION IN SIMULATION ENVIRONMENTS   **1**
    1.1 Introduction 1
    1.2 Knowledge Representation Schemes and Formalisms . 2
    1.3 Simulation Model Specification Formalisms 3
    1.4 AI Knowledge Representation Schemes 3
    1.5 Representation and Knowledge 5
    1.6 System-theoretic Representation 7
    1.7 Modular, Hierarchical Models and Object-Oriented Paradigms Contrasted 8
    1.8 Framework for Knowledge Representation in Simulation 10
    1.9 What Kinds of Modelling and Simulation Knowledge Are There? 11
    1.10 Endomorphic Models, Simulations, and Agents 15

2 BASICS   **17**
    2.1 Object-Oriented Programming Concepts 17
    2.2 The System Entity Structure/Model Base 26
    2.3 Independent Testability 27
    2.4 Artificial Worlds Example 32
    2.5 SES Pruning and Model Synthesis 37

CONTENTS

3 DEVS FORMALISM AND DEVS-SCHEME   **41**
    3.1   Discrete Event Dynamic Systems 41
    3.2   Brief Review of the DEVS Formalism 44
    3.3   Basic Models 48
    3.4   Coupled Models 55
    3.5   DEVS-Scheme Simulation Environment 58

4 ATOMIC-MODELS: SIMPLE PROCESSOR EXAMPLE   **69**
    4.1   Performance of Simple Architectures 70
    4.2   A Simple Processor Model 72
    4.3   Normal Form Atomic Model Specification 75
    4.4   DEVS-Scheme Atomic Model Implementation of Simple Processor 77
    4.5   Simulation of Atomic Models 79
    4.6   Stand-alone Testing of an Atomic Model 82
    4.7   Simple Processor with Buffering and Random Processing Times 88

5 DIGRAPH-MODELS AND EXPERIMENTAL FRAMES   **89**
    5.1   Experimental Frame for Simple Computer Architectures 90
    5.2   Development of Digraph-Models 94
    5.3   Co-ordinator of Coupled-Models 105
    5.4   Applicability of Frames to Models: Model Instrumentation 112

6 A MODEL BASE FOR SIMPLE MULTI-COMPUTER ARCHITECTURES   **117**
    6.1   Co-ordinators and Architectures 118
    6.2   Testing the Architectures 141

7 SYSTEM ENTITY STRUCTURES   **145**
    7.1   System Entity Structure Definitions and Axioms . . . 146
    7.2   Using the System Entity Structure in DEVS-Scheme . 149

CONTENTS

    7.3 System Entity Structure Organization of Model Bases 155
    7.4 Operations on Hierarchical Model Structures: Flatting and Deepening 165

8 ADVANCED DEVS CONCEPTS AND KERNEL-MODELS   169
    8.1 More Advanced Processor Models 169
    8.2 Kernel-Models: Homogeneous Structures 179
    8.3 Example: Parallel Processor Broadcast Architecture . 183
    8.4 Methods Make-new and Make-class 190
    8.5 System Entity Structure Representation of Kernel Models 192
    8.6 Multilayered Models and Distributed Experimental Frames 200

9 RULE-BASED SPECIFICATION OF ATOMIC-MODELS   205
    9.1 Activities as Rules 205
    9.2 Class Forward-Models 210
    9.3 Inheritance and Specialization 216
    9.4 Specialization and Multiple Entities 229
    9.5 DEVS-Scheme Methodology Reviewed 231

10 A ROBOT-MANAGED LABORATORY OF THE FUTURE   233
    10.1 Multilevel Hierarchical Robot Model 235
    10.2 Space Management for Mobile Components 238
    10.3 Robot Cognition System 239
    10.4 Robot-Managed Laboratory Model 247

11 ENDOMORPHY: MODELS WITHIN INTELLIGENT AGENTS   249
    11.1 Approach to Endomorphy: Multifacetted Modelling Methodology 252
    11.2 Process Laboratory Model 254

- 11.3 Robot Models: Designing Model-Plan Units 256
- 11.4 DEVS Representation of Dynamic Systems 258
- 11.5 Obtaining the Characteristic Functions of the DEVS Model 262
- 11.6 Robot Fluid Handling MPUs 264
- 11.7 Table-Models: Deriving Internal Models from External Models 267
- 11.8 Windows in Table-Models: Parameter Sensitivity Analysis 272

12 ENDOMORPHY: MODEL USAGE WITHIN INTELLIGENT AGENTS   275

- 12.1 Event-Based Control 275
- 12.2 Using DEVS Models of Processes to Construct Event-Based Control Models 279
- 12.3 Introspection and Super-Simulation 285
- 12.4 Table-Models: Command Sequence Planning 287
- 12.5 Breakdown Diagnosis 290
- 12.6 Testing MPU Designs 292
- 12.7 Summary: Methodology for Event-Based Control ... 292

13 MODEL BASE MANAGEMENT AND ENDOMORPHIC SYSTEMS   299

- 13.1 Reuse of Pruned Entity Structures 300
- 13.2 Hierarchical Reuse of PES Versions 303
- 13.3 Partitioned System Entity Structures 304
- 13.4 Context Sensitive Pruning 305
- 13.5 Model Coherence and Context Sensitive Constraint Rules 307
- 13.6 Model Bases in Endomorphic Systems and Intelligent Agents 311
- 13.7 Minsky's Views on Models and Knowledge 316

14 DEVS-SCHEME IN THE LARGER SCHEME OF THINGS 325
14.1 Layers of DEVS-Scheme 326
14.2 Other Properties, Other Views 334

15 EPILOGUE: THE CHALLENGE OF HIGH AUTONOMY SYSTEMS 347

A ADVANCED CONCEPTS AND FACILITIES 351
A.1 Continuous Model Extensions to DEVS-Scheme 351
A.2 Simulation of Multi-formalism Non-homogeneous Networks 353
A.3 Distributed Simulation of DEVS Models 354
A.4 Automated Hierarchical Model Simplification 356
A.5 Variable Structure Models 358
A.6 Using Object-Oriented Concepts to Support Extensibility of Layer 1 with Respect to Layer 2 . . . 360
A.7 Converting Non-modular to Modular Form 361

B DEVS AND GSMP: SOME RELATIONS 363
B.1 Some Simple Behaviors of DEVS 364
B.2 Proof that the DEVS Behaviors Require Uncountable State Sets 365
B.3 Expressing GSMP within DEVS 366

Bibliography 369

Index 387

I am not only located in space and in time and in personal relationships. I am also located in a world of how things operate ... I live ... in a world of reasonably stable relationships, a world of "ifs" and "thens", of "if I do this, then that will happen".

What I have been talking about is knowledge. Knowledge, perhaps, is not a good word for this. Perhaps one would rather say my "Image" of the world ... It is my Image that largely governs my behavior.

... This means in all probability that (the salamander's) image does not include a self-image. It is aware of some sort of universe around it. It interprets the messages which come to its sense organs, as for instance, food out there toward which it will run ... It does not, however, see its legs as performing those running functions. The higher mammal on the other hand is capable of retraining its lower nervous center to conform to the image which it has of itself.

— Kenneth E. Boulding*

*Boulding, K.E., The Image: Knowledge in Life and Society, ©1956, The University of Michigan Press, Ann Arbor, MI.

PREFACE

Why this book?

This book shows how the concepts of multifacetted modelling methodology, developed in *Multifacetted Modelling and Discrete Event Simulation*, (Academic Press, 1984), are implemented in the DEVS-Scheme modelling and simulation environment. The result is a practical step toward treating models as knowledge — chunkable, inspectable, archivable, and reusable. Since model-making is patently an activity of intelligent agents, the latter part of the book applies the DEVS-Scheme environment to modelling artificial intelligent agents. A new concept of *endomorphism* emerges to characterize the use of self-embedded models, including models of self.

To reach a broad audience, the style of presentation is informal, differing from that of the *Multifacetted* book and its predecessor, *Theory of Modelling and Simulation* (Wiley, 1976; reissued by Krieger, 1987). A more rigorous basis for the developments discussed here is available in these two sources.

The DEVS-Scheme environment will interest simulation theorists and practitioners because of its fundamental use of the *object-oriented paradigm*. More generally, people concerned with building intelligent, autonomous systems (including researchers in artificial intelligence (AI), systems engineering, computer science and engineering, and operations research) should have simulation at their fingertips. They will find the concepts of reusable, multifacetted, multi-abstraction, model bases and endomorphic systems particularly interesting.

What is DEVS-Scheme?

Discrete event simulation and AI knowledge representation schemes form a powerful combination, called *knowledge-based simulation*, for studying intelligent systems in a realistic manner. DEVS-Scheme is a knowledge-based simulation environment for modelling and design that facilitates construction of families of models in a form easily reusable by retrieval from a model base.

In contrast to other knowledge based simulation systems, DEVS-Scheme is based on the *DEVS formalism*, a theoretically well-grounded means of expressing hierarchical, modular discrete event simulation models.

The DEVS-Scheme environment is engineered in a set of layers so that all of the underlying Lisp-based and object-oriented programming language features are available to the user. This layering also lends itself to model base organization using a knowledge representation scheme called the *system entity structure*.

The architecture of the DEVS-Scheme simulation system is derived from the abstract simulator concepts associated with the hierarchical, modular DEVS formalism. Since such a scheme is naturally realized in multiprocessor architectures, models developed in DEVS-Scheme are readily transportable to distributed simulation systems. Since structure descriptions in DEVS-Scheme are accessible to runtime modification, the environment provides a convenient basis for development of variable structure simulation models.

The software is written in the PC-Scheme language which runs on IBM compatible microcomputers and on the Texas Instruments Explorer Systems.

What the book is not

The book is not a manual for DEVS-Scheme. However, the system is described in sufficient detail to give the reader an idea of its syntactic and semantic features.

What the book is

The book is a principled development of an approach to object-oriented discrete event simulation in the context of a convincing implementation. The concepts of *hierarchical, modular model* construction are described in sufficient detail so that they can be reproduced in object-oriented programming systems other than the one used here.

Preface

What are the contents?

To set the background, the book reviews the following:

- representation formalisms, both dynamic and symbolic
- knowledge in modelling and simulation methodology
- object-oriented programming concepts
- contrast of modular systems and object-oriented paradigms
- system entity structure knowledge representation
- the DEVS formalism for hierarchical, modular model specification.

With this as background, we discuss the DEVS-Scheme environment in greater detail.

Layer 1 includes presentation of

- structure of DEVS-Scheme
- atomic-models specification and testing
- digraph-models specification and testing
- experimental frame construction
- simulation of hierarchical models.

Layer 2 deals with

- system entity structure construction
- hierarchical models synthesis from pruned system entity structures
- multiple entities and their realization in class kernel-models
- rule-base modelling paradigm
- representation of continuous systems in DEVS
- simplification and abstraction.

These new concepts are introduced:

- model-making and using agents within intelligent systems
- endomorphic models and simulation environments
- constraint-driven pruning of the system entity structure.

Throughout, detailed examples are given to present and illustrate the concepts.

The examples include the following:
- considerations for design of life support systems
- a performance study of simple multi-processor architectures
- more advanced distributed, multi-level architectures
- co-operative, communicating organizations of robots
- modelling of intelligent, autonomous robots.

The latter robot application is a "real life" example, based on continuing research in our laboratory to develop autonomous robots for managing space-borne experiments.

The book concludes with an extensive recapitulation of DEVS-Scheme features and a comparison with other knowledge-based simulation approaches.

An epilogue discusses the challenge of higher autonomy systems from the perspective of multifacetted modelling methodology.

Appendix A presents some technical considerations in, and extensions to, the development of DEVS-Scheme. Appendix B provides a view of the DEVS formalism in the context of the Generalized Semi-Markov Processes.

Who helped?

There are many people operating behind the scenes who helped to make this book possible. In no particular order: The student research assistants in the AI-Simulation Research Lab, especially, Tag-Gon Kim, Jeff Hu, S. Sevinc, and Jim Luh reduced my high-level (in other words, vague) sketches to working software and to polished word/picture processor files. AI-Simulation Lab collaborators Francois Cellier and Jerzy Rozenblit supplied key pieces to the emerging puzzle. Colleagues Tuncer Ören, Yu-Chi Ho, Paul Davis, and Paul Fishwick were invaluable in offering their course-correcting feedbacks. The enthusiastic support of short-course "students" David Castillo, of McDonnell Douglas and Frank Grange, of Martin-Marietta offered crucial assurance that all was not ivory tower speculation. Franz Pichler and Ken Anderson (our Siemens Europe and USA connections) offered further confidence-building measures. Sari Kalin, at Academic Press, moved the writing project along with steady persistence.

The development of DEVS-Scheme was supported through a series of grants from the National Science Foundation Computer Research Division. Its application to autonomous laboratory robots continues under research funded by NASA Ames AI Research Branch. Peter Friedland, Silvano Colombano and Monte Zweben encouraged us to stretch our limits to new territory. For such support I am truly grateful.

Bernard P. Zeigler
Tucson, Arizona

Object-Oriented Simulation with Hierarchical, Modular Models
Intelligent Agents and Endomorphic Systems

Chapter 1

DIMENSIONS OF KNOWLEDGE REPRESENTATION IN SIMULATION ENVIRONMENTS

1.1 Introduction

The inclusion of specific modules for knowledge representation within simulation models results in so-called *knowledge-based simulation systems* (Reddy *et al.*, 1986; Kerckhoffs *et al.*, 1986). Knowledge representation tools are effective organizers of information about the objects involved in a simulation. Also, they can be used within components themselves to model intelligent agents (Davis, 1986; Robertson, 1986). Such combinations of artificial intelligence (AI) and conventional simulation methodologies call for new concepts in knowledge representation and utilization (Ören, 1986, 1989a).

1.2 Knowledge Representation Schemes and Formalisms

In everyday life, the term "knowledge" has a wide spectrum of interpretations. To a philosopher, "knowledge" is reduced to "true, justified belief".[1] AI workers generally identify "knowledge" with particular knowledge representation schemes or languages. Often, for example, if a program uses rules, or is written in Prolog, it is assumed to embody knowledge. Given the gap between our everyday interpretations and current technical assumptions, it is worth spending some time, before proceeding, on the question: what is knowledge? (or better, how will the term be used here?). Roughly, "knowledge" is "valid representation" (Zeigler, 1986a). So let us consider the concepts of "representation" and "validity".

A *representation scheme* is a means of representing reality in computerized form. Each representation adhering to the pattern laid down by the scheme consists of four kinds of features or slots. Operations are procedures which can create, modify and destroy representations or their components. Questions are procedures that can be used to interrogate the representation to get answers. Operations and questions are internal features of the representation in that they are meaningful independently of outside reality. However, a representation is not useful as a thing onto itself, but only in reference to something else. Thus the third feature of a representation designates exactly what real world entity it represent. Finally, there must be a means of putting into correspondence the features of the representation with the entity it claims to represent. The validity of the representation hinges on this correspondence as we shall see. Both AI representation schemes and simulation model formalisms fit within this umbrella concept.

---

[1] The philosophical literature relating to "knowledge" is vast. Yet perhaps due to its foundational bent, it seems to have had no direct influence on AI concepts. One approach to reconciliation, on the pessimistic side, is that of Herbert and Stuart Dreyfus (1986).

1.3 Simulation Model Specification Formalisms

Consider simulation model formalisms first. Differential equation models, for example, have operations which include the writing of the equations, and assignment of values to initial conditions and parameters. Questions that can be addressed to the model concern the dynamic behavior of its variables and can be answered with suitable analysis or simulation methods. Differential equations specify continuous system models of a wide variety of real world systems, including astronomical, aeronautical, biological, systems and many others.

Formalisms in simulation are best regarded as set-theoretic shorthands for specifying mathematical dynamic systems (see below). Often, formalisms are associated with particular simulation languages. For example, the break down of discrete event formalisms into event-based, activity scanning, and process interaction subclasses, is mirrored by simulation languages which support the corresponding world views (Zeigler, 1984). Nevertheless, formalisms have an independent conceptual existence (Concepcion and Zeigler, 1988). No one formalism is best to represent the variety of behaviors in real systems of interest. Depending on a variety of factors, including the domain of application, the modelling objectives and the level of abstraction, some formalisms are more natural (correspond more directly with the perceived operation) and (usually at the same time) lead to more computationally efficient simulation than others. Indeed, the same real system may have a variety of related models, expressed in different formalisms (Zeigler, 1984; Fishwick, 1987, 1989c).

1.4 AI Knowledge Representation Schemes

Knowledge representation schemes developed in artificial intelligence research, such as rule-based systems and frame-base systems, have received extensive exposition(see for example: Buchanan and Shortliffe (1984), Waterman (1985), Harmon and King (1985)). Elzas

(1986a,b) provides an insightful review of such schemes and their applicability to modelling and simulation methodology. The distinguishing feature of AI schemes is their ability to represent knowledge in *declarative*, as opposed (and in addition to), procedural form. In declarative knowledge representation, states of an entity are presented in propositional form as facts, amenable to general purpose logical manipulation. In other words, such knowledge is explicitly isolated as "data" rather than intermingled with the "code" that uses it (Winograd, 1975).

In retrospect it seems like a very natural thing to do: isolate the knowledge initially given to a program, and acquired during its operation, from the procedures for processing it. Yet the concept that knowledge is somehow different from the rest of computer code and can be treated as a thing in, and of, itself, was slow in coming. Implications of the power of such knowledge modularization are only now becoming widely appreciated. When knowledge is interlaced with the rest of the code of a program, there is no easy way of using it for more than one related purpose. In contrast, if the program has a separate declarative component, called the knowledge base, this knowledge is then usable not only for its primary purpose but also for other subsidiary, but equally important, purposes. A system that is designed in such a way that there is a recognizable knowledge component is called a *knowledge-based system*.

A variety of *object-oriented programming languages* have been developed: Smalltalk (Goldberg and David, 1983) (LOOPS (Bobrow and Stefik, 1983), Flavors (Weinreb *et al.*, 1983), C++ (Stroustrup, 1986), and CLOS (Keene, 1988). The object based paradigm provides a computational basis for integrating the features of the popular AI knowledge representation formalisms. In such programming systems, an object is a conglomerate of data structures and associated operations, usually representing a real world counterpart. *Objects* are usually given generic descriptions so that *classes* of objects are defined and individual instances of such classes may be generated at will. Classes of objects form a *taxonomical hierarchy* in which they are arranged according to their degree of generality. Special kinds of objects have *slots* for both attributes and methods that are unique as well as those that are *inherited* from more general classes (Adelsberger et al., 1986). *Methods* (procedures) can perform operations on the global object state (the ensemble of its slots) and invoke each other in a manner called *message passing*. The massage passing paradigm differs from subroutine invocation in allowing a much greater degree of discretion to the receiver in interpreting a message. A subroutine call is a command sent to by an omniscient master to a completely subservient slave; a message is a polite request by one peer to another to perform an action that the latter may or may not be able, or choose, to do. Slots can have so-called *active values*. These are procedures that are triggered when a slot is accessed or modified. Active values can be likened to *demons* that watch over slots to determine their values and propagate information to other slots.

1.5 Representation and Knowledge

Having a representation of an entity is obviously not enough to claim knowledge about that entity. A *homomorphism* is a correspondence between the states of a pair of objects which is preserved under all relevant operations. For a representation to be valid, the correspondence in question should be have this homomorphic character: we associate states of the real world entity with those of its representation in such a way that when we ask a question about the entity we get the same answer from the representation that we would get by making a corresponding observation on the entity (Zeigler, 1984, 1987). The states of the entity and its representation will stay in correspondence if for each real world action that changes the entity state, there is a corresponding operation which correctly updates the representation state.

Put succinctly, *dynamic systems formalisms* are concerned with the time related changes in entities' states while AI formalisms generally are concerned with relationships that do not take time into account. Correspondingly, the preservation of state correspondence over time is crucial for assessing the validity of dynamic models and there is a rich literature on such morphism concepts (see (Zeigler, 1984) for discussion and review). Although traditional AI has tended to view knowledge in a static frame, new directions, e.g., in qualitative modelling and in planning, are finding it necessary to take time into account (Allen, 1984). Accordingly, morphism concepts should be borrowed and applied.

Entities in some domain are *knowable* by a computer system if it has a representation scheme to generate representations for them. In this sense, only a small (but important) fraction of reality is knowable with classical modelling formalisms. For example, a Newtonian model of the earth-sun system represents orbital trajectories, but it can not represent other immediately relevant knowledge. Indeed, it has no way of expressing what are the real world entities (planets and stars) involved or their parameters, such as masses, appearing in the equations (we can ask it about the dynamical properties of the orbit but not about whether it is that of the earth around the sun). Of course, non-mechanical properties, i.e., those not appearing in the equations, are not at all knowable. And the model can not infer new facts from known ones, can not access its representations and compare them, nor does it possess any meta-knowledge about them as AI-based schemes can (Bobrow 1975).

As Elzas (1986b) makes clear, current AI representation schemes can certainly organize much of the knowledge about a system that was unknowable using conventional modelling formalisms, but they are not adept at representing the dynamics that latter were invented for. Thus, there needs to be a paradigm whose scope of representation includes both classical and AI schemes. This is an area of research with at least two sources of inspiration. One stems from the hypothesis that for a computer to reason about physical systems it must have more of a qualitative and common sense representation than exists in the classical modelling formalism (Bobrow, 1985; de Kleer, 1989)). (See Rajogopalan (1986) for an excellent review.) For example, differential equations cannot easily represent knowledge that a string can not be used to push, only to pull. In attempting to capture common sense knowledge about physical systems, qualitative modelling tends to drastically coarsen the state descriptor space from the real numbers to small discrete sets. Accordingly, intractable ambiguity may arise in generating the behavior (reasoning) of such models (Kuipers, 1989). Some recent approaches employ symbolic means to summarize dynamic system behavior rather than to generate it (Reddy *etal.*, 1985, 1986; Hardt, 1988; Cellier, 1988) or as point of departure for further model refinement (Fishwick and Luker, 1989; Allen and Wilson, 1988). We return to discuss these issues in more depth in Chapter 14.

Another source of inspiration for a wider paradigm comes from computer simulation. Here the world views of discrete event simulation have been found to be highly compatible with the representation schemes of Artificial Intelligence (O'Keefe, 1986; Zeigler, 1986, 1987). Actually already in 1965, the discrete event simulation language Simula (Dahl and Nygaard, 1966) introduced class inheritance and association of both procedures and data structures with class instances. It is not surprising therefore, that languages are being developed to express both the dynamic knowledge of discrete event formalisms and the declarative knowledge of AI paradigms (Klahr, 1986; Middleton and Zancanato, 1986, Ruiz-Mier and Talavage, 1989).

1.6 System-theoretic Representation

Mathematical systems theory provides a framework for representing and studying dynamical systems (Zadeh and Dosoer, 1963; Wymore, 1967; Mesarovic and Takahara, 1975; Pichler, 1986). Systems modelling concepts are an important facet in a movement to develop a methodology under which simulation can be performed in a more principled and secure manner (Zeigler *etal.*, 1979; Ören *etal.*, 1984). The recent advent of high performance artificial intelligence software and hardware has facilitated the transfer of this simulation methodology from research to practice (Elzas 1986b). System theory distinguishes between system structure (the inner constitution of a system) and behavior (its outer manifestation). Regarding structure, the theory has given us the concept of *decomposition*, i.e., how a system may be broken down into component systems, and *coupling*, i.e., how these components may be combined to reconstitute the original system. Thus decomposition and coupling should be fundamental relations in a knowledge representation scheme. System theory however has not focussed on a third fundamental kind of relation, taxonomic, which concerns the admissible variants of a component and their specializations, exhibited for example, in object class hierarchies.

Regarding system behavior, we distinguish between *causal* and *empirical representations*. By empirical representation we refer to actual records of data (time history of variable values) gathered from a real system or model. Causal relationships are integrated into units called models which can be interpreted by suitable simulators to generate data in empirical form.

1.7 Modular, Hierarchical Models and Object-Oriented Paradigms Contrasted

Model specifications arising from mathematical system theory (Ören, 1984; Zeigler, 1976,1984; Futo, 1986) bear a resemblance to concepts of object-oriented programming. Both objects and system models share a concept of *internal state*. However, *modular system models* operate on a *time base* and have recognized input and output ports through which all interaction with the environment occurs. Modular system models can have a *hierarchical structure* in which component systems are coupled together to form larger ones. The formalism in which models are expressed must be closed under such coupling to make such recursive structuring possible.

Objects in typical object-oriented paradigms are not modular systems in that they do not have a time base nor are they hierarchical or modular in the above sense. While objects communicate with other objects by message passing, the sender must have an explicitly given set of receivers — the latter *acquaintances* must exist for the transmission to be well defined (Agha, 1989). The coupling concept

Dimensions of Knowledge Representation

in modular systems provides a level of *delayed binding* — a system model places a value on one of its ports, the actual destination of this output is not determined until the model becomes a component in a larger system and a coupling scheme is specified. Clearly, a system model may place an output on a port which has no receiver coupled to it. It can therefore a) be developed and tested as a stand alone unit, b) be placed in a model base and reloaded at will (an object must have its acquaintances specified), and c) reused in any applications context in which its behavior is appropriate and coupling to other components makes sense.

Communication in a modular systems paradigm involves a more complex *communication protocol* than that of a conventional object oriented one. In conventional object paradigms, a component A can send a message to a component B expecting a value to be returned immediately as in a subroutine call. In concurrent object-oriented systems (Yonezawa and Tokorro, 1987), objects are simultaneously active and message transmission is more complex: an arbitrary time will elapse between A's sending to B and B's responding to A. During this interval, both A and B may also be engaging in their individual activities. Indeed, B may be busy when A's message arrives and may ignore it or buffer it for later examination. A concurrent object oriented environment must clearly specify the details of the message handling protocols so that the user can design his object behaviors accordingly.

The modular systems paradigm, on the other hand, does not impose specific message passing protocols.[2]

The modeller is therefore completely free to specify, as an integral part of his models, how communication is handled. Note that information flow is only one of many interactions that may be modelled, e.g., material flow. Finally, since system models operate on a time-base, times involved in communication and other interaction are explicitly modelled. In concurrent object oriented computing, the underlying computational model must shield the user, who does

---

[2] Perhaps it would be fairer to say that it imposes only a minimal one; we invite the reader to decide after reading the details in succeeding chapters.

not concern himself with time explicitly, from indeterminacies that could arise due to transmission delays, buffering, etc. DEVS-Scheme and other implementation of the hierarchical, modular formalism for discrete event models demonstrate that conventional object-oriented paradigms can be serve well as a basis to implement the modular systems paradigm (Zeigler, 1986; Thomasma and Ulgen, 1988; Kim, 1988). After presenting the DEVS-Scheme approach, we return to continue this discussion in Chapter 14.

1.8 Framework for Knowledge Representation in Simulation

The *Systems Entity Structure/Model Base (SES/MB)* framework was proposed by Zeigler (1986) as a step toward marrying the dynamics-based formalism of simulation with the symbolic formalisms of AI. It consists of two components: a system entity structure and a model base. The system entity structure, declarative in character, (Zeigler, 1987b and Kim, 1988; Kim *et al.*, 1988) represents knowledge of decomposition, component taxonomies, and coupling specifications and constraints. The *model base* contains models which are procedural in character, expressed in classical and AI-derived formalisms. The *entities*[3] of the entity structure refer to conceptual components of reality for which models may reside in the model base. Also associated with entities are slots for attribute knowledge representation. An entity may have several *aspects*, each denoting a decomposition and therefore having several entities. An entity may also have several *specializations*, each representing a classification of the possible variants of the entity.

The SES/MB framework is intended to be *generative* in nature. The SES provides a compact representation scheme which can be unfolded to generate the family of all possible models synthesizable from components in the model base. The user, whether human or artificial, should be a goal-directed agent which can interrogate the

---

[3] No relation to the Entity-Relation Database model; see Higa (1988).

knowledge base and synthesize a model using *pruning operations* that ultimately reduce the SES to a structure called a *composition tree*. The composition tree contains all the information needed to synthesize a model in hierarchical fashion from components in the model base (Zeigler, 1985; Rozenblit, 1985; Rozenblit *et al.*, 1986)

1.9 What Kinds of Modelling and Simulation Knowledge Are There?

Having reviewed the fundamental concepts of knowledge representation, we are in a position to ask what kinds of knowledge are relevant to the modelling and simulation enterprise. In doing so, we shall conclude that although state-of-the-art knowledge representation provides powerful tools, there are many developments still needed to exploit much of this knowledge in simulation environments.

1.9.1 Knowledge of the Real World

The system entity structure/model base scheme is not complete. For example, it does not deal with the fine grained causal relations from which models are synthesized nor with the empirical data they must replicate. Elzas (1986b) has sketched an epistemology that views modelling, simulation and AI approaches to knowledge representation within a wider scientific scope. The epistemology addresses itself to what forms of knowledge there are about particular domains and how they are organized into more encompassing units. In Elzas's hierarchy, one starts with known facts. Reasoning organizes such facts into relations. These are grouped into blocks or mini-knowledge bases that are applicable in many contexts. Blocks are grouped together to form knowledge bases for specific application domains. Such knowledge bases are the aggregations usually considered in knowledge-based system design. Scientific knowledge corresponds to meta-knowledge concerning the regularities found within relations, blocks and knowledge-bases.

From this perspective it is possible to understand the essential difference between knowledge in general, knowledge in expert systems, and models. *Knowledge in general*, refers to representation of reality in the full Elzas hierarchy. *Expert system* methodology concerns itself with acquiring knowledge from an expert at the knowledge-base level (in Elzas's hierarchy), hence with knowledge of limited, but useful, application. *Models* are representations that also package knowledge about a particular system domain to meet specific objectives. The knowledge so packaged however is usually derived from scientific knowledge of a general character in combination with empirical data sources. Expert systems may be regarded as models, not directly of a real system, but of a human who is expert in dealing with some aspect of it. We return to this discussion later when we consider issues in modelling of intelligent agents.

1.9.2 Knowledge of Simulation Modelling Methodology

In modelling of systems, the full spectrum of knowledge levels must be considered whether from the top-down (postulational) approach (Zeigler, 1986) typical in simulation methodology or the bottom-up (discovery) approach of inductive modeling (Klir, 1985; Cellier, 1988). In the following we consider the knowledge involved in simulation modelling methodology. This is meta-knowledge with respect to the real world knowledge just discussed.

1.9.3 Knowledge Relating to Objectives

Modelling and simulation activities are carried out to achieve a *multiplicity of objectives* which arise from the goals of either gaining knowledge about a real system or of exerting control, management or design interventions on it. Although when approached with differing objectives a real system may yield various, seemingly disparate, models, there is nevertheless an underlying unity that binds these models together — namely, their common origin. Rather than consider each model as a distinct entity, *multifacetted modelling methodol-*

Dimensions of Knowledge Representation

ogy (Zeigler, 1984) attempts to organize models so that a coherent whole emerges. With such support, the construction of models to meet new objectives may be accelerated, since components already existing in the model base may be exploited. To gain full advantage of the knowledge in the model base, there must be provided a strong capability for representing the components of models, their variations and their interconnection. To facilitate synthesis, models must be readily disassembled into components, and these must be able to be easily assembled into new combinations. The SES/KB framework provides a basis for such model *reusability* (Kim, 1988).

1.9.4 Knowledge Relating to Aggregation

Models may be constructed at different levels of *aggregation (resolution, abstraction)*: the differences are not always clear (see Fishwick 1987, 1988)). The level of aggregation is jointly determined by the objectives at hand, the available knowledge, and the given resource/time constraints. The objectives, including the accuracy desired of the answers, dictate the minimal degree of disaggregation needed in the model to be able to satisfy the objectives. Beyond this level further disaggregation may be futile or even counterproductive. The concepts of (generic) experimental frame and applicability of frames to models have been introduced to link the objectives with the models (Zeigler, 1984; Rozenblit and Zeigler, 1986) Available domain knowledge places a lower limit on the aggregation limit — in principle (from a reductionist standpoint), one could always sink to the level of basic physical particles in every model provided that relationships were available to express the desired behavior of interest (Simon, 1969). Likewise, since as resolution increases, the complexity of the model almost always rapidly increases, time and money determine how much disaggregation can be considered.

Thus, models oriented to fundamentally the same objectives may be constructed at different aggregation levels due to tradeoffs in accuracy achievable versus complexity costs incurred. An environment can support construction of such aggregation-related models by facilitating elaboration of models (constructing a new model related to an existing one by adding new variables or refining their ranges) (e.g., Allen and Wilson, 1988) and simplification of models (constructing a new model by dropping variables, coarsening their ranges, or grouping several together to form aggregated variables). Moreover, relationships among such collections of models should form part of the knowledge base of the environment and be available for use in model validation (against the real system) and cross-validation (against each other). The experimental frame concept (Zeigler, 1976; Ören and Zeigler, 1979) provides a basis for rigorously characterizing the behavioral regions in which validity is expected to hold.

1.9.5 Knowledge Relating to Behavior and Structure

Considering a real system as a black box, there is *hierarchy of levels* (Zeigler, 1984) at which models may be constructed ranging from the purely behavioral — in which the model claims to represent only the observed input/output behavior of the system, up the strongly structural — in which much is claimed about preserving the structure of the system. Simulation models are usually placed at the higher levels of structure and they embody many supposed mechanisms to generate the behavior of interest. In contrast, behavior descriptions obtained by curve fitting represent lowest level models. High structural detail usually implies a high degree of disaggregation in model variables needed to express the relationships involved. However, the converse is not necessarily true: one can employ a high degree of resolution in defining variables and corresponding measurement and still use only curve fitted relationships to express the values of variables over time.

While simulation models are, by nature, formulated at high levels of structure, an environment may support the development of other kinds of models at lower levels. Behavioral descriptions obtained by curve fitting, statistical correlations, or inductive systems modelling may complement the simulation models by providing summaries of real system behavior. Such summaries may replace the original extensive records and therefore may be more economical to use in such activities as validation of simulation models of the same phenom-

Dimensions of Knowledge Representation

ena. The same kinds of techniques can be applied to simulation generated behavior. For example, statistical metamodels (Kleinen, 1982) summarize the dependence of a performance index on model parameters. Introspective simulation (Reddy *etal.*, 1986)) employs artificial intelligence to discover causal relationships in simulation records to form symbolic cause-effect models. Such abstraction and inference processes are understood as level transitions within the hierarchy of systems specifications. Those going from lower to higher levels (hence inferring structure from behavior) require justification principles (Zeigler, 1984; Fishwick, 1989).

Conventional simulation systems adequately support only a single level at which change occurs in the model, that of changes in the model descriptive variables, viz. its behavior. Although changes in the model structure may be introduced, and to some extent, tracked in such systems, specific and powerful support is not provided for such activities. Biological, and other adaptive, systems are most readily perceived as exhibiting changes simultaneously at structural and behavioral levels. A new paradigm, structural simulation (as opposed to conventional "trajectory" simulation) is needed to avoid having to force structural changes down to the same level as behavioral ones (Ören 1975; Zeigler 1986; Davis 1986; Hogeweg and Hesper 1986; Elbert and Salter, 1986; Sampson, 1984). Modelling of intelligent, endomorphic agents (see below) ultimately requires an environment supporting structural simulation.

1.10 Endomorphic Models, Simulations, and Agents

To achieve realism, models of intelligent agents must be able to represent not only their decision making capabilities but also the models on which such capabilities are based, — and their methodologies for building such models. Thus modelling of intelligent agents raises a host of issues requiring not just the application of principles of simulation methodology *per se*, but also the embedding of such knowledge within the simulation model itself.

We use the term *endomorphy* to refer to objects (systems, models, agents) in which some sub-objects use models of other sub-objects. Endomorphism is a hoary mathematical concept which refers to the existence of a homomorphism from an object to a sub-object within it, the part (sub-object) then being a model of the whole. The term is the closest I could find but falls short of what is needed. For one thing it fails to allow homomorphic relations between pairs of sub-objects — the object, as the largest sub-object being a special case. More fundamentally, it fails to deal with the *construction and use* of internally embedded models.

In this book, we shall understand endomorphy to include the broader senses just mentioned. For example, an *endomorphic simulation model* can be one containing an agent and environment such that the agent has, and uses, a model of the environment. This has elements of endomorphy since the environment is modeled twice within the simulation model. Simulation engines that can recursively invoke themselves to generate the behavior of such endomorphic models (as does the pioneering RAND war game simulator (Davis and Hall, 1988)) are *endomorphic simulators*. Going one step further, among the models that an agent may possess may be those of itself. Thus, we use the term *endomorphic agent* to refer to an agent that incorporates, uses (and possibly constructs) models of itself in its decision making.

Endomorphy, then, establishes the conceptual context for considering self-embedding issues in the modelling of intelligent agents. We shall return to it in the last third of the book after presenting the DEVS-Scheme implementation of the SES/MB framework.

Chapter 2
BASICS

This chapter introduces the foundations for the rest of the book. First, we discuss object-oriented programming since the DEVS-Scheme environment is built upon this paradigm. Then we introduce the concepts of modular, hierarchical models and the system entity structure which we elaborate in the rest of the book.

2.1 Object-Oriented Programming Concepts

Object-oriented programming is a paradigm in which a software system is decomposed into subsystems based on objects. Computation is done by objects exchanging messages among themselves. The paradigm enhances software maintainability, extensibility and reusability.

Conventional software systems tend to consist of collections of subprograms based on functional decomposition techniques that concentrate on algorithmic abstractions. In conventional programming languages such as LISP or Pascal, we tend to write programs around a main routine which calls on other routines to work at appropriate times. Decision making power is concentrated in the main routine. The other routines play supporting roles, coming alive only when the flow of control passes through them. In contrast, object-oriented programming encourages a much more decentralized style of decision making by creating objects whose existence may continue throughout the life of the program. We can make such objects act as experts in their own task assignments by providing them with the appropriate knowledge. Such distribution and localization of knowledge simplifies the main routine and relieves it of much of its decision making burden.

Indeed in object-oriented programming, we abandon the concept of main routine. Instead we design an interface to the user which sends messages to the objects directing them to carry out desired tasks. This interface exists at a higher level of control than the objects in the sense that it co-ordinates their activities. One of the main advantages of object-oriented programming is that the interface need not change as more and more specialized objects are introduced. This greatly simplifies program design and enhances *evolvability*. Program evolvability is the ability to easily modify a program as we learn more about the problem domain.

2.1.1 Objects

As just indicated, an object-oriented program contains components called *objects*. Each object has its own variables and procedures to manipulate these variables called *methods*. Only the methods owned by the object can access and change the values of its variables. The values originally assigned to variables of an object will persist indefinitely throughout its lifetime — unless changed by some method. They will stay this way until a subsequent change is brought about by some — the same or another — method. Thus the variables collectively constitute the state of the object. In these terms, only the methods of an object can alter its state.

Objects can communicate with each other, and with higher levels of control, to cause changes in their states, by a process called message passing. The general form of a message is:

> to object: O
> apply method: m
> with arguments: a1,..., an

Basics

This represents a message sent to object O telling it to apply its method named m with the argument values a1,..., an. Carrying out the orders of this message may result in the method changing the state of the object and/or producing an output in response to the message.

One of the most useful concepts afforded by the object oriented paradigm is that different objects can have variables or methods having the same name. Such methods may exhibit a basic similarity in purpose despite a difference in the detailed manner in which this purpose is achieved. We will see why this is important soon.

As an example, consider objects representing various barn yard animals. Each such object will have a method called *make-sound*, but the result produced by the method will be different for different objects. For example,

 send cat make-sound(soft) $\rightarrow$ returns "meow"
 send cat make-sound(loud) $\rightarrow$ returns "meow meow meow"
 send dog make-sound(soft) $\rightarrow$ returns "woof"
 send dog make-sound(loud) $\rightarrow$ returns "woof woof woof"

A higer level control procedure might be the following:

 Procedure: Make-racket
  For each object in the barn yard list,
   send object make-sound(loud) and
   collect these in a list called *racket*.

Note that the procedure *make-racket* does not know what sound is generated by an object. Nor does it have to know how the individual objects do this generation. It relies only on the fact that each object has a method called *make-sound*, and leaves the details of this method to the designer of the object. The process of shielding the user of an object from its details is called *abstraction*. Such abstraction has an important consequence, called *extensibility*, the ability to extend a software system by adding in new definitions without modifying earlier ones. In our example, the procedure *make-racket* does not have to be modified when new objects are added to the barn yard list — provided that each new object is given a method called *make-sound*.

2.1.2 Object classes

In object orient programming systems, objects are usually not defined individually. Instead, a class definition provides a template for generating any number of instances, each one an identical copy of a basic prototype. Thus in our example above, we might define a class called *barn-yard-animals*, from which the various instances, *dog, cat, pig, horse*, etc., would be generated. The basic form for such a class definition is given in Figure 2.1.

```
Define class: name       (name to be used for the class)
   class variables:      (variables describing the class per se)
   instance variables:   (variables owned by each instance)
   methods:              (methods owned by each instance)
   constructor:          (procedure for creating instances)
   destructor:           (method for destroying instance)
   inheritance:          (other classes from which to inherit definitions)
```

Figure 2.1. Basic form of Class Definition.

In our example, we might provide the following definition:

```
Define class: barn-yard-animals
   class variables: barn-yard-list
   instance variables: name, sound
   methods:
      (set-sound(sound-string) sound:= sound-string)
      (get-sound() return sound )
      (get-name() return name)
      (make-sound(strength)
```

```
            (if (strength = loud)
                return: concatenate (sound ,sound, sound)
            else if (strength = soft) return: sound
            else return: wrong input argument ))
        constructor:
            (make-barn-yard-animal(name-string)
            — make an instance with name, name-string,
                and place it on the barn-yard-list — )
        destructor:
            (destroy() — remove this instance from
                            the barn-yard-list — )
        inheritance: none
```

This definition specifies a class variable called *barn-yard-list*, which will be used to keep track of the instances of the class that are currently in existence. When an instance is created using the defined constructor, it is placed on the *barn-yard-list*. To remove it from this list, we send it a message to apply its method destroy. Note that each instance has a destructor method. However, to construct an instance, we cannot be employ one of its methods — the instance does not yet exist, so we cannot send a message to it.

There are two instance variables, *name*, and *sound*, respectively, to hold the name of the instance and a string for the sound it makes. As indicated above, the only way to change values of an object's variables is to apply one of its methods. The only exception to this rule pertains at the birth of an instance. The constructor can assign initial values to the instance variables individually, or such values can be specified in the class definition as default values assigned to each instance upon creation. In our example, the constructor assigns the name to the newly created instance and a method, *set-sound*, can be employed to initially assign a sound to the instance. Note that the sound can be changed at any time by applying the *set-sound* method. However, the *name* cannot be changed, since no method has been defined to do this. (There is a method to obtain the *name*). In general, we may define *set-* and *get-* methods for those instance variables whose values we wish to modify and access, respectively.

In our example, we can create the instances mentioned previously and assign them appropriate values as follows:

>   make-barn-yard-animal(cat)
>   send dog set-sound "meow"
>   make-barn-yard-animal(dog)
>   send dog set-sound "woof"

Having done so, calling the procedure, *make-racket*, will return the list

>   racket: "woof woof woof" "meow meow meow"
>   "oink oink oink" "neigh neigh neigh"

(remember that barn-yard-list employed by *make-racket* contains the created instances). The following would destroy *horse* and create *cow*:

>   send horse destroy
>   make-barn-yard-animal(cow)
>   send cow set-sound "moo"

Make-racket would now return a correspondingly modified list of sounds. Once again, note that such a procedure need not be modified whenever we create new instances or destroy existing ones. What's more it does not have to be changed when new classes are added to the system as we next consider doing.

For comparison, Figure 2.2 shows a class definition of animals as it is done in SCOOPS (Scheme Object-oriented Programming System). It is beyond the scope of this book to delve into the details of object-oriented programming systems in Scheme (see Texas Instruments (1986) PC-Scheme Users Manual; also see Smith (1989) or Eisenberg (1988) for introductions to Scheme programming). However, from time to time, we shall touch upon some facets of the implementation of DEVS-Scheme in SCOOPS when it is of special interest to do so.

```
;;;;class definition of animals

(define-class animals
(classvars
   (barnyard-list '())   ;;the list of instances, initially empty
)
(instvars
   name                  ;;name of animal, a symbol
   self                  ;;this object itself
   (sound "")            ;;the sound it makes, a string
)
(options
  settable-variables     ;;each instance variable has a corresponding
                         ;;set method
  gettable-variables     ;;each instance variable has a corresponding
                         ;;get method
  inittable-variables)   ;;each instance variable can be initialized in
                         ;;the general constructor, make-instance
)

(compile-class animals)  ;;needed to make instances of the class
                         ;;not needed if class is only used as a source
                         ;;hereditable material

;;;;;;;;methods for animals

(define-method (animals make-sound)(strength)
 (if (equal? strength 'loud)
     (string-append sound sound sound)
     sound
 )
)

(define-method (animals destroy)()
(delete! self barnyard-list)
)

;;;;;;; example of construction of an instance
;;;;;;; uses set methods existing due to class definition

(define cat (make-instance animals))
(send cat set-sound "meow ")       ;;uses set method for sound
(send cat set-name 'cat)           ;;name is symbol, 'cat
(send cat set-self cat)            ;;self is object, cat

;;;;;;;; another example of instance construction
;;;;;;;; uses inittable capability defined in class definition

(define dog (make-instance animals 'sound "woof " 'name 'dog))
(send dog set-self dog)
(setcv animals barnyard-list (cons dog (getcv animals barnyard-list)))
```

Figure 2.2. Class definition of animals.

```
;;;;;;; a constructor for class animals would package these altogether
;;;;;;; for example, (make-animal dog "woof"), would accomplish
;;;;;;; the instance variable initialization and the insertion in
;;;;;;; the classvar, barnyard-list
```

Figure 2.2. (continued).

```
;;;;;;;;; specialized classes of animals
(define-class foul
  (classvars price-of-eggs)    ;;foul have an additional class variable
  (instvars
    (sound "cluck")            ;;foul have a default sound
    egg-laying-frequency)      ;;foul have an additional instance variable
  (mixins animals)             ;;everything else is inherited from animals

(define-method (foul market-value)()
  (* price-of-eggs egg-laying-frequency)
                               ;;foul differ in their egg production
)                              ;;but the price of eggs is common

(define-class cattle
  (classvars price-of-milk)    ;;cattle have a different class variable
  (instvars
    (sound "moo")              ;;cattle have a different default sound
    milk-production)           ;;cattle have a different instance variable
  (mixins animals)

(define-method (cattle market-value)()  ;;cattle have a different way of
  (* price-of-milk milk-production)     ;;computing market value
)
```

Figure 2.3. Specialized classes of animals.

2.1.3 Class inheritance

Often objects can be organized into a family of homogeneous classes, which are mutually distinct, but do share certain fundamental properties in common. The object oriented paradigm provides a natural way to exploit such situations to afford an economy of definition as well as the extensibility just referred to. As in Figure 2.1, a class definition can specify from which classes the new class will inherit, i.e., automatically obtain all their definitions. This saves having to copy or rewrite such common variables and methods and helps maintain consistency in definitions when code modifications are made.

In the most straightforward case, a class inherits only from at most one other class, called its parent. In this case, the classes form a tree structure, called a specialization hierarchy under a root class. The root class is the most general class. Its children inherit all its features and are more specialized, in that they may have additional ones as well. Their children may be even more specialized, inheriting from the parents (and hence from the grandparent). For example, we could define specialized classes *foul* and *cattle* of *barn-yard-animals*. Each class definition would have *barn-yard-animals* in its inheritance slot. Objects in such classes would automatically be given all the instance variables and methods defined for *barn-yard-animals*. In addition, we could add new class and instance variables and methods to *foul* that are particular to chicken, geese, etc. as opposed to *cattle*, such as cows, oxen, etc. Figure 2.3 shows how this may be done in SCOOPS.

The root class generally provides general definitions for methods needed to interface with higher level procedures. The more specialized classes may override such general definitions by providing methods of their own with the same name. For example, in Figure 2.3, foul and cattle each have methods with the same name but with different behavior. The term *polymorphism* is used to refer to such multi-valued definition: object-oriented programming systems obviously must interpret the meaning of a method name in its proper context, a process called *dynamic binding*. Polymorphism and dynamic binding are important features which distinguish message passing from ordinary procedure calls.

The system may evolve by adding more and more specialized classes, while the higher level procedures need not change so long as the newly introduced specialized methods are compatible (same input and output) as the general ones. Thus extensibility and ease of program evolution are inherent in the object-oriented programming approach.

The more general form of organization in which classes may inherit from several classes, called multiple inheritance, provides additional flexibility in certain situations but is harder to keep track of. Layer 1 of the DEVS-Scheme environment uses mainly the hierarchical organization but Layer 2 provides extensive support of multiple inheritance by means of the system entity structure.[1]

2.2 The System Entity Structure/Model Base

While object-oriented programming provides the means for implementing knowledge-based simulation environments, the The System Entity Structure/Model Base (SES/MB) framework provides the ends to which these means are applied. Here we provide a general overview of these concepts so as to provide a context for later detailed discussion.

2.2.1 Modularity and Model Base Concepts

Hierarchical synthesis and reuse of models are greatly facilitated if the objects in the model base are modular in the sense we now describe. As in Figure 2.4, suppose that we have models A and B in

---

[1] The recent standardization of object oriented approaches in CLOS (Common Lisp Object System; Keene, 1988) takes things one step further. It supports a very flexible scheme of associating a generic method call with a particular method based on the classes of its arguments. Ordinary inheritance is then the simple case in which only one argument determines how a generic method is to be interpreted.

Basics

the model base. If such model descriptions are in the proper modular form, then we can create a new model by specifying how the input and output ports of A and B are to be connected to each other and to external ports, an operation called *coupling*. Ören (1980,1984) was the first to introduce this concept into simulation languages. The resulting model, AB, called a coupled model is once again in modular form. As can be seen, the term *modularity*, as used here, means the description of a model in such a way that it has recognized input and output ports through which all interaction with the external world is mediated. Once placed into the model base, AB can itself be employed to construct yet larger models in the same manner used with A and B. This property, called closure under coupling enables hierarchical construction of models.

A coupling specification has three parts:

- external input coupling tells how the input ports of the coupled model are identified with the input ports of the components.

- external output coupling tells how the output ports of the coupled model are identified with the output ports of the components.

- internal coupling specifies how the components inside the coupled model are interconnected by telling how the output ports of components are connected to input ports of others.

It is important to remember that the resulting coupled model cannot be used in further model construction unless external coupling is specified. However, internal coupling can be omitted: a non-interacting, parallel composition of components results in this case.

2.3 Independent Testability

An important benefit of such modular construction is that any model in the model base can be readily, and independently, tested by injecting the proper test message sequences and comparing the results

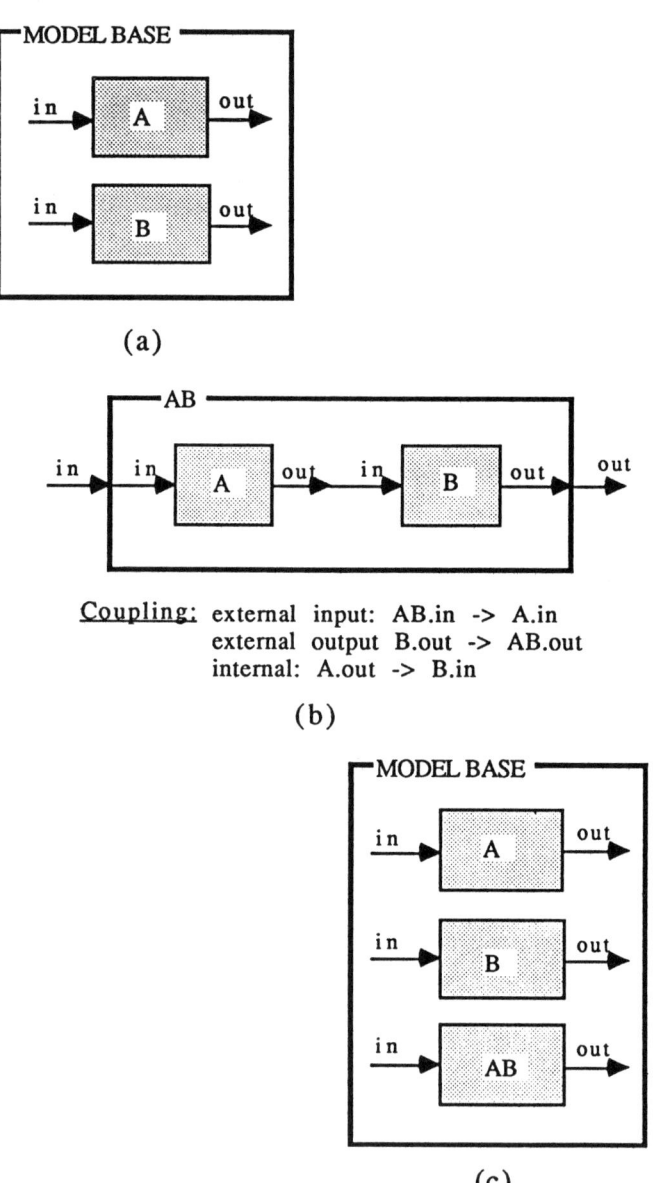

Figure 2.4. Modularity and Model base concepts.

with those expected. The ability to do such testing at each stage of a hierarchical construction facilitates reliable and efficient verification of large simulation models. Such systematic testing is not possible in standard simulation languages which do not support modular and hierarchical model development. Test modules for models can be developed in a systematic manner using the concept of experimental frame, which specifies the input, control and output variables and constraints desired of the experimentation. Models that have been validated in experimental frames can be put into the model base for reliable reuse as components in larger models. A caveat: such validation is relative only to the tests that have been done. In reusing a model we should be aware that the behavior elicited in its new context may not have been covered in earlier validation experiments.

2.3.1 Hierarchical Construction: The Composition Tree

A *hierarchical* model is inductively defined:

- an atomic model is a hierarchical model

- a coupled model whose components are hierarchical models is a hierarchical model

- nothing else is a hierarchical model.[2]

The structure of a hierarchical model is exhibited in a *composition tree* such as that in Figure 2.5. The components of the outermost coupled model, or root model, are shown as its children (e.g., A1, A2, B and C are the children of ABC). A child, which is also a coupled model, has its components descending from it as children (e.g., B and C). Children which are atomic models become leaves in the tree (e.g., B1, B2, C1, and C2). The coupling specification needed to construct a coupled model is attached to vertical line descending from the parent to its children. In other words, the coupling specification

---

[2]The last clause is not superfluous: it says the only way to get hierarchical models is by following the inductive process defined in the first two clauses.

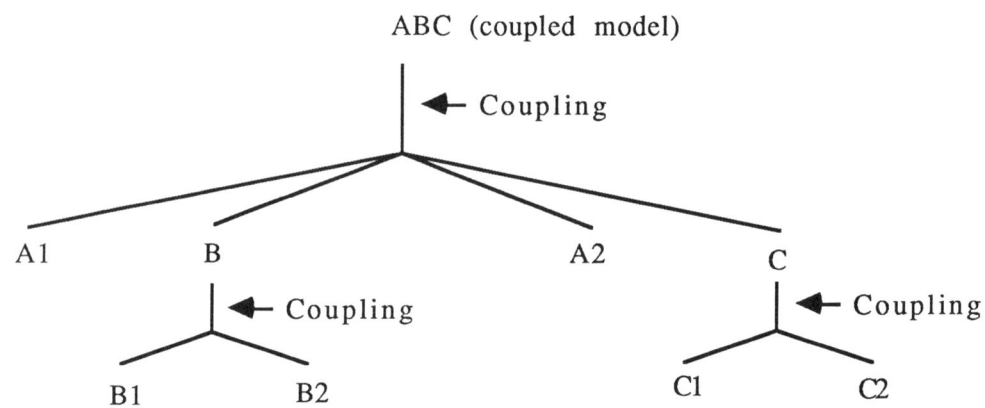

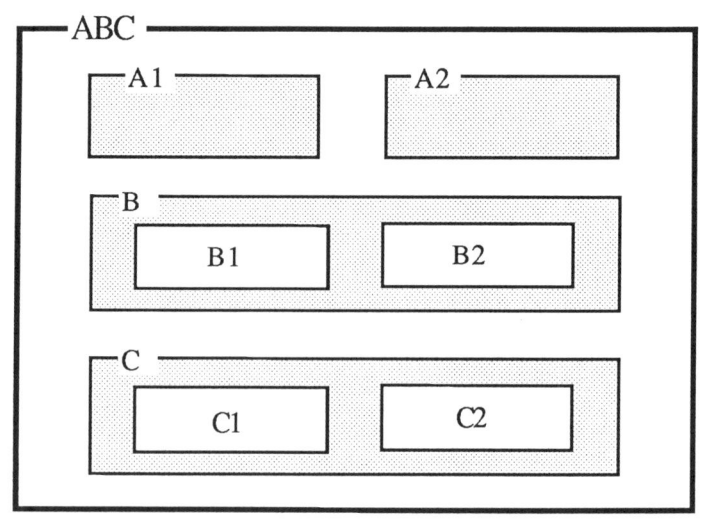

Figure 2.5. Composition tree.

Basics

is associated with a decomposition of the parent into its children. The system entity structure, to come next, generalizes this concept. In it, an entity may have several decompositions, called aspects, associated with it. Each such aspect carries with it the coupling specifications needed to construct the parent by coupling together the children of that aspect.

Thus a composition tree represents the information needed to construct a particular hierarchical model. The SES represents the possible construction of a whole family of hierarchical models.

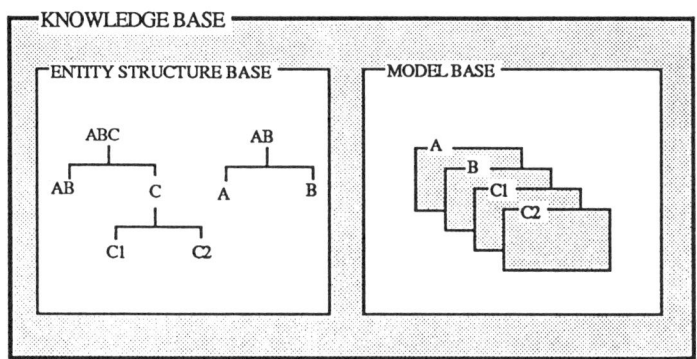

Figure 2.6. The System Entity Structure/Model Base (SES/MB) framework.

2.3.2 System Entity Structure

The *system entity structure* (SES) directs the synthesis of models from components in the model base (Figure 2.6). The SES is a knowledge representation scheme that combines the decomposition, taxonomic, and coupling relationships. Associated with an SES is a model base which contains models which may be expressed in any of dynamical formalisms mentioned earlier. The *entities* of the SES refer to conceptual components of reality for which models may reside in the *model base*. Also associated with entities (as with other object types we shall discuss) are slots for attribute knowledge representation. An entity may have several *aspects*, each denoting a representation. An entity may have several *aspects*, each denoting a decomposition and therefore having several entities. An entity may also have several *specializations*, each representing a classification of the possible variants of the entity.

Whereas the entity-aspect relation conveys decomposition knowledge, the entity-specialization relation represents taxonomic knowledge. Specializations (classification schemes) also have several entities. Specializations, can be thought of as partitions; the product of two partitions forms a finer partition whose blocks are the intersections of the originals. In pruning, when one entity from a specialization is selected, it *inherits* the substructure (slots, aspects and remaining specializations) of its parent. The selected entity also replaces the parent in any coupling specifications involving the latter. Specializations may form a hierarchy analogous to the object class hierarchy. It may happen that not all combinations of specialization choices represent actual possibilities. In this case, *constraints* can be added to the specializations to express the allowable combinations. A *multiple entity* represents the set of all members of an entity class. Such a multiple entity always has an aspect which is its multiple decomposition into the individual entities of the class. Class variables, carrying aggregation and distribution information, are associated with the multiple entity, whereas instance variables, belonging to each instance of the class are associated with the entity.

One application of the SES/MB framework is to the design of systems. Here the SES serves as means of organizing and generating the possible configurations of a system to be designed. Although we will discuss the SES formalism in greater depth later, we discuss an example at this point so as to facilitate the reader's visualization of the concept.

2.4 Artificial Worlds Example

There is increasing interest in design and construction of "artificial" worlds, in the sense of large scale enclosures supporting human, animal and plant habitation placed in environments, such as the moon, which would otherwise not support life. Modern materials technology has made it possible to build and isolate such systems from interaction with external environments. Modern high technology has supplied the information processing hardware needed to "wire" the system for the necessary observation and control. Modern design methodology must be invoked to marshall these powerful means toward achieving desired objectives. Proper design entails intensive application of techniques of modelling and simulation and of knowledge representation. Artificial worlds engineering is a prime example of the need for multifacetted modelling methodology to deal in a coherent manner with the multiplicity of facets involved in large scale systems.

A *biosphere* is a stable, complex, evolving system containing life, composed of various ecosystems operating in a synergetic equilibrium, completely closed to material input or output, and open to energy and information exchanges. The earth ecosystem is the only such biosphere currently known. Biosphere II (Hayes, 1989) is a unique, non-governmentally sponsored project to create an analog of the earth ecosystem (Biosphere I) in an encapsulated structure spanning 2.5 acres located 20 miles north of Tucson Arizona. The knowledge gained in experimenting with Biosphere II, a faster responding replica of the earth, could be invaluable in solving the latter's ecosystemic problems. Such a biosphere would provide a potential means of establishing permanent manned stations in space, or on other planets, as research and observation bases and eventually colonization.

Complete material closure implies recycling of wastes and regeneration of all consumable resources: a major set of problems for which Biosphere II may demonstrate solutions. However, complete material closure is not a necessity in many life support environments such as projected space stations, antarctic colonies, manned expeditions below the earth's surface, radiation impregnable habitats, etc. In such circumstances, although recycling of wastes and regeneration of vital resources would be advantageous, disposal of some wastes and resupply of some consumables might prove more feasible than complete closure. The point to be made is that there are a great variety of alternatives in the continuum between partial closure and complete closure to be explored in the engineering of such artificial worlds.

2.4.1 SES for Life Support Systems

Figure 2.7 is a system entity structure for designing life support systems in artificial worlds. The figure shows that a LSS (life support system), the top-most, or root, entity, in its broadest context consists of number of subsystems including: (reading from left to right) a radiation protection subsystem, an expendables resupply subsystem, an energy supply system, etc. These subsystems are identified as entities falling under an aspect called LSS-DEC, which represents the decomposition of the LSS into the just mentioned components. Generally, entities may have one or more ways of being decomposed, each represented by an aspect (labelled decomposition). For example, the food supply system has a decomposition, FOOD-SUP-DEC which breaks it into food production and food storage subsystems. The food production subsystem is further decomposed, under food-prod-dec, into several entities, the growth medium, the harvesting subsystem, nutrient supply subsystem, and plant waste recycling system.

Also ubiquitous in Figure 2.7a is a third organizational concept (besides entity and aspect), namely SPECIALIZATION. SPECIALIZATION is a means of representing the possible variants or forms that an entity might assume. For example, the LSS might be biologically based, physical/chemical based, or a hybrid of both. This is represented in the specialization LSS-SPEC, shown with a double line, as are all specializations to visually distinguish them from aspects. A biologically based LSS has a specialization, BIO-SPEC, which has as one variant an earth biome-based bioregenerative LSS such as Biosphere II, and other biologically based alternatives that do not attempt to replicate the function of the earth's biomes.

A property of the entity structure formalism is that it automatically brings to bear all the defining features of a component in every context in which it appears. For example, since biological LSS is a

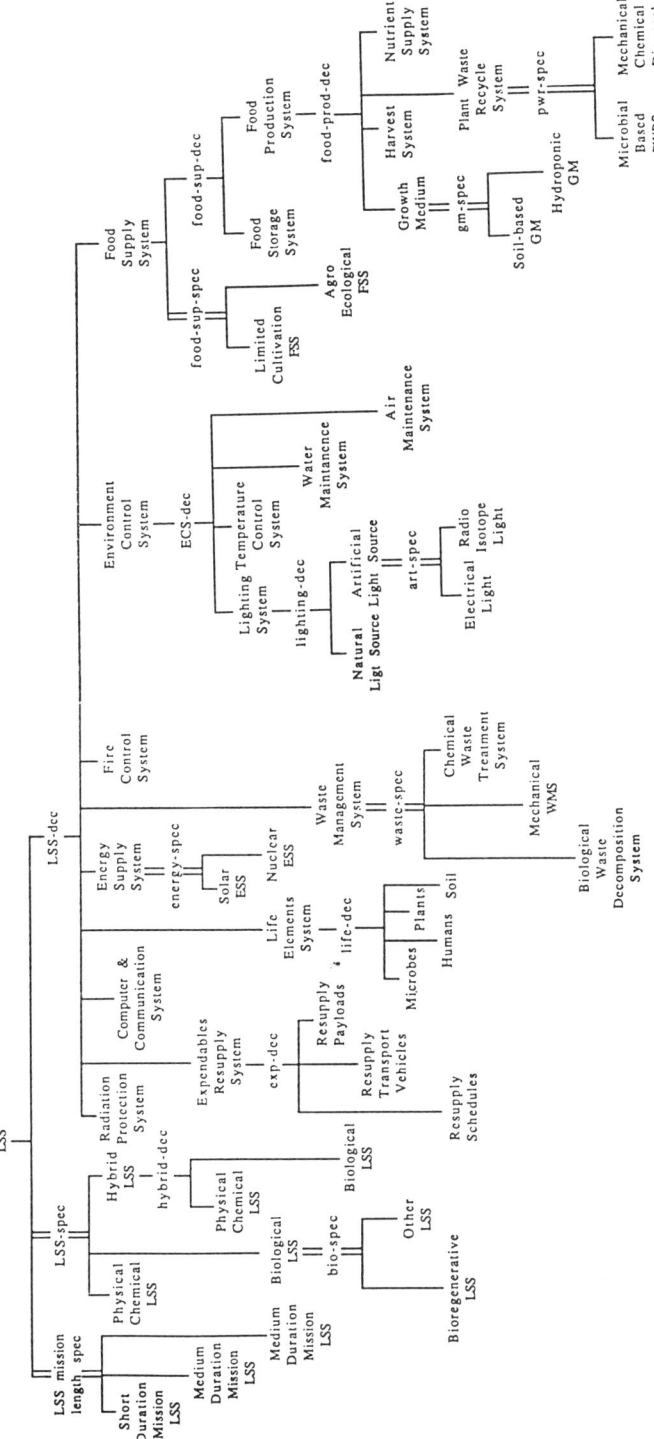

Figure 2.7a. SES for life support system.

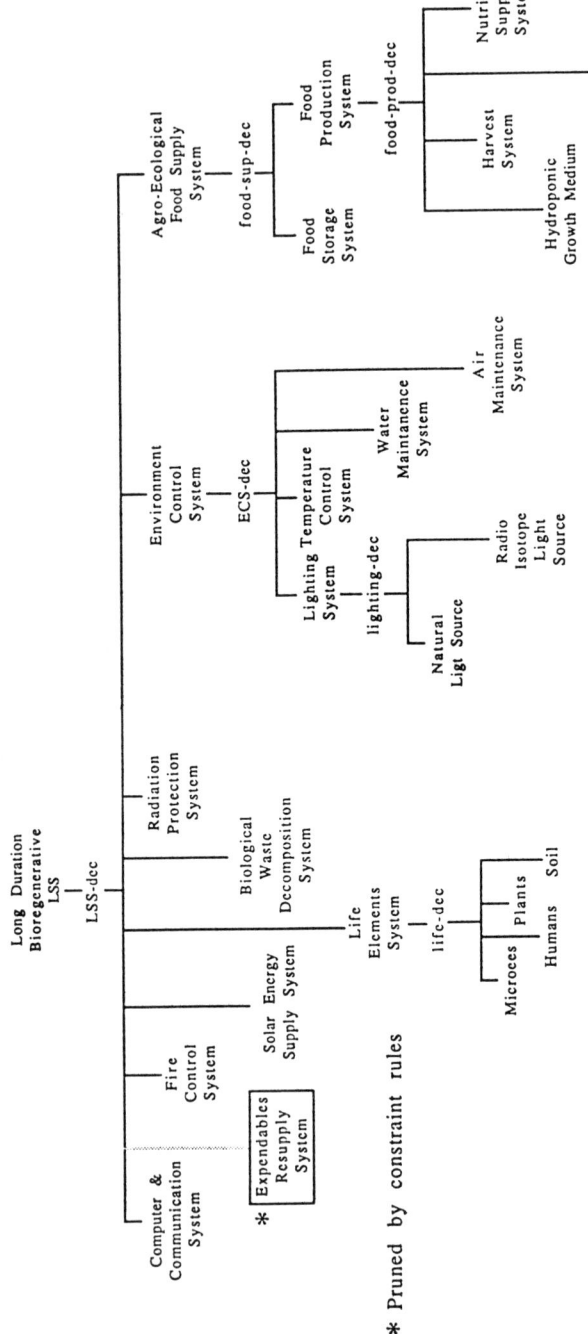

Figure 2.7b. Pruned system entity structure for long duration mission using bioregenerative LSS.

component of a hybrid LSS, the alternatives for biological LSS, shown under the BIO-SPEC specialization, also present themselves as choices in this context, as well as in the non-hybrid alternative. This means that when considering hybrid life support systems, we should consider the various combinations of alternatives that will be available for both its biological and physical/chemical components. Although many of these combinations may not be feasible, some very good ones may emerge that might not have considered in a non-systematic approach.

System design is the process of generating candidate designs and ranking them with respect to design objectives. To start generating a candidate we use a process called *pruning* which reduces the SES to a so-called *pruned entity structure* (PES). An example of such a pruned structure is shown in Figure 2.7b. Note that such structures are derived from the governing structure by a process of selecting from alternatives where ever such choices are presented (we shall have much more to say about pruning later). Not all choices may be selected independently. Once some alternatives are chosen at a high level, some options are closed and others are enabled. Moreover, rules may be associated with the entity structure which further reduce the set of configurations that must be considered. For example, a long duration bioregenerative mission would not need an expendables resupply system — having selected this type of mission from the specializations under LSS a constraint rule would automatically eliminate expendables-resupply-system from LSS-DEC.

2.5 SES Pruning and Model Synthesis

As shown in Figure 2.8, pruned entity structures are stored along with the SES in files forming the *entity structure base*. Hierarchical simulation models may be constructed by applying the *transform* function to pruned entity structures in working memory. As it traverses the pruned entity structure, *transform* calls upon a retrieval process to search for a model of the current entity. If one is found, it is used and transformation of the entity subtree is aborted.

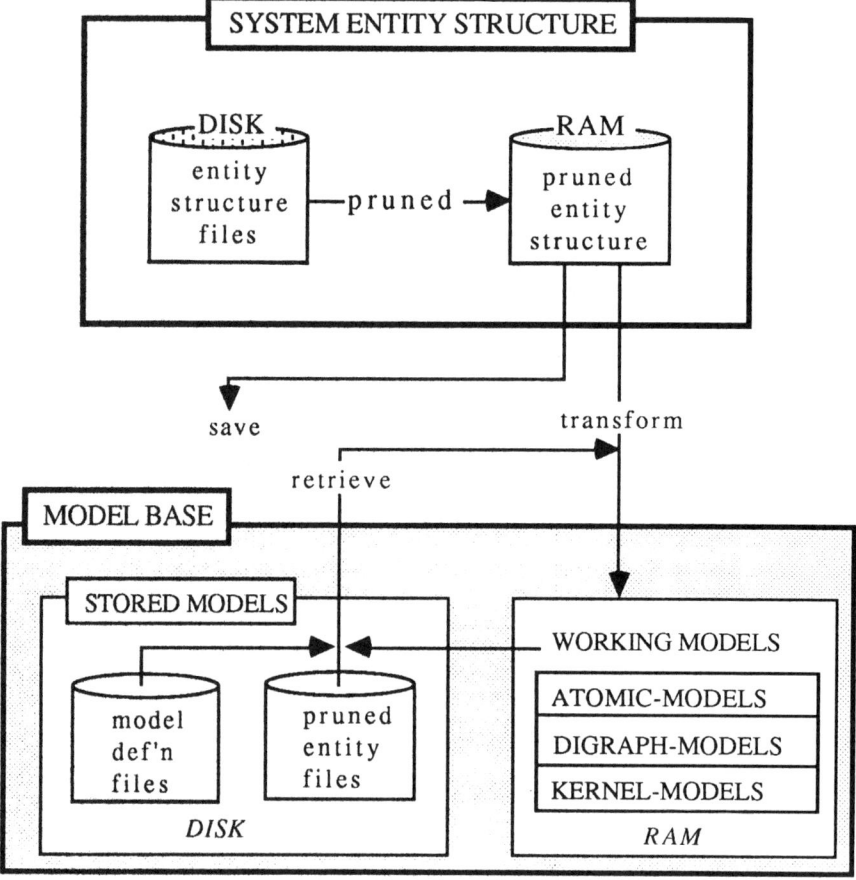

Figure 2.8. The System Entity Structure/Model Base (SES/MB) Environment.

Basics 39

Retrieve looks for a model first in working memory (we shall see that such a model may be an instance of the classes *atomic-models* or *coupled-models*, whose main subclasses are *digraph-models* and *kernel-models*). If no model is found in working memory, then the *retrieve* procedure searches through model definition files, and finally, provided that the entity is a leaf, in pruned entity structure files. A new incarnation of the *transform* process is spawned to construct the leaf model in the last case. Once this construction is complete, the main *transform* process is resumed.

The result of a transformation is a model expressed in an underlying simulation language such as DEVS-Scheme which is ready to be simulated and evaluated relative to the modeler's objectives.

The fact that the *transform* process can look for previously developed pruned entity structures, in addition to basic model files, has an important consequence for reusability — as we shall see in Chapter 13. The reader is certainly allowed to peak ahead to see why. However, before proceeding with the more advanced ideas, let us build up our understanding of DEVS-Scheme: Layer 1.

Chapter 3

DEVS FORMALISM AND DEVS-SCHEME

This chapter reviews the DEVS formalism and its implementation in DEVS-Scheme. Although we don't dwell on the mathematical properties of the DEVS formalism, understanding its basic features helps to understand how hierarchical, modular simulation models are specified in DEVS-Scheme.

3.1 Discrete Event Dynamic Systems

Discrete event modelling is finding ever more application to analysis and design of complex manufacturing, communication, and computer systems among others. Long overdue recognition of the importance of the field emerged with the publication of a special issue of *IEEE Proceedings* on DEDS (Discrete Event Dynamic Systems) edited by Yu-chi Ho (1989). Powerful languages and workstations been developed for describing such models for computer simulation (see Garzia *et al.*, 1986 for a general review). Yet general understanding of the nature of discrete event systems *per se* (as distinct from their computer representations) is still in relative infancy compared to that of continuous systems.

3.1.1 A Bit of History

Differential equations employed to describe continuous systems have a long history of development whose mathematical formalization came well before the advent of the computer. In contrast, discrete event simulations were made possible by, and evolved with, the growing computational power of computers. The prime requirement for conducting such simulation was to be able to program a computer appropriately. Not of immediate utility, computer-independent model description formalisms for discrete event systems, paralleling the differential equations for continuous systems, were late in coming. Yet, it is now being recognized that our understanding of complex systems may be greatly enhanced with such mathematically based formalisms.

Since the early 70's work has been proceeding on a mathematical formalism for modelling discrete event systems. One approach, inspired by the systems theory concepts of Zadeh and Dosoer (1963), Wymore (1967), Mesarovic and Takahara (1975), and Arbib and Padulo (1974), attempted to cast both continuous and discrete event models within a common systems modelling framework. This approach was elaborated in a number of publications primarily summarized in the books (Zeigler, 1976) and (Zeigler, 1984a), and is reviewed in (Zeigler, 1984b). Systems modelling concepts were an important facet in a movement to develop a methodology under which simulation could be performed in a more principled and secure manner (see for example Ören et al., 1984). The recent advent of high performance artificial intelligence software and hardware has facilitated the transfer of this simulation methodology from research to practice (Elzas et al., 1986).

3.1.2 The DEVS Approach

The Discrete Event System Specification (DEVS) formalism introduced by Zeigler (1976) provides a means of specifying a mathematical object called a system. Basically, a system has a time base, inputs, states, and outputs, and functions for determining next states and outputs given current states and inputs (Zeigler, 1984b). Discrete event systems represent certain constellations of such parameters just as continuous systems do. For example, the inputs in discrete event systems occur at arbitrarily spaced moments, while those in continuous systems are piecewise continuous functions of time. The insight provided by the DEVS formalism is in the simple way that it characterizes how discrete event simulation languages specify discrete event system parameters. Having this abstraction, it is possible to design new simulation languages with sound semantics that are easier to understand. Indeed, the DEVS-Scheme environment to be described later is an implementation of the DEVS formalism in Scheme (a Lisp dialect) which enables the modeler to specify models directly in its terms. DEVS-Scheme supports building models in a hierarchical, modular manner described above. This is a systems oriented approach not possible in popular commercial simulation languages such as SIMSCRIPT, SIMULA, GASP, SLAM and SIMAN (all of which are discrete event based) or CSMP and ACSL (which are for continuous models). [1]

The DEVS formalism is more than just a means of constructing simulation models. It provides a formal representation of discrete event systems capable of mathematical manipulation just as differential equations serve this role for continuous systems. Such manipulation includes behavioral analysis whereby properties of the behavior of a system are deduced by examining its structure. Although this is an area of intense investigation, such analysis is difficult — we return to this thought in a moment. Therefore, direct computer simulation will remain a primary means of generating, and studying, model behavior. However, other kinds of processing, are equally important: mathematical representations may be compared, transformed into other forms, simplified, decomposed and reconstituted in a great variety of ways (Ören, 1987; Pichler, 1986). Much of this type of processing can be automated within a symbol manipulation such as Scheme, as we shall see.

---

[1] DEVS-Scheme can be used to map into such languages however; see Appendix A.1.

3.1.3 DEVS in Relation to Other Approaches

A number of other approaches to modelling DEDS are brought together in the above-mentioned special issue (Ho, 1989). Many are algebraic or graphical in character and do not include the time element that DEVS inherits from its system theoretic origins. The most closely related formalisms are those emerging under the framework of Generalized Semi-Markov Processes (GSMP), in which we can include the stochastic generalizations of Petri Nets (Sanders, 1988). GSMP, as formulated by Glynn (1989) and Cassandras and Strickland (1989), attempt to formalize discrete event simulation models as Markov processes with countable state sets that are amenable to mathematical analysis. The relationship between DEVS and GSMPs needs to be explored. However, in Appendix B, we show that DEVS appears to the more powerful formalism, trading mathematical tractability for expressive power.

Chapter 14 provides an in-depth comparison of DEVS-Scheme with other knowledge-based simulation environments.

3.2 Brief Review of the DEVS Formalism

Figure 3.1 depicts the conceptual framework underlying the DEVS formalism (Zeigler, 1976). The modelling and simulation enterprise concerns three basic objects:

- the *real system*, in existence or proposed, which is regarded as fundamentally a source of data.

- the *model*, which is a set of instructions for generating data comparable to that observable in the real system. The structure of the model is its set of instructions. The behavior of the model is the set of all possible data that can be generated by faithfully executing the model instructions.

- the *simulator* which exercises the model's instructions to actually generate its behavior.

The basic objects are related by two relations:

- the *modelling relation*, linking real system and model, defines how well the model represents the system or entity being modelled. In general terms a model can be considered valid if the data generated by the model agrees with the data produced by the real system in an experimental frame of interest.
- The *simulation relation*, linking model and simulator, represents how faithfully the simulator is able to carry out the instructions of the model.

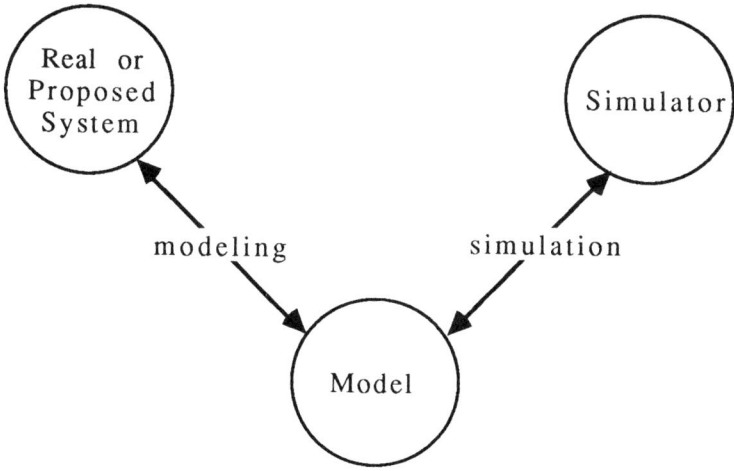

Figure 3.1. Entities and relations in simulation.

There is a crucial element which must be brought into this picture — the experimental frame.[2] This captures how the modeller's

---

[2]The interpretation of the experimental frame concept in simulation languages is still evolving. GEST (Ören, 1980) was the first conceptual language to sharp

objectives impact on model construction, experimentation and validation. As we shall see later, in DEVS-Scheme, experimental frames are formulated as model objects in the same manner as the models of primary interest. In this way, model/experimental frame pairs form coupled model objects with the same properties as other objects of this kind. It will become evident later, that this uniform treatment yields immediate benefits in terms of modularity and system entity structure representation. For an alternate formulation, see Ören (1989).

The basic items of data produced by a system or model are *time segments*. These time segments are mappings from intervals defined over a specified time base to values in the ranges of one or more variables. The variables can either be observed or measured. An example of a data segment is shown in Figure 3.2.

The structure of a model may be expressed in a mathematical language called a *formalism*. The discrete event formalism focuses on the changes of variable values and generates time segments that are piecewise constant. Thus an event[3] is a change in a variable value which occurs instantaneously as shown in Figure 3.3.

In essence the formalism defines how to generate new values for variables and the times the new values should be take effect. An important aspect of the formalism is that the time intervals between

---

distinguish model and experiment specifications. SIMAN (Pedgen, 1983) was the first commercial language to incorporate a modicum of separation between model and experimental frame along the lines suggested by Zeigler (1976) and Ören and Zeigler (1979). The uniform treatment of experimental frame objects and models objects in DEVS-Scheme implements a more recent formalization (Zeigler, 1984). The situation is somewhat complicated in continuous simulation where execution control parameters, such as step size and communication interval, can be considered to be part of the experimentation specification. In contrast to perhaps a more widely held view expressed by Ören (1989), I believe that execution control specification should be not be included in the experimental frame. The implementation of continuous simulation within DEVS-Scheme by Wang (1989) shows how this can be done (see Appendix A.1).

[3]We distinguish events, which are changes in value, from event generating mechanisms. The latter are simulation constructs (e.g., event routines) that at certain (scheduled) times determine whether an event actually occurs and what new values for variables are established.

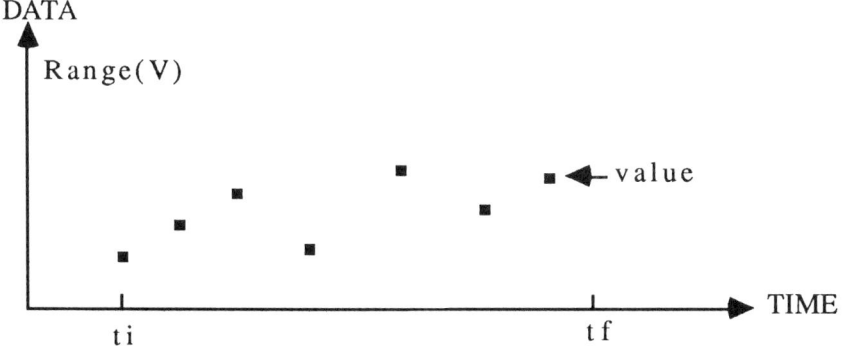

Range(V): set of values that V can assume

ti: initial (starting) time

tf: final (terminating) time

Figure 3.2. Generalized data segment produced by a system or model.

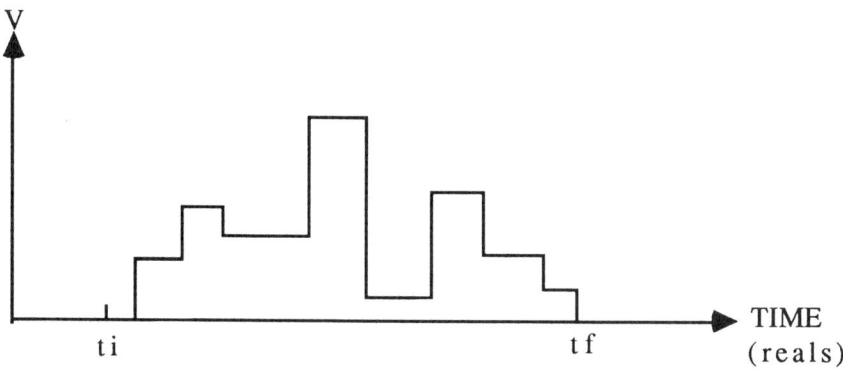

Figure 3.3. Discrete event time segment.

event occurrences are variable (in contrast to discrete time where the time step is a fixed number).

3.3 Basic Models

In the DEVS formalism, one must specify 1) basic models from which larger ones are built, and 2) how these models are connected together in hierarchical fashion. In this formalism basic models are defined by the structure

$$M = \langle X, S, Y, \delta_{int}, \delta_{ext}, \lambda, ta \rangle$$

where X is the set of external input event types, S is the sequential state set, Y is the set of external event types generated as output, δ_{int} (δ_{ext}) is the internal (external) transition function dictating state transitions due to internal (external input) events, λ is the output function generating external events at the output, and ta is the time-advance function. Rather than reproduce the full mathematical definition here (Zeigler, 1984), we proceed to describe how it is realized in DEVS-Scheme.

To specify modular discrete event models requires that we adopt a different view than that fostered by traditional simulation languages. As with modular specification in general, we must view a model as possessing input and output ports through which all interaction with the environment is mediated. In the discrete event case, events determine values appearing on such ports. More specifically, when external events, arising outside the model, are received on its input ports, the model description must determine how it responds to them. Also, internal events arising within the model, change its state, as well as manifesting themselves as events on the output ports to be transmitted to other model components.

A basic model contains the following information:

- the set of input ports through which external events are received

- the set of output ports through which external events are sent

DEVS Formalism and DEVS-Scheme

- the set of state variables and parameters: two state variables are usually present — *phase* and *sigma* (in the absence of external events the system stays in the current *phase* for the time given by *sigma*)

- the time advance function which controls the timing of internal transitions — when the *sigma* state variable is present, this function just returns the value of *sigma*.

- the internal transition function which specifies to which next state the system will transit after the time given by the time advance function has elapsed

- the external transition function with specifies how the system changes state when an input is received — the effect is to place the system in a new *phase* and *sigma* thus scheduling it for a next internal transition; the next state is computed on the basis of the present state, the input port and value of the external event, and the time that has elapsed in the current state.

- the output function which generates an external output just before an internal transition takes place.

3.3.1 Pseudo-code Description of Basic Models

A pseudo-code facilitates such model specification and its expression within DEVS-Scheme. Each input port requires specification of an external transition, in the form of a

> when receive x on input port p ...

phrase.

The internal transition function can be specified in the form of a process-like description with phases and their transitions. The output function uses phrases of the form

> send y to output port p.

As an example, consider a simple buffering model in Figure 3.4a. There are three input ports: *in*, for receiving items to be buffered, *done*, for receiving the acknowledgement of the down stream process, and *stop_send* for flow control from the up stream process. The output port out, is for sending items down stream. The pseudo-code description is in Figure 3.4b.

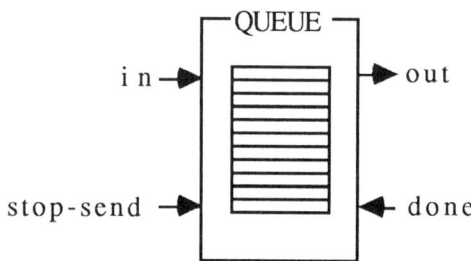

Figure 3.4a. Simple buffering model.

The pseudo-code makes use of the variables e (elapsed time in current phase) and σ (time left in current phase) which are essential to achieving modularity in discrete event models. These variables are assumed to be managed by the simulation executive. Although, such management takes the form of a global event list in the case of conventional simulation languages, other implementations, such as that in DEVS-Scheme, may be more advantageous in conventional as well as multiprocessor simulation architectures.

Note that the external transition specification has three *when receive* phrases, one for each input port. The first says that when an input value x is received on the in port, it should be inserted in a queue; if it is the only member of the queue, control should be sent to the phase SEND, otherwise the model should continue (no new internal event will be scheduled). The internal transition specification has only one phase, SEND, in which the model stays for a period, *preparation-time* — this causes the scheduling of an internal transition to occur at *time = current time + preparation-time*. Upon occurrence of the event, the model sends the first value in its queue to the output port *out*, removes it from the queue, and then passivates. The PASSIVE phase (in which the model passivates) represents a "ground" phase of the model in which it waits for external events while engaging in internal activity of its own.

```
----------------- external transition specification----------
    when receive x on port in
        insert(x,queue)
        if one(queue) then
                e := preparation-time
                hold-in SEND for e
            else continue

    when receive done on port done
        if not empty(queue) then
                e := preparation-time
                hold-in SEND for e
            else continue

    when receive x on port stop_send with elapsed time e
        if phase = SEND and x = stop then
                processing-time-left := e - e
                passivate

        if passive and x = start then
                e := processing-time-left
                hold-in SEND for e
            else continue

----------------- internal transition specification----------
    If phase = SEND then
        queue:=rest(queue)
        passivate
-------------------- output specification -----------------
    If phase = SEND then
        send first(queue) to port out
```

Figure 3.4b. The pseudo-code description of a simple buffering model.

The phrase "continue" indicates that the time remaining in the phase in which the model finds itself is not to be changed as result of the external event processing. To express an interruption requiring a change in scheduling we replace continue statements by those manipulating σ, as the specification for the input port *stop_send* shows. This external event, if indicating stop, causes the model to leave phase SEND, where it is holding, and abort the current transmission; if indicating start, transmission is re-initiated.

Change in scheduling is brought about as σ is changed from a finite value to infinity in the first case. Supposing that the time already spent in preparing the output need not be repeated when transmission is resumed, we store the remaining time (σ - e) in *processing-time-left* for restoration to σ upon re-entry to the SEND phase. Were there several jobs that could be in suspended states of this kind at once, we would save a processing-time-left with each one.

3.3.2 DEVS-Scheme Implementation of DEVS Basic Models

In the DEVS-Scheme realization, the DEVS formalism is refined so that both the input and output sets X, Y consist of pairs of the form (port, value). Thus, an external input event of the form $x = (p, v)$ signals the fact that a value v has been received at an input port p. Similarly, $y = (p, v)$ represents the sending of a value v to output port p.

Port-value pairs are specified using the structure definition:

(define-structure content port value).

This definition creates a template for a structure type named content so that an instance may be created using the *make-content* function. The slots *port* and *value* are accessed using the *content-port* and *content-value* procedures created by Scheme.

The set-theoretic components of the DEVS formalism take the form of Figure 3.5. Due to the absence of typed variables, the abstract input, state and output sets of the formalism cannot be completely characterized in Scheme. Indeed, this fact makes it possible for DEVS-Scheme to be completely general. However, the four basic functions are expected to receive and return arguments consistent with the DEVS formalism as indicated in Figure 3.5.

To illustrate consider a simple model (itself of no significance beyond illustration). The model state is numerical, each internal transition causes a doubling in value; internal transitions occur every

DEVS Formalism and DEVS-Scheme

```
Let
    s represent a data object standing for sequential state
    e be a non-negative number
    x represent a content structure for a port-value pair

Then definitions in DEVS-Scheme adhere to the forms:
```

* internal transition function:

    (define (int s)...)

    returns same type as s

* external transition function:

    (define (ext s e x)...)

    returns same type as s

* output function:

    (define (out s)...)

    returns a content structure

* time advance function:

    (define (ta s)...)

    returns a non-negative number or 'inf (symbol for infinity)

The ... represent function body definitions expressed in Scheme.

Figure 3.5. How the set theoretic components of the basic DEVS formalism are realized in DEVS-Scheme.

1 unit. Formally,

$$S = \text{Reals}$$
$$\delta_{int}(s) = 2 * s$$
$$ta(s) = 1$$

In DEVS-Scheme, this model is represented by the definitions:

(define (int s)   (* 2 s))
(define (ta s)   1)

Note that *(int s)* will yield a numerical value so long as *s* is initially set to a number. This meets the requirement that the internal transition function map values from the state set back into itself. Similarly, *(ta s)* always returns a non-negative number (namely, 1) as required by the formal definition.

Let us add an external transition function which causes the input value to be added to the current state:

$$\delta_{ext}\ (s\ e\ x) = s + x.$$

Note that the external transition function has three arguments: *s* (the current state), *e* (the elapsed time in this state), and *x* (the external input causing this event).[4] The DEVS-Scheme representation is:

(define (ext s e x)   (+ s (content-value x)))

Note that the input *x* is expected to be in the form of a content structure as indicated above. Moreover, the value field in this content structure must be a number for the addition to the current state to make sense. For example, we might generate such a content structure by:

(define x1   (make-content 'port 'in 'value 3))

Here *(content-value x1)* = 3, so that 3 will be added to the current state when *x1* is received. So long as content structures with numerical values are applied as input to the model, the external transition function returns a numerical value. Thus, it also meets the requirement of mapping to the state set expected by the internal transition.

As it stands, our external transition function does not check for the port on which the input event is occurring. This can be remedied with the definition:

(define (ext s e x)
  (if (equal? (content-port x) 'in)
    (+ s (content-value x))
    (bkpt "input not on port 'in "(content-port x))))

The *content-structure x1*, defined above, meets the requirement that *(ext 7 0 x1)* evaluates to 10. However, the input *(make-content 'port*

---

[4]The fact that the arguments spell a popular three-letter word is purely coincidental!

'*enter 'value 2)* will cause a breakpoint to occur in processing when given as an argument to *ext*.

Adding an output function follows the same principles:

$$\lambda(s) = s.$$

causes the output generated just before a state transition to be the current value of the state. In DEVS-Scheme, this is:

(define (out s)(make-content 'port 'out 'value s))

Although the sequential state can be an arbitrary data object, usually we use a so-called normal form representation. In this representation, the state is specified as a structure with a definition of the form:

(define-structure state phase sigma ...)

where the "..." indicates additional state variables may be added. In this case, the s argument in Figure 3.5, is an instance of the state structure and both internal and external transition functions must return state structures of the same form. We shall discuss further details using the examples in the next chapter.

3.4 Coupled Models

Basic-models may be coupled in the DEVS formalism to form a multicomponent model which is defined by the structure:

$DN = \langle D, \{M_i\}, \{I_i\}, \{Z_{i,j}\}, select \rangle$.
where
D is a set of component names;
for each i in D,
M_i is a component basic model
I_i is a set, the influences of i

and for each j in I_i,
$Z_{i,j}$ is a function, the i-to-j output translation
and
select is a function, the tie-breaking selector.

Multi-component models are implemented in DEVS-Scheme as coupled models. A coupled model, tells how to couple (connect) several component models together to form a new model. This latter model can itself be employed as a component in a larger coupled model, thus giving rise to hierarchical construction. A coupled model contains the following information:

- the set of components

- for each component, its influencees

- the set of input ports through which external events are received

- the set of output ports through which external events are sent

- as discussed earlier in Chapter 2, the coupling specification consisting of:

    - the external input coupling which connects the input ports of the coupled to model to one or more of the input ports of the components — this directs inputs received by the coupled model to designated component models

    - the external output coupling which connects output ports of components to output ports of the coupled model — thus when an output is generated by a component it may be sent to a designated output port of the coupled model and thus be transmitted externally

    - the internal coupling which connects output ports of components to input ports of other components — when an input is generated by a component it may be sent to the input ports of designated components (in addition to being sent to an output port of the coupled model)

- the select function which embodies the rules employed to choose which of the imminent components (those having the minimum time of next event) is allowed to carry out its next event.

A multi-component model DN can be expressed as an equivalent basic model in the DEVS formalism (Zeigler, 1984). Such an basic model can itself be employed in a larger multi-component model. This shows that the formalism is closed under coupling as required for hierarchical model construction. Expressing a multi-component model DN as an equivalent basic model captures the means by which the components interact to yield the overall behavior. We shall briefly discuss this interaction (the reader is free to skip this section and to return to it for reference later when the simulation process in DEVS-Scheme is described).

3.4.1 Expressing a Multi-component Model as a Basic Model

At any event time t, each component, i is in a state s_i and has been there for an elapsed time e_i. The time advance in state s_i is $ta_i(s_i)$ so that component i is scheduled for an internal event at time $t + (ta_i(s_i) - e_i)$. The next event in the system will occur at a time which is the minimum of these scheduled times, namely, at time $t + \sigma$, where σ is the minimum of the residual times, $(ta_i(s_i) - e_i)$, over the components i in DN. Of those components whose remaining times $(ta_i(s_i) - e_i)$ are equal to the minimum, we choose one using the tie breaking *select* function. Let i^* be this selected, or imminent, component. At time $t + \sigma$, just before i^* changes state, it computes its output $y^* = \lambda_i^*(s_i^*)$. This output is sent to each of the influencees of i^* in the form of a translated input: for influencee j, the input, x_{i*j} is $Z_{i*j}(y^*)$. The elapsed time at any component i at time $t + \sigma$ is just $e_i' = e_i + \sigma$. An influencee, j responds to the external event generated by i^* by applying its external transition function, to obtain the next state $s_j' = \delta_{ext}(s_j, e_j', x_{i*j})$ and to reset its elapsed time to 0. Other components not in the influencee set are unaffected by the activation of i^* except that their elapsed time clock is incremented by σ as just described. Finally, the imminent component i^* executes its internal transition by going to state $s_i^{*\prime} = \delta_{int}(s_i^*)$ and resetting its elapsed time to 0.

Let the state of the basic DEVS model M, representing the overall system, be the vector of states $s = (s_i, e_i)$ of the components. The the above describes how M's time advance and internal transition functions work. Namely, the time advance in state s, $ta(s) = \sigma$, the smallest of the residual times of each of the components. At the next event, M's internal transition function transforms the given state to a new vector (s'_i, e'_i) computed according to the above recipe. We can similarly follow the effect of an external input event arriving to some of the components and thereby derive the external transition function of the basic model.

3.5 DEVS-Scheme Simulation Environment

The DEVS formalism underlies DEVS-Scheme, a general purpose environment for constructing hierarchical discrete event models. DEVS-Scheme is written in the PC-Scheme language (Texas Instruments, 1986) which runs on DOS compatible microcomputers and under a Scheme interpreter for the Texas Instruments Explorer. DEVS-Scheme is implemented as a shell that sits upon PC-Scheme in such a way that all of the underlying Lisp-based and objected oriented programming language features are available to the user. The result is a powerful basis for combining AI and simulation techniques.

The architecture of the DEVS-Scheme simulation system is derived from the abstract simulator concepts (Concepcion and Zeigler, 1987) associated with the hierarchical, modular DEVS formalism. Since such a scheme is naturally implemented by multiprocessor architectures, models developed in DEVS-Scheme are readily transportable to distributed simulation systems designed according to such principles. Finally, since structure descriptions in DEVS-Scheme are accessible to run-time modification, the environment provides a convenient basis for development of learning or evolutionary models which adapt or change their own internal structure.

This section provides a brief overview of DEVS-Scheme.

3.5.1 Classes

DEVS-Scheme is principally coded in SCOOPS, the object-oriented superset of PC-Scheme (Texas Instruments, 1986). The class specialization hierarchy is illustrated in Figure 3.6.

All classes in DEVS-Scheme are subclasses of the universal class *entities* which provides tools for manipulating objects in these classes. The inheritance mechanism ensures that such general facilities need only be defined once and for all. Entities of a desired class may be constructed using *mk-ent* and destroyed using *destroy*. More specifically, *mk-ent* makes the entity and places it in the list of members of the given class, *lst*; destroy removes the entity from this list. Every entity has a *name*, assigned to it upon creation,

Models and *processors*, the main subclasses of entities, provide the basic constructs needed for modelling and simulation. *Models* is further specialized into the major classes *atomic-models* and *coupled-models*, which in turn are specialized into more specific cases, a process which may be continued indefinitely as the user builds up a specific model base. Class *processors*, on the other hand, has three specializations: *simulators*, *co-ordinators*, and *root-co-ordinators*, which serve to handle all the simulation needs.

3.5.2 Modelling: The Class Models

Models and *processors* are intermediary classes which serve to provide basic slots needed by their specializations. For example, *models* has instance variables *processor* (which records the processor responsible for handling it), *parent* (its parent coupled-model, if it is a component in one. Class *atomic-models* realizes the atomic level of the underlying model formalism. It has variables corresponding to each of the parts of this formalism. For example, in the DEVS formalism, *atomic-models* has instance variables *int-transfn*, *ext-transfn*, *outputfn*, and *time-advancefn* which specify a model's internal transition function, external transition function, output function, and time-advance function, respectively. These functions are applied to

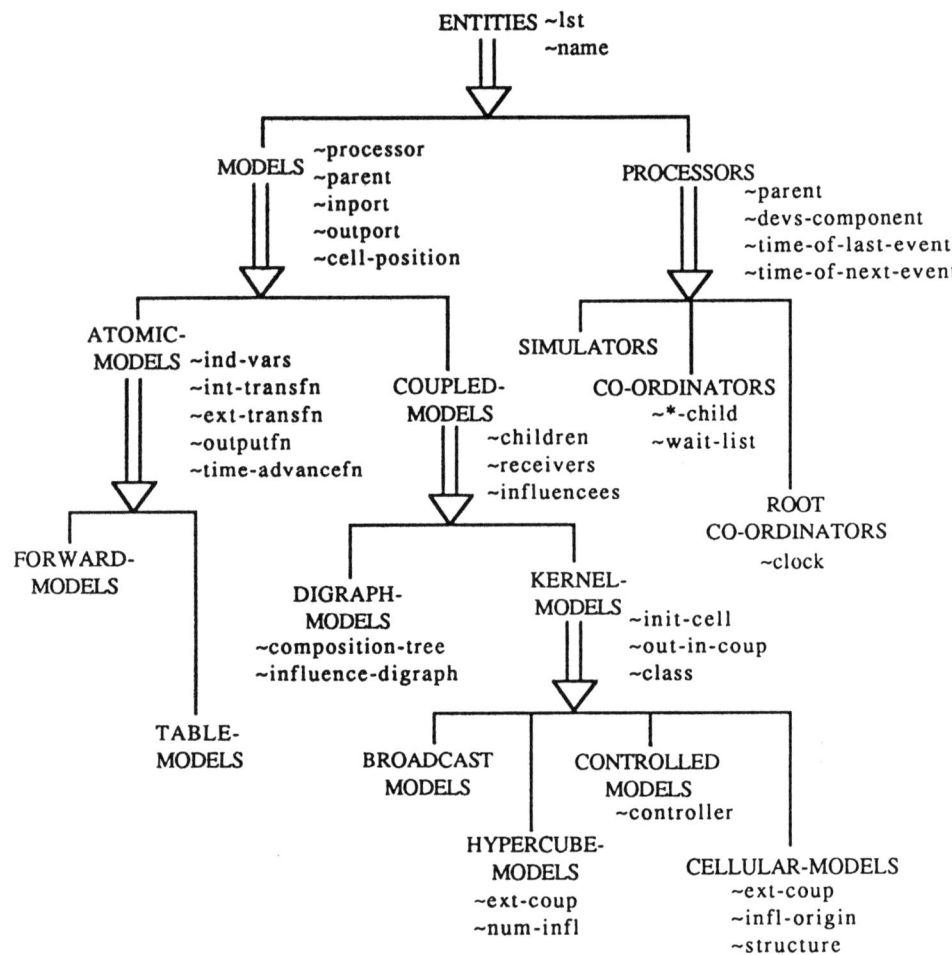

Figure 3.6. Class hierarchy of DEVS-Scheme.

DEVS Formalism and DEVS-Scheme

the state of the model by the methods *int-transition*, *ext-transition*, *output?* and *time-advance?*.

Coupled-models is the major class which embodies the hierarchical model composition constructs of the DEVS formalism; *digraph-models* and *kernel-models* are specializations which enable specification of coupled models in specific ways. A coupled model is defined by specifying its component models, called its *children*, and the coupling relations which establish the desired communication links. Accordingly, any specialization of *coupled-models* is expected to supply the methods:

- *get-children*, which returns the list of components,

- *get-influencees*, which determines those siblings to which the output of the imminent component will be sent,

- *get-receivers*, which determines which subcomponents will receive an external event input to the parent coupled model,

- *translate* which provides port-to-port translation.

Instances of the class *kernel-models* are coupled models which link together all existing instances of a specific model class or models generated from the same entity structure. The *children*, *influencees*, and *receivers* are uniquely determined by the particular specialization of *kernel-models*, of which there are currently four: *broadcast-models*, *hypercube-models*, *cellular-models* and *controlled-models*. The idea of broadcasting is that all subcomponents of a coupled model communicate directly with each other and with the outside world. *Controlled-models* provides a means for representing centrally controlled systems and perhaps surprisingly, spatial relationships for mobile objects as will be illustrated later. *Hypercube-models* and *cellular-models* provide for coupling of components via a geometrically based neighborhood relations. The only additional information required is how to translate output ports to input ports. Method *add-port-pair* of *kernel-models* enables the modeller to provide this specification.

In contrast to *kernel-models*, *digraph-models* provides a means of specifying coupled models which are composed of a finite set of explicitly given components with explicitly specified coupling. Methods are available to build the *composition-tree* and *influence-digraph* structures which encode the external and internal coupling relationships, respectively. External input coupling couples the input ports of a coupled model to the input ports of its components. Likewise, external output coupling couples the output ports of the components to output ports of the coupled model. Internal coupling couples output ports of components to input ports of other components. Digraph models provides the required methods *get-influencees*, *get-receivers* and *translate* by inspecting the information provided in the *composition-tree* and *influence-digraph*.

3.5.3 Simulation: The Class Processors

The *simulators, co-ordinators,* and *root-co-ordinators* specialization classes of processors carry out the simulation of DEVS models by implementing the abstract simulator principles developed as part of the DEVS theory (Zeigler, 1984; Concepcion and Zeigler, 1988). In essence, an abstract simulator is an algorithmic description of how to carry out the instructions implicit in DEVS models to generate their behavior. The implementation in DEVS-Scheme has the characteristics of a "virtual multiprocessor" in that each of the processor objects could in principle be assigned to a different physical computer. This renders modelling in DEVS-Scheme a natural basis for implementing discrete event models on multi-computer architectures. An overall view of the simulation process is given here. Later, we return to provide further detail.

Simulators and co-ordinators are assigned to handle atomic models and coupled models in a one-to-one manner, respectively (Figure 3.7). The model-processor pairing is recorded in the variables *processor* and *devs-component* of the model and processor, respectively. A root-co-ordinator manages the overall simulation and is linked to the co-ordinator of the outermost coupled model. Simulation proceeds by means of messages passed among the processors which carry

DEVS Formalism and DEVS-Scheme

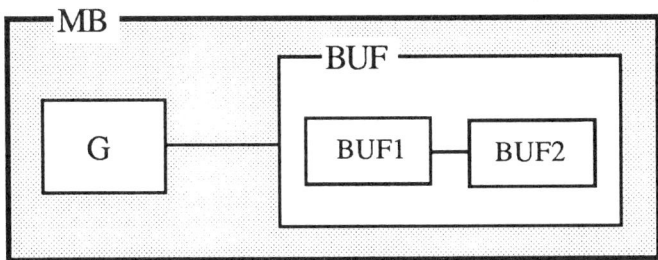

Figure 3.7a. A hierarchical model composed of a generator (G) and a buffer complex (BUF) which is a serial composition of two queuing buffers: BUF1 and BUF2.

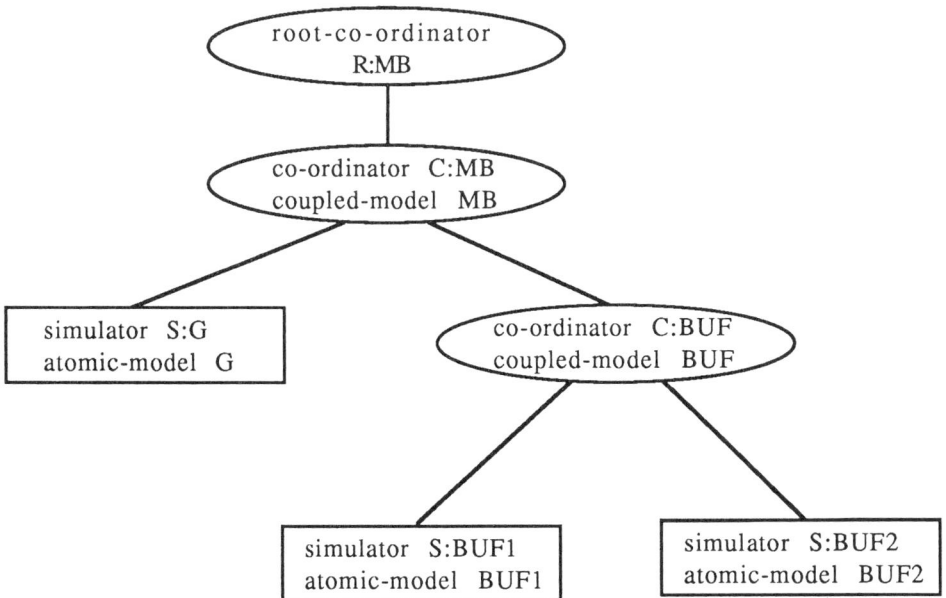

Figure 3.7b. The abstract simulator structure formed by assigning processors to the model components.

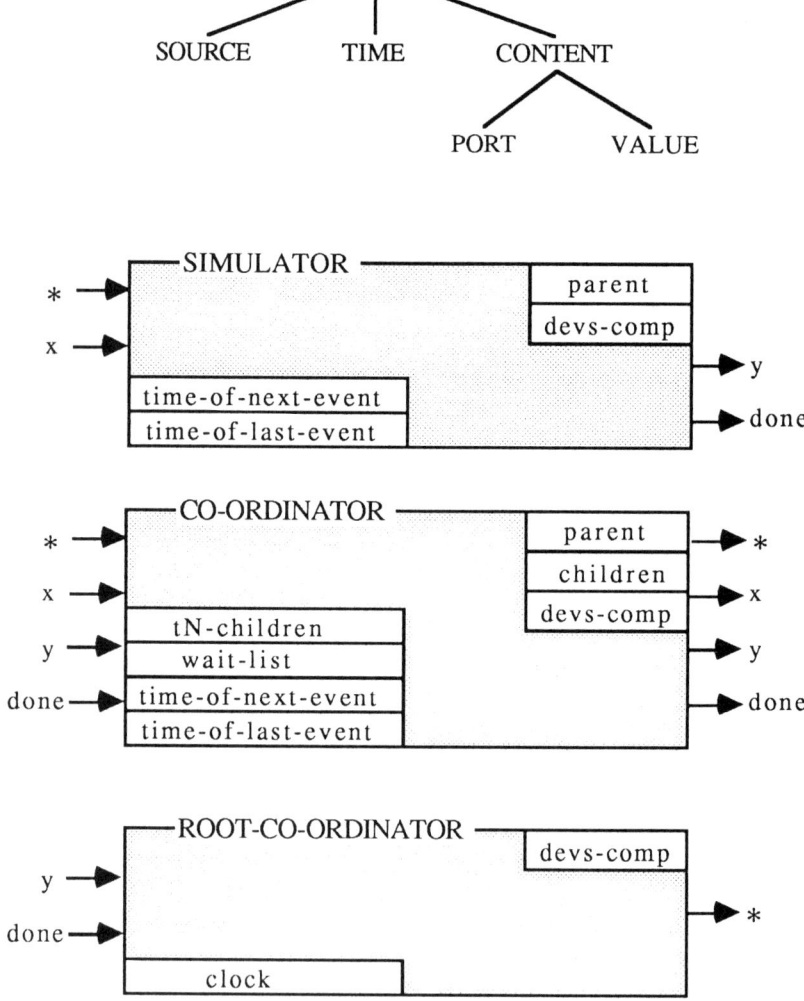

Figure 3.8. Illustrating the structure of messages exchanged among processors which manage simulation according to the abstract simulator scheme.

DEVS Formalism and DEVS-Scheme

information concerning internal and external events, as well as data need for synchronization. As in Figure 3.8a, messages have fields for *source* of origination, *time* (carrying local or global time stamps, depending on the use), and *content* consisting of a *port* designation and a *value*, both determined by atomic model output functions. There are four types of messages: *, x, y, and *done*.

As shown in Figure 3.8b, a processor receives and sends several types of messages. An *x-message* represents the arrival of an external event to a processor's *devs-component*; it bears the global model time and comes from its parent. A co-ordinator transmits this message to the processors of its *devs-component*'s receivers, using its *get-receivers* and *translate* methods. When a simulator receives an *x-message* it calls the external transition function of its *devs-component* (using the *ext-transition* method) and then responds with a *done-message*. The latter indicates to the parent that the state transition has been carried out and carries with it the model time at which the next internal event of its component is scheduled (obtained by calling the *time-advance?* method).

A *-message* arriving at a processor indicates that the next internal event is to be carried out within its scope. Thus a co-ordinator responds to a *-message* by transmitting it to its imminent child, the child with minimum *time-of-next-event* (or selected by tie-breaking rules embodied in the *selectfn*, if more than one has the minimum *time-of-next-event*).

A simulator processes the *-message* by computing the internal transition function of its *devs-component* (which is the imminent atomic-model) and responding with a *y-message* followed by a *done-message*. The former message carries as content, the *port* and *value* obtained by computing the output function of its atomic model. The latter *done-message* indicates that the state transition has been carried out and provides the new *time-of-next-event*.

When a co-ordinator receives a *y-message* from its imminent child, it consults the external output coupling scheme to see whether it should be transmitted to its parent, and its internal coupling scheme to obtain the children and their respective input ports to which the message should be sent. This processing uses the *get-influencees* and *translate* methods of its coupled model.

When a co-ordinator has received the *done-messages* from all the influencees (in the ascending *y-message* case) or receivers (in the descending *x-message* case) it computes the minimum of its *tN-children* (maintained list of times of next event) and determines its new imminent child for use upon receiving the next **-message*. Also it sends this new minimum as the time of its own next internal event in a *done-message* to its parent.

3.5.4 DEVS-Scheme Simulation Modes

Simulation is initiated by initializing the states of the atomic models, thereby also determining each one's *time-of-next-event*. These times are propagated upwards by *done-messages* and thus set up a path of imminent subcomponents from the outermost coupled model to an innermost atomic model. When the root-co-ordinator receives a *done-message* from its child (the co-ordinator of the outermost coupled-model), it returns a **-message* to it bearing its *time-of-next-event*. This starts the simulation, since the **-message* will be transmitted down the imminent path to the imminent simulator. There will result an upward wave of *y-messages*, a downward wave of *x-messages*, and an upward wave of *done-messages*, the last of which, transmitted to the root co-ordinator initiates the next round of simulation (processing of the next internal event).

Make-pair creates both a model M as well as the appropriate processor P:M assigned to it, obviating the need to separately create (using *mk-ent*), and assign (using a function called *attach*), models and processors. If the desired class is a specialization of *atomic-models*, *make-pair* takes the required processor to be simulator, otherwise a co-ordinator.

Initialize links a root-co-ordinator r (created with *mk-ent*) to the processor P:M. Since both types of processor present the same interface to a root-co-ordinator, its behavior does not depend on the nature, atomic or coupled, of the underlying model. *Initialize* proceeds to establish all the structural conditions necessary to start a simulation run. Descent through the model structure is provided by access paths recursively calling *get-children* until the atomic models are reached. The attached processors are linked in a hierarchical configuration via these access paths.

Once initialization has been performed *restart* (re)establishes the state of the simulator configuration. The user is queried for any changes desired in the states of the atomic models. From these state settings, the *time-of-next-event* and *time-of-last-event* variables of all the processors in the hierarchy are determined by upwards propagation. Having the *time-of-next-event* of its child, the root-co-ordinators generates a **-message* bearing this time to start the simulation.

DEVS-Scheme runs interactively in two modes: *run* and *pause*. In the *pause* mode, the simulation pauses with each message receipt and the contents of the received message are displayed in the window of the affected component. In the *run* mode, the simulation advances without interruption and only the states of the atomic models are displayed in their respective windows. In *pause* mode, a simulation run can be terminated anywhere during the root-co-ordinator's cycle. This leaves the model in a partial state, which may well manifest the source of an error. In *run* mode however, a request for termination can be issued at any time, but the simulation will stop only when the current cycle is complete. This leaves the model in a completed state from which the simulation can be validly continued. The run can be restarted from the resulting state after any desired modification, whether to the model or to the state.

With this a brief overview, we proceed to illustrate the development of a simple family of models in DEVS-Scheme.

Chapter 4

ATOMIC-MODELS: SIMPLE PROCESSOR EXAMPLE

We now begin to build models in DEVS-Scheme and organize them using the system entity structure. The model domain to be discussed is that of simple computer architectures. We are interested in comparing the performance of single processor systems with multiprocessor systems including the multiserver, the pipeline, and the divide and conquer configurations. Performance evaluation is to be based on two fundamental measures, *turnaround time*, the average time taken by the system to process jobs (for example, solve a problem) and *throughput*, the rate at which completed jobs emerge from the system.

The multiprocessor configurations to be modelled each have a coordinator that sends problems (jobs) to some sub-ordinate processors and receives solutions from them. In the *multiserver* architecture, the co-ordinator re-routes incoming problems to whichever processor is free at the time. In the *pipeline* architecture, problems pass through the processors in a fixed sequence, each processor performing a part of the solution. In the *divide and conquer* architecture, problems are decomposed into subproblems that are worked on concurrently and independently by the processors before being be put together to form the final solution.

4.1 Performance of Simple Architectures

Table 4.1 shows typical performance characteristics of the architectures. To obtain these results, we assume that problems arrive to the system with a fixed interarrival time and all have the same difficulty. In other words, problems all require the same processing time, whose value we associate with the relevant processor. Thus, for a single processor with processing time p, the turnaround time for each problem is (by definition in this case) p. The maximum throughput occurs when the processor is always kept busy, i.e., it always has a next problem to work on as soon as it has finished the previous one. In this case, the processor can send out solved problems every p units of time, i.e., at the rate 1/p.

ARCHITECTURE	PARAMETERS	TURNAROUND TIME	MAXIMUM THROUGHPUT
simple processor	processing-time, p	p	1/p
multiserver	processing-times, 1) p1,p2,p3	3/throughput	1/p1 + 1/p2 + 1/p3
	2) p1=p2=p3=p	p	3/p
pipeline	processing-times, 1) p1,p2,p3	p1 + p2 + p3	1/max{pi}
	2) p1=p2=p3=p/3	p	3/p
divide & conquer	processing-times, 1) p1,p2,p3, cp, cm	cp + cm + max{pi}	1/max{pi,cp,cm}
	2) p1=p2=p3=p/3	cp + cm + p/3	1/max{p/3,cp,cm}

Table 4.1. Performance characteristics of simple architectures.

Atomic-Models: Simple Processor Example

The multiserver architecture in Table 4.1 is assumed to have three subordinate processors. If each processor has the same processing time p then the turnaround time is also p. The maximum throughput again occurs when all of the processors are always kept busy, and with three processors the combined rate is 3 times that of the single processor. If there were n processors, the throughput could be increased by n (this ideal result neglects overhead due to co-ordination and communication time).

The pipeline architecture can also increase throughput without much effect on turnaround time. The turnaround time in this case is the sum of the times taken by each stage and the maximum throughput is that of the slowest stage (the bottleneck). Ideally, a problem can be divided into identically time consuming stages whose total time is less than the original processing time (any savings is due the fact that each stage can be optimized to perform only its specialized task).

Practically speaking, the only architecture that can both significantly reduce turnaround time and increase throughput is the divide and conquer configuration. For analysis purposes, this can be regarded as a pipeline consisting of the problem partitioner, the subproblem processors, and the compiler of partial results. For the subproblem processing stage to be finished, all of the subproblem processors must be finished, so the processing time of this stage is the maximum of the individual processing times. Ideally, each of n subprocessors takes time p/n, where p is the original problem solution time, and the partitioner and compiler times are much smaller than this. In this case, both the time for an individual problem to be solved (turnaround time) and the time for a large group of problems to solved (inverse of throughput) are reduced by a factor of n.

Insight into way these results arise can be gained by following the processing events as they happen in simulated models of these architectures. We shall show how to define simple, yet illuminating, versions of these architectures in DEVS-Scheme.

4.2 A Simple Processor Model

We start with a rather simplistic model of a processor. Expressed in architecture, it takes the form of an atomic model called P. Basically, we represent only the time it takes to complete a job or solve a problem not the detailed manner in which such processing is done. Thus if the processor is idle, i.e., in *phase* 'passive, when a job arrives on the input port 'in, it stores the *job-id* (a distinct name for the job) and goes to work. This is achieved by the phrase "hold-in busy processing-time", which sets the *phase* to 'busy and *sigma* (the time-left state variable) to *processing-time*. Such handling of incoming jobs is represented in the external transition function. Since this processor has no buffering capability, when a job arrives while the processor is busy it simply ignores it. This is achieved by the "continue" phrase which updates *sigma* to reflect the passage of elapsed time, but otherwise leaves the state unchanged.

When the processor has finished processing, it places the job identity on port 'out and returns to the 'passive *phase*. Sending of the job is done by the output function which is called just before the state transition function. The latter contains the phrase "passivate" which returns the model to the idle state in which the *phase* is 'passive and *sigma* is 'inf.

Note that P has two state variables, *job-id* and *processing-time*, in addition to the standard ones *sigma* and *phase*. Since *processing-time*, once initialized, does not change during the run, it is actually a *parameter* (fixed characteristic) of the model.

Simple as this processor is, we can combine it with other components to create models of computer architectures that provide some insight into their performance. The basic model can also be refined to represent more complex aspects of computer operation as we shall see later.

It is important to note here that there is no way to generate an output directly from an external input event. An output can only occur just before an internal transition. To have an external event cause an output without delay, we have it "schedule" an internal state with a hold time of zero (see the multi-server model in Chapter 5,

Atomic-Models: Simple Processor Example

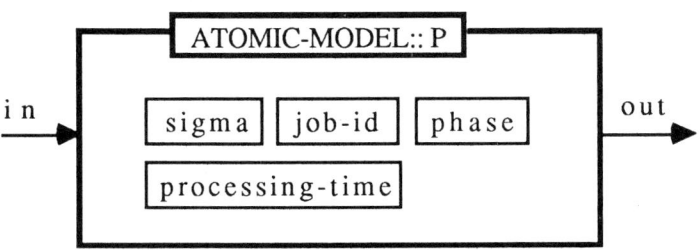

ATOMIC-MODEL: P

> state variables: sigma = inf
> phase = passive
> job-id = ()
>
> parameters: processing-time = 5
>
> external transition function:
> case input-port
> in: case phase
> passive: store job-id
> hold-in busy processing-time
> busy: continue
> else: error
>
> internal transition function:
> case phase
> busy: passive
> passive: (does not arise)
>
> output function:
> send job-id to port out
>
> Figure 4.1. Pseudo-code for a simple processor.

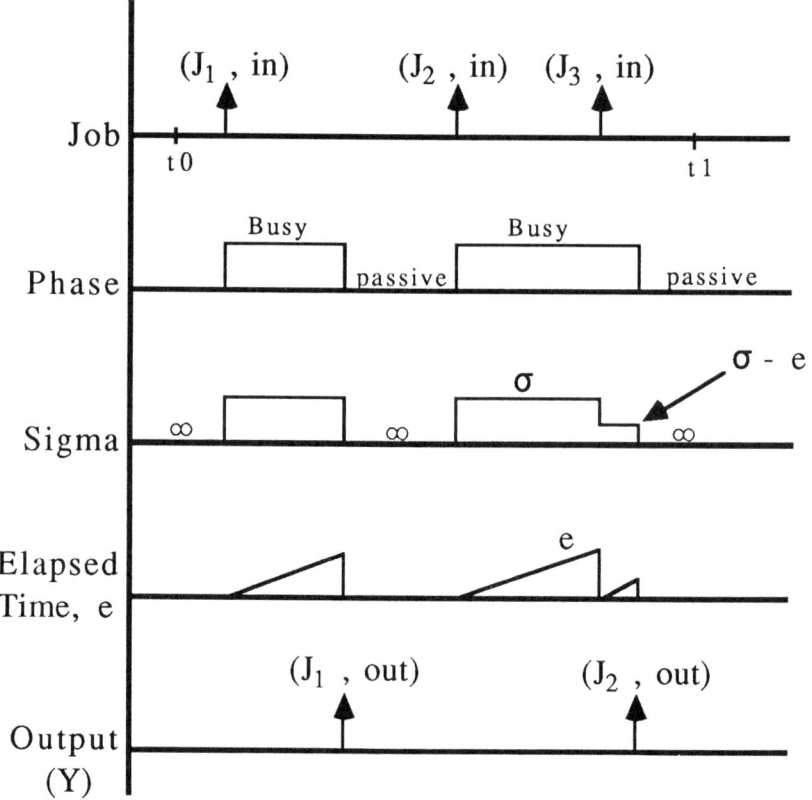

Figure 4.2. Trajectory for simple processor.

Atomic-Models: Simple Processor Example

for example). The relationship between external transitions, internal transitions, and outputs are as shown in Figure 4.2.

4.3 Normal Form Atomic Model Specification

To explain how the simple processor model is coded in DEVS-Scheme, we consider the class *atomic-models* in more depth. From its class definition (Figure 4.3), we see that *atomic-models* has instance variables *x*, *s*, *y*, and *e*, corresponding to the sets of the DEVS formalism. It also has instance variables *int-transfn*, *ext-transfn*, *outputfn*, and *time-advancefn* to hold the corresponding functions in the formalism.

Usually, we employ the normal form of *atomic-models*. This sets up the state as a Scheme structure by calling:

(define-structure state sigma phase ...)

where the ... denotes other state variables supplied by a method called *def-state*. *Sigma* holds the time remaining to the next internal event. This is precisely the time-advance value to be produced by the time-advance function. Thus, as in Figure 4.3, every atomic model is created with its *time-advancefn* slot set to the access procedure supplied by Scheme, *state-sigma*. The normal form can be overridden simply by redefining the values of instance variables *s* and *time-advancefn*.

Several macro definitions help manipulate *sigma* and *phase*. Their Scheme definitions are given in Figure 4.4.

* (hold-in '⟨phase⟩ ⟨time⟩)

sets state-variable *phase* to '⟨phase⟩ and *sigma* to ⟨time⟩. This causes the model to stay in the given phase for the specified time.

* (passivate-in '⟨phase⟩)

is the equivalent of (hold-in '⟨phase⟩ 'inf), where 'inf plays the role of infinity in DEVS-Scheme. This means that the arithmetic properties of infinity are extended to 'inf. For example, subtracting any finite

```
(define-class atomic-models
    (instvars
            (ind-vars '(phase sigma))
            (x (make-content 'port 'in 'value '()))
            (s (make-state 'sigma 'inf 'phase 'passive))
            (y (make-content 'port 'in 'value '()))
            (e 0)
            int-transfn
            ext-transfn
            outputfn
            (time-advancefn (lambda(s)(state-sigma s)))
            )
    (mixins models)
)
```

Figure 4.3. Atomic-models class definition (partial presentation).

```
(macro hold-in (lambda (expr)              ;;(hold-in '<phase> <time>)
   (let (
         (phase (cadr expr))
         (time (caddr expr))
         )
'(begin
 (set! (state-phase s) ,phase)
 (set! (state-sigma s) ,time)
))))

(macro passivate-in (lambda (expr)         ;;(passivate-in '<phase>)
   (let (
         (phase (cadr expr))
         )
'(begin
 (set! (state-phase s) ,phase)
 (set! (state-sigma s) 'inf)
))))

(macro passivate (lambda(expr)             ;;(passivate)
   '(begin
        (set! (state-phase s) 'passive)
        (set! (state-sigma s) 'inf)
)))

(macro continue (lambda(expr)              ;;(continue)
   '(when (not (equal? (state-sigma s) 'inf))
        (set! (state-sigma s) (- (state-sigma s) e))
))
```

Figure 4.4. Macros for *sigma* and *phase*.

Atomic-Models: Simple Processor Example

number r from 'inf returns 'inf. Also the minimum of any finite number r and 'inf is r; thus a passive component (which has time-advance equal 'inf) is never selected as the one with smallest next event time.

* (passivate)

sets *phase* to 'passive and *sigma* to 'inf, it is thus the equivalent of (passivate-in 'passive).

* (continue)

reduces *sigma* by the elapsed time, e. This allows the next internal event to occur at the the same time it was scheduled for despite an external event interruption.

4.4 DEVS-Scheme Atomic Model Implementation of Simple Processor

Using normal form tools, the pseudo-coded description of the simple processor in Figure 4.1 is readily translated into the atomic-model specification of Figure 4.5.

Let us examine the role of each of the parts of this definition. The constructor

(make-pair atomic-models 'p)

creates both the atomic-model P as well as the simulator S:P assigned to it. The use of *make-pair* obviates the need to separately create (using *mk-ent*), and link together (using a function called *attach*), models and processors. The message

(send p def-state ...)

is used to set up the additional state variables required for the model. Recall that all atomic models have *sigma* and *phase* upon creation by default. In this case, additional state variables are defined for the name of the job to be processed (*job-id*) and the time required to process a job (*processing-time*).

The message

   (send p set-s (make-state ...))

creates an instance of the state structure and sets the instance variable s of the model to this structure. In this way the state variables are initialized. Note that in particular *sigma* and *phase* must be initialized. When *sigma* has the value 'inf, this indicates that the model will not have an internal transition unless an external transition occurs.

The definition

   (define (ext-f s e x) ...)

specifies the external transition function. Every external transition function must be defined using s,e,x as arguments (actually, any names can be used so long as the types are correct). The external transition begins by looking at the *content-port* of input x. If this input port equals 'in, the *phase* of the processor must be checked. If the *phase* equals 'passive the following actions are taken: First, the state variable *job-id* is set to the value of the message content appearing on port 'in; second the *phase* is set to 'busy with a *sigma* equal to the state variable processing time. For the case of *phase* equals 'busy the processor will ignore the input and continue in its current state.

The definition

   (define (int-f s)...)

specifies the internal transition function. The internal transition function first checks the *phase* of the processor. If *phase* equals 'busy the macro *passivate*, is used to set the *phase* to 'passive and *sigma* to 'inf.

The definition

   (define (out-f s)...)

specifies the output function This function first checks the *phase* of the processor. If the *phase* equals 'busy, an output will be generated. The output must always return a content structure. Here it is created with

   (make-content 'port 'out 'value (state-job-id s))

which generates an output on the port called 'out with value *job-id*. Again note that an output is produced just before the internal transition occurs. Here this transition is that from *phase* 'busy to 'passive.
The three forms

(send p set-ext-transfn ext-f)
(send p set-int-transfn int-f)
(send p set-outputfn out-f)

are used to assign the procedures defined for external transition, internal transition, and output functions to the corresponding slots of atomic-model P. The atomic model is now ready for testing and simulation.

4.5 Simulation of Atomic-Models

Recall that an atomic-model P is handled by its attached simulator S:P. We can understand the workings of a DEVS-Scheme atomic model by examining the simulation process performed by its simulator.

Recall that there are two message types arriving to a simulator. A *-message* indicates that the next internal event is that of its model. An *x-message* is an arrival of an external event to the model.

- A simulator S:M of an atomic model M processes an *-message* as follows:

    - checks if the time carried by the *-message* agrees with the *time-of-next-event*; this should agree because a *-message* should only arrive to S:M if its model is imminent, i.e., has the smallest *time-of-next-event*.
    - emits:
        (send M output?)
        thereby causing M to apply its output function; the result is a content structure containing a *port* and a *value*.

This is where the output is generated prior to the internal transition.
- embeds the above content in a *y-message* and sends it out to the next higher level, i.e., the parent co-ordinator if M is a component in a coupled model or to the root-co-ordinator otherwise.
- emits:

  (send M int-transition)

  thus causing M to apply its internal transition function (*int-transfn s*) to update its state, s.
- updates the *time-of-last-event* and *time-of-next-event* slots:

  time-of-last-event = *time-of-next-event*

  time-of-next-event = *time-of-next-event* +

  (send m time-advance?)
- creates a *done-message* which indicates that the state transition has been carried out and which reports the new *time-of-next-event* to the next higher level, i.e., the parent co-ordinator if M is a component in a coupled model or to the root-co-ordinator otherwise.

- When a simulator S:M receives an *x-message* it:
  - checks if the time carried by the *x-message* lies between the times in its time-of-last event and *time-of-next-event* slots; this should be so because an *x-message* should only arrive to S:M after the last event and before its next internal event.
  - computes the elapsed time,

    e = time carried by *x-message* - *time-of-last-event*

    and sends it to M:

    (send M set-e e)
  - sends the content of the *x-message*, to M

    (send M set-x (message-content *x-message*))

Atomic-Models: Simple Processor Example

- emits:

    (send M ext-transition)

    thus causing it to apply its external transition function *(ext-transfn s e x)* where it has just received the updated values of *e* and *x*.

- updates the *time-of-last-event* and *time-of-next-event* slots:

    time-of-last-event = *time-of-next-event*

    time-of-next-event = *time-of-next-event* +
    (send m time-advance?)

- creates a done message which indicates that the state transition has been carried out and which reports the new *time-of-next-event* to the next higher level, i.e., the parent co-ordinator if M is a component in a coupled model or to the root-co-ordinator otherwise.

4.5.1 Significance of Model/Simulator Separation

The foregoing simulator is *generic* for the *atomic-models* class. This means it works with any model in this class or any of its subclasses. The interface between a model and its attached simulator is defined by methods, such as *int-transition*, *ext-transition*, etc. representing queries and operations that the simulator requests of the model. The details of the model's internal structure are hidden behind this interface.

There are important consequences of DEVS-Scheme's object-oriented approach to behavior generation. First, any model may be simulated by a simulator if it has the methods required by the interface. This underlies the genericity just mentioned and makes it easy to add sub-classes to the *atomic-models* class. Second, the removal of all simulation-related information from model specification enables us to treat models as knowledge, i.e., to be placed in a model base. Later we shall see how a decision-making device, other than a simulator, can interrogate and exercise a model (Section 12.3).

4.6 Stand-alone Testing of an Atomic Model

As indicated before, one of the most important features of DEVS-Scheme is that models at any level of complexity can be independently tested. Let us see how this applies to the ultra-important atomic model level. To test the model, one sends it message sequences that would be sent by its simulator to have it execute internal transitions and respond to external events.

Consider for example, a test message sequence that sends a job to the atomic model P, forces the associated external transition (in which the *job-id* should be recorded) and then the resulting internal transition (in which the job is completed). We assume that P starts in an idle state, i.e., any state with *phase* = 'passive and *sigma* = 'inf.

    a. (send p set-x (make-content 'port 'in 'value 'x1))

The effect should be that x is assigned a content (IN X1) (the order is: *port, value*).

    b. (send p set-e 0)

    c. (send p ext-transition)

The effect should be that s becomes the state (5 BUSY X1 5) (the order is: *sigma, phase, job-id, processing-time*).

    d. (send p output?)

The effect should be that y is assigned the content (OUT X1).

    e. (send p int-transition)

The effect should be that s becomes (INF PASSIVE X1 5).

Message a) causes P to set its external input event (x) slot to a content structure consisting of a port 'in and 'value x1. Message b. tells P to set the elapsed time (e) slot to 0. These messages mimic those generated by S:P when it receives an *x-message* on port 'in with value X1 and determines the elapsed time of P to be 0.

Message c) causes P to execute its external transition function. Again this is what the simulator would send to P in order to have it respond to the current *x-message*.

Atomic-Models: Simple Processor Example

Messages d) and e) cause P to execute its output and internal transition functions respectively. Again, note the output occurs prior to the internal transition. S:P would request this to be done when it receives a *-message indicating that the time has arrived for its model to execute its internal event. In this case, the stored *job-id* is output on port 'out and the model returns to an idle state.

Messages a), b), and c), may be replaced by a single message which performs the same functions. This message uses a method called *inject*. The *inject* method creates a content-structure with the given *port* and *value*, sets the elapsed time, e, to the value supplied (optional), and calls for an *ext-transition*. The format of the message using *inject* is:

(send ⟨atomic-model⟩ inject ⟨'port⟩ ⟨'value⟩ {⟨elapsed-time⟩}).

With *inject*, the message sequence testing for P's handling of a job arrival while it is idle is reduced to the following:

f. (send p inject 'in 'x1 0)

The result is state s = (5 BUSY X1 5)

g. (send p output?)

The result is output y = (OUT X1)

h. (send p int-transition)

The result is state s = (INF PASSIVE X1 5)

To test the "continue" alternative of the external transition function a job must be sent into the processor when it is busy. The following sequence of messages is used to test that condition:

i. (send p inject 'in 'x1 0)

The result is state s = (5 BUSY X1 5)

j. (send p inject 'in 'x2 3)

The result is state s = (2 BUSY X1 5)

Notice: The job being processed is still X1. Thus job X2 was ignored as it should be. *Sigma* is now 2 as it should be since, the continue statement reduced *sigma* by e to get the the time remaining, i.e., 5-3 = 2.

k. (send p output?)

The result is output y = OUT X1

1. (send p int-transition)

The result is state s = (INF PASSIVE X1 5)

In case a test fails, the modeller must locate and correct the error. Usually, the requires resetting the model's state. There are several ways to do this, appropriate to different circumstances. To inspect and alter a single state variable, we can use the methods, *get-sv* and *set-sv* as in:

(send p get-sv 'phase)

which returns the value of the *phase* state variable, and

(send p set-sv 'phase 'busy)

which sets the *phase* state variable to 'busy.

To reset the state completely, we can use the *make-state* function as in Figure 4.5. Sequences of messages may be put into a test file (e.g., p.tst for testing the simple processor P, shown in Figure 4.6). The test file can be archived in a subdirectory of the appropriate modelling domain (for example, test is a subdirectory of simparc). Test sequences should cover the different combinations of inputs and states in which the model must respond correctly. The expected responses are shown as comments and may be compared with the actual ones. If all comparisons succeed then we may gain full confidence in the model and place it into the model base as a verified model. The stored test file can be reused when modifications are made in the model.

If an error occurs in a coupled model, and all components have been verified in the foregoing way, we can look for the source to be in the coupling or tie-breaking specifications of the coupled model. This bottom-up testing makes it possible to confidently build up successively higher level subcomponents until the final model is achieved. We return to consider testing of hierarchical models later.

Atomic-Models: Simple Processor Example

```
;;;;;;;;;;;;;;;;;;;;;;;;;;;;;;;;;;;;;;;;;;;;;;;;;;;;;;;;;;;;;;
;;   Content of the simple processor definition file p.m   ;;
;;;;;;;;;;;;;;;;;;;;;;;;;;;;;;;;;;;;;;;;;;;;;;;;;;;;;;;;;;;;;;
;----------------------------------------------------------------
; This file contains the definition of a simple processor
; without buffering capability
;----------------------------------------------------------------
; It performs following tasks:
; Gets a job from input and sends the job to the output after
; its processing time.
;----------------------------------------------------------------

;;;;;;;;; make a pair for the processor and its simulator

(make-pair atomic-models 'p)

;;;;;;;;; set up additional variables job-id and processing-time

(send p def-state
      '(
        ;;;state-variables:

           job-id            ;name of the processed job

        ;;;parameters

           processing-time   ; processing time of this processor
        )
)

;;;;;;;;; initialize variables

(send p set-s
      (make-state 'sigma          'inf
                  'phase           'passive
                  'job-id          '()
                  'processing-time 5
      )
)

;;;;;;;;; define the external transition function

(define (ext-f s e x)
        (case (content-port x)
              ('in (case (state-phase s)
                         ('passive
                             (set! (state-job-id s) (content-value x))
                             (hold-in 'busy (state-processing-time s))
                         )
                         ('busy (continue))
                   )
              )
        )
)
```

Figure 4.5. Atomic model specification of simple processor.

```
;;;;;;;; define the external transition function
(define (ext-f s e x)
        (case (content-port  x)
              ('in (case (state-phase s)
                    ('passive
                        (set! (state-job-id s) (content-value x))
                        (hold-in 'busy (state-processing-time s))
                    )
                    ('busy (continue))
                    )
              )
        )
)
;;;;;;;; define the internal transition function
(define (int-f s)
  (case (state-phase s)
    ('busy (passivate))
) )

;;;;;;;; define the output function
(define (out-f s)
  (case (state-phase s)
    ('busy
        (make-content 'port 'out 'value (state-job-id s))
    )
    (else (make-content))
) )

;;;;;;;; assignment to the model

(send p set-ext-transfn ext-f)
(send p set-int-transfn int-f)
(send p set-outputfn out-f)
```

Figure 4.5. (continued).

Atomic-Models: Simple Processor Example

```
;;;;;;;;;;;;;;;;;;;;;;;;;;;;;;;;;;;;;;;;;;;;;;;;;;;;;;;;;;;;
;;;;                Content of the test file p.tst          ;;;;
;;;;;;;;;;;;;;;;;;;;;;;;;;;;;;;;;;;;;;;;;;;;;;;;;;;;;;;;;;;;
;;;-----------------------------------------------------------
; This file contains the test sequence for the simple processor
;;;-----------------------------------------------------------
; in case the model-base_directory is not already defined:
(define model-base_directory "/scheme/devs/simparc/mbase/")
; load the file containing the processor
(load-from model-base_directory p.m)
; arrival of external event job_in_1 on  port 'in at elapsed time 0
(send p inject 'in 'job_in_1 0)
; STATE S = (5 BUSY JOB_IN_1 5) processor is now processing job_in_1
; after 5 time units have elapsed the following should happen
(send p output?)            ;;; execute the output function
; OUTPUT Y = OUT JOB_IN_1             ;;;; output the job
(send p int-transition)   ;; execute the internal transition function
; STATE S = (INF PASSIVE JOB_IN_1 5) ;;;; back to passive state
; repeat external event arrival with job_in_2
(send p inject 'in 'job_in_2)
; STATE S = (5 BUSY JOB_IN_2 5) ;;;; sigma is 5 and phase is BUSY
; input when the processor is busy   ---> job_in_3 at elapsed time 2
(send p inject 'in 'job_in_2 2)
; state s = (3 BUSY JOB_IN_2 5) ;;;; job_in_3 is lost,
                                ;;;; job_in_2 has 3 time units left
                                ;;;; due to the continue statement
; finally after 3 units the following should happen
(send p output?)
; OUTPUT Y = OUT JOB_IN_2  ;; still output only the previous job_in_2
(send p int-transition)
; STATE S = (INF PASSIVE JOB_IN_2 5)  ;; back to passive state
```

Figure 4.6. Test sequence for the simple processor.

4.7 Simple Processor with Buffering and Random Processing Times

The simple processor model introduced in this chapter can be made more realistic in a variety of ways. Often the processing time in such a model is not constant but is sampled from a probability distribution. This is easy to arrange in DEVS-Scheme by modifying the external transition function in Figure 4.5 by adding a statement such as:

(set! (state-processing-time s) (random 100))

before the hold-in statement. This samples the processing time from a uniform distribution in the range [0,99]. Other distributions such as the exponential or normal may be used as explained in many books on discrete-event simulation.

Buffering such as described in the model of Figure 4.4 in Chapter 3 is also readily specified. In Figure 4.5, we need only treat the *job-id* state variable as able to hold a list of jobs rather than a single one. When a job arrives, we add it to this list (for first-in-first-out queueing, we add it at the end). A statement to this effect can be placed right at the beginning of the external transition function. The rest of the function need not be altered! The internal transition function however, is modified so that after removing the first job in the queue, if the queue is not empty, we start processing the next job. The output function is modified so that the first job in the queue is sent out.

Discrete-event simulation is often associated with simulation of queueing models and one might imagine that queueing is an inevitable factor in any such model. However, as new approaches to manufacturing such as just-in-time production (Manivannan, 1989) have shown, queues are evidence of inadequate process co-ordination and impose a costly overhead that often can be avoided. In the models to be discussed in this book, we intentionally do not incorporate queues, in favor of more sophisticated co-ordination schemes. The reader may wish to compare performance of the models in the ensuing chapters with, and without, queues. Modularity, and model base concepts, facilitate exploration of such alternatives.

Chapter 5

DIGRAPH-MODELS AND EXPERIMENTAL FRAMES

Although a model, such as that of the processor, can be tested in a stand-alone fashion, it really does not "come to life" until it is coupled with a module capable of providing it input and observing its output. An experimental frame module is a coupled-model, which when coupled to a model, generates input external events, monitors its running, and processes its output (Figure 5.1). The design of an experimental frame reflects the objectives one has in experimenting with a model. Thus the same model might be coupled to different experimental frame modules which observe it under different conditions. (If desired, experiments under different experimental conditions can all be done in parallel by coupling a copy of the model to each frame.) Conversely, the same experimental frame module may be employed to experiment with different models under the same conditions.

We now show how to construct an experimental frame module to measure turn-around time and throughput in any of the simple computer architecture models.

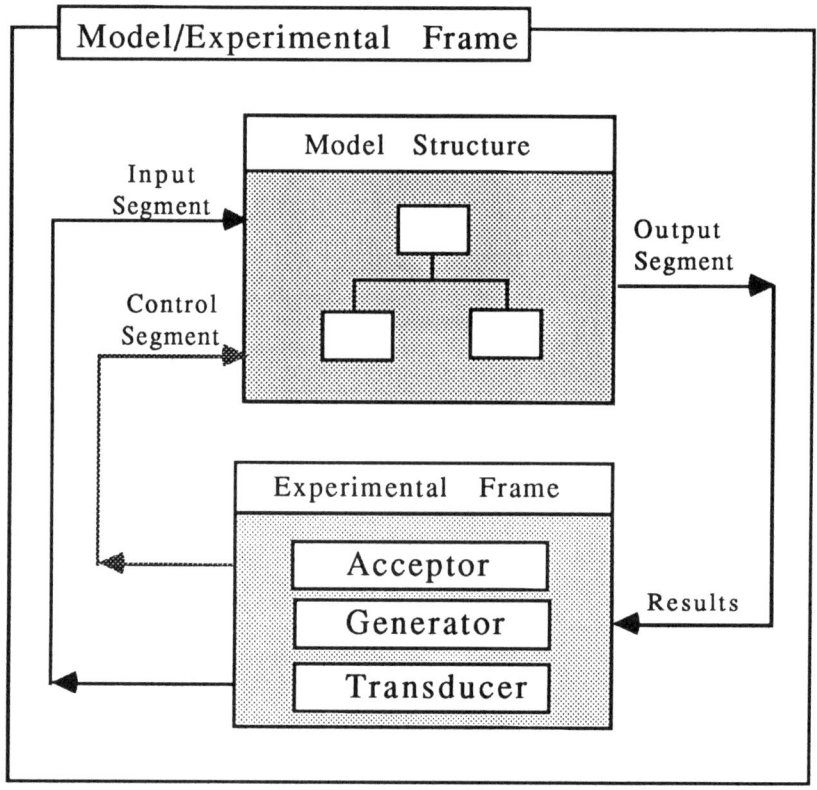

Figure 5.1. Structure of model/experimental frame pair.

5.1 Experimental Frame for Simple Computer Architectures

An example of such an experimental frame module, shown in Figure 5.1, is a digraph model consisting of a generator, GENR and transducer, TRANSD.

Digraph-Models and Experimental Frames

5.1.1 Generator

The generator (Figure 5.2) outputs a sequence of job identifiers spaced equally in time. The basic mechanism that produces this behavior is the "hold-in active inter-arrival-time" phrase in GENR's internal transition function. This phrase returns the model to the same phase, ACTIVE after each internal transition and schedules it to undergo a next transition in a time given by *inter-arrival-time* (which is constant in this case, but could vary in general). Just before the internal transition takes place, the output of a randomly determined *job-id* symbol is produced. Since GENR is itself a DEVS model, it can be tested in stand-alone fashion.

In principle, a generator is an autonomous model, (its behavior is self induced by recurring internal events) hence, it does not need an external transition function to dictate its response to external input events. However, we have added an input port 'stop which, when stimulated, stops the generator from producing any more outputs.

5.1.2 Transducer

The transducer (Figure 5.3) is designed to measure two performance indexes of interest for computer processors: the *throughput* and average *turnaround time* of jobs in a simulation run. Recall that *throughput* is the average rate of job departures from the architecture, estimated by the number of jobs processed during the observation interval, divided by the length of the interval. A job's *turnaround time* is the length of time between its arrival to the processor and its departure from it as a completed job (i.e., solved problem). Note that for the simple processor P, the turnaround time is the same as the processing time. However, for more complex architectures, this relationship is not necessarily true as we shall see.

To compute the performance measures, the transducer, TRANSD places job-ids that arrive at its 'ariv input port on its *arrived-list* together paired with their arrival times. When, and if, the *job-id* also appears at the 'solved input port, TRANSD places it on the *solved-list* and also computes its turnaround time. TRANSD maintains

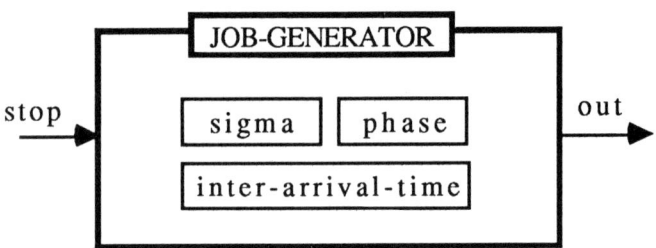

ATOMIC-MODEL: GENR

    <u>state variables:</u> sigma = inf
                           phase = active

    <u>parameters:</u> inter-arrival-time = 10

    <u>external transition function:</u>
      case input-port
        stop: passive
        else: error

    <u>internal transition function:</u>
      case phase
        active: hold-in active inter-arrival-time
        passive: (does not arise)

    <u>output function:</u>
      case phase
        active: send random-job-name to port out
        passive: (does not arise)

Figure 5.2a. Pseudo-code for job generator.

```
;----------------------------------------------------------------
; This file contains the definition of the job generator
;----------------------------------------------------------------
; It should perform following tasks:
; generates a job every inter-arrival-time
; Option: stops the generating sequence when receiving a stop
;         signal (stop)
;----------------------------------------------------------------

;; create a generator

(make-pair atomic-models 'genr)

; add another state variable: inter-arrival time

(send genr def-state '(inter-arrival-time))

; initialization

(send genr set-s (make-state 'sigma              0
                              'phase             'active
                              'inter-arrival-time 10
                 )
)

;; Add external transition function to terminate the generator
;; when the experiment is over instead of using keyboard interrupt

(define (ext-genr s e x)
  (case (content-port x)
        ('stop (passivate))    ;when receive stop signal passivate
        (else (continue))
))

;; definition of internal transition function

(define (int-genr s)
  (case (state-phase s)
        ('active
            (set! (state-sigma s) (state-inter-arrival-time s))
        )          ;;;reset sigma each time an internal transition occurs
))                 ;;; Note: not really necessary for fixed inter-arrival
                   ;;; time

;; definition of output function

; output the jobname (gensym) to port 'out

(define (out-genr s)
  (case (state-phase s)
        ('active
           (make-content 'port 'out 'value (gensym))
        )
        (else (make-content))
) )
```

Figure 5.2b. Atomic-model specification of job generator.

```
;; connect the definitions of functions to generator

(send genr set-int-transfn int-genr)
(send genr set-ext-transfn ext-genr)
(send genr set-outputfn out-genr)
```

Figure 5.2b. (continued).

its own local clock to measure arrival and turnaround times. The DEVS formalism does not make available the simulation clock time to model components. Thus models have to maintain their own clocks if timing is needed. They can easily do so by accumulating elapsed time information which is available in the form of *sigma* and *e*.

Note that, in contrast to a generator, a transducer is essentially driven by its external transition function. In TRANSD, an internal transition is used only to cause an output at the end of the observation interval. In a more general experimental frame, the role of terminating the simulation run would be handled by a component called an acceptor.

As illustrated in the atomic-models specification of TRANSD, any atomic model, can write directly into DOS files to maintain a log of events over time.

5.2 Development of Digraph-Models

Recall that *digraph-models* is a specialized subclass of *coupled-models*. A digraph model is a coupled model which is composed of a set of explicitly given components with explicitly specified coupling. As Figure 5.4, a digraph model has instance variables corresponding to the parts of the DEVS mult-component formalism. Methods are used to specify the components of the digraph-model (*build-composition-tree*) and to specify the coupling of the components (*set-inf-dig, set-int-coup, set-ext-out-coup, set-ext-inp-coup*).

Digraph-Models and Experimental Frames

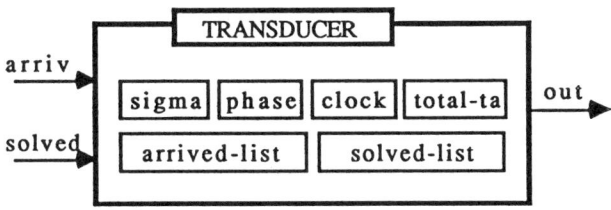

ATOMIC-MODEL: TRANSD

<u>global variable:</u> observation-interval

<u>state variables:</u> sigma = observation-interval
phase = active
arrived-list = ()
solved-list = ()
clock = 0
total-ta = 0

<u>external transition function:</u>
   advance local clock to agree with global clock
   case input-port
      ariv: append job to arrived-list
      solved: find job arrival time
             total-ta = clock - arrival time
             put the job to solved-list
   continue

<u>internal transition function:</u>
   case phase
      active: passive
   ;; end of observation interval

<u>output function:</u>
   case phase
      active: average-turnaround-time =
             total-ta / solved-job-number
             thruput = solved-job-number / clock
      else: no output

Figure 5.3a. Pseudo-code for transducer.

```
;----------------------------------------------------------------
; This file contains the definition of transducer
;----------------------------------------------------------------
;
; Transducer designed for the measurement of
;
;           1. average turnaround time of processed jobs
;           2. thoughput
;
; observation-interval must be set (default is 100)

(define observation-interval 100)

; now start model definition

(make-pair atomic-models 'transd)

(send transd def-state '(arrived-list    ;; all jobs which have arrived
                         solved-list     ;; all jobs which have been
                                         ;; processed
                         clock           ;; local clock
                         total-ta)       ;; total turnaround time of
                                         ;; processed jobs
)

(send transd set-s (make-state
                        'sigma          observation-interval
                        'phase          'active
                        'arrived-list   '()
                        'solved-list    '()
                        'clock          0
                        'total-ta       0
)           )

;; external transition function takes care of recording arriving
;; and departing jobs and of accumulating total turnaround time

(define (ext-t s e x)
    (let (
        (problem-id (content-value x))
        )
      (set! (state-clock s) (+ (state-clock s) e))
      (case (content-port x)
       ('ariv (set! (state-arrived-list s)
                    (cons (list problem-id (state-clock s))
                          (state-arrived-list s)))
       )
       ('solved (let* (
                    (pair (assoc problem-id (state-arrived-list s)))
                    (prob-arrival-time (cadr pair))
                    (turn-around-time
                        (- (state-clock s) prob-arrival-time))
                    )
```

Figure 5.3b. Atomic-model specification of transducer.

```
                        (when (not (null? prob-arrival-time))
                           (set! (state-total-ta s)
                               (+ (state-total-ta s) turn-around-time))
                           (set! (state-solved-list s)
                               (cons problem-id (state-solved-list s)))
                        )
                     )
                  )
            (else
               (bkpt "error: invalid input port name --> " (content-port x)))
            )
            (continue)
)

;; internal transition function is called only at end of run
(define (int-t s)
   (case (state-phase s)
      ('active (passivate))
))


;; output function serves to compute summary indexes: throughput and
;; average turnaround time
(define (out-t s)
   (case (state-phase s)
      ('active
         (let (

   ; a port log-file is opened to record transducer output in file "log"

            (log-file (open-output-file "log"))
   ; average turn-around time: total-ta divided by number of processed
   ;                           jobs
            (avg-ta-time
               (if (NULL? (state-solved-list s))
                  '()
                  (/ (state-total-ta s) (length (state-solved-list s)))
               )
            )
   ; thruput: number of processed jobs divided by observation interval
            (thruput
               (if (= (state-clock s) 0)
                  '()
                  (/ (length (state-solved-list s)) (state-clock s))
               )
            )
         )
```

Figure 5.3b. (continued).

```
            (newline log-file)
            (display "The arrived list: " log-file)
            (display (state-arrived-list s) log-file)
            (newline log-file)
            (display "The solved list:  " log-file)
            (display (state-solved-list s) log-file)
                (newline log-file)
            (display "Avg. turnaround time: " log-file)
                (display avg-ta-time log-file)
            (newline log-file)
            (display "ThruPut: " log-file)
                (display thruput log-file)
            (newline log-file)
            (close-output-port log-file)
            (make-content 'port 'out 'value (list avg-ta-time thruput))
         ) ;;let
       ) ;;active
       (else (make-content))
  ))

(send transd set-ext-transfn ext-t)
(send transd set-int-transfn int-t)
(send transd set-outputfn out-t)
```

Figure 5.3b. (continued).

```
(define-class digraph-models
   (instvars
            this-model          ;actual object this instance is
            (composition-tree (bi-tree))
            (children '())
            (influence-digraph (digraph))
            (selectfn (lambda (l) (car l)))
            (priority-list '())
   )
   (mixins coupled-models)
```

Figure 5.4. Digraph model class definition (partially shown).

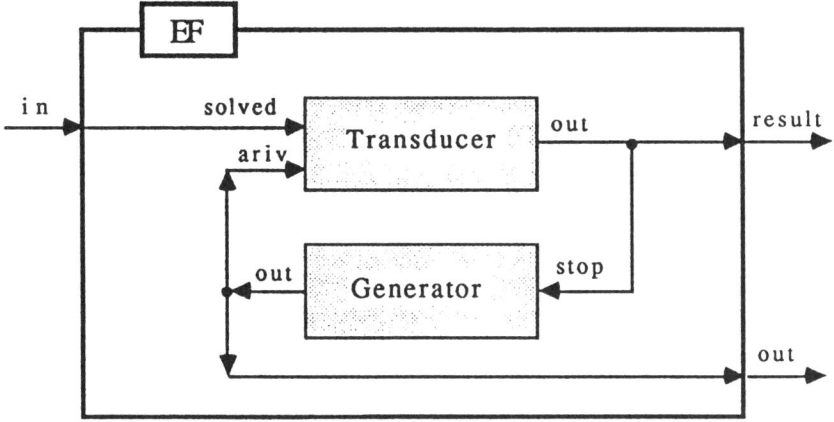

Figure 5.5. Experimental frame digraph-model.

To show how to specify a digraph model we will construct an experimental frame module by coupling the generator and transducer components just discussed.

5.2.1 Experimental Frame Digraph Model

GENR and TRANSD are coupled together to form the experimental frame EF, a digraph model shown in Figure 5.5. The input port 'in of EF is for receiving solved jobs which are sent to the 'solved input port of TRANSD via the external input coupling. There are two output ports: 'out, which transmits job identifiers sent to it by GENR, and 'result which transmits the performance measures computed by TRANSD. Both these transmissions are brought about by external output couplings. Finally, there are two internal couplings: the output port 'out of GENR sends job identifiers to the 'ariv port of TRANSD and the output port 'out of TRANSD which couples to the 'stop input port of GENR.

It should be noted that output lines may diverge to indicate the occurrence of simultaneous events. Thus for example, when GENR sends out a job identifier on port 'out, it goes at the same clock time, both to the 'ariv port of TRANSD and port 'out of EF, hence eventually to some processor model. Also, convergence of input lines, i.e., two or more source ports connected to the same destination port, can occur. Convergence does not pose a problem since at most one component is active and can be sending an output at any given moment.

The composition tree (Figure 5.6) depicts the digraph model (EF) as the root of a tree with its leaves being the component models (GENR, TRANSD) comprising the digraph model. In the general case the leaves can be either coupled models or atomic models. As shown, port pairs in the external-input coupling specification are assigned to appropriate arcs from the root to the leaves; port pairs in the external-output coupling are associated with arcs in the other direction.

The influence digraph (Figure 5.6) depicts how the components influence each other. In EF, GENR influences TRANSD and TRANSD influences GENR. In the general case there does not have to be a bidirectional influence. The influencees of a component are those components whose input ports are coupled to it's output ports. Port pairs in the internal coupling specification are assigned to appropriate arcs in the influence digraph.

The DEVS-Scheme implementation of EF (Figure 5.7a) illustrates the general approach to defining *digraph-models*. Recall that *composition-tree* and *influence-digraph* are instance variables of a digraph model which are assigned directed graph objects. The methods *build-composition-tree* and *set-inf-digraph* construct the respective objects and the other methods add port pairs to designated arcs in the directed graphs. The input required from the modeller can be reduced to a minimum using more "intelligent" methods (Figure 5.7b). Since, as will be shown, the system entity structure provides a yet more user-friendly approach to specifying digraph-models, we do not delve into greater detail here.

Digraph-Models and Experimental Frames

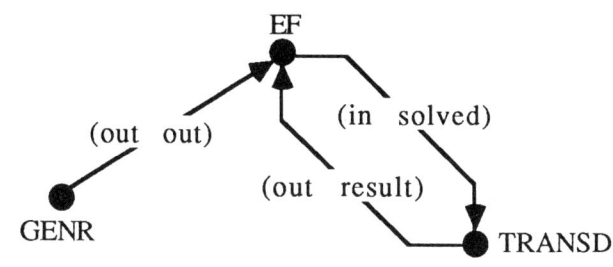

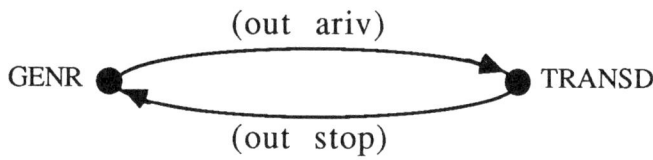

DIGRAPH-MODEL: EF

COMPOSITION TREE: root: EF
 leaves: GENR, TRANSD

EXTERNAL INPUT COUPLING:

EF.in -> TRANS.solved

EXTERNAL OUTPUT COUPLING:

GENR.out -> EF.out
TRANSD.out -> EF.result

INFLUENCE DIGRAPH:

GENR -> TRANSD
TRANSD -> GENR

INTERNAL COUPLING:

GENR.out -> TRANSD.ariv
TRANSD.out -> GENR.stop

Figure 5.6. Composition tree and influence digraph for experimental frame.

```
;----------------------------------------------------------------
; This file contains the construction of the experiment frame
; by using digraph-models. The components
; are retrieved from the models.m defined in model-base.
;; components: One generator (genr.m)   -- genr
;              one transducer (transd.m) -- transd
;----------------------------------------------------------------

;; load components of experimental frame, generator and transducer

(load "/scheme/devs/simparc/mbase/genr.m")
(load "/scheme/devs/simparc/mbase/transd.m")

;; couple them in a digraph-model

(make-pair digraph-models 'ef)

;; specify the root and leaves of the composition-tree

(send ef build-composition-tree ef (list genr transd))

;; add the external input port pairs to the arcs of the
;; composition-tree

(send ef set-ext-inp-coup transd (list (cons 'in 'solved)))

;; add the external output port pairs to the arcs of the
;; composition-tree

(send ef set-ext-out-coup genr (list (cons 'out 'out)))
(send ef set-ext-out-coup transd (list (cons 'out 'result)))

;; specify the influencees of each component

(send ef set-inf-dig (list (list genr transd) (list transd genr)))

;; add the internal port-pairs to the arcs of the influence-digraph

(send ef set-int-coup transd genr (list (cons 'out 'stop)))

(send ef set-int-coup genr transd (list (cons 'out 'ariv)))
```

Figure 5.7a. Digraph-model specification of EF showing how the composition and influence digraph are constructed.

Digraph-Models and Experimental Frames

```
;; load components of experimental frame, generator and transducer

(load "/scheme/devs/simparc/mbase/genr.m")
(load "/scheme/devs/simparc/mbase/transd.m")

;; couple them in a digraph-model

(make-pair digraph-models 'ef)

;; method specify-children calls build-composition-tree and
;; set-inf-dig

(send ef specify-children (list genr transd))

;; method add-couple figures out where to place the specified
;; port pairs from the source and destination given in each case

(send ef add-couple ef transd 'in 'solved)
(send ef add-couple genr ef   'out 'out)
(send ef add-couple transd ef  'out 'result)
(send ef add-couple transd genr 'out 'stop)
(send ef add-couple genr transd 'out 'ariv)
```

Figure 5.7b. Digraph-model specification of EF using more user-friendly methods *specify-children* and *add-couple*.

5.2.2 Model/Experimental Frame Pairs

To experiment with the simple processor model P we couple it together with the experimental frame component EF to form the digraph model EF-P (Figure 5.8). Note that coupling together an experimental frame and a model forms a closed, input-free, system. Thus there is no external-input coupling in EF-P. The external-output coupling makes the transducer output available at the port 'result of EF-P. The internal coupling is rather simple: the 'out ports of each of the components are coupled to the 'in ports of the other. The experimental frame EF can be coupled to any other model in this way. Of course, to make sense, the model has to use its input port for receiving job-identifiers and its produce such job-identifiers at its output port. This will be true for a selection of simple architecture models we shall discuss. Used in such a way, the experimental frame will generate jobs for the architecture and measure its throughput and turnaround time.

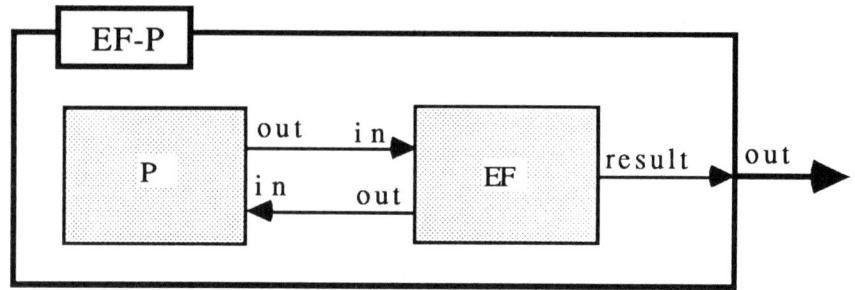

DIGRAPH-MODEL: EF-P

COMPOSITION TREE:
> root: EF-P
> leaves: EF, P

EXTERNAL INPUT COUPLING: none

EXTERNAL OUTPUT COUPLING:
> EF.result -> EF-P.out

INFLUENCE DIGRAPH:
> P -> EF
> EF -> P

INTERNAL COUPLING:
> P.out -> EF.in
> EF.out -> P.in

PRIORITY LIST: (P EF)

Figure 5.8. Composition tree and influence digraph for model/frame pair.

Digraph-Models and Experimental Frames 105

Figure 5.9 contains the specification for digraph model EF-P and also enables this model-frame pair to be simulated using a root-co-ordinator called R.

5.2.3 The Select Function: Breaking Schedule Ties

Recall that in the DEVS coupled-model formalism, the select function contains the the rules for breaking scheduling ties. Such ties are relatively rare, but nevertheless can cause unpleasant behavior distortions. For example, in EF-P, if the generator and processor have inter-arrival-times and processing-times which are equal (or more generally, exact multiples of each other), they will have equal next-event-times when both are ready to send out a job simultaneously. In particular, if the generator inter-arrival-time and the processing-time are equal, every second job is lost if the generator carries out its next-event first: the generator output encounters a busy processor and is ignored. To prevent this obvious distortion from occurring, the *select-fn* instance variable of EF-P can be defined so that the processor is always chosen as the imminent component when there is tie.

As shown in Figure 5.9, there are two ways of specifying the *select-fn*. It can be defined directly or the *set-priority* method can be used. In the latter case, a particular kind of select function is implemented, namely that based on a priority scheme. In the EF-P example, the direct definition (*sel-p*) is actually equivalent to the *select-fn* defined by the *set-priority* method. The priority-based approach is usually adequate and is properly handled by the *flattening* and *deepening* methods to be discussed later. Direct definition can be used when the linear ordering of the priority scheme is not sufficient.

5.3 Co-ordinator of Coupled-Models

Figure 5.10 shows the hierarchical structure of the processor configuration employed in DEVS-Scheme to simulate the model EF-P.

```
;----------------------------------------------------------------
; This file uses a digraph model to couple the simple processor
; with the experimental frame.
;----------------------------------------------------------------

;; load the components

(load "/scheme/devs/simparc/mbase/p.m")
(load "/scheme/devs/simparc/coupbase/ef.m")

;; couple the experimental frame with the processor by p-ef

(make-pair digraph-models 'ef-p)

;; build the composition tree and influence digraph

(send ef-p specify-children (list p ef))

;; internal coupling

(send ef-p add-couple p ef 'out 'in)
(send ef-p add-couple ef p 'out 'in)

;; external coupling

(send ef-p add-couple ef ef-p 'result 'out)

;; define the select function to avoid losing a job when it
;; arrives at the time the processor is finishing: processor first
;; then generator

(define (sel-p slst)
   (cond ((member p slst) p)
         ((member ef slst) ef)
) )

(send ef-p set-selectfn sel-p)

;; equivalently

 (send ef-p set-priority (list p ef))

;; is shorter and preferable when using flat-devs and deep-devs

;; the final touch, attach a root co-ordinator

(mk-ent root-co-ordinators r)

;; initialize it with the co-ordinator for ef-p

(initialize r c:ef-p)

;; start a simulation run

(restart r)
```

Figure 5.9. Digraph-model specification of EF-P.

Digraph-Models and Experimental Frames

We shall discuss the simulation process with reference to this example. Since we have already considered the simulation of atomic-models, we can assume the handling of the leaf components, GENR, TRANSD and P by their respective simulators is understood.

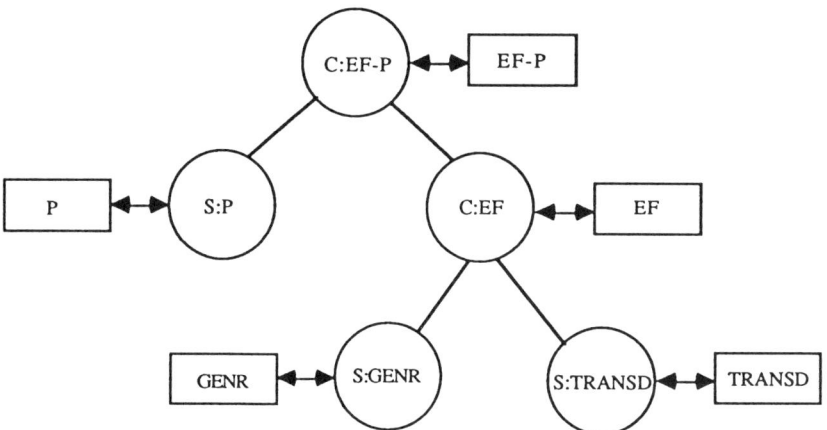

Figure 5.10. DEVS-Scheme processor hierarchy for simulation of EF-P.

Recall that a simulation cycle starts with a *-message sent by the root-co-ordinator to the co-ordinator of the outermost model, namely C:EF-P in Figure 5.10.

Consider then how a co-ordinator C:M of a coupled model M works. For example, M could be the model/frame pair EF-P or the frame EF. Arrival of a *-message at a co-ordinator indicates that the next internal event is to be carried out within its scope. Thus C:M responds to a *-message by transmitting it to its imminent child, the child with minimum time-of-next-event (or selected by selectfn), if more than one has the minimum time of next event). C:M places the imminent child in the *wait-list*. For C:EF-P, the imminent child may be either EF (when it is time to generate a new job) or P (when a job has been processed). For C:EF, GENR is repeatedly the imminent child until TRANSD becomes imminent to stop the simulation. We have seen that when S:GENR receives a **-message* it sends a *y-message* (applying its output function to produce a content with *port* 'out and *value* a job-id) to its parent C:EF. S:GENR also forces the execution of GENR's internal transition function, and sends a *done-message* with GENR's *time-of-next-event*.

When a C:M receives a *y-message* from its imminent child, it consults its internal coupling scheme to obtain the children and their respective input ports to which the message should be sent. C:M employs the methods *get-influencees* and *translate* to do this. Recall that in the case of digraph-models, the influencees of a component are explicitly specified in the influence-digraph. Thus the *get-influencees* method for digraph-models looks under the entry for the imminent child in the *influence-digraph* to obtain its influencees. The internal coupling port-pairs are also kept in the *influence-digraph*. For each influencee, *translate* gets the input port corresponding to the output content-port in the *y-message*. Each influencee is sent an *x-message* which is contains the input-port just found in the content-port slot and is otherwise identical to the *y-message*. For C:EF, when GENR is imminent, the *y-message* it puts out on port 'out is translated to an *x-message* on port 'ariv and sent to its influencee, TRANSD. C:M then places each of the influencees in its *wait-list*: used to keep track of the processors of its components which have not yet completed their transitions.

Similarly, C:M consults the external output coupling table to see whether the *y-message* should be transmitted to its parent. The method *translate* is used again. For digraph-models, it looks up the port-pairs associated with the edge I-M (where I is the imminent child) in the *composition-tree*, to get the output port associated with content-port in the *y-message*, if there is one. If so the appropriately amended *y-message* is transmitted to the parent of C:M or to the root-co-ordinator. If there is no output port then nothing is sent

Digraph-Models and Experimental Frames 109

since there is no external output to be derived from that generated by the imminent child in this transition. For C:EF, when GENR is imminent, the *y-message* its puts out on port 'out appears as a *y-message* appearing at port 'out of parent EF. Since EF is the imminent child of EF-P, the latter *y-message* is sent to C:EF-P, where it will be sent as an *x-message* (as just discussed) to the simulator of P, the influencee of EF. Handling of such an *x-message* by a simulator has already been discussed. In this case, assuming P is idle, P is set into phase 'BUSY. When the processing-time has elapsed, S:P generates a *y-message* (a job-id on port 'out) which goes to its parent C:EF-P and then as an *x-message* to C:EF, the influencee of P. Let us see how this is sent as an *x-message* to S:TRANSD.

An *x-message* to C:M represents the arrival of an external event to M; it bears the global model time and comes from C:M's parent if M is itself a component in a more encompassing model. To carry out the external input coupling scheme, C:M transmits this message to the processors of M's receivers, using its *get-receivers* and *translate* methods. Every sub-class of coupled models can have its own *get-receivers* and *translate* methods. In the case of digraph-models, we have seen that the external input coupling is specified by attaching port-pairs to the composition tree. For digraph-models, the method *get-receivers* returns the subset of children of M that are coupled to the content-port in the *x-message*. For each receiver, R, the method *translate* looks up the set of external-input port-pairs associated with the edge M-R, to find the appropriate input port. For C:EF, the only receiver for an *x-message* on external input port 'in is TRANSD and translate maps port 'in to port 'solved. Thus the *x-message* that C:M sends on to S:TRANSD is the same as it receives except that the content-port is changed to 'solved. After retransmitting the *x-message* to all the receivers, C:M puts them in the *wait-list*.

Consider now that C:M is waiting to receive *done-messages* from the children on its *wait-list* (i.e., its imminent child as well as from all its influencees in the ascending *y-message* case or the receivers in the descending *x-message* case). With the arrival of each *done-message*, C:M updates its *tN-children*, associating the *time-of-next-event* carried by the *done-message* with the child that sent it. When all *done-messages* have arrived, C:M computes the minimum of the *tN-children* and determines its new imminent child (using the *select-fn*) to use when receiving the next *-message. Also it sends this new minimum as the time of its own next internal event in a *done-message* to its parent. For example, if C:EF's *tN-children* is ((GENR 10)(TRANSD 1000)), this indicates that GENR is imminent and C:EF's own *time-of-next-event* is also 10. Then C:EF send a *done-message* with time set to 10 to its parent, C:EF-P. The latter having received all its *done-messages*, sends a *done-message* to the root-co-ordinator. Assuming its *tN-children* is ((EF 10)(P 15)), C:EF-P's *done-message* contains the *time-of-next-event* 10. The *done-message* is sent to the root-co-ordinator and turned around to appear as a *-message to C:EF-P with time 10. This starts a new simulation cycle, in this case with a GENR generating a second job.

In pause mode, a DEVS-Scheme simulation displays all the messages as they are processed. This aids understanding of the simulation process. With regard to model verification, it permits step-by-step tracking of the events, and hence makes for quicker discovery of sources of error.

5.3.1 Sample Simulation Results

Table 1 illustrates results obtained by simulating the single processor/frame pair. The processing time required by each job is fixed at 15. Each row represents a simulation run with a different job inter-arrival time. There are three cases:

1. When the inter-arrival time is greater than the processing time, the processor finishes a job before the next one arrives. Thus, departures are determined solely by arrivals and the throughput should be the same as the inter-arrival rate (1/inter-arrival time).

2. When the inter-arrival time is the same as the processing time, the processor is always kept busy, and the maximum throughput is attained. Note that in this case, both the generator and

Digraph-Models and Experimental Frames 111

the processor are imminent at the same time. Moreover, the processor has no queuing capability so that it loses an incoming job if it has not released the current one. Thus, when both generator and processor are imminent, the selectfn must choose the processor to enable it to finish first.

3. When the inter-arrival time is less than the processing time, if the processor had unlimited queuing capability, maximum throughput would be maintained. However, the current processor does not have such ability, and will lose jobs if they come in while it is busy. Thus, maximum throughput will be attained only when the inter-arrival time exactly divides into the processing time.

The actual results obtained with simulation agree with the above expectations. Differences are attributable to well known end-effect inaccuracies due to the relatively short observation interval (100) (see Delany and Vacari (1989) for discussion of simulation output analysis).

As expected, the average turnaround time of jobs is identical to the processing time.

Similar considerations to those expressed in cases 1), 2) and 3) above can be applied to the basic multi-computer architectures to derive the results in Table 4.1. We next consider implementations of these architectures in DEVS-Scheme.

Inter-arrival time:	Throughput		Average turnaround time	
	theoretical	experimental	theoretical	experimental
25	0.0400	0.0444	15	15.0
20	0.0500	0.0526	15	15.0
15	0.0667	0.0666	15	15.0
10	0.0500	0.0525	15	15.0
5	0.0667	0.0630	15	15.0

Table 5.1. Performance of simple processor.

5.4 Applicability of Frames to Models: Model Instrumentation

An experimental frame E is *applicable* to a model M if when E is coupled to M, the experimentation objectives that gave rise to E can be achieved. A rigorous definition of the general concept of applicability requires considerable work as in Chapter 13 of Zeigler (1984). Here we are concerned with a more limited issue in applicability: whether the output variables specified in a frame E can be observed in a model M. The practical significance of this issue is the following:

M has output ports that enable it to send external events to other model components. If information desired by a frame E is available through such a port, we may couple this port to an input port of E. For example, the departing job-id that a simple processor places on port 'out is available to the 'solved port of TRANSD (via the 'in port of EF). However, what happens if information desired by a frame is not available through an existing output port of a model M?

One approach is to modify M so that it computes the desired values and sends them out on a newly created output port. There are three problems with this approach: 1) we must manually modify the code of M thereby possibly introducing error, 2) there are now two kinds of output ports, those that are necessary for M to interact with other components (presumably matching corresponding "ports" in reality) and those invented to couple M to an observation process (which may not exist in reality), and 3) due to the modifications and additional ports, the code of M has been rendered more difficult to understand and modify later.

A second approach which is supported by DEVS-Scheme obviates these problems at the cost of somewhat reduced simulation speed. We can "instrument" an atomic-model so that the value of any expression computable in its environment can be output prior to external or internal events. Such values appear on two special ports: '%ext-event% and '%int-event%, for external, and internal, events, respectively. The code of M, as it appears in its file specification, is not modified in this instrumentation. It therefore remains uncom-

Digraph-Models and Experimental Frames

promised, and can be just as easily be instrumented to satisfy the needs of other experimental frames one may desire to apply to the model.

The methods, *add-int-event-observation* and *add-ext-event-observation*, which perform the foregoing instrumentation, are shown in Figure 5.11. For example, we can cause a model M to output the value of an expression, *exp*, in its environment on port '%int-event% just before every internal transition by appending the command to the end of its file:

(send M add-int-event-observation exp)

This modifies the object M (not the file code for M) so that its output function now sends out the value of *exp* to port '%int-event% in addition to its original output. One kind of transition is excepted: no output on port transitions whose time advance is 0. Such transitions are assumed not to be informative of model behavior, arising for example, due to the instrumentation for external events as below.[1] As an example of external event instrumentation, consider the following:

(send P add-ext-event-observation
       '(when (equal? (state-phase s) 'busy)
        (list (content-value x) 'lost))).

This will cause P to put out the list '(j lost) on port '%ext-event% whenever a job, j arrives while P is busy; the empty list is output on port '%ext-event% if a job arrives when P is free. Notice, in Figure 5.11b, that the expression *exp* is evaluated before the external transition takes place. Thus, if P is free when a job arrives, it will still be in phase PASSIVE when the (equal? (state-phase s) 'busy) test is performed. This results in an empty *content-value* for port '%ext-event% as desired.

---

[1] *exp* is any expression which is preceded by a quote to prevent its evaluation in user-initial-environment. To be meaningful it must have a value in the environment of M. Every SCOOPS object is a actually a Scheme environment, i.e., an association list of identifiers and bound values, in which expressions can be evaluated. Thus expressions that can be evaluated in the environment of M are either state-variables, or other instance variables (such as x, e, or y), or contain such variables.

```
(define-method (atomic-models add-int-event-observation)(exp)
(let (
    (old-out outputfn)
    (model (eval name user-initial-environment))
    )
(set! outputfn (lambda(s)
    (cond
     ( (> (state-sigma s) 0) ;; no observation in transient state
       ; (not (member (state-phase s) '(%ext-report% %report%)))
        (list
           (make-content 'port '%int-event%
                         'value (eval exp model))
           (old-out s)
        )
     ))
     (else (old-out s))
     )
))))
```

Figure 5.11a. The add-int-event-observation method.

```
(define-method (atomic-models add-ext-event-observation)(exp)
(def-state '(%ext-phase% %ext-sigma% %ext-result%))
(let (
    (old-int int-transfn)
    (old-ext ext-transfn)
    (old-out outputfn)
    (model (eval name user-initial-environment))
    )
(set! int-transfn (lambda(s)
   (if (equal? (state-phase s) '%ext-report%)
      (hold-in (state-%ext-phase% s) (state-%ext-sigma% s))
      (old-int s)
   )))
(set! ext-transfn (lambda (s e x)
    (let* (
         (result (eval exp model))
         )
    (old-ext s e x)
    (eval '(begin
       (set-sv '%ext-result% ',result)
       (set-sv '%ext-sigma% (get-sv 'sigma))
       (set-sv '%ext-phase% (get-sv 'phase))
       (hold-in '%ext-report% 0)
      ) model)
  )
))
(set! outputfn (lambda(s)
 (if (equal? (state-phase s) '%ext-report%)
    (make-content 'port '%ext-event%
                  'value (state-%ext-result% s))
    (old-out s)
    )))
))
```

Figure 5.11b. The add-ext-event-observation method.

Digraph-Models and Experimental Frames

Outfitting P with capability to report ignored jobs by direct means is discussed in Chapter 8. If the real world counter-part of P does not have such a capability, it is best if the model, P, does not have it either. Note however, that an experimental frame for P may legitimately wish to get such information. The *add-ext-event-observation* method permits us to satisfy the frame requirements without corrupting the file specification of P.

A model can be given both internal and external event instrumentation. For example, we can add the command

   (send P add-int-event-observation
        '(get-vals '(job-id processing-time))).

Processor model P will now output information about lost jobs on port '%ext-event% and about accepted jobs on port '%int-event% as shown in Figure 5.12. Note that we can omit all instrumentation ports from graphical displays, thus showing only intra-model related couplings. Likewise, we can omit all non-special ports from a display to emphasize model/frame couplings.

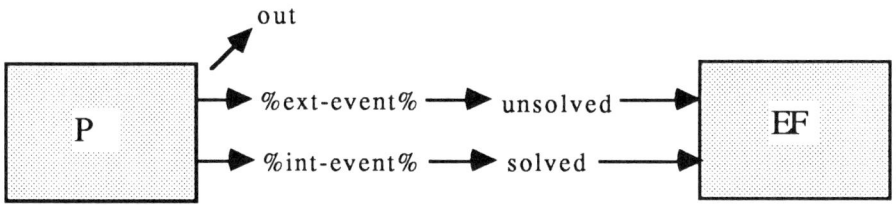

Figure 5.12. Coupling a processor to frame EF which makes use of its internal and external event observations.

In summary, we have demonstrated a partial implementation of the applicability relation proposed in Chapter 13 of (Zeigler, 1984). In this approach, a frame E is applicable to a model M if the variables required by E can be evaluated in the environment of M. If E is applicable to M, we can outfit M with the %int-event% and %ext-event% output ports and couple them to appropriate input ports of E. This avoids corruption of of M's specification. Once more, this separation of model and frame properties fosters reusability and better comprehension.

Chapter 6

A MODEL BASE FOR SIMPLE MULTI-COMPUTER ARCHITECTURES

At this point, we have seen how to express atomic-models and digraph-models in DEVS-Scheme. Specifically, a simple processor model/experimental frame pair was constructed. We can now design other simple architectures to replace the simple processor in such a pair and study each one's performance under the same conditions.

Three basic multiprocessing configurations will be modelled, each having a co-ordinator which sends problems (jobs) to some subordinate processors and receives solutions from them. In the *multiserver* architecture, the co-ordinator re-routes incoming problems to whichever processor is free at the time. In the *pipeline* architecture, problems pass through the processors in a fixed sequence, each processor performing a part of the solution. In our model, in contrast to typical hardware pipelines, the problems are routed by the co-ordinator from one processor to the next. In the *divide and conquer* architecture, problems are decomposed into subproblems that are worked on concurrently and independently by the processors.

When all partial solutions are available, they are then sent to a compiling processor to be put together to form the final solution. In each of the architectures, problems arrive at the co-ordinator and emerge from it.

6.1 Co-ordinators and Architectures

We want to study the throughput and turn-around time performance measures of the foregoing architectures and will do so by coupling the experimental frame in Chapter 5 to each of them. In this way, the performance relations presented in Table 4.1 can be tested . The architectures themselves are built up in the following manner:

1. define the co-ordinator — an atomic model — appropriate to each case,

2. create copies of the simple processor to serve as the subordinate processors, and

3. define each architecture as a digraph model coupling together the corresponding co-ordinator and the subordinate processors.

In what follows, for each architecture, we provide a pseudo-code description of the co-ordinator, its DEVS-Scheme implementation, and the DEVS-Scheme implementation of the architecture. Later we discuss testing and simulating the architectures. Although the models are highly simplified — problems are represented only by time of processing not by actual content — they illustrate significant aspects of model definition in DEVS-Scheme.

6.1.1 Multiserver Co-ordinator

As described in Figure 6.1, the co-ordinator, MUL-C keeps track of the status of its processors in corresponding state variables. A problem arrives at the input port 'in and is routed to the first passive

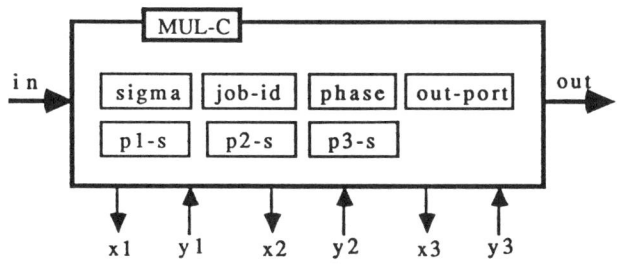

ATOMIC-MODEL: MUL-C

<u>state variables:</u> sigma = inf
phase = passive
p1-s = passive
p2-s = passive
p3-s = passive
out-port = ()
job-id = ()

<u>external transition function:</u>

store job-id
case   input-port
    in: sequentially select an idle subordinate and set the
        out-port (destination) to the corresponding value. i.e.
        if p1-s passive then set out-port = x1 and p1-s = busy
        if p2-s passive then set out-port = x2 and p2-s = busy
        if p3-s passive then set out-port = x3 and p3-s = busy
    when receive solution from a subordinate send to out:
        y1: reset p1-s to passive and set out-port = out
        y2: reset p2-s to passive and set out-port = out
        y3: reset p3-s to passive and set out-port = out
        hold-in busy 0

<u>internal transition function:</u>

case phase
    busy: passive
    passive: (does not arise)

<u>output function:</u>

case phase
    busy: case out-port
        x1, x2,x3,out: output job-id to out-port
        else make a null output

Figure 6.1a. Pseudo-code for co-ordinator of multiserver architecture.

```
;;;;;;;;;;;;;;;;;;; Multi-server Co-ordinator ;;;;;;;;;;;;;;;;;
;----------------------------------------------------------------
; This file contains the definition of the co-ordinator in
; Multi-server architecture.
;----------------------------------------------------------------
; It should perform following tasks:
; 1) Gets a job from input and sends the job to any of the three
;    processors that is not busy. If all processors are busy,
;    job is lost.
; 2) When finished job is returned from one of the processors,
;    sends it to output.
;----------------------------------------------------------------

;;;;;;;;; make a pair for the co-ordinator in multi-server module

(make-pair atomic-models 'mul-c)

(send mul-c def-state '(
                        p1-s        ;;phase of p1
                        p2-s        ;;phase of p2
                        p3-s        ;;phase of p3
                        out-port    ;;holds next destination port
                        job-id      ;;holds job id
                        )
)
;; initialize the state

(send mul-c set-s      (make-state    'sigma 'inf
                                      'phase 'passive
                                      'p1-s 'passive
                                      'p2-s 'passive
                                      'p3-s 'passive
                                      'out-port '()
                                      'job-id   '()
                       )
)
;; external transition function

(define (ext-mc s e x)
    (set! (state-out-port s) '()) ; default, no port to be sent to
    (set! (state-job-id s) (content-value x))
    (case   (content-port x)

        ; case 1. input from outside of the world

        ('in
            ; find a processor not busy and send the job to it

            (cond
            ( (equal? (state-p1-s s) 'passive)
                  (set! (state-out-port s) 'x1)
                  (set! (state-p1-s s) 'busy))
```

Figure 6.1b. Atomic-model specification of co-ordinator of multi-server architecture.

```
              ( (equal? (state-p2-s s) 'passive)
                       (set! (state-out-port s) 'x2)
                       (set! (state-p2-s s) 'busy))

              ( (equal? (state-p3-s s) 'passive)
                       (set! (state-out-port s) 'x3)
                       (set! (state-p3-s s) 'busy))
       ))

       ;case 2. input for the subordinate processors

       ('y1  (set! (state-p1-s s) 'passive)
             (set! (state-out-port s) 'out)
       )
       ('y2  (set! (state-p2-s s) 'passive)
             (set! (state-out-port s) 'out)
       )
       ('y3  (set! (state-p3-s s) 'passive)
             (set! (state-out-port s) 'out)
       )
    ) ; end of case

    (hold-in 'busy 0)
)

;;;;;;;; internal transition function

(define (int-mc s)
  (case (state-phase s)
    ('busy
        (passivate)
)))

;;;;;;;; output function
;;;;;;;; output the value to corresponding port

(define (out-mc s)
  (case (state-phase s)
    ('busy
        (case (state-out-port s)
          ((x1 x2 x3 out)
               (make-content 'port (state-out-port s)
                             'value (state-job-id s))
          )
          (else (make-content))    ;;null output needed
))))

;;;;;;;; assignment to the model

(send mul-c set-ext-transfn ext-mc)
(send mul-c set-int-transfn int-mc)
(send mul-c set-outputfn out-mc)
```

Figure 6.1b. (continued).

processor by being sent out on a corresponding to output port, 'x1, 'x2, or 'x3. If no processor is free, the problem is lost. When a solved problem returns on corresponding ports, 'y1, 'y2, or 'y3, MUL-C reroutes it to the output port 'out. For simplicity, we have MUL-C taking 0 time to do such work, as indicated by the "hold-in busy 0" phrase in the external transition function. This causes the output function to be invoked immediately after the external transition. Note that in the case of a problem arriving when all processors are busy, the output function creates a null content structure (one with empty port and value slots). Since the output function must always produce a content object, such a null structure should be the default. Since its port slot is empty, a message containing this null content has nowhere to go.

Multiserver Architecture Specified Directly as a Digraph Model

Figures 6.2a,b describe the digraph model, MUL-ARCH that implements the multiserver architecture. Note how the external-input coupling connects the 'in port of MUL-ARCH to the 'in port of MUL-C, while the external-output coupling similarly connects the 'out ports together. The internal coupling connects the sending and receiving ports of MUL-C to corresponding ports of the subordinate processors.

State Trajectories and Performance Indexes

Let us trace a typical state trajectory to illustrate the operation of coupled models in general, and the multiserver architecture in particular. We start in an initial state in which the multiserver coordinator and all subordinate processors are idle. Imagine that the experimental frame, ef, is coupled to the architecture in the same manner as it was for the simple processor architecture. This will result in jobs arriving on port 'in of MUL-ARCH from GENR and leaving on port 'out for TRANSD. Figure 6.2c shows how we can represent the time behavior for a coupled model. The incoming job

Model Base for Multi-Computer Architectures

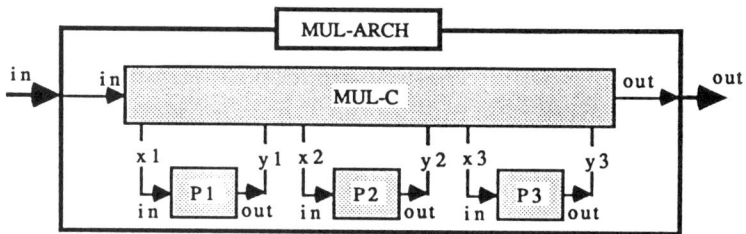

DIGRAPH-MODEL: MUL-ARCH

COMPOSITION TREE:

root: MUL-ARCH
leaves: MUL-C, P1, P2, P3

EXTERNAL-INPUT COUPLING:

MUL-ARCH.in -> MUL-C.in

EXTERNAL-OUTPUT COUPLING:

MUL-C.out -> MUL-ARCH.out

INFLUENCE DIGRAPH:

MUL-C -> P1, P2, P3
P1 -> MUL-C
P2 -> MUL-C
P3 -> MUL-C

INTERNAL COUPLING:

MUL-C.x1 -> P1.in   MUL-C.x2 -> P2.in
MUL-C.x3 -> P3.in   P1.out -> MUL-C.y1
P2.out -> MUL-C.y2   P3.out -> MUL-C.y3

PRIORITY LIST:

P1 P2 P3 MUL-C

Define the select function in order to avoid the loss of jobs which arrive at the same time the processors finish their jobs. Thus, the processors all have higher priority than the co-ordinator.

Figure 6.2a. Pseudo-code for the multiserver architecture.

```
;;;;;;;;;;;;;;;; multi-server architecture ;;;;;;;;;;;;;;;;;;;;;
;------------------------------------------------------------------
; This file contains the construction of the multi-server
; architecture  using a digraph-model. The components
; are retrieved from prototypes in the model-base.
; Components: Three sub-processors are copies of p in file "p.m"
;              One co-ordinator : mul-c  defined in "mul-c.m"
;------------------------------------------------------------------

(load-from model-base_directory p.m)
(load-from model-base_directory mul-c.m)

;; make three copies from original p processor and copy its
;; initial state

(send p make-new 'p1)
(send p make-new 'p2)
(send p make-new 'p3)

;;now couple them to the multi-server

(make-pair digraph-models 'mul-arch)

;;build composition tree and influence digraph

(send mul-arch specify-children (list mul-c p1 p2 p3))

;; external-input coupling

(send mul-arch add-couple mul-arch mul-c 'in 'in)

;; external-output coupling

(send mul-arch add-couple mul-c mul-arch  'out 'out)

;;internal coupling between processors and co-ordinator

(send mul-arch add-couple mul-c p1  'x1 'in)
(send mul-arch add-couple p1 mul-c  'out 'y1)
(send mul-arch add-couple mul-c p2  'x2 'in)
(send mul-arch add-couple p2 mul-c  'out 'y2)
(send mul-arch add-couple mul-c p3  'x3 'in)
(send mul-arch add-couple p3 mul-c  'out 'y3)

;; define the select function to avoid  job loss when it
;; is sent from co-ordinator to a processor just as the
;; process is finishing its current job: processors first,
;; then co-ordinator

(send mul-arch set-priority (list p1 p2 p3 mul-c))
```

Figure 6.2b. Digraph model specification of the multiserver architecture.

Model Base for Multi-Computer Architectures

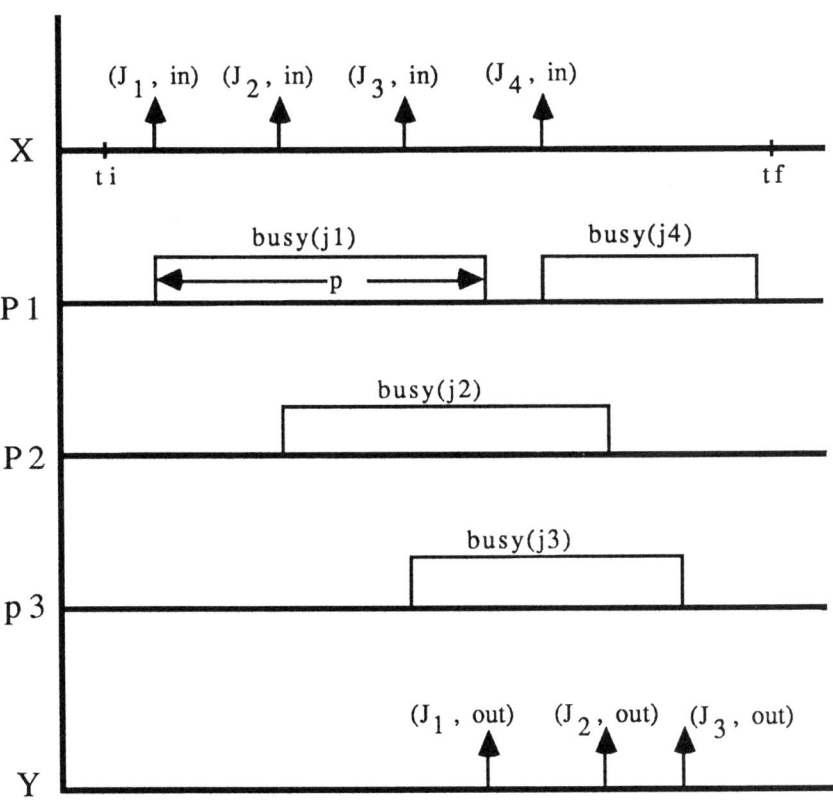

Figure 6.2c. Sketch of trajectory for multiserver architecture.

stream is represented by the segment of external input events shown on the top horizontal axis. The co-ordinator and each of the three processors is assigned its own axis.

Following the course of the first job arrival, J1, on port 'in of MUL-ARCH, the external input coupling scheme will send J1 to port 'in of the co-ordinator, MUL-C.[1] Having received J1 and being passive, MUL-C goes into state BUSY (dictated by its external transition function). After waiting there for a very short time (actually zero), the co-ordinator puts J1 on port 'x1 (as dictated by the output function) and immediately returns to the passive phase (due to the internal transition function).

The internal coupling of MUL-ARCH then causes J1 to be appear on port 'in of processor P1. Since the latter is idle, it accepts the job and enters the BUSY phase for a time given by its *processing-time* parameter (recall the description of the simple processor P in Section 4.2, of which P1 is an isomorphic copy). Let p represent the value of the processing time. For simplicity in the sequel, we shall assume that p is a constant and the same for all processors. After time p has elapsed, P1 will place J1 on port 'out. The external output coupling now determines that J1 appears on port 'out of MUL-ARCH and leaves the architecture as a processed job as illustrated in Figure 6.2c.

Now let a second job, J2, arrive T time units after J1's arrival. If T is bigger than p, then P1 will be passive by the time J2 arrives and will start processing it. However, if T is smaller than p, then P1 will be busy when J2 arrives. Rather than losing J2 as was the case for the simple processor, here the multi-server co-ordinator comes into play. Knowing that P1 is busy, MUL-C sends J2 to the next free processor, which happens to be P2. More truthfully, MUL-C places J2 on its output port 'x2, which is coupled by the internal coupling

---

[1] Recall that in DEVS-Scheme this transmission is realized by having a co-ordinator C:MUL-ARCH call on its *devs-component* MUL-ARCH to use its *get-receivers* and *translate* methods to return the receivers (here only MUL-C) of the external event, J1 and the port on which it will be sent. Please do not confuse the co-ordinator C:MUL-ARCH used in the simulation engine with the co-ordinator MUL-C, a model component.

Model Base for Multi-Computer Architectures

of MUL-ARCH to P2's input port 'in. J2 will be sent out of MUL-ARCH p units later in a manner similar to J1's processing. A third job, J3, arriving while both P1 and P2 are busy, will be sent to P3. However, a fourth job that arrives while all processors are busy will be lost. As illustrated in Figure 6.2c, if the job inter-arrival-time, T, is a constant, equal to $p/3$, then the fourth and subsequent jobs arrive just after a (exactly one) processor has finished its work. The figure makes clear that this is an arrival pattern in which processors are always kept busy. The emerging jobs are separated in time by $p/3$ so that the throughput is $3/p$. Since the processors are always kept busy, there is no way to produce a higher rate of job completions. Thus we can justify the entry for the multi-server architecture with constant processing time in Table 4.1. Clearly, each job still takes time p units to be processed, so that the average turnaround time is p as in the Table.

In the case of heterogeneous processing times $\{p_i\}$, the fastest that each processor, P_i, can emit jobs is at rate $1/p_i$. The maximum throughput is the sum of these rates. The average turnaround time associated with this departure rate can be derived from Little's relation (Sauer and Chandy, 1980). It is the number of jobs in the system (i.e., 3) divided by the departure rate, accounting for the corresponding entry in Table 4.1. Note that Little's formula relates the two performance indexes, throughput and turnaround time, as inverses of each other, just as intuition would have us imagine. However, it holds only for certain kinds of systems in which jobs are distributed uniformly around the processors at all times.

6.1.2 Pipeline Co-ordinator

The pipeline co-ordinator follows the same form as the multiserver co-ordinator except it does not keep track of the phases of its subordinates. As described in Figures 6.3a,b, PIP-C merely takes problems arriving at one input port and routes then to another output port. Thus a problem traverses the following sequence of ports:

'in → 'x1
'y1 → 'x2
'y2 → 'x3
'y3 → 'out

Pipeline Architecture

The coupling of the pipeline architecture follows exactly the form of the multiserver architecture with PIP-C replacing MUL-C as the co-ordinator of the processors. Specifying the digraph-model, PIP-ARCH is therefore a straightforward revision of the specification of MUL-ARCH. Later we shall show how the system entity structure formulation enables us to take advantage of such isomorphisms to reduce the amount of specification needed.

Figure 6.3c displays a typical state trajectory for the pipeline architecture. Note the progress of jobs through the successive stages of the pipeline. Clearly, the turnaround time is sum of the processing times a job encounters. How soon can job J2 arrive after J1 and not be lost? Let T be the time separating their arrivals. So long as J2 encounters only idle processors, this time difference is preserved as J2 follows J1 through the system. However, if T is smaller than some processing time, p_i, then Pi will be busy with J1 when J2 arrives. Said another way, the maximum throughput is the rate at which jobs can emerge from the slowest, or *bottleneck* processor. Jobs emerging from a faster processor upstream of the bottleneck will eventually encounter the bottleneck; a faster processor downstream can only get its input at the rate emerging from the bottleneck. Since $max\ \{p_i\}$ is the largest processing time, its inverse is the maximum throughput as in Table 4.1.

Consider the problem: minimize $max\ \{p_i\}$ subject to $\Sigma p_i = p$. The answer is p/n as can be shown by induction on n. This means that the best partitioning of a problem for pipeline processing with n stages occurs when each stage takes the same time, p/n.

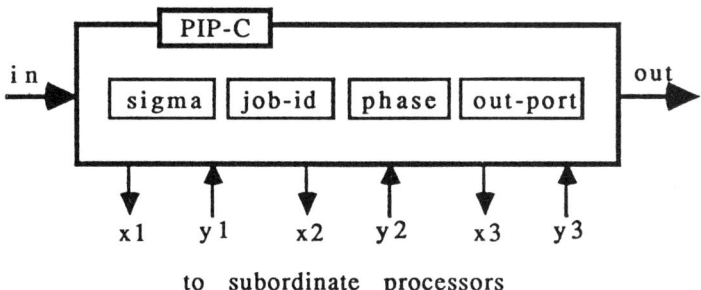

ATOMIC-MODEL: PIP-C

state variables: sigma = inf
　　　　　　　　phase = passive
　　　　　　　　out-port = ()
　　　　　　　　job-id = ()

external transition function:

　　store job-id
　　case input-port
　　　　in: set out-port to x1
　　　　y1: set out-port to x2
　　　　y2: set out-port to x3
　　　　y3: set out-port to out
　　hold-in busy 0

internal transition function:
　　case phase
　　　　busy: passive

output function:
　　case phase
　　　　busy: case out-port
　　　　　　　　x1, x2,x3,out: output job-id to out-port
　　　　　　　　else make a null output

Figure 6.3a. Pseudo-code for co-ordinator of pipeline architecture.

```
;;;;;;;;;;;;; Pipeline Co-ordinator ;;;;;;;;;;;;;;;;;;;;;;
;----------------------------------------------------------------
; This file contains the definition of the co-ordinator in
; Pipe-line architecture.
;----------------------------------------------------------------
; It should perform following tasks:
; 1) Gets a job from input and sends the job to the first
; processor.
; 2) If a finished job is returned from one of the processors,
; sends it to next processor in the pipeline.
; If the returning processor is the last processor, sends the
; job to output.
;----------------------------------------------------------------

;;;;;;;; make a pair for the co-ordinator in pipeline module

(make-pair atomic-models 'pip-c)

(send pip-c def-state '(
                        out-port    ;;holds next destination port
                        job-id
                        )
)

;; initialize the state

(send pip-c set-s (make-state 'sigma        'inf
                              'phase        'passive
                              'out-port     '()
                              'job-id       '()
)                 )

;; external transition function

(define (ext-ppc s e x)
        (set! (state-out-port s) '())
        (set! (state-job-id s) (content-value x))
        (case (content-port x)
        ; case 1. input from outside world
          ('in
           ; always send to first processor

             (set! (state-out-port s) 'x1)
           )
         ;case 2. input from the subordinate processors

           ('y1  (set! (state-out-port s) 'x2 ))
           ('y2  (set! (state-out-port s) 'x3 ))
           ('y3  (set! (state-out-port s) 'out))
                  ;send last result out
         ) ; end of case
         (hold-in 'busy 0)
)
```

Figure 6.3b. Atomic-model specification of co-ordinator of pipeline architecture.

```
;;;;;;;; internal transition function

(define (int-ppc s)
  (case (state-phase s)
    ('busy
        (passivate)
) ) )

;;;;;;;; output function
;;;;;;;; output the value to corresponding port

(define (out-ppc s)
  (case (state-phase s)
    ('busy
        (case (state-out-port s)
          ((x1 x2 x3 out)
              (make-content   'port (state-out-port s)
                              'value (state-job-id s))
          )
          (else (make-content))
) ) )   )

;;;;;;;; assignment to the model

(send pip-c set-ext-transfn ext-ppc)
(send pip-c set-int-transfn int-ppc)
(send pip-c set-outputfn out-ppc)
```

Figure 6.3b. (continued).

132   Object-Oriented Simulation

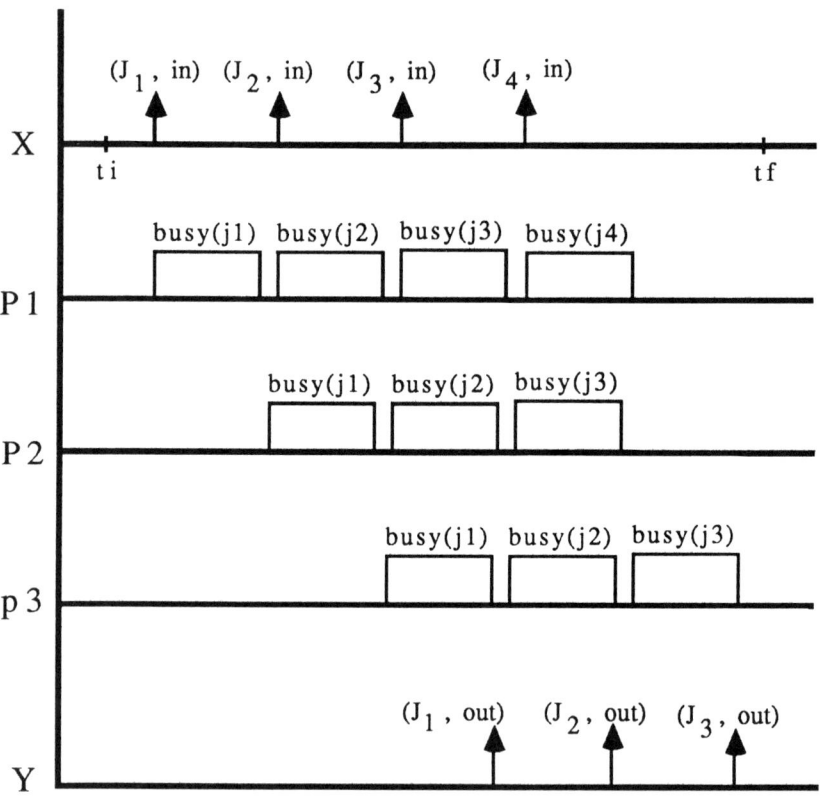

Figure 6.3c. Sketch of trajectory for pipeline architecture.

6.1.3 Divide and Conquer Co-ordinator

As described in Figure 6.4, the divide and conquer co-ordinator, DC-C is somewhat more complex than the proceeding co-ordinators. Part of its operation is like that of the pipeline. It routes an incoming problem first to the partitioner, then to the processors, to the compiler, and then out. Conceptually, the partioner divides the problem into sub-problems to be sent to the individual processors. In our simplified model, the partioning time is accounted for but the problem is not actually partitioned. Instead the job identifier is sent to each of the processors simultaneously. This is done in the output function *out-dc* using a list of content structures:

```
(list
  (make-content 'port 'x1 'value (state-job-id s))
  (make-content 'port 'x2 'value (state-job-id s))
  (make-content 'port 'x3 'value (state-job-id s))
).
```

In general, the simulation process in DEVS-Scheme will output the successive content structures in any normal list one after another without advancing the simulation clock, thus effectively outputting them simultaneously. Before sending out the "partial problems" to the processor, DC-C checks that they are all free. This keeps the processors all working on the same problem.

Divide and Conquer Architecture

As illustrated in Figure 6.5a, the coupling required to form the divide and conquer architecture is very similar to the previous cases. The only difference is that five, rather than just three processors are connected to the co-ordinator. Indeed, if we group the partioner and the compiler together with the co-ordinator, to form a new co-ordinator (now itself a digraph model), we once again have an architecture isomorphic to the multiserver. We shall take this approach when creating a compact system entity structure for this model family (Section 7.3.3).

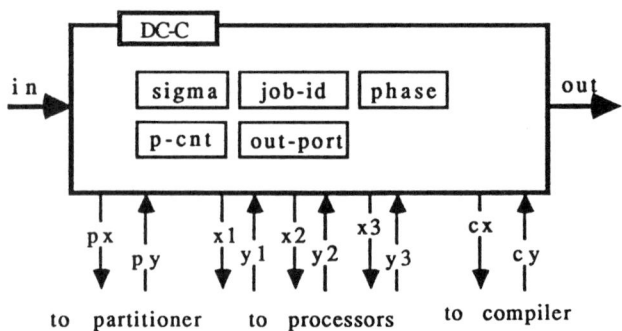

ATOMIC-MODEL: DC-C   ;;; divide & conquer co-ordinator

<u>state variables:</u> sigma = inf   phase = passive
out-port = ()   job-id = ()
p-cnt = 3   ;; count of free processors

<u>external transition function:</u>
store job-id
case input-port
    in: always send to problem partitioner by setting out-port to 'px
    py: if three sub-processors are free then set out-port to 'xin indicating to output function that a job is available in job-id (problem is not partitioned in this simple model). Otherwise job is lost.
    y1, y2, y3: partial result returned by one of the processors
        increment p-cnt by one.
        if p-cnt = 3 then send job-id to the port cx
            set out-port to cx
            clear p-cnt
hold-in busy 0

<u>internal transition function:</u>
case phase
    busy: passive

<u>output function:</u>
case phase
    busy: case out-port
        xin: send job-id to each processor
        px,cx,out: output to given port
        else make a null output

Figure 6.4a. Pseudo-code for co-ordinator of divide and conquer architecture.

Model Base for Multi-Computer Architectures 135

```
;;;;;;;;;;; Divide and conquer co-ordinator ;;;;;;;;;;;;;;;;;;
;------------------------------------------------------------------
; This file contains the definition of the co-ordinator in
; divide and conquer architecture.
;------------------------------------------------------------------
; It should perform following tasks:
; 1) Gets a problem from input and sends the problem to
;    problem-partitioner
; 2) When the divided problem is sent back, decides whether the
;    sub-processors are ALL available. If they are, the sub-problems
;    will be send to all sub-processors. If not, problem is lost.
; 3) After collecting all the returned results from sub-processors,
;    sends the returned partial results to post-compiler.
; 4) Gets the final result from compiler and sends it to output.
;------------------------------------------------------------------

;; make a pair for the co-ordinator in divide and conquer module

(make-pair atomic-models 'dc-c)

(send dc-c def-state '(
                       p-cnt     ;; number of partial solutions
                                 ;; received
                       out-port  ;; destination for next output
                       job-id
)                      )

;; initialize the states of this module

(send dc-c set-s (make-state 'sigma    'inf
                             'phase    'passive
                             'p-cnt    3
                             'out-port '()
                             'job-id   '()
)                )

;;;;;;;; Definition of divide and conquer co-ordinator

;; external transition function

(define (ext-dc s e x)
        (set! (state-out-port s) '())
        (set! (state-job-id s) (content-value x))
        (case (content-port x)

          ; case 1. arrival of a problem

          ('in   ;; Always send to partition processor
            (set! (state-out-port s) 'px)
          )

          ;case 2. input from partition processor

            ('py   ;; check whether the processors are all free
               (if (= (state-p-cnt s) 3)
```

Figure 6.4b. Atomic-model specification of co-ordinator of divide and conquer architecture.

```
                        (begin
                            (set! (state-p-cnt s) 0)
                            ;; send to three processors at the same time
                            (set! (state-out-port s) 'xin)))
                    )
                ;case 3. input from partial solution processors

                    ((y1 y2 y3)     (set! (state-p-cnt s) (1+ (state-p-cnt s)))
                                    (when (= (state-p-cnt s) 3)
                                        ; send the partial results to compiler
                                        (set! (state-out-port s) 'cx)
                    )               )

                ;case 4. input from the compiler

                    ('cy    (set! (state-out-port s) 'out))
                ) ; end of case

                (hold-in 'busy 0)
)
;;;;;;;;; output function

(define (out-dc s)
    (case (state-phase s)
      ('busy
        (case (state-out-port s)
            ('xin
                (list
                    (make-content 'port 'x1   'value (state-job-id s))
                    (make-content 'port 'x2   'value (state-job-id s))
                    (make-content 'port 'x3   'value (state-job-id s))
                )
            )
            ((px cx out)
                (make-content   'port (state-out-port s)
                                'value (state-job-id s))
            )
            (else (make-content))  ; no valid output to be made
)   )   )   )

;;;;;;;; internal transition function

(define (int-dc s)
  (case (state-phase s)
    ('busy
        (passivate)
)   )   )

;;;;;;;; assignment to the  model

(send dc-c set-ext-transfn ext-dc)
(send dc-c set-int-transfn int-dc)
(send dc-c set-outputfn out-dc)
```

Figure 6.4b. (continued).

Model Base for Multi-Computer Architectures

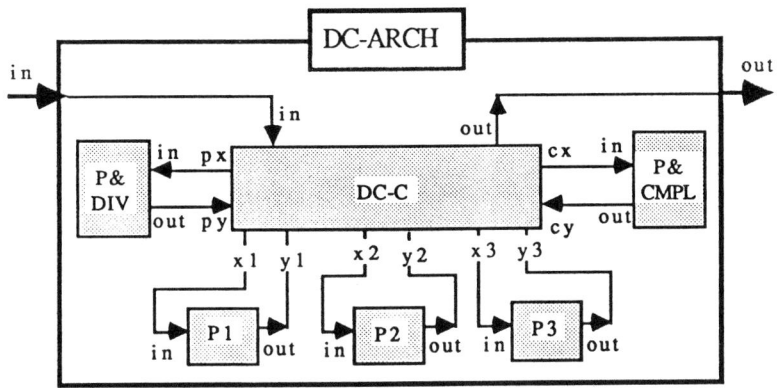

DIGRAPH-MODEL: DC-ARCH

COMPOSITION TREE:
> root: MUL-ARCH
> leaves: DC-C, P&DIV, P1, P2, P3, P&CMPL

EXTERNAL-INPUT COUPLING: DC-ARCH.in -> DC-C.in

EXTERNAL-OUTPUT COUPLING: DC-C.out -> DC-ARCH.out

INFLUENCE DIGRAPH:
> DC-C -> P1, P2, P3, P&DIV, P&CMPL
> P1 -> DC-C   P2 -> DC-C   P3 -> DC-C
> P&DIV -> DC-C   P&CMPL -> DC-C

INTERNAL COUPLING:
> DC-C.x1 -> P1.in   P&DIV.out -> DC-C.py
> DC-C.x2 -> P2.in   P1.out -> DC-C.y1
> DC-C.x3 -> P3.in   P2.out -> DC-C.y2
> DC-C.px -> P&DIV.in   P3.out -> DC-C.y3
> DC-C.cx -> P&CMPL.in   P&CMPL.out -> DC-C.cy

define the selection function to avoid collision when a job arrives at the same time the processor finishes:

PRIORITY LIST: P&CMPL P1 P2 P3 P&DIV DC-C

Figure 6.5a. Pseudo-code for divide-and-conquer architecture.

```
;;;;;;;;;;;; Divide and Conquer Architecture ;;;;;;;;;;;;;;;;;
;----------------------------------------------------------------
; This file contains the construction of the divide and conquer
; architecture by using digraph-model. The components
; are retrieved from the models.m defined in model-base.
;; components: One job partition process (p.m) -- p&div.
;              Three sub-processors (p.m) -- p1, p2, p3.
;              One post-compiler (p.m) -- p&cmpl.
;              One co-ordinator (dc-c.m) --- dc-c.
;----------------------------------------------------------------

;; get processor and co-ordinator

(load-from model-base_directory p.m)
(load-from model-base_directory dc-c.m)

;; make five copies from the original p processor
; first the pre-job-partition processor

(send p make-new 'p&div)

; and the post-compiler

(send p make-new 'p&cmpl)

; three sub-processors

(send p make-new 'p1)
(send p make-new 'p2)
(send p make-new 'p3)

;; now couple them together

(make-pair digraph-models 'dc-arch)

(send dc-arch specify-children (list dc-c p&div p1 p2 p3 p&cmpl))

;; external-input coupling

(send dc-arch add-couple dc-arch dc-c 'in 'in)

;; external-output coupling

(send dc-arch add-couple dc-c dc-arch 'out 'out)

;; internal coupling

(send dc-arch add-couple dc-c p&div 'px 'in)
(send dc-arch add-couple p&div dc-c 'out 'py)
```

Figure 6.5b. Digraph-model specification of divide-and-conquer architecture.

```
(send dc-arch add-couple dc-c p1 'x1 'in)
(send dc-arch add-couple p1 dc-c 'out 'y1)
(send dc-arch add-couple dc-c p2 'x2 'in)
(send dc-arch add-couple p2 dc-c 'out 'y2)
(send dc-arch add-couple dc-c p3 'x3 'in)
(send dc-arch add-couple p3 dc-c 'out 'y3)
(send dc-arch add-couple dc-c p&cmpl 'cx 'in)
(send dc-arch add-couple p&cmpl dc-c 'out 'cy)


;; define the select function
(define (sel-dcc slst)
        (cond   ((member p&cmpl slst) p&cmpl)
                ((member p1    slst) p1)
                ((member p2    slst) p2)
                ((member p3    slst) p3)
                ((member p&div slst) p&div)
                ((member dc-c  slst) dc-c)
        )
)

(send dc-arch set-selectfn sel-dcc)

;;equivalently,

(send dc-arch set-priority (list p&cmpl p1 p2 p3 p&div dc-c)))
```

Figure 6.5b. (continued).

A typical state trajectory for the divide and conquer architecture is shown in Figure 6.5c. You will see that the three processors, act in effect, as one stage in the sequence from input to output. This is so since to accept a new problem the co-ordinator DC-C requires that all processors have finished the subproblems of the current one. Since they are processed concurrently, the time to solve all subproblems is the time taken to finish the longest one, i.e., $max\ \{p_i\}$. Considering DC-ARCH as a pipeline, and using the results just obtained for the latter, verifies the results in Table 4.1.

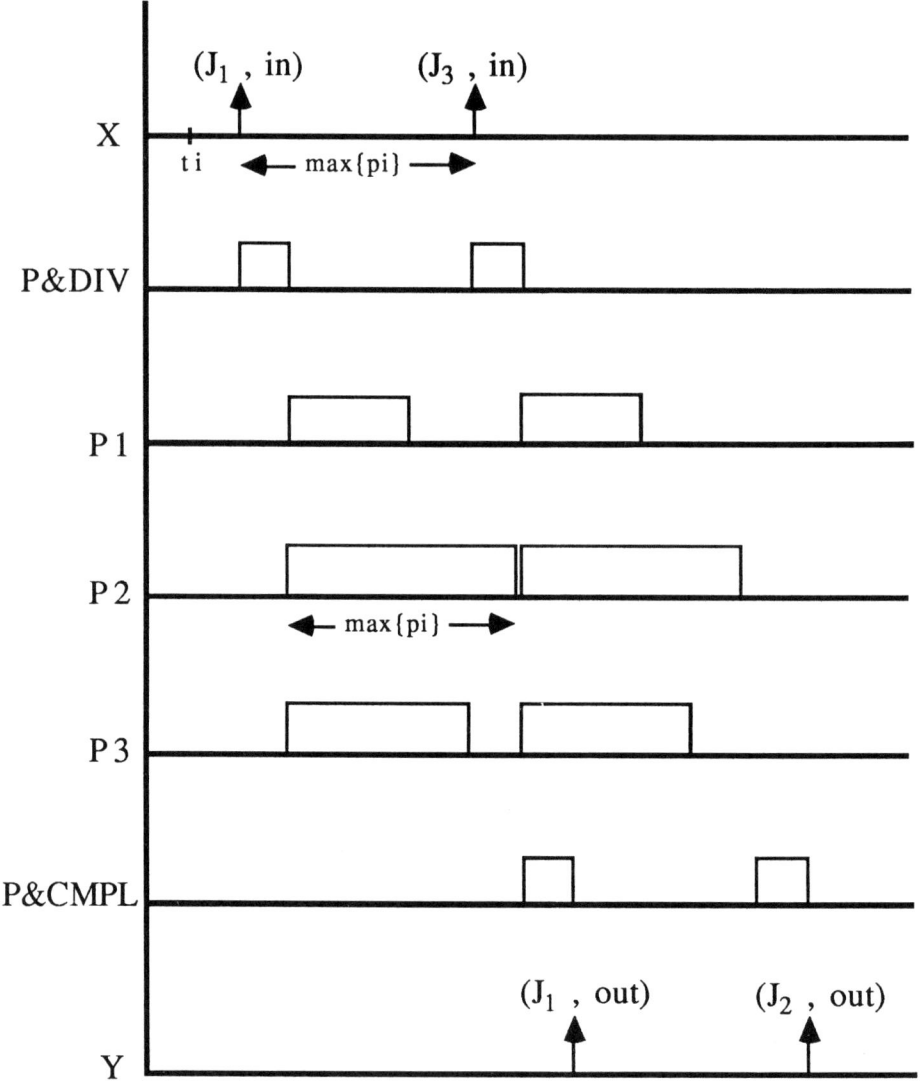

Figure 6.5c. Sketch of trajectory of divide and conquer architecture.

Model Base for Multi-Computer Architectures 141

6.2 Testing the Architectures

Testing of digraph models for correctness can be done conveniently using the simulation process. After loading the file containing the multi-server architecture, for example, we can start simulation with the command (*restart* r) where r is the root-co-ordinator created and initialized to C:MUL-ARCH. However, since all atomic-model components are in their passive phases, the simulation will immediately terminate. In general, the state of a coupled model is determined by the states of its atomic models. These must be set as desired to put the coupled model in a non-passive state.

There are two ways to start atomic-model components in different states: 1) internally, by entering the desired state variable values when queried by the restart command or 2) externally, by sending external events to the components.

6.2.1 Internal Initialization

In internal initialization we must know what states we wish to establish. For example, we could set the co-ordinator, MUL-C into the state that it would be in after receiving the first job:

STATE S = (0 BUSY BUSY PASSIVE PASSIVE X1 JOB_IN1)

This state can be established by interactively responding to the prompt of the restart command for entering state variable values for MUL-C. Alternatively, we can put the following in a file such as test.s:

(send mul-c set-s (make-state 'sigma 0
                              'phase 'busy
                              'p1-s 'busy
                              'p2-s 'passive
                              'p3-s 'passive
                              'out-port 'x1
                              'job-id 'job_in1
)
)

This message will automatically be loaded if we issue the *restart* command with the file as an argument: (restart r "test.s").

6.2.2 External Initialization

External initialization requires that we send an appropriate external event to the component we wish to initialize. For example, by entering:

(send mul-c inject 'in 'job_in1)

with MUL-C in its idle state, we send MUL-C into the same state as given above. Here we rely on the fact that we have already tested the component for its response to external inputs, so that we are confident that it will enter the correct state.

External initialization can also be done at any level in a hierarchical model since the method inject is also defined for coupled-models. For example,

(send mul-arch inject 'in 'job_in1)

will produce the same effect as above. The method, *inject*, for coupled-models behaves similarly to a co-ordinator when receiving an external event. It sends the translated content structure to the receivers determined by the external-input coupling. Since the receivers may also be coupled-models, the method is recursive. Figure 6.6 displays the code for the inject method for both coupled and atomic models. This illustrates how recursive calling of methods works. Such recursion is often needed in DEVS-Scheme methods due to the hierarchical structure.

Having one or more components set to desired initial states, we can run the simulation in pause mode. This will enable viewing the messages as they are created and routed through the components. If a message does not get created as it should, or go to the right destination, then we can terminate the simulation and view the current state of the model as a start toward analyzing the source of the error.

The *inject* method is also very useful in testing a model for response to external events. Often, we run a simulation until it reaches a particular state. If the time advance for this state is infinity, (the model passivates in this state), then the simulation stops naturally. Otherwise, we can terminate the simulation before the next transition takes place. Now we can inject an external event into the model to test its response in this state both statically, i.e., by examining the new state after an external event, and dynamically, i.e., by restarting the simulation from the new state.

```
(define-method (coupled-models inject) (port value . elapsed-time)
                        ;; the " . " makes the arguments following it
                        ;; into a list; a null list is also accepted
                        ;; effectively yielding optional arguments
  (let (
        (e (when (number? (car elapsed-time)) (car elapsed-time)))
        (destinations (get-receivers))
        )
     (for-each (lambda(child)
               (let (
                    (tr-port (translate this-model child port))
                    )
                 (when tr-port
                   (send child inject tr-port value e)
                   )        ;; note no check of the child's class is needed
                 ))
                 destinations)
  ))



(define-method (atomic-models inject)(port  value . elapsed-time)
  (set-x (make-content 'port port 'value value))
  (when (number? (car elapsed-time)) (set-e (car elapsed-time)))
  (ext-transition)
  )
```

Figure 6.6. Definition of the *inject* method for atomic-models and coupled-models.

Chapter 7

SYSTEM ENTITY STRUCTURES

This chapter discusses the use of the *Systems Entity Structure (SES)* to specify hierarchical models and to organize them for reuse from an archival model base. We illustrate these concepts in modelling and simulating simple computer architectures. We begin with a review of SES concepts.

Recall that a knowledge representation scheme for managing a family of models must support the following three relationships: *decomposition*, *taxonomy*, and *coupling*. Knowledge about *decomposition* means that there are schemes for representing the manner in which an object is decomposed into components. The schemes are hierarchical since components themselves may be decomposed into subcomponents, and so on, to a depth determined by the modeller's objectives.

The requirement for *taxonomic* knowledge means that there must be a method of organizing the different kinds of objects, i.e., how they can be categorized and subclassified. For example, a scheme could "know" that automobile transmissions are automatic or manual, and that the latter can be of the four-speed or five-speed variety.

The requirement for *coupling* knowledge means that there must be a way of representing how models are coupled together and what constraints apply to component combinations.

7.1 System Entity Structure Definitions and Axioms

The *System Entity Structure* (SES) is defined as labeled tree with attached variable types which satisfies the following axioms:

1. *uniformity*: Any two nodes which have the same labels have identical attached variable types and isomorphic subtrees.

2. *strict hierarchy*: No label appears more than once down any path of the tree.

3. *alternating mode*: Each node has a mode which is either *entity*, *aspect*, or *specialization*; if the mode of a node is *entity* then the modes of its successors are *aspect* or *specialization*, if the mode of a node is *aspect* or *specialization*, then the modes of its children are *entity*. The mode of the root is *entity*.

4. *valid brothers*: No two brothers have the same label.

5. *attached variables*: No two variable types attached to the same item have the same name.

6. *inheritance*: every *entity* in a *specialization* inherits all the variables, *aspects* and *specializations* from the parent of the *specialization*

The SES is completely characterized by its axioms (Zeigler, 1984; Zhang and Zeigler, 1989). However, the interpretation of the axioms cannot be specified and thus is open to the user. When constructing a SES it may seem difficult to decide how to represent concepts of the real world. How to choose between *entity*, *aspect* or *specialization*?

System Entity Structures

To help make this decision the following points should be kept in mind:

An *entity* represents a real world object that either can be independently identified or postulated as a component of a decomposition of another real world object.

An *aspect* represents one decomposition out of many possible of an entity. The children of an aspect are entities representing components in a decomposition of its parent.

A *specialization* is a mode of classifying entities and is used to express alternative choices for components in the system being modelled. The children of a specialization are entities representing variants of its parent. For example, in an SES for a computer system, the entity *printer* could have such specializations as: *size, typeface,* and *interface-type*. The children of interface-type might be *parallel interface* and *serial interface*. These are variants for the interface of printer. That printers also come in various sizes is represented in the specialization *size*.

The entities of an aspect represent distinct components of a decomposition. A model can be constructed by connecting together some or all of these components. The aspects of an entity do not necessarily represent disjoint decompositions. A new aspect can be constructed by selecting from existing aspects as desired.

The properties of a SES are illustrated in a computer example (Figure 7.1). The root entity is COMPUTER and it has a specialization, shown by two vertical lines, called CLASS-SPECIALIZATION with entities ANALOG, DIGITAL, and HYBRID. In such a specialization relation, COMPUTER is referred to as a generic type relative to the entities, ANALOG, DIGITAL, and HYBRID, which are called special types. Besides having their own distinctive attributes, HYBRID, ANALOG, and DIGITAL inherit all of the attributes (variables and substructures) possessed by COMPUTER. To make this true, we must be sure to assign to COMPUTER only those attributes that are common to all its variants.

HYBRID is shown as having a decomposition into ANALOG and DIGITAL, i.e., it is a system built from two component systems. By the uniformity axiom, the DIGITAL part of a HYBRID computer has the same PHYSICAL-DECOMPOSITION shown under the occurrence of DIGITAL as a special type of COMPUTER. In other words, when a DIGITAL_COMPUTER is combined with an ANALOG_COMPUTER, its internal structure is the same as if it were free standing.

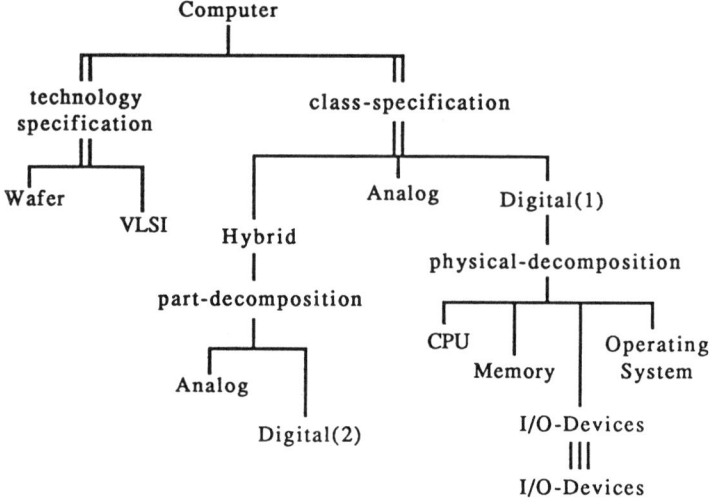

Note: Digital(2) has the same attributes and sub-structure as Digital(1)

Figure 7.1. System entity structure for electronic computers.

The SES makes it possible to represent, and distinguish between, two types of property transfer related to multiple inheritance in object-oriented programming (Chapter 2). The first kind is illustrated above in the fact that HYBRID, being decomposed into DIGITAL and ANALOG components, "inherits" properties from both

System Entity Structures 149

through the uniformity axiom. In this case, the sources of the "inheritance" are represented as distinct components and it is possible to take account of their interaction through coupling specification associated with the parent decomposition. This contrasts with object-oriented inheritance in which attributes are simply accumulated.

The second kind of property transfer is that directly corresponding to multiple inheritance in object oriented systems. This occurs when a succession of selections is made from a set of specializations under the same entity. For example, first select DIGITAL from CLASS-SPECIALIZATION under COMPUTER. Then the TECHNOLOGY-SPECIALIZATION of COMPUTER is inherited by DIGITAL. Selecting VLSI from it, we have a result VLSI_DIGITAL_COMPUTER which has inherited from both DIGITAL and VLSI. Later (Chapter 9), we shall see that to be meaningful for models, this kind of accumulation of properties assumes a underlying superposition principle.

The triple vertical bars connecting I/O_DEVICES and I/O_DEVICE in Figure 7.1 represent a special type of decomposition called a *multiple decomposition*. A *multiple decomposition* is used to represent entities whose number in a system may vary. For example a digital computer may have 0, 1, 2, or more I/O_DEVICEs.

As you may recall, the coupling relationship defines how the entities (models) communicate with each other. Since the aspects define the decompositions of the system, the coupling relationships must be associated with their respective aspects.

7.2 Using the System Entity Structure in DEVS-Scheme

In the first place, the SES provides an alternative to the digraph model approach for specifying coupled models. In DEVS-Scheme this is a high level of specification which is then transformed into an equivalent coupled model, similar to the way in which a procedural language is compiled into assembly language. Using a higher level specification considerably simplifies the model description task in the same way that writing a program in a procedural language simplifies writing the equivalent code in machine language. However, we shall see that the primary feature of the SES is that it serves as a knowledge representation scheme to organize a family of models in a model base.

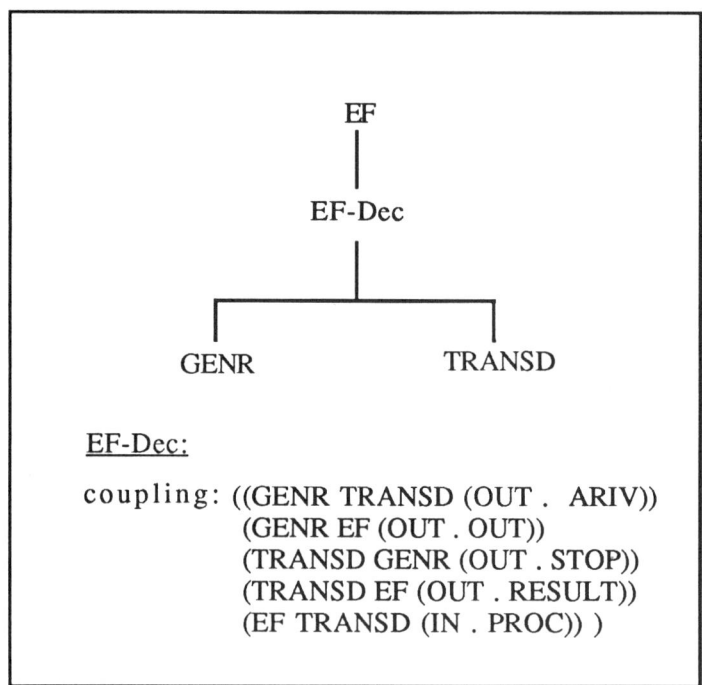

Figure 7.2. Entity structure for experimental frame component.

Figure 7.2 illustrates an entity structure for the experimental frame component discussed earlier. The SES asserts that an entity EF, the root of the structure, is decomposed into entities TRANSD and GENR using aspect EF-DEC. The coupling specification which

System Entity Structures

is employed to synthesize EF from TRANSD and GENR is associated with the aspect EF-DEC. This coupling is presented as a list of elements of the form (comp1 comp2 (port1 . port2)) in Figure 7.2. The type of coupling (external-input, external-output, or internal) is recognizable from the component sequence: comp1 comp2. For example, (GENR TRANSD (OUT . ARIV)) specifies the internal coupling from GENR's outport 'out to TRANSD's input port 'ariv. (GENR EF (OUT . OUT)) specifies external-output coupling from GENR to the enclosing digraph model, EF. Note that the digraph model's instance variables, *composition-tree* and *influence-digraph*, can be inferred from the decomposition and coupling information in the SES.

Figure 7.3 shows how the SES of Figure 7.2 is specified. First the SES object E:EF, is constructed using *make-entstr*. In creating E:EF, *make-entstr* makes a root entity with name EF. Then the aspect, EF-DEC is added to the root, EF using the operation, *add-item*. To add entities to this aspect, we must first move the current-item pointer from EF, where it starts to EF-DEC. In general, all operations are performed with respect to the current-item (i.e., the item designated by the last *set-current-item* operation). Using *add-item* again, the entities GENR and TRANSD, are added to the EF-DEC aspect. Without moving the *current-item*, the couplings to be associated with EF-DEC are added using the operation *add-couple*. The *save-en* command compiles the information defining E:EF in a file, ef.e. Subsequently, E:EF is known to the entity structure manager and it can be quickly loaded with the command (*load-entstr e:ef*).

An entity structure for the simple processor/experimental frame pair EF-P is shown in Figure 7.4. The coupling associated with the aspect is the same as that represented in the digraph model EF-P described earlier. The same approach to specifying t.is SES is used as just discussed, except that now we use the operation:

(*add-priority e:ef-p '(p ef)*)

to specify that the select function will be based on the priority scheme in which P takes priority over EF.

```
;---------------------------------------------------------------------
; This file contains the experimental frame for all architectures
;---------------------------------------------------------------------

;; make an entity structure with root EF

(make-entstr 'ef)

;; add an aspect for decomposition

(add-item e:ef asp 'ef-dec)

;; experimental frame consists of generator and transducer

(set-current-item e:ef 'ef-dec)
(add-item e:ef ent 'transd)
(add-item e:ef ent 'genr)

;-------- coupling ---------------------------------

(add-couple e:ef 'ef 'transd 'in 'solved)
(add-couple e:ef 'transd 'ef 'out 'result)
(add-couple e:ef 'transd 'genr 'out 'stop)
(add-couple e:ef 'genr 'ef 'out 'out)
(add-couple e:ef 'genr 'transd 'out 'ariv)

; save e:ef in a file ef.e

 (save-en e:ef)
```

Figure 7.3. Specification of SES for EF.

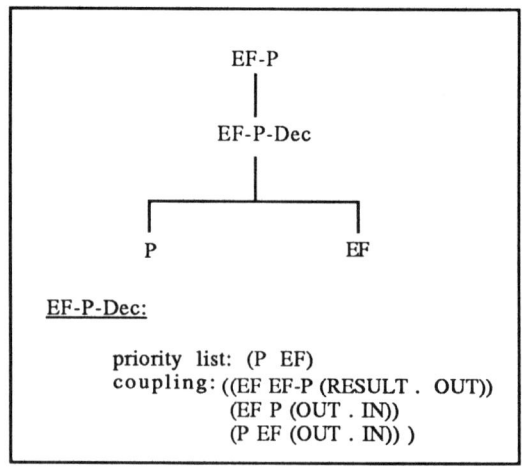

Figure 7.4. SES for processor/frame pair.

System Entity Structures

Later we shall see how the *transformation* procedure conveniently handles the situation where a leaf entity, such as EF in Figure 7.4, is itself a coupled model, specified by another SES. For now we extend the SES of Figure 7.4 to include the specification for entity EF as shown in Figure 7.5.

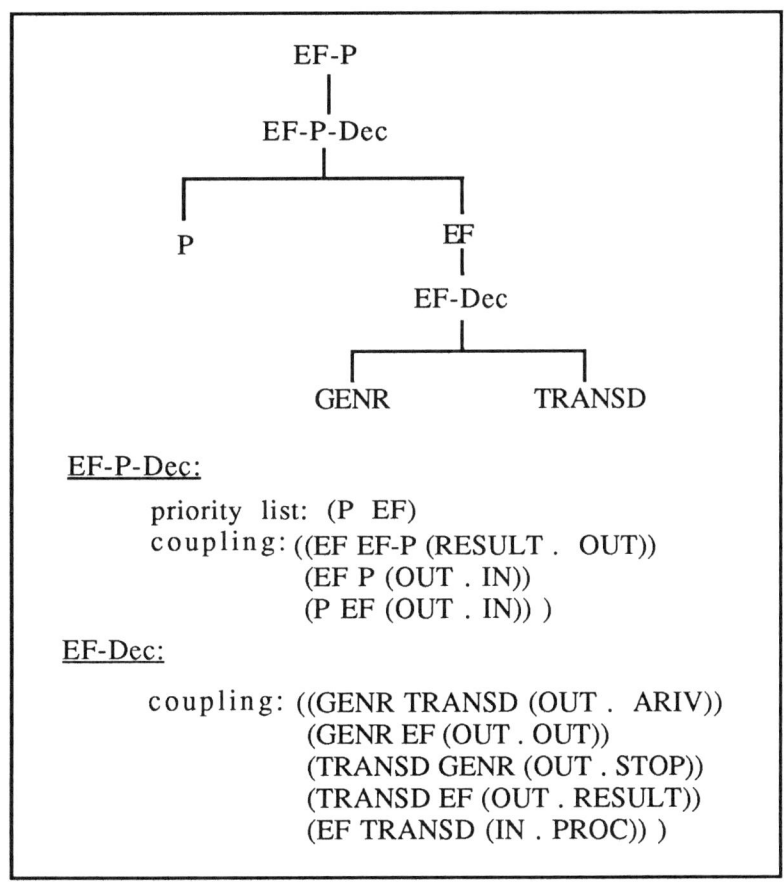

Figure 7.5. Extended SES for processor/frame pair.

7.2.1 Simulating Directly from an Entity Structure

The SES, E:EF-P is said to be *pure*, i.e., it has no specializations and at most one aspect under each entity. Such an SES can be directly transformed into a hierarchical model and simulated. The transformation procedure expects that models for the leaves of the SES will be available: having files p.m, genr.m and transd.m in the model base directory will satisfy this requirement. After synthesizing the digraph model EF-P, the transformation procedure makes a root-co-ordinator R:EF-P and initializes it to the co-ordinator C:EF-P, it has also made. Thus, as shown below, after transforming, the model is ready to be simulated and awaits the command (*restart r:ef-p*) to do so.

```
;; load the entity structure
(load-entstr e:ef-p)
;; transform it into a hierarchical model and initialize it
;; with a root-co-ordinator r:ef-p
(transform e:ef-p)
;; start a simulation run
(restart r:ef-p)
```

Comparing the SES manner of constructing EF-P with the direct digraph-model approach of Chapter 5 we see that

- it the SES is declarative, while the digraph-model specification is procedural, in character, and

- the SES relieves the modeller of specifying many of the details required by the digraph-model that can be inferred from other information (c.f., the coupling specification).

- the transformation process, besides synthesizing the model, also can relieve the user of associated actions (namely, creating, naming and initializing a root-co-ordinator.)

However, the SES provides much more power to specify and organize models as we shall now show.

7.3 System Entity Structure Organization of Model Bases

The various computer architecture models and model/frame pairs synthesized earlier in Chapter 6, are all built from the atomic-models shown in Figure 7.6. Files describing these models are the only ones that actually must be present in the model base directory for the system entity structure to direct synthesis of all of the hierarchical models.

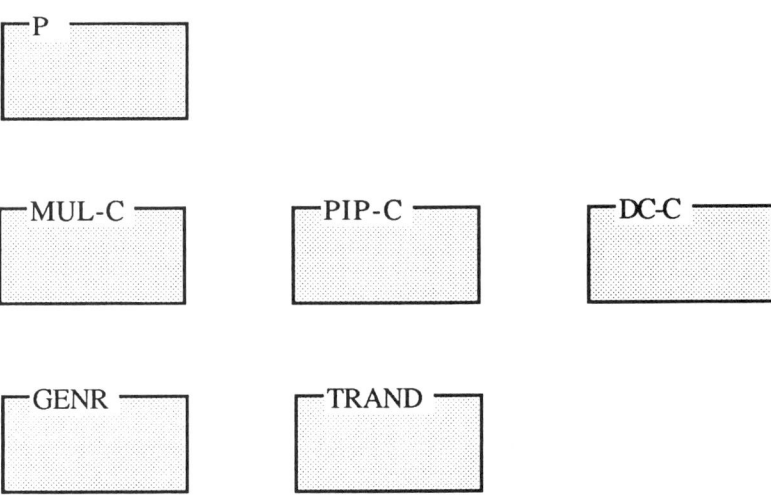

Figure 7.6. Model base for simple architecture study.

In general, files for all the atomic entities in the SES must exist in the model base with the following exception: entities with names ending in numbers or having a "&" in the name.

The transform procedure treats names ending in numbers or having an "&" as instance names for an underlying "class" corresponding to the first part of the name. For example, the entities P1, P2, P3, P&DIV, and P&CMPL are all transformed into models which are copies of the model P (including its initial state). In this example, P is called the *base-name* and the file *base-name.m* should be in the model base. Alternatively, the base-name model must be constructable by the transformation procedure to be discussed soon. Note however that no explicit class definition corresponding to base-name model is required.

The organization of the directories for a model domain takes the following form:

scheme directory:	\scheme
DEVS-Scheme directory:	\scheme\devs
domain directory:	\scheme\devs\simparc
model base directory:	\scheme\devs\simparc\mbase
entity structure directory:	\scheme\devs\simparc\enbase

Each of the top three directories contains a scheme initialization file (scheme.ini) which respectively, loads the PCScheme system, loads the DEVS-Scheme system, and informs DEVS-Scheme of the model domain directory and its subdirectories. The model and entity structure directories are assumed to be subdirectories of the domain directory with names, *mbase* and *enbase*, respectively. These directories can be changed with the DEVS-Scheme command (*change-dir*). Global variables *model_base-directory* and *entstr_base-directory* hold the path information to the respective subdirectories.

To start up ESP-Scheme, the entity structure layer of DEVS-Scheme, the user has only to set the current directory to the domain directory and call the extended or expanded version of PCScheme. For example:

⟩cd   \scheme\devs\simparc
⟩pcsext

System Entity Structures 157

When loading has finished, the variable, *model_base-directory* is bound to the string "\\scheme\\devs\\simparc\\mbase\\" and the variable, *entstr_base-directory* is bound to the string "\\scheme\\devs\\simparc\\enbase\\" (note: / may be used instead of \\).

7.3.1 SES/Model Base for Simple Computer Architectures

Files corresponding to the models of Figure 7.6 are placed in the model base directory:

> model base directory: \scheme\devs\simparc\mbase
> files:
>> p.m
>> mul-c.m
>> pip-c.m
>> dc-c.m
>> genr.m
>> transd.m

An SES for this model domain is shown in Figure 7.7 and specified in file ef-a.s which is contained in the entity structure base. After ef-a.s is loaded the first time, the compiled form of the SES it specifies, is stored in the entity structure directory as ef-a.e. Hence, we have:

> entity structure directory: \scheme\devs\simparc\enbase
> files:
>> ef-a.s
>> ef-a.e

The SES of Figure 7.7 makes it clear that the same experimental frame is to be used with each of the four architectures under study. To see this, notice that the model/frame combination is represented by the root entity, EF-A. The components of this combination are specified through an aspect, EF-A-DEC. which has as components

158   *Object-Oriented Simulation*

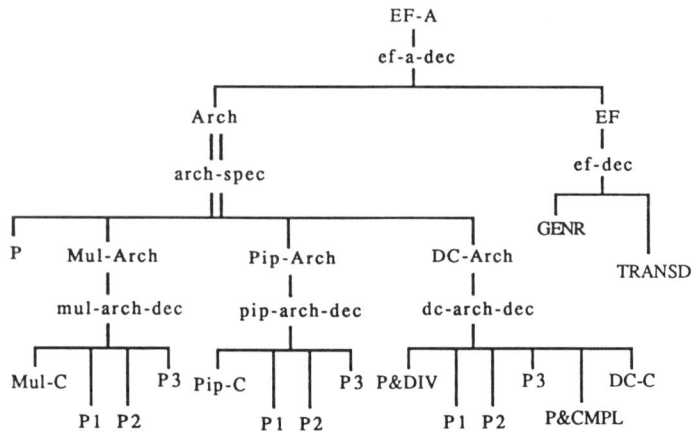

EF-A-DEC: priority list: (EF ARCH)
              coupling: ((EF EF-A (RESULT . OUT)) (EF ARCH (OUT . IN))
                     (ARCH EF (OUT . IN)))

EF-DEC: coupling: ((GENR TRANSD (OUT . ARIV)) (GENR EF (OUT . OUT))
                     (TRANSD GENR (OUT . STOP)) (TRANSD EF (OUT . RESULT))
                     (EF TRANSD (IN . PROC)))

MUL-ARCH-DEC:
    priority list: (P1 P2 P3 MUL-C)
    coupling: ((P3 MUL-C (OUT . Y3)) (P2 MUL-C (OUT . Y2))
              (P1 MUL-C (OUT . Y1)) (MUL-C P3 (X3 . IN))
              (MUL-C P2 (X2 . IN)) (MUL-C P1 (X1 . IN))
              (MUL-C MUL-ARCH (OUT . OUT)) (MUL-ARCH MUL-C (IN . IN)))

PIP-ARCH-DEC:
    priority list: (P3 P2 P1 PIP-C)
    coupling: ((P3 PIP-C (OUT . Y3)) (P2 PIP-C (OUT . Y2))
              (P1 PIP-C (OUT . Y1)) (PIP-C P3 (X3 . IN))
              (PIP-C P2 (X2 . IN)) (PIP-C P1 (X1 . IN))
              (PIP-C PIP-ARCH (OUT . OUT)) (PIP-ARCH PIP-C (IN . IN)))

DC-ARCH-DEC:
    priority list: (P&CMPL P3 P2 P1 P&DIV DC-C)
    coupling: ((P&CMPL DC-C (OUT . CY)) (P&DIV DC-C (OUT . PY))
              (DC-C P&CMPL (CX . IN)) (DC-C P&DIV (PX . IN))
              (P3 DC-C (OUT . Y3)) (P2 DC-C (OUT . Y2))
              (P1 DC-C (OUT . Y1)) (DC-C P3 (X3 . IN))
              (DC-C P2 (X2 . IN)) (DC-C P1 (X1 . IN))
              (DC-C DC-ARCH (OUT . OUT)) (DC-ARCH DC-C (IN . IN)))

Figure 7.7. SES for simple architectures study.

the frame, EF and an entity, ARCH. ARCH generically represents the four architectures since it has a specialization, ARCH-SPEC which contains the architectures as variants.

The coupling between ARCH and EF is attached to the aspect, EF-A-DEC. In pruning, when a particular specialized entity is selected from ARCH-SPEC, this particular entity replaces all references to ARCH in the coupling specification. Thus, the general entity, ARCH, can be viewed as a kind of place holder for any of its specialized versions in the coupling specification. For example, if P is selected as the specialized entity from ARCH-SPEC, the coupling between EF and P becomes:

$$\text{coupling} \rightarrow ((\text{EF EF-A (RESULT . OUT)})$$
$$(\text{EF P (OUT . IN)})$$
$$(\text{P EF (OUT . IN)})).$$

We see that this is the same as the coupling established earlier when P was coupled to EF in the digraph model EF-P.

Clearly, for ARCH to validly represent its specialized versions, the coupling between each of the versions and the experimental frame must be isomorphic, i.e., essentially the same except for replacement of one variant for another. Fortunately, this is the case here. Indeed, the frame was designed so that it could consistently be coupled with any job processing model to measure average turnaround time and throughput.

The priority order attached to an aspect is treated similarly to the attached coupling by the pruning procedure. Thus when P is selected for ARCH from ARCH-SPEC, the priority list attached to EF-A-DEC becomes

priority-list: (P EF).

7.3.2 Pruning the System Entity Structure

Recall that a pure entity structure is one having no specializations and at most one aspect hanging from every entity. *Pruning* is required to create a such a pure SES. The result of pruning is a *Pruned*

Entity Structure (PES) which contains fewer aspects and specializations than the original and therefore specifies a smaller family of alternative models than the latter. Ultimately, pruning terminates in a pure entity structure which specifies the synthesis of a particular hierarchical model. We employ the pruner by issuing the command (*prune es*) for a desired entity structure *es*.

For example, let us prune the entity structure of Figure 7.7 to construct a model/frame pair suitable for experimenting with the divide & conquer architecture. Then we issue the command:

(*prune* e:ef-a),

and follow the interaction shown in Figure 7.8.

First the pruner requests an extension to distinguish this particular pruning from others (line 1). The starting entity for pruning is then requested (line 2). The pruned entity structure (PES) that results will have as its root the chosen starting entity. This PES will have the name of the starting entity with the above extension suffixed to it. Note that since the starting entity can be chosen by the user, models of components or subsystems of the the overall system, may be constructed by pruning.

The next choice (line 3, and later line 8) is whether the current entity is to be made a leaf or not. Making an entity a leaf has the effect of terminating subsequent pruning of its subtree and requires that a model for the entity be accessible to the transform procedure. This is appropriate for example, if we want to employ a simplified model for the current entity rather than the more elaborate one that would result from synthesis directed by the subtree.

A single aspect must be chosen for the current entity from those available (line 4). Since, in this case, only one aspect, EF-A-DEC, is available, the pruning procedure automatically selects it.

Pruning proceeds in a depth-first traversal of the SES. For example, the first child of aspect EF-A-DEC, ARCH, is visited next. If more than one specializations are hanging under the current entity, the user is queried to select one (line 5). If only one exists, we proceed to make a selection from it (line 6).

```
1)   give extension for pruned-entstr name :
**   dc
2)   select starting entity from the following: (GENR TRANSD P&CMPL
     P&DIV DC-C MUL-C P3 P2 P1 PIP-C P DC-ARCH MUL-ARCH PIP-ARCH EF
     ARCH EF-A)
**   ef-a
     working from entity EF-A
3)   make this a leaf? (y/n)
**   n
4)   select an aspect from the following: (EF-A-DEC)
     aspect EF-A-DEC selected
     working from entity ARCH
5)   select a specialization from the following: (ARCH-SPEC)
     specialization ARCH-SPEC is selected
6)   select an entity from the following: (P PIP-ARCH
     MUL-ARCH DC-ARCH)
**   dc-arch
     entity DC-ARCH from specialization ARCH-SPEC selected
7)   select an aspect from the following: (DC-ARCH-DEC)
     aspect DC-ARCH-DEC selected
     working from entity DC-C
     working from entity P1
     working from entity P2
     working from entity P3
     working from entity P&DIV
     working from entity P&COM

     working from entity EF
8)   make this a leaf? (y/n)
**   n
     select an aspect from the following: (EF-DEC)
     aspect EF-DEC selected
     working from entity TRANSD
     working from entity GENR

9)   save this entity-structure? (y/n)
**   y
     Pruned entstr P:ef-a-dc made.
```

Figure 7.8. Transcript of a pruning interaction to construct divide-and-conquer model.

Pruning in this manner continues until all leaf entities (which remain after subtree abortion) have been visited.

Figure 7.9 shows the PES resulting from the above pruning. When transformed, this SES will result in a digraph model which couples the divide and conquer architecture with the experimental frame. Notice that the coupling associated with the aspect ef-a-dec has automatically been modified to reflect the replacement of the

162   Object-Oriented Simulation

generic entity ARCH by the specialized choice DC-ARCH. In general, replacement of a generic entity by its selected specialized entity is made in all contexts in which the generic entity appears.

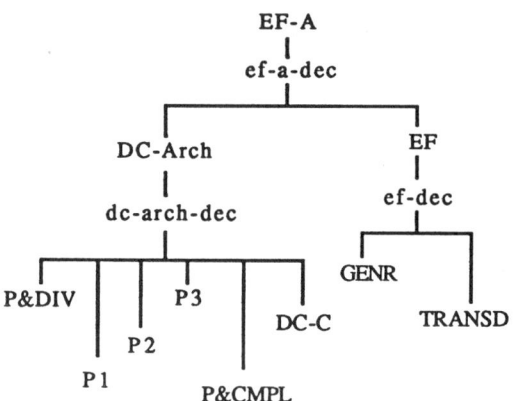

EF-A-DEC: priority list: (EF DC-ARCH)
          coupling: ((EF EF-A (RESULT . OUT)) (EF DC-ARCH (OUT . IN))
                     (DC-ARCH EF (OUT . IN)))

EF-DEC: coupling: ((GENR TRANSD (OUT . ARIV)) (GENR EF (OUT . OUT))
                    (TRANSD GENR (OUT . STOP)) (TRANSD EF (OUT . RESULT))
                    (EF TRANSD (IN . PROC)))

DC-ARCH-DEC:
       priority list: (P&CMPL P3 P2 P1 P&DIV DC-C)
       coupling: ((P&CMPL DC-C (OUT . CY)) (P&DIV DC-C (OUT . PY))
                   (DC-C P&CMPL (CX . IN)) (DC-C P&DIV (PX . IN))
                   (P3 DC-C (OUT . Y3)) (P2 DC-C (OUT . Y2))
                   (P1 DC-C (OUT . Y1)) (DC-C P3 (X3 . IN))
                   (DC-C P2 (X2 . IN)) (DC-C P1 (X1 . IN))
                   (DC-C DC-ARCH (OUT . OUT)) (DC-ARCH DC-C (IN . IN)))

Figure 7.9. PES resulting from pruning interaction of Figure 7.8.

System Entity Structures

To construct a simulation model ready for execution we need only issue the command (*transform p:ef-a@dc*). Should we desire to construct the same model in subsequent sessions, we need only load the PES, P:EF-A@DC and issue the same *transform* command.

7.3.3 Alternative SES for Simple Architectures Domain

An alternate SES for the simple architectures model domain is shown in Figure 7.10. Notice that in this case the four architectures of interest are not listed individually under the ARCH-SPEC specialization as they are in Figure 7.7. Instead, a common structure for the co-ordinated architectures is described under the specialized entity, CO-ARCH. The decomposition CO-ARCH-DEC specifies this common structure consisting of a co-ordinator, CO-ORD and three subordinate processors, P1, P2, and P3. The fact that the co-ordinator is different in each case is reflected in the specialization, COORD-SPEC which contains the three types: MUL-C, PIP-C, and DC-COORD.

This SES is superior to the original one in Figure 7.7 in two ways:

1. The specification is more compact, requiring less information to be provided.

2. It makes explicit the common features of the co-ordinated architectures, leading to better comprehension.

The coupling between the general entity COORD and the subordinate processors is attached to the enclosing aspect CO-ARCH-DEC. When COORD is replaced by any of its specialized entities, the coupling is specialized accordingly. Thus, although each of the co-ordinator alternatives manages the subordinate processors differently, the coupling between co-ordinators and subordinates is essentially the same (isomorphic) in each case.[1]

---

[1] The situation here is reminiscent of writing grammars for natural languages: a syntactic class, such as verbs, can be formed if it expresses a valid generality, namely that all members of that class are treated alike in the construction of sentences.

Object-Oriented Simulation

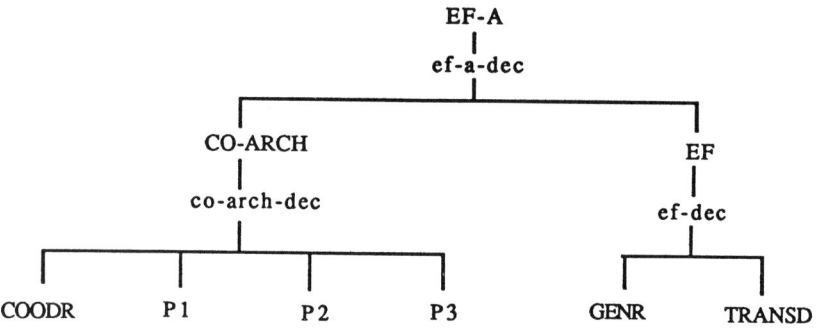

EF-A-DEC: priority list: (EF CO-ARCH)
coupling: ((EF EF-A (RESULT . OUT))
(EF CO-ARCH (OUT . IN))
(CO-ARCH EF (OUT . IN)))

CO-ARCH-DEC: priority list: (P1 P2 P3 COORD)
coupling: ((P3 COORD (OUT . Y3))
(P2 COORD (OUT . Y2))
(P1 COORD (OUT . Y1))
(COORD P3 (X3 . IN))
(COORD P2 (X2 . IN))
(COORD P1 (X1 . IN))
(COORD CO-ARCH (OUT . OUT))
(CO-ARCH COORD (IN . IN)))

Figure 7.10. An alternative SES for the simple architecture model base.

System Entity Structures 165

The divide and conquer co-ordinator is this case is actually a digraph model containing the co-ordinator DC-C proper and its helpers, the partitioner and compiler: P&DIV and P&CMPL. An entity structure for DC-COORD is shown in Figure 7.11. It is shown as a pruned entity structure P:DC-COORD in order to make it available to the transform procedure, as described at the end of Chapter 2. (This PES was derived from the original DC-ARCH model by a process called deepening which we will discuss later.) The entity structure directory in this case contains the file dc-coord.p for the model DC-COORD as well as the file ef-a.e for the overall SES. Thus we have:

entity structure directory: \scheme\devs\simparc\enbase

files:

ef-a.s
ef-a.e
dc-coord.p

In general, *.e files describe system entity structures (SES) while *.p files describe pruned entity structures (PES). When such files are loaded into RAM, the structures they describe are given names prefixed by e: and p:, respectively. Thus after loading, ef-a.e and dc-coord.p, the entity structures E:EF-A and P:DC-COORD exist in RAM.

7.4 Operations on Hierarchical Model Structures: Flatting and Deepening

To create a common structure for the co-ordinated architectures we had to group the divide & conquer co-ordinator, DC with its helpers, the partitioner, P&DIV and compiler, P&CMPL to form a new component, DC-COORD. This is an example of a structure modifying operation called *deepening*. A procedure, *deep-devs*, is provided which automatically does the desired restructuring in such a way that behavioral equivalence is preserved. To group the components DC, P&DIV and P&CMPL together, we use the command:

(*deep-devs* dc-arch '(dc p&div p&cmpl) 'dc-coord 'digraph-models)

where *deep-devs* takes as arguments:

- the name of the model some of whose components are to be grouped (dc-arch),
- the list of components to be grouped, (dc p&div p&cmpl),
- the name of the model to be constructed by grouping, (dc-coord),
- the class to which the new model will belong (digraph-models or a sub-class of it).

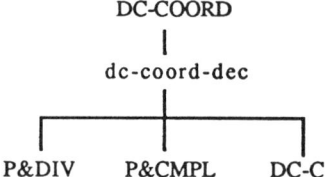

DC-COORD-DEC:
  coupling: ((P&CMPL DC-C (OUT . CY)) (P&DIV DC-C (OUT . PY))
            (DC-C P&CMPL (CX . IN)) (DC-C P&DIV (PX . IN))
            (DC-C P2 (X2 . IN)) (DC-C P1 (X1 . IN))
            (DC-C DC-COORD (OUT . OUT4)) (DC-C DC-COORD (X1 . OUT3))
            (DC-C DC-COORD (X2 . OUT2)) (DC-C DC-COORD (X3 . OUT1))
            (DC-COORD DC-C (IN4 . IN)) (DC-COORD DC-C (IN3 . Y1))
            (DC-COORD DC-C (IN2 . Y2)) (DC-COORD DC-C (IN1 . Y3)))

Figure 7.11. PES for DC-COORD which includes Co-ordinator proper, partitioner and compiler.

As shown in Figure 7.12, the effect of this operation is to restructure DC-ARCH so that a new level is introduced into its hierarchical structure. The couplings internal to the new digraph-model, DC-COORD are the original ones involving its components (Figure 7.11); new external input and output couplings are added so that the original connections to other components are preserved (Figure 7.10).

The inverse operation of deepening is *flattening*. Here a digraph model is removed from a larger model and its components (children) are coupled to their grandparent. For example,

(*flat-devs* dc-coord)

will remove DC-COORD from the model in which it is found, DC-ARCH, and reconnect its children to its parent in such a way that the original model, DC-ARCH, is restored. Clearly, the model to be removed cannot be the highest level digraph model of a hierarchical structure.

To flatten a hierarchical model down to a single level, we can employ

(*flat-all* dc-arch)

which repeatedly applies *flat-devs* until a completely flat model (digraph model with atomic children) is obtained.

Flattening and deepening are useful manipulations of a model structure. They produce alternative structures that are all behaviorally equivalent. Such alternative structures may, for example, have better properties in relation to execution speed on either a serial or parallel computer. Or as we have seen, these restructuring operations may be employed to facilitate a better system entity structure representation of the model base.

The command, *inverse-transform*, takes a coupled-model and writes a pure entity structure for it. Thus (*transform* (*inverse-transform* M)) reconstructs M. After flattening or deepening in the model domain, we can use *inverse-transform* to obtain an entity structure representing the result. We obtained the PES for DC-COORD by applying *inverse-transform* to it after deepening DC-ARCH.

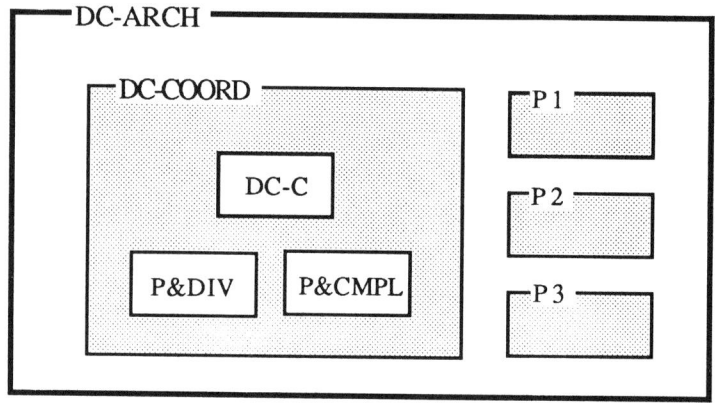

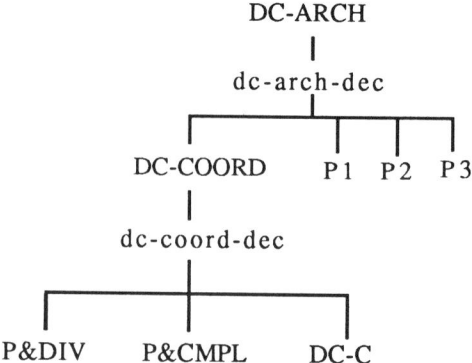

Figure 7.12. DC-ARCH digraph-model and its equivalent deepened SES (coupling not shown).

Chapter 8

ADVANCED DEVS CONCEPTS AND KERNEL-MODELS

This chapter introduces concepts that help create more meaningful models. On one hand, we learn to make more powerful atomic-models by exploiting the *phase* and *elapsed time* variables. On the other hand, we shall show how the class *kernel-models* and its subclasses make it easy to specify coupled models with great flexibility and power.

8.1 More Advanced Processor Models

Models of processors can be made ever-more complex and realistic. The objectives of the simulation study should determine what features will be incorporated and at what level of abstraction (recall Chapter 1). We now discuss some processor designs which illustrate use of more advanced concepts in DEVS modelling.

8.1.1 Interruptable Processor: Phases and Use of the Elapsed Time Component

The *phase* state variable in the atomic model state structure is useful for breaking complex dynamics into sections corresponding to what might, in other contexts, be called "states".[1] Thus, for example, one can model a system as a finite state machine by representing its states as phases of an atomic DEVS model. However, because of the state of a DEVS model also contains components for timing, it has far greater expressive power than does the finite state formalism. The timing components, *sigma* (the time left in the current state) and e (the *elapsed time* in the current state), have already been introduced. Here we illustrate how the *elapsed time* is a useful component of the current state of a model.

Figure 8.1 describes a model which extends the simple processor to handle interrupts. Such an interrupt occurs when a job arrives while another job is in process. In the interruptable processor, IP, the processor stops working on the current job and takes note of the incoming one before resuming processing. There are now three phases: PASSIVE, BUSY, and INTERRUPTED. Normally, the model transits between PASSIVE and BUSY. When the processor receives a job while it is busy, it transits to INTERRUPTED before returning to BUSY. Just before the internal transition to BUSY, the output function is called to send out a message reporting the interruption. As remarked earlier, in this and later models, we intentionally forego storing the interrupting job in a queue in favor of mechanisms that could yield better performance in distributed systems.

Use of the elapsed time component enables us to resume the processing of the interrupted job from the point it was interrupted. To do this, the processing time remaining is reduced by the elapsed time, e when an interruption occurs. Note that processing time remaining may be different from *sigma*, the time remaining in the current state, since it represents the processing of a job which may be interrupted

---

[1] "Phases" here correspond to what are often called "states" but we cannot use "states" since "state" is already being used and "phase" is only one component of the state.

Advanced DEVS Concepts and Kernel-Models

several times. *Sigma* applies only to the current state while the job in process may remain with the model over several state transitions.

```
ATOMIC-MODEL:    IP              ; a simple interruptable processor

state-variables:                 initial-values:
    sigma                            inf
    phase                            passive
    job-id                           ()
    temp                             ()
    time-remaining                   0
    processing-time                  5
    interrupt-handling-time          0.1

parameters:                      default values:
    processing-time                  5

external transition function:

case input port
    in:  case phase
            passive:   store incoming job-id in job-id
                       set time-remaining to processing-time
                       hold-in busy processing-time

            busy:      reduce time-remaining by elapsed time e
                       store job-id in temp
                       hold-in interrupted interrupt-handling-time

            interrupted: continue

        else: error

internal transition function:

case phase
    busy: passivate
    interrupted: hold-in busy time-remaining
    passive: (does not arise)

output function:

case phase
    busy: send job-id to port out
    interrupted: send  temp to port interrupted
```

Figure 8.1a. Pseudo-code for interruptable processor IP.

```
;----------------------------------------------------------------
; This file contains the definition of a simple processor with
; simple interrupt handling
;----------------------------------------------------------------
; It performs following tasks:
; Gets a job from input and sends the job to the output after
; its processing time.  If interrupted it saves the processing
; time remaining and outputs a message containing the interrupting
; job, before resuming the processing.
;----------------------------------------------------------------

(make-pair atomic-models 'ip)

(send ip def-state
        '(
          ;;;state-variables:

             job-id           ;name of the processed job
             temp             ;temperary storage for interrupting job
             time-remaining   ;processing time remaining

          ;;;parameters

             processing-time    ; processing time of this processor
             interrupt-handling-time ;time to handly interrupt
           )
)

;;;;;;;; initialize variables

(send ip set-s
          (make-state 'sigma      'inf
                      'phase      'passive
                      'job-id     '()
                      'temp       '()
                      'time-remaining 0
                      'processing-time 5
                      'interrupt-handling-time 0.1
          )
)
(define (ext-i s e x)
  (case (content-port x)
    ('in
      (case (state-phase s)
        ('passive  (set! (state-job-id s) (content-value x))
                   (set! (state-time-remaining s)
                         (state-processing-time s))
                             ;;time-remaining will be saved for
                             ;;recovery from interruptions
                   (hold-in 'busy (state-processing-time s))))
    )
```

Figure 8.1b. Atomic-model specification of interruptable processor IP.

Advanced DEVS Concepts and Kernel-Models

```
       ('busy (set! (state-time-remaining s)
                    (- (state-time-remaining s) e))
              (set! (state-temp s) (content-value x))
              (hold-in 'interrupted (state-interrupt-handling-time s))
        )
        ('interrupted (continue)
        )
      )
  )
  (else (bkpt "error: invalid input port" (content-port x)))
))

(define (int-i s)
(case (state-phase s)
  ('busy (passivate))
  ('interrupted (hold-in 'busy (state-time-remaining s)))
  (else (passivate))
))

(define (out-i s)
(case (state-phase s)
  ('busy (make-content 'port 'out 'value (state-job-id s)))
  ('interrupted (make-content 'port 'interrupted
                              'value (state-temp s))
  )
  (else (make-content))
))

(send ip set-int-transfn int-i)
(send ip set-ext-transfn ext-i)
(send ip set-outputfn out-i)
```

Figure 8.1b. (continued).

8.1.2 Selective Interruptable Processor

Consider now extending the interruptable processor so that it accepts problems for processing only under certain conditions. As specified in Figure 8.2, if the selective interruptable processor (SIP) is busy, it will allow itself to be interrupted, also under certain conditions, and transfer the incoming problem to the output port 'unsolved. The problem acceptance conditions are based on the level (or priority) of the problem and the level of the processor. While such acceptance conditions are fairly simple, more elaborate conditions can be readily modelled. In fact, the class *forward-models* is ideal for such rule-based modelling as we shall show later.

```
;;;;;;;;;;;;;;;;;;;;selective interruptable processor;;;;;;;;;;;;

(make-pair atomic-models 'sip)

(send sip def-state '(time-remaining job-id
                      temp processor-level transfer-time max-level))

(send sip set-s (make-state 'sigma 'inf 'phase 'passive
                            'transfer-time 1))

(define (ext-1 s e x)
(let* (
    (val (content-value x))
    (job-id (car val))            ;;the value of the incoming message
    (processing-time (cadr val))  ;;is a list of three elements
    (problem-level (caddr val))
    )
(case (content-port x)
  ('in
      (case (state-phase s)
        ('passive (when (>= problem-level (state-processor-level s))
                   (set! (state-job-id s) val)
                   (set! (state-time-remaining s) processing-time)

                              ;;time-remaining will be saved for
                              ;;recovery from interruptions

                   (hold-in 'busy processing-time)
                   )
                 )
        ('busy  (if (= problem-level (state-processor-level s))
                  (begin
                    (set! (state-temp s) x)
                    (set! (state-time-remaining s)
                      (- (state-time-remaining s) e))
                    (hold-in 'transfer (state-transfer-time s))
                  )
                  (continue)
                )
              )
        ('transfer (continue)
        )
      )
  )
  (else (bkpt "error: invalid input port" (content-port x)))
)))

(define (int-1 s)
(case (state-phase s)
  ('busy (passivate))
  ('transfer (hold-in 'busy (state-time-remaining s)))
  (else (passivate))
))
```

Figure 8.2. Atomic-model specification of selective interruptable processor SIP.

```
(define (out-1 s)
 (case (state-phase s)
   ('busy (make-content 'port 'solved 'value (state-job-id s)))
   ('transfer
                (let* (
                        (val (content-value (state-temp s) ))
                        (job-id (car val))
                        (processing-time (cadr val))
                        (problem-level (caddr val))
                        )
                   (set! (content-value (state-temp s))
                         (list job-id processing-time (+ 1 problem-level)))
                   (set! (content-port (state-temp s))
                         (if (< problem-level (state-max-level s))
                             'unsolved
                             'special))
                   (state-temp s)
                   )
   )
   (else (make-content))
 ))

(send sip set-int-transfn int-1)
(send sip set-ext-transfn ext-1)
(send sip set-outputfn out-1)
```

Figure 8.2. (continued).

In the external transition function of Figure 8.2, when in phase PASSIVE the processor will accept an incoming problem only if the level of the problem is not lower than that of the processor. In BUSY, an incoming problem can interrupt processing only if its level is equal to that of the processor. If interruption occurs, the current problem's remaining processing time is reduced by the processing it has received.

Recall that internal transition function is called when an internal event occurs, we see that when SIP has finished processing (in phase BUSY), it should *passivate* (phase is set to PASSIVE). When finished transferring the interrupting problem (in phase TRANSFER), it resumes processing.

Recall that the output function is called just before the internal transition takes place. Thus, in phase BUSY, the id of the solved problem is placed on the port 'solved. In phase transfer, the interrupted problem packet is placed on port 'unsolved with its level increased so as to enable it to accepted by more processors; if its level has reached a too high value, *max-level*, it is sent out on port 'special.

Figure 8.3 depicts an alternative design for realizing the same kind of problem acceptance behavior. In this case, it is a digraph model PEL, (short for processing element) consisting of a "active buffer" ACT-BUF (Figure 8.3a), and a processor P (Figure 8.3b). P is a slightly modified version of the simple processor of Chapter 5 and is responsible only for actual problem solution. The acceptance decisions are now made by ACT-BUF, which also stores an accepted incoming problem for solution or retransmission. In this arrangement, the processing of a problem is never interrupted so that we can expect better turnaround time than with SIP, the equivalent atomic-model formulation. Note that ACT-BUF needs two input ports, 'in, to receive the problems and 'done to synchronize itself with P.

The digraph model PEL is specified using a pruned entity structure (Figure 8.3c) which is placed in the enbase directory of the model domain.

```
;;;;;;;;;;;;;;;;;;;;;;; processing element ;;;;;;;;;;;;;;;;;;;;;;;;;;
;;;;;;;;;;;;;composed of processor and active buffer;;;;;;;;;;;;;;;;;

(make-pair atomic-models 'act-buf)

(send act-buf def-state '(
                   ;;; state variables
                      p-free temp processor-level
                   ;;; parameters
                      transfer-time max-level))

(define (ext-ab s e x)
  (set! (state-temp s) x)
  (case (content-port x)
    ('in
      (let* (
            (val (content-value x))
            (problem-level (caddr val))
            )
        (case (state-phase s)
           ('passive (if (state-p-free s)
                        (when (= problem-level (state-processor-level s))
                              (hold-in 'send 0)
                     )
```

Figure 8.3a. Atomic-model specification of active buffer ACT-BUF.

```
                        (when (> problem-level (state-processor-level s))
                              (hold-in 'transfer (state-transfer-time s))
                        )
                  )
            )
            ('send     (continue))
            ('transfer (continue))
      ))
)
('done    (set! (state-p-free s) #!true)
          (case (state-phase s)
                ('transfer (hold-in 'send 0))
                (else (continue))
          )
)
(else (bkpt "error: invalid input port" (content-port x)))
))


(define (int-ab s)
(when (equal? (state-phase s) 'send)
      (set! (state-p-free s) #!false))
(passivate)
))


(define (out-ab s)
(case (state-phase s)
('send     (set! (content-port (state-temp s)) 'out)
           (state-temp s)
)
('transfer (let* (
                  (val (content-value (state-temp s) ))
                  (job-id (car val))
                  (processing-time (cadr val))
                  (problem-level (caddr val))
                  )
             (set! (content-value (state-temp s))
                   (list job-id processing-time (1+ problem-level)))
             (set! (content-port (state-temp s))
                   (if (< problem-level (state-max-level s))
                         'unsolved
                         'special))
             (state-temp s)
             )
)
(else (make-content))
))


(send act-buf set-int-transfn int-ab)
(send act-buf set-ext-transfn ext-ab)
(send act-buf set-outputfn out-ab)
```

Figure 8.3a. (continued).

```
;;;;;;;;;;;;;;;;;;;; processor p ;;;;;;;;;;;;;;;;;;;;;;;;;
(make-pair atomic-models 'p)

(send p def-state '(
      ;;;;;; state-variables
                 job-id
      ))

(send p set-s (make-state 'sigma 'inf 'phase 'passive))

(define (ext-pe s e x)
(let* (
      (val (content-value x))
      (job-id (car val))
      (processing-time (cadr val))
      )
(case (content-port x)
  ('in
      (case (state-phase s)
        ('passive
             (set! (state-job-id s) val)
             (hold-in 'busy processing-time)
        )
        (else (bkpt "input received when not passive" val))
      )
  )
  (else (bkpt "error: invalid input port" (content-port x)))
)))

(define (int-pe s)
(passivate)
)

(define (out-pe s)
(case (state-phase s)
  ('busy (make-content 'port 'solved 'value (state-job-id s)))
  (else (make-content))
))

(send p set-int-transfn int-pe)
(send p set-ext-transfn ext-pe)
(send p set-outputfn out-pe)
```

Figure 8.3b. Atomic-model specification of simple processor P.

Advanced DEVS Concepts and Kernel-Models

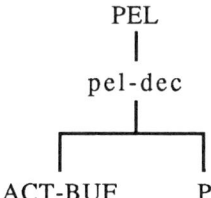

PEL-DEC:

    coupling: ((ACT-BUF P (OUT . IN))
              (ACT-BUF PEL (UNSOLVED . UNSOLVED))
              (ACT-BUF PEL (SPECIAL . SPECIAL))
              (P ACT-BUF (SOLVED . DONE))
              (P PEL (SOLVED . SOLVED))
              (PEL ACT-BUF (IN . IN)))

Figure 8.3c. PES for coupling ACT-BUF to P for PEL.

8.2 Kernel-Models: Homogeneous Structures

As already indicated, *kernel-models* and its subclasses provide convenient facilities for constructing models having arbitrary numbers of components, generated from a prototype, the kernel, and coupled in a uniform manner. The contrast with the *digraph-models* class becomes apparent by examining any one the architectures discussed in Chapter 6. Notice, for instance, that the multi-server architecture contains 3 processors, all isomorphic to each other. The coupling involving these components has to specified in detail. Now what if we want to have the same kind of architecture but with only 2 components? or with 5 components? with 10? In each case, we will have to construct a new digraph model, which although it follows the general pattern, has to be specified in detail. In contrast, a *kernel-models* representation of such an architecture would encode the coupling pattern as a formula applicable to whatever number of components is chosen. Each of the simple architectures can be conveniently represented as a controlled-model as we shall see later.

Before proceeding, we provide a brief overview of *kernel-models* and some of its existing sub-classes.

8.2.1 Class Kernel-Models

In contrast to *digraph-models*, instances of *kernel-models* are coupled models whose components (children) are isomorphic models or are generated from a common entity structure (Chapter 9). In the isomorphic component case, method *make-members* creates the isomorphic children using an instance variable of *kernel-models* called *init-cell*. The children are all members of the same class called the kernel class, stored in instance variable, *class*, of the instance of *kernel-models*. An important point to note is that modeller is spared from specifying the coupling scheme in a brute force manner. Indeed, as will now be explained, the coupling specification is determined by a parameterized formula characteristic of each sub-class of *kernel-models*. Thus, the modeller specifies only the parameter values, DEVS-Scheme does the rest.

An instance variable, *out-in-coup* of *kernel-models* tells how to translate output ports to input ports of the internally coupled children. Different specialized classes of *kernel-models* realize different internal and external coupling schemes. Four coupling schemes are representative of the possibilities: broadcast, hypercube, cellular and centrally co-ordinated coupling which are realized by the subclasses *broadcast-models, hypercube-models, cellular-models* and *controlled-models* , respectively. Constructors *make-broadcast, make-hypercube, make-cellular* and *make-controlled* create models in the respective classes.

Advanced DEVS Concepts and Kernel-Models

Class broadcast-models

Broadcast-models is a simple but important subclass of *kernel-models*. All members (children) of a broadcast coupled model communicate directly with each other and with the outside world. Thus methods, *get-children*, *get-influencees* and *get-receivers* uniquely determine children, influencees, and receivers of the coupled model, respectively. For example, influencees of any child of a broadcast model are all children of the broadcast model except itself. The receivers of a broadcast model are all the children of the broadcast model. The only additional information on the coupling scheme of broadcast models is how to translate output ports to input ports. Method *add-port-pair* inherited from *kernel-models* enables the modeller to specify pairs of ports for internal coupling by inserting the pairs in *out-in-coup* table inherited from *kernel-models*.

Class hypercube-models

Hypercube-models is a specialization of *kernel-models* whose children are 2^n instances of the kernel class, where n is the dimension of the hypercube. To specify positions of all the children in the hypercube, each instance has *cell-position* as an instance variable. In a hypercube model the modeller has a choice in both internal and external coupling schemes. The external coupling can be either *broadcast* or *origin-only*. In broadcast external coupling, inputs and outputs of all the children in a hypercube coupled model are coupled to input and output of the hypercube coupled model, respectively. On the other hand, only the cell at origin is coupled to the hypercube coupled model in the origin-only external coupling scheme. Method *set-ext-coup* selects one of the coupling schemes.

Method *add-port-pair* inherited from *kernel-models* is similar to that of *broadcast-models* except that it stores triples of the form (neighbor, outport, inport) in the *out-in-coup* table. For example, the triple ((0 0 1) out in) specifies that the output port 'out of any component with cell-position (x1 x2 x3) is connected to the input port 'in of its neighbor (x1 x2 x3+1), where the addition is taken modulo 2.

Class cellular-models

A specialization of *kernel-models*, cellular models provides for coupling of a fixed or variable set of geometrically located cells, each of which is connected to other cells in a uniform way. The class *cellular-models* described here realizes the formalism for discrete event cell space models (Zeigler, 1984). Influencees of a cell in a cellular model can be computed by translating the influencees pattern of the origin cell, *infl-origin*. The translated influencees pattern is called a neighborhood. For a *fixed* structure cellular model, the influencees of a cell C are those cells in its neighborhood which currently exist (of which, for example, there may be none). However, for a *variable* structure cellular model, cells in the cell positions of the neighbors which do not exist will be created as needed. Therefore, all cells have the same number of influencees and the space is potentially infinite (more precisely, finite but unbounded). An instance variable, *structure* is used to specify whether the model has fixed or variable structure. Methods *set-ext-coup* and *add-port-pair* parallel those of *hypercube-models*. Details are in (Kim, 1988).

Class controlled-models

In contrast to the foregoing kernel-model subclasses, *controlled-models* enables the modeller to impose centralized control over a class of components in a dynamic fashion. The central co-ordinator is an atomic-model specified in the instance variable, *controller*. This atomic-model must have a state variable called *influencees* whose current value determines to which of the existing members of the class its output will be sent. Thus, internal coupling from the controller to members of the class is variable. Internal coupling in the reverse direction is fixed: each member can send output only to the controller. External coupling is also fixed: only the controller is coupled to the overall model (similar to origin-only above). Method *add-port-pair*

Advanced DEVS Concepts and Kernel-Models 183

plays a role similar to that in broadcast models. Indeed, here each component communicates with its siblings via the controller instead of directly. Accordingly, the *out-in-coup* table determines how an output port of the controller is mapped to (the same) input ports of its influencees.

Controlled-models thus provides facilities for conveniently representing a variety of centralized architectures. Such schemes would otherwise have to be modelled using a combination of an atomic-model (for the controller), a digraph model (to impose the centralized topology) and a kernel model (to obtain an arbitrary number of components).

8.3 Example: Parallel Processor Broadcast Architecture

As already indicated, *kernel-models* are well suited to model the multi-processor architectures involving selectable numbers of processors of the same type. As an example, Figure 8.4 depicts a model/frame pair for such an architecture. The model/frame pair is a digraph model consisting of an experimental frame module EXPERIMENT and a broadcast model br-SIPS. Such broadcasting is especially germane to the high bandwidth communications that may be afforded by computer architectures employing optical processing in the future. The "kernel" model of |br-SIPS| is the atomic model SIP. When coupled in the broadcast model |br-SIPS|, such processors will carry out con trolled recirculation of problems. In such recirculation, jobs never get stuck in queues. The problem in designing such a system, to be investigated with simulation, is how to take advantage of the speed in searching for free processors afforded by broadcasting, while minimizing the overhead of problems solved more than once and also not at all. Accordingly, EXPERIMENT is a digraph model containing a GENERATOR component (for sending problems to the broadcast model), and ACCEPTOR (which makes decisions concerning run termination) and a TRANSDUCER (which keeps performance statistics: problem solution time, throughput, per-cent multiply solved problems, per-cent lost problems).

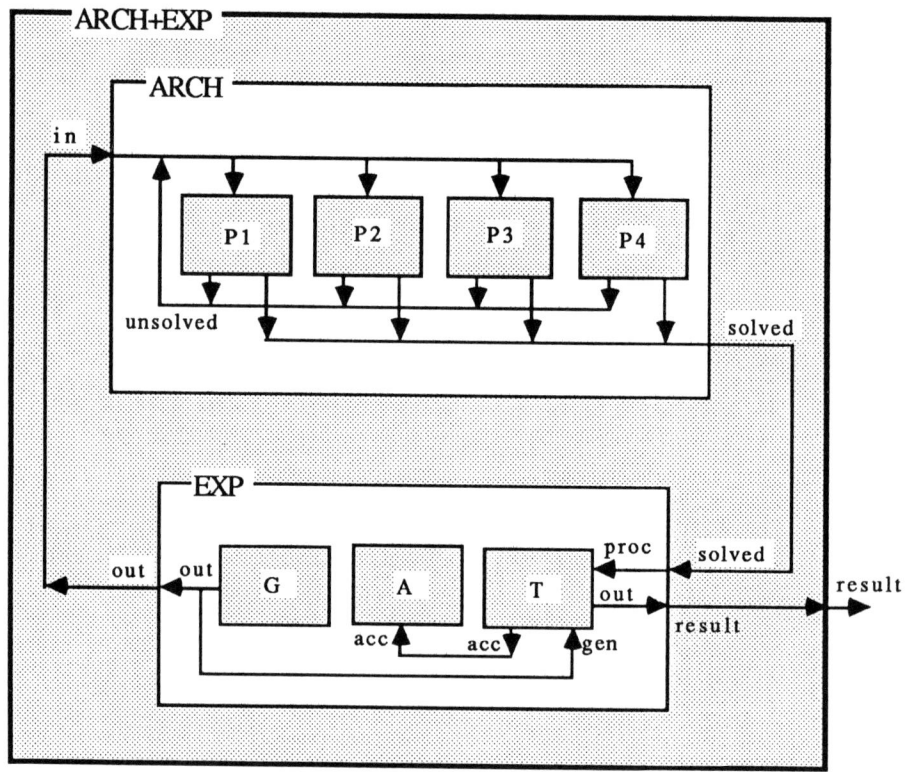

Figure 8.4. Model/frame pair for broadcast architecture.

Figure 8.5 depicts the experimental frame components. The definitions are straightforward extensions of similar components discussed in Chapter 5. The GENERATOR outputs a stream of jobs

Advanced DEVS Concepts and Kernel-Models 185

```
;;;;;;;;;;;;;;;;;;;;; generator.m
;;;;;;;;;;;;;;;;;;;;; Generator for architecture
;
;     output packet:  (job-id, processing-time, problem-level)
;
;

(make-pair atomic-models 'generator)

(send generator def-state '(
          ;;state-variable

          ;;parameter
              interarrival-time
              processing-time
              problem-level
                        )
 )

(send generator set-s
    (make-state 'sigma 0 'phase 'busy
                      'interarrival-time 5
                      'processing-time 10   'problem-level 1
    ))


(define (int-g s)
 (case (state-phase s)
    ('busy
          (hold-in 'busy  (expon (state-interarrival-time s) 1)))
    (else (passivate))
 )
)

(define (out-g s)
   (make-content 'port 'out
          'value (list (gensym)
                       (expon (state-processing-time s) 2)
                       (state-problem-level s))
   ))


(send generator set-int-transfn int-g)
(send generator set-outputfn out-g)
```

Figure 8.5a. Generator for broadcast architecture.

```
;;;;;;;;;;;;;;;; transducer.m
;;;;;;;;;;;;;;;; Transducer designed for the measurement of
;
;          1. average turnaround time
;          2. thru-put
;          3. %unsolved
;          4. %multiply solved (solved more than once)
;

(make-pair atomic-models 'transducer)

(send transducer def-state '(sigma phase arrived-list solved-list
                             multiple-solved-list clock report-time
                             total-ta))

(send transducer set-s (make-state 'sigma 0 'phase 'active
                        'arrived-list '() 'solved-list '()
                        'multiple-solved-list '() 'clock 0
                        'report-time 100 'total-ta 0))

(define (ext-t s e x)
  (let ((problem-id (content-value x)))
    (continue)
    (set! (state-clock s) (+ (state-clock s) e))
    (case (content-port x)
      ('gen (set! (state-arrived-list s)
                  (cons (list problem-id (state-clock s))
                        (state-arrived-list s))))
      ('proc (cond
               ((member problem-id (state-multiple-solved-list s)) '())
               ((member problem-id (state-solved-list s))
                (set! (state-multiple-solved-list s)
                      (cons problem-id (state-multiple-solved-list s))))
               ((assoc problem-id (state-arrived-list s))
                (set! (state-total-ta s)
                      (+ (state-total-ta s)
                         (- (state-clock s)
                            (cadr (assoc problem-id
                                         (state-arrived-list s))
                            ))))
                (set! (state-solved-list s)
                      (cons problem-id (state-solved-list s))))))
      (else
        (bkpt "error: invalid input port name --> " (content-port x)))))
))

(define (int-t s)
  (case (state-phase s)
    ('active (set! (state-clock s) (+ (state-clock s) (state-sigma s)))
             (hold-in 'temp 0))
    ('temp (hold-in 'active (state-report-time s)))
    (else (passivate))
    ))
```

Figure 8.5b. Transducer for broadcast architecture.

```
(define (out-t s)
  (case (state-phase s)
    ('active (make-content 'port 'out 'value (list
; average turn-around time
               (if (NULL? (state-solved-list s))
                   'nil
                   (/ (state-total-ta s) (length (state-solved-list s))))
; thruput
               (if (= (state-clock s) 0)
                   'nil
                   (/ (length (state-solved-list s)) (state-clock s)))
; percentage of unsolved-packets
               (if (NULL? (state-arrived-list s))
                   'nil
                   (/ (- (length (state-arrived-list s))
                         (length (state-solved-list s)))
                      (length (state-arrived-list s))))
; percentage of multiple-solved packets
               (if (NULL? (state-solved-list s))
                   'nil
                   (/ (length (state-multiple-solved-list s))
                      (length (state-solved-list s))))
    )))
    ('temp (make-content 'port 'acc 'value
                         (list (state-clock s)
                               (length (state-arrived-list s)))))
    (else (make-content 'port 'dum 'value '()))
  ))

(send transducer set-ext-transfn ext-t)
(send transducer set-int-transfn int-t)
(send transducer set-outputfn out-t)
```

Figure 8.5b. (continued).

```
(make-pair atomic-models 'acceptor)

(send acceptor def-state '(sigma phase observation-packet
                           observation-time))

(send acceptor set-s (make-state 'sigma 'inf 'phase 'passive
                     'observation-packet 8 'observation-time 20))

(send acceptor set-ext-transfn (lambda(s e x)
  (case (content-port x)
    ('acc (if (or (> (car (content-value x))
                     (state-observation-time s))
                  (> (cadr (content-value x))
                     (state-observation-packet s)))
              (set! pause #!true)))
  )))
```

Figure 8.5c. Acceptor for broadcast architecture.

all starting with level 1. In a basic configuration of |br-SIPS|, successive processors are assigned level s starting with 1 and successively increasing by 1. In such a configuration, the first job to arrive, will be accepted by the level 1 processor. The second job will be transmitted by the level 1 processor (if it is busy) to the level 2 processor for execution. The third job will be finds its way to the level 3 processor if the lower level processors are busy. And so on. As processors finish they are immediately available for work. Thus as a job increases in level it may be recirculated down to more than one lower level processor and so be solved more than once. It is also possible that a job is dropped from circulation if there are no processors able to process it or retransmit it:– the system has a maximum capacity. Setting of a threshold priority above which a job is sent out of the system (possibly to another cluster as we shall see) should reduce loss of jobs.

To understand the operation of such a broadcast model, let us run through the sequence of steps necessary to construct it. Later, we will see that, once specified by an SES, and pruned, these steps are performed by the transform and initialization methods without user intervention.

First we load the kernel:

(define model-base_directory "/scheme/devs/proc/mbase/")
(load-from model-base_directory "sip.m"))

Now make a class, called SIPS, with model SIP as the template:

(send sip make-class 'sips)

Then make a broadcast-model based on class SIPS:

(make-broadcast sips)

The model will automatically be called |br-SIPS|. We can use an alias for convenience if desired:

(alias br1 |br-SIPS|)

When |br-SIPS| is made, its *init-cell* is assigned a model made from class SIPS (note however that the *init-cell* is not included in the instances of the class SIPS).

Advanced DEVS Concepts and Kernel-Models

We now specify the *out-in-coup* table:

(send br1 add-port-pair 'unsolved 'in)

Since the broadcast paradigm is in effect, this is all that is needed to set up the appropriate coupling. This port pair establishes that whenever a value appears on output port 'unsolved of any processor, it will be sent to the input port 'in of all other processors currently in the model, viz., the current instances of class SIPS. This establishes the internal coupling. The external coupling is already established: for a broadcast model, the external input (resp., output) ports are in one-one correspondence with those of the kernel; moreover, every input (resp. output) port of the broadcast model is connected to the input (resp. output) port of all of the components. Thus, when a problem arrives on port 'in of |br-SIPS|, it is broadcast to all processors in the model. When a problem is solved by a processor (appears on its output port 'solved), it is sent to the 'solved port of |br-SIPS|.

The above is all that is required to construct a broadcast model. As it stands however, the model has no components. The following sequence generates such components, initializes their states and starts the simulation.

Components of |br-SIPS| are the current members of the class SIP S. The method, *make-members*, of *broadcast-models*, makes it convenient to generate such instances. It takes as argument a name and the number of instances desired. The name is used as a basic name for each of the instances generated. It can, but need not, be related to the kernel.

(send br1 make-members 'p 3)

Models P0, P1, and P2 have been made and added as components |br-SIPS|. Such members of SIPS are made by sending the *make-new* message to the *init-cell* of |br-SIPS| (see Section 8.4).

From here on, the sequence is quite standard:

Initialize the states of the components:

(send p0 set-s (make-state 'sigma 0 'phase 'transfer
                           'time-remaining 0 'job-id 0
                           'temp (make-content 'port 'in 'value '(1 3 1))
                           'processor-level 1 'transfer-time 1))

(send p1 set-s (make-state 'sigma 'inf 'phase 'passive
                           'time-remaining 0 'job-id 0 'temp '()
                           'processor-level 2 'transfer-time 1))

(send p2 set-s (make-state 'sigma 'inf 'phase 'passive
                           'time-remaining 0 'job-id 0 'temp '()
                           'processor-level 3 'transfer-time 1))

Make a root co-ordinator:

(mk-ent root-co-ordinators r:br1)

Initialize it

(init r:br1 |C:br-SIPS|)

and run

(res r:br1).

8.4 Methods Make-new and Make-class

As we have seen above, isomorphic copies of existing models are needed to conveniently construct complex coupled models. DEVS-Scheme provides two main alternatives for creating such copies. The first method, *make-new*, when sent to a model creates an isomorphic copy of the original. The copy is an instance of the same class as the original. It is also given a copy of the current state assignment of the original (using method *copy-state*). The primary classes (atomic-models, *digraph-models*, and the specializations of *kernel-models*) require their own versions of the *make-new* method since each has features that are unique to itself. (Sub-classes of these primary classes, if they do not add additional structure, can inherit the

Advanced DEVS Concepts and Kernel-Models

make-new method from the primary class.) Since coupled-models instances are hierarchical in structure, the *make-new* method must be recursive in the sense that components at each level must replicate themselves with their own *make-new* methods (c.f., the *inject* method in Chapter 4).

The second method, *make-class*, when sent to a model, creates a class definition with the original model as template. Instances created for such a class will be isomorphic to the original. However, in contrast to the effect of *make-new*, such instances are members of a different class than the original. For example, for the atomic-model SIP, consider the following:

(send sip make-class 'sips)

(mk-ent sips p).

The first command will create a class named SIPS whose instances are isomorphic to SIP. The second will create an instance of SIPS called P. Note however, that SIP is an member of atomic-models while P is a member of class SIPS.

Method *make-new* may be employed whenever an isomorphic copy of a model is desired. Method *make-class* must be employed in order to establish a class to serve as the kernel *class* for an instance of *kernel-models*. Note that we can create different instances of such *kernel-models* each having a different *class*, but all classes having the same template. For example, two networks of IBM PCs may be modeled as distinct instances of *broadcast-models*, as in:

(send ibm-pc make-class 'ibm-pc1s)

(send ibm-pc make-class 'ibm-pc2s)

(make-broadcast ibm-pc1s)

(make-broadcast ibm-pc2s).

The last two commands create the distinct broadcast models, |br-IBM-PC1S| and |br-IBM-PC1S| respectively. In an example application, these broadcast models may be linked together as components in a digraph model to represent connected local area networks. We return to consider such issues soon under "Multilayered Models".

In general, there may be any number of instances of *kernel-models* having "isomorphic" classes, i.e., classes whose instances are all isomorphic to each other.

Since models in DEVS-Scheme may be complex, hierarchical structures special attention has been paid to replicating such structures. To test the methods for creating copies of models we employ a novel approach: a parallel set of methods is used for checking isomorphism between models. The criteria for correct copying are formalized in the isomorphism methods. For a copying method to be valid, a copy of a model must be isomorphic to the original as determined by the isomorphism test (Kim, 1988).

8.5 System Entity Structure Representation of Kernel Models

Having constructed a kernel-model, it can be coupled with other models within *digraph-models* and even larger *kernel-models* in ways already discussed. However, it is much more convenient and productive to employ the entity structure representation for this purpose. Figure 8.6 shows a SES for creating a model/frame pair ready for simulation for the multi-processor architecture studies. The main novel feature of the entity structure is the multiple entity relationship shown by the three parallel vertical lines connecting PROCS and PROC. PROCS is called a multiple-entity, PROC is its single entity, and the three lines represent an aspect, PROCS-MULT-ASP as shown below:

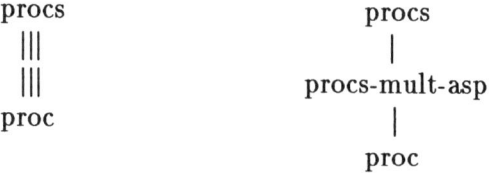

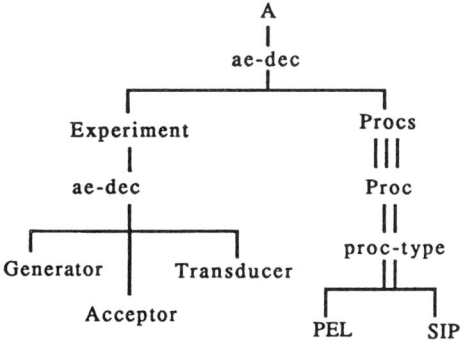

```
(make-entstr 'a)
(add-item e:a asp 'ae-dec)
(set-current-item   e:a 'ae-dec)
(add-item e:a ent 'experiment)

(add-couple e:a 'experiment 'procs 'out 'in)
(add-couple e:a 'procs 'experiment 'solved 'solved)
(add-couple e:a 'experiment 'arch-exp 'result 'result)

(add-mult e:a 'proc)

(set-current-item e:a 'proc)
(add-item e:a spec 'proc-type)
(set-current-item   e:a  'proc-type)

(add-item e:a ent 'pel)
(add-item e:a ent 'sip)

(set-current-item   e:a  'experiment)
(add-item e:a asp 'exp-dec)
(set-current-item   e:a  'exp-dec)
(add-item e:a ent 'generator)
(add-item e:a ent 'transducer)
(add-item e:a ent 'acceptor)

(add-couple e:a 'generator 'transducer 'out 'gen)
(add-couple e:a 'transducer 'acceptor 'acc 'acc)
(add-couple e:a 'experiment 'transducer 'solved 'proc)
(add-couple e:a 'generator 'experiment 'out 'out)
(add-couple e:a 'transducer 'experiment 'out 'result)
```

Figure 8.6. SES specification of kernel model architecture.

The right hand side represents the actual manner in which the multiple entity relation is represented in an entity structure. As mentioned earlier, the meaning of such a relation is that the multiple entity, e.g., PROCS, represents the current set of instances of a class of the same name. Thus, in transforming the entity structure, the multiple entity PROCS is mapped to a kernel model with kernel-class, PROCS.

To add a multiple entity to an entity structure, we use the command *add-mult*. Thus, for example, to add PROCS to E:A, set the current-item pointer to AE-DEC (if not already there)

(set-current-item e:a 'ae-dec)

and add the multiple entity using add-mult with single entity name as argument

(add-mult e:a 'proc).

The effect is to add the items PROCS, PROCS-MULT-ASP, and PROC to the entity structure. The current-item pointer ends up at PROC. The order of commands (i.e., with the add-mult trailing all operations involving AE-DEC) in Figure 8.6 was chosen so as not to have to restore the current-item pointer to AE-DEC after the add-mult.

Note that in coupling specification, a multiple entity is treated as is any other entity. For example,

(add-couple e:a 'experiment 'procs 'out 'in)

establishes that the output port 'out of EXPERIMENT is coupled to the input port 'in of PROCS, representing the kernel model that it will transform to.

Since PROC has a specialization containing the two processor models, SIP and PEL, there are actually 6 architectures that can be generated from this entity structure: 3 compatible kernel-model choices (*controlled-models* is not compatible), and 2 processor choices. In pruning, we select one option from each category. Later we shall see that it is possible to specify a mixture of the components

Advanced DEVS Concepts and Kernel-Models

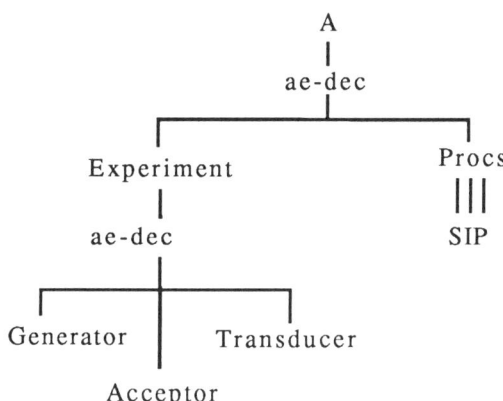

AE-DEC:

    coupling: ((EXPERIMENT A (RESULT . RESULT))
                   (PROCS EXPERIMENT (SOLVED . SOLVE))
                   (EXPERIMENT PROCS (OUT . IN)))

EXP-DEC:

    coupling: ((TRANSDUCER EXPERIMENT (OUT . RESULT))
                   (GENERATOR EXPERIMENT (OUT . OUT))
                 (EXPERIMENT TRANSDUCER (SOLVED . PROC))
                 (TRANSDUCER ACCEPTOR (ACC . ACC))
                 (GENERATOR TRANSDUCER (OUT . GEN)))

PROCS-MULT-ASP:

    mult-coup-type: BROADCAST
    coupling: ((() () (UNSOLVED . IN)))

Figure 8.7. PES broadcast model with SIP as kernel.

of *kernel-models* from the choices available for its kernel (Chapter 10).

Figure 8.7 shows the pruned entity structure, P:A-BR@SIP resulting from a pruning in which broadcast was chosen as the kernel-model type and SIP was chosen from the PROC-TYPE specialization. Note that the multiple entity retains the name PROCS even though, its single entity is now SIP. The *transform* operator is aware of this difference and correctly interprets the situation.

Applying the *transform* operator to this entity-structure, (*transform* p:a-br@sip), results in the model/frame pair shown in Figure 8.4. During the transformation, all simulators and and co-ordinators are attached to their respective models and a root-co-ordinator R:A, is initialized. Thus to start simulation, we use (*restart r:a*) which will also then let us populate the broadcast-model with components and initialize their states.

8.5.1 Controlled-Models

As indicated before, *controlled-models* realizes a centralized control structure which sets it apart from the other kernel-model classes. A controlled model has both a *controller* component as well as a its controllees, which are instances of the kernel class. Consider for example, implementing the simple computer architectures of Chapter 6 as *controlled-models*. The SES of Figure 8.8 shows the configuration required. Note that the architecture decomposes into a co-ordinator CO-ORD and a multiple entity PROCS. When pruned and transformed, such a configuration will be converted to a controlled-model, |co-PROCS|, whose *controller* slot is filled with the particular co-ordinator selected from the CO-ORD-SPEC specialization. Note also, that the existence of a sibling, CO-ORD, for PROCS in ARCH-DEC is necessary for *controlled-models* to be an allowed selection in pruning PROCS.

The simulation model, |co-PROCS|, has as components the *controller* (e.g., MS-CO, the multiserver co-ordinator, if selected in pruning) and the controllees, i.e., instances of class PROCS (Figure 8.9). In such a controlled-model, the *controller* acts as central

Advanced DEVS Concepts and Kernel-Models

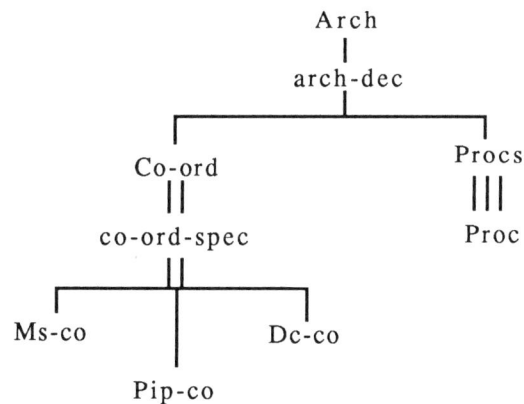

Figure 8.8. SES for controlled-model formulation of simple architecture.

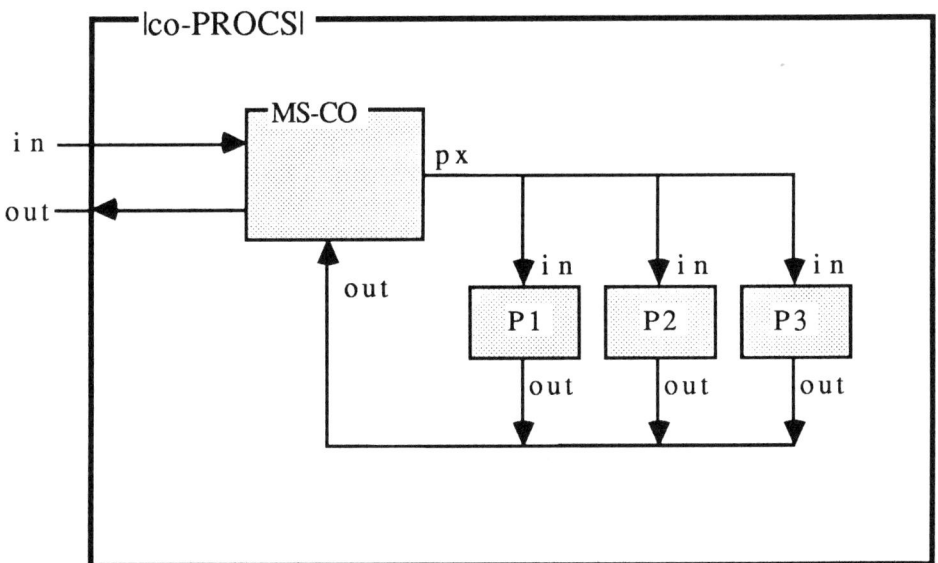

Figure 8.9. Controlled-model for multiserver.

switchboard through which all communication must pass. Thus |co-PROCS| has input (resp. output) ports corresponding to the input (resp. output) ports of the *controller*; a value placed on an input port of |co-PROCS| is sent to the same input port of the *controller*; a value placed on an output port of the *controller* is sent to the same output port of |co-PROCS|. This external input and output coupling is implemented in the *get-receivers* and *translate* methods of controlled-models.

A controlled model also has internal coupling between the *controller* and controllees. The *controller* has input ports corresponding to output ports of any controllee. Thus, a value placed on an output port 'out of a controllee, P will appear on the input port 'out of the *controller*, MS-CO (this input port is distinct from MS-CO's output port 'out). Also, a value placed on an output port of the *controller* will appear on an input port of each of certain controllees, the influencees of the *controller*. The method *add-port-pair* builds the *out-in-coup* table, which will translate output po rts of the *controller* into input ports, of the controllee. For example, the output port 'px of MS-CO is coupled to the input port 'in of an influencee, P. (If coupling is not specified in *out-in-coup*, the output port of the *controller* is coupled to the like-named input port of a controllee.) In contrast to all other models, the influencee set of the *controller* in a controlled model is not fixed, but is determined dynamically, by the *controller* itself. This is done through the setting of its state-variable, INFLUENCEES. The method, *get-influencees*, of *controlled-models* accesses this state-variable to determine where to send an output of the *controller*.

Dynamic setting of influencees is illustrated by the definition of the multi-server co-ordinator MS-CO (Figure 8.10). Note that MS-CO has the requisite state-variable, INFLUENCEES, as it must to be a *controller*. It also has a state-variable called IDLE-PROCESSORS in which it keeps a queue of processors (controllees) which are idle. When a job arrives, MS-CO sends it to the first processor on the IDLE-PROCESSORS list. The way it does so is to set the INFLUENCEES state-variable to the list containing the selected processor

```
(make-pair atomic-models 'ms-co)
(send ms-co def-state '(job-id idle-processors influencees))
(send ms-co set-s (make-state
                    'sigma 'inf
                    'phase 'passive
                    'job-id '()          ;;incoming job-id
                    'outport '()         ;;output port
                    'idle-processors '() ;;free processors
                    'influencees '()     ;;needed for controlled-models
                  ))
(define (ext-ms-co s e x)
    (case (content-port x)
       ('in    ;; send job to first idle processor
          (cond
           ((state-idle-processors s)
              (set! (state-job-id s) (content-value x))
              (set! (state-influencees s)
                    (list (car (state-idle-processors s))))
              (set! (state-idle-processors s)
                    (cdr (state-idle-processors s))))
              (hold-in 'send-to-processor 0))
           (else (continue))
          )
       ('out ;; finished job received from processor, send it out
          (set! (state-influencees s) '())
          (set! (state-job-id s) (car (content-value x)))
          (let (
                (proc (cadr (content-value x)))
               ) ;; return processor to idle list
          (set! (state-idle-processors s)
                (append (state-idle-processors s) (list proc)))
          (hold-in 'send-out 0)
          ))
       (else (bkpt "error: invalid input port" (content-port x)))
))
(define (int-ms-co s)
   (passivate)
)
(define (out-ms-co s)
   (case (state-phase s)
      ('send-to-processor
         (make-content 'port 'px 'value (state-job-id s)))
      ('send-out
         (make-content 'port 'out 'value (state-job-id s)))
      (else
         (make-content))
))
(send ms-co set-ext-transfn ext-ms-co)
(send ms-co set-int-transfn int-ms-co)
(send ms-co set-outputfn out-ms-co)
```

Figure 8.10. Atomic-model specification of multi-server co-ordinator for use in controlled model.

as the only member. The job-id placed on port 'px goes to the 'in port of the selected processor since the pair ('px 'in) is in *out-in-coup*.

When a completed job is returned to MS-CO, it is sent out on port 'out. This time it does not go to any controllee, since the INFLUENCEES state-variable is set to the empty list. The name of the sending processor is placed in at the end of the IDLE-PROCESSORS queue. Clearly, each processor must have a state-variable for recording its name which can be used to identify itself as needed. Apart from this addition, the processor model is identical with that described earlier for simple architectures.

8.6 Multilayered Models and Distributed Experimental Frames

One outcome of the hierarchical, modular construction facilities is the specification of architectures employing compounds of clusters. Figure 8.11 shows an example of a multi-level hypercube architecture. Computer models placed at the nodes of the hypercube (|hc-NODES|) are themselves clusters, i.e., kernel models, either broadcast or cellular. Each member of the broadcast or cellular model at a node is a processor, either PEL or SIP.

When the hypercube model receives an incoming problem on port 'in, it sends the problem to all nodes (if its external coupling is *broadcast*) or the origin node only (if its external coupling is *origin-only*). If it receives a solution of a problem from its nodes, the hypercube model sends it out on port 'solved. When a node of the hypercube receives a problem, it sends it to all processors in the node (if the node has a *broadcast* architecture) or to the neighboring processors (if the node has a *cellular* architecture). The structure of a node is characterized by the broadcast-model within Figure 8.4.

Leaf processors are responsible for actual problem solving. Recall that a processor accepts an incoming problem under certain conditions. If the conditions for acceptance are not met, and the level of the problem has not reached a threshold, the processor transfers the incoming problem to the output port 'unsolved . The unsolved

Advanced DEVS Concepts and Kernel-Models

problem is retransmitted to other processors (the destination is based on the architecture of nodes) in the same node. If the interrupting problem level has reached the threshold value, the problem is put on output port 'special.

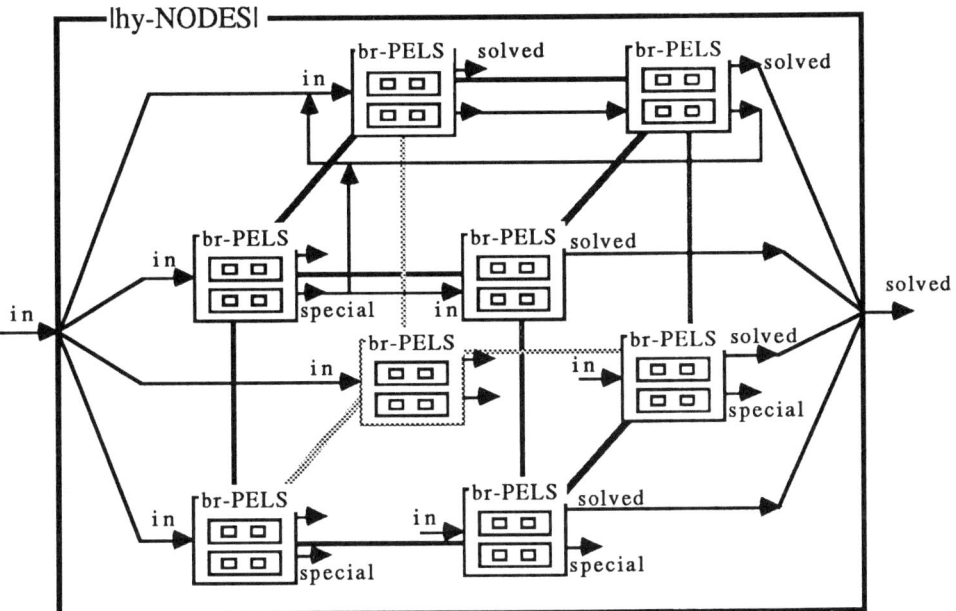

Figure 8.11. Hypercube model with components which are broadcast models.

The external coupling of a node is such that the output port 'special of processor is coupled to the output port 'special of the node. The internal coupling of nodes in the hypercube model specifies the pair ('special 'in). Thus a problem emerging from a node on port 'special is retransmitted on port 'in to the closest node(s) in the hypercube. This implements a locally determined load balancing mechanism: when the load in a cluster is too high, work is automatically sent to neighboring clusters.

To extend the SES of Figure 8.6 to incorporate the specification of the layered architecture, we use the command

(add-mult-mult e:a 'node 'proc)

to create the sequence of multiple entities NODES, PROCS. The *add-mult-mult* command will take a list of any length and produce a SES with as many layers as there are names in the list. Figure 8.12 shows the extended SES of Figure 8.6. The second option under ARCH-SPEC is the result of sending the add-mult-mult command to E:A when the current item is ARCH-SPEC. The third option under ARCH-SPEC includes a TRANSDUCER with each cluster (*add-mult-mult* is not used here). After pruning and selecting the second option for ARCH-SPEC, the PES will transform into a multi-layered model such as shown in Figure 8.11.

Note that the performance questions as embodied in the experimental frame previously developed still apply to the new architecture. However, now there are two layers of architectures which can be evaluated: a) for the overall architecture, we can obtain global measures using the original experimental frame, and b) we can obtain each cluster using a local experimental frame, in fact using just the same transducer as before will do nicely; such local measures can provide insight on how evenly work is being distributed among the clusters (existence of "hot spots", need for additional load balancing strategies).

Note that due to uniformity, the substructure of PROC under NODES is the same as that under ARCH-SPEC; likewise, TRANSDUCER as a component of NODE&TR refers to the same model as in EXPERIMENT. The TRANSDUCER in NODE&TR will work properly if it receives its input from NODE&TR rather than from GENERATOR as in EXPERIMENT.

This example illustrates two general ideas. The first is that one can specify complex, multilayered models in a straightforward manner in the SES representation. The second is that along with such layered models, or indeed in other hierarchical models, one may wish to distribute the experimental frame components on both *global and local levels* (Rozenblit, 1985).

Advanced DEVS Concepts and Kernel-Models

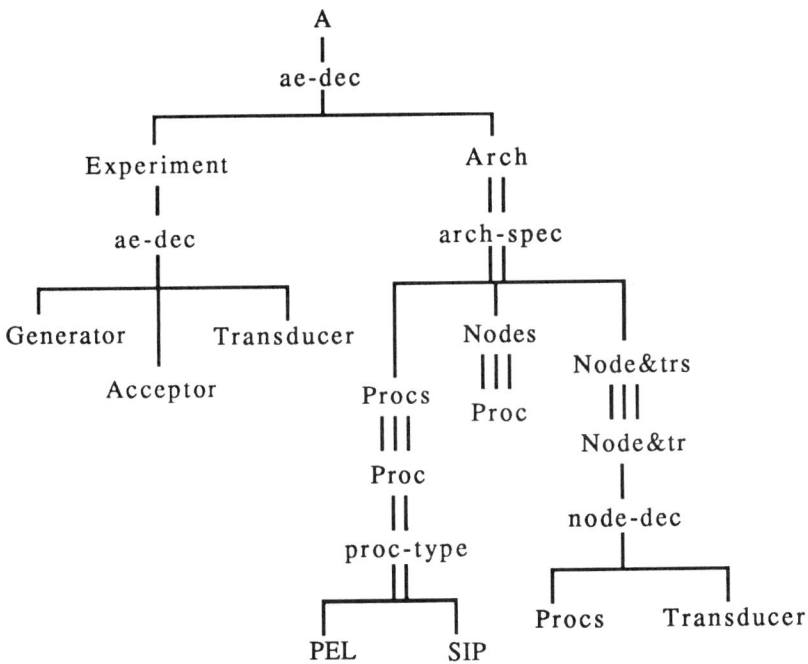

Figure 8.12. SES for Figure 8.6 extended to provide a choice of one layer or two layered architectures.

Chapter 9

RULE-BASED SPECIFICATION OF ATOMIC-MODELS

The DEVS formalism expressed in the *atomic-models* class of DEVS-Scheme serves as a basis on which higher level formalisms can be implemented. In particular, a convenient rule-based programming style is supported by *forward-models*, a specialized class of *atomic-models*. *Forward-models* is based on a forward chaining paradigm. This is one of many alternatives that might be implemented for writing models in a rule based manner.

9.1 Activities as Rules

To develop a model of type *forward-models* we write rules which together specify the internal transition, external transition and output functions of a DEVS model. As shown in Figure 9.1, a rule, called an *activity* is a structure defined by:

(define-structure activity condition action before-output after-output)

Such a structure contains *condition* and *action* slots, as usual, and in addition, slots for specifying outputs to be produced before and/or after the *action* is performed. An *action* specifies a change in the state of the model. Rules for specifying both internal and external transitions have the same format. Internal transition rule conditions test the *phase* and other state-variables of the model. External transition rules also include tests of the input content structure and elapsed time in their conditions.

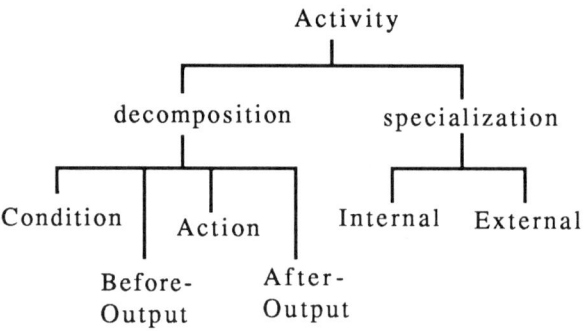

Figure 9.1. Structure of an activity.

As an example, consider some of the rules for an agent that requests help when needed, first informally presented:

external activity:

R1.   if phase is wait-for-info
    and receive x on port motion-info
        then record value of x as current position
    and hold in phase active for 1 unit

internal activities:

R2.   if phase is active
    and need help in executing task
        then send out request for help
    and passivate in wait-for-help

Rule-Based Specification of Atomic-Models

R3.   if phase is active
        then send to port 'starting
    and hold-in working for 100 units
    and send to port 'finished

R4.   if phase is working
        then passivate

Rule R1 is an external activity which activates the model when an external event arrives on port 'motion-info while the model is in phase WAIT-FOR-INFO. The DEVS-Scheme version of this activity is provided to the model by use of the *forward-models* method *add-ext-activities*:

```
(make-pair forward-models 'assistance-requestor)
(send assistance-requestor def-state '(need-help position))
(send assistance-requestor set-s (make-state 'sigma 'inf
          'interpreter-phase 'test-condition 'phase 'wait-for-info))
(send assistance-requestor add-ext-activities
   (list
;;;R1:
       (make-activity
           'condition '(and
                           (equal? (content-port x) 'motion-info)
                           (equal? (state-phase s) 'wait-for-info)
                           )
           'action '(begin
                           (set! (state-position s)
                               (car (content-value x)))
                           (hold-in 'active 1)
                       )
       )
   )
)
```

No output is specified in activity R1 as only *condition* and *action* slots are given non-nil values. Note that these values are quoted text fragments since they should only be evaluated under the appropriate circumstances: the *condition* slot when the condition is being tested and the *action* slot when the action is being executed. Note that expression forms already known for writing atomic models can be used.

Rules R2, R3, and R4 are internal activities following on from rule R1. Rules R2 and R3 provide alternative courses of action that follow once R1 has placed the model in phase ACTIVE. R2 starts a sequence of activities dictating what to do if help is needed. R3 bypasses this request for help and immediately starts the model working. R4 dictates what happens once the model finished its work (with or without help). DEVS versions of these activities may be sent to the model with the method *add-int-activities*:

```
(send assistance-requestor add-int-activities
    (list
;;;R2:
        (make-activity
            'condition '(and (equal? (state-phase s) 'active)
                            (state-need-help s))
            'before-output '(make-content 'port 'ask-for-help
                                        'value (state-position s))
            'action '(passivate-in 'wait-for-help)
        )
;;;R3:
        (make-activity
            'condition '(equal? (state-phase s) 'active)
            'before-output '(make-content 'port 'starting)
            'action '(hold-in 'working 100)
            'after-output '(make-content 'port 'finished)
        )
;;;R4:
        (make-activity
            'condition '(equal? (state-phase s) 'working)
            'action ' (passivate)
        )
```

Rule-Based Specification of Atomic-Models 209

```
 )
)
```

Note that R2 specifies a value for the *before-output* slot. This sends out a request for help just before the model passivates in phase WAIT-FOR-HELP. Since the model passivates, there is no point in specifying a value for the *after-output* slot (it will never get executed anyway). However, Rule R3 provides an example where both before and after outputs are specified.

The before-output is generated just before the action is evaluated while the after-output is generated at the end of the interval specified by the hold-in primitive. Graphically,

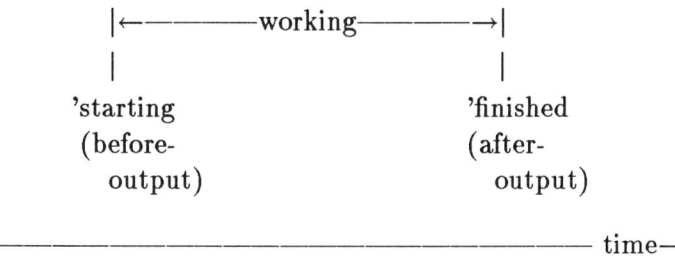

The inference engine underlying *forward-models* evaluates the rules in the order that they are added to the model. Thus rules can be ordered by *context specificity*. For example, R2's condition is more specific than R3's. Since R2 comes first, its condition will be tested before R3's. If R2's condition is satisfied its action will be executed. R3 will get a chance for activation only when R2's condition is not satisfied. In general, one can express multiway decisions by serializing a set of rules partially ordered by specificity. The complexity of the conditions can be reduced by exploiting the sequential order of evaluation: when a condition is tested, all the preceding conditions are known to be false.

9.1.1 Advantages of Rule-based Model Formalism

One advantage of employing rules is apparent in the above example. Whether internal or external, activities that are closely associated can be placed contiguously. This avoids breaking sequences of external and internal transitions apart and thus aids model comprehension. A second benefit: since outputs may be specified within the rules, output specification is not separated from transition specification as in *atomic-models*.

The ability to write models using rules provides an additional level of decomposition or granularity to model specification. Until now the smallest meaningful chunks of a models were the basic functions: internal transition, external transition, and output function (and possibly, time advance). *Atomic-models* could share such functions but they could not share smaller parts of them. Rules, as more granular knowledge units, make it possible to "mix and match" specifications among models. Sets of rules can readily be copied from one model and added to those of another. We will show that sharing of rule sets can be directed from the entity structure level using the specialization and inheritance concepts.

Benefits of rule-based model specification as outlined above are achieved at some cost in execution time but no cost in expressive power. The implementation of *forward-models* will make this clear.

9.2 Class Forward-Models

As a specialization of *atomic-models*, the class *forward-models* generates model objects which inherit all the instance variables and methods of *atomic-models*. However, *forward-models* overrides some of these to implement an inference engine, as shown in the class definition of Figure 9.2. The state-variables of *forward-models* are specified in the instance variable *ind-vars*. They include *int-activities* and *ext-activities* which are to contain lists of internal and external activities, respectively. Also included is a state-variable, *interpreter-phase* which keeps track of the phase of the inference engine as well as other state-variables for temporary storage of information.

The forward chaining inference engine is implemented by the functions *int-for*, *ext-for* and *out-for* which fill the *int-transfn*, *ext-transfn* and *outputfn* slots of all forward models, respectively. Thus, all instances of *forward-models* have the same underlying inference engine. What makes them different are the rules expressed as data in their *int-activities* and *ext-activities* state-variable.

```
;;;;;;;;;;;;;;;;;;;;;;;;;;;;; forw-cl.s ;;;;;;;;;;;;;;;;;;;;;;;;;;;;
(define-class forward-models
              (classvars)
              (instvars
               (ind-vars '(sigma phase saved-sigma name interpreter-phase
                           before-output-buffer after-output-buffer
                           action-buffer ext-activities int-activities))
               (int-transfn int-for)
               (ext-transfn  ext-for)
               (outputfn out-for)
               )
 (options
     gettable-variables
     settable-variables
     inittable-variables)
 (mixins atomic-models)
 )

(compile-class forward-models)
```

Figure 9.2. Class definition of *Forward-models*.

The transition and output functions employed by *forward-models* are shown in Figure 9.3. Both transition functions use the function *first-satisfied* to check their respective lists of activities for the first one whose condition is satisfied. This is done only in *interpreter-phase* TEST-CONDITION, the phase in which the inference engine starts and to which it returns after executing a test-act cycle. *Ext-for* also does this testing when it receives an input while in *interpreter-phase* DOING. The model is in *interpreter-phase* DOING while the model is doing its action, i.e., during the interval specified by the *hold-in* primitive in an executed action. Thus external events arriving during such an interval can have the same effect of causing an immediate state transition as they do in *atomic-models*. In particular, the elapsed time since the last event is available in the variable e as before.

Once *first-satisfied* returns an activity the following occurs:

- its *after-output* component is stored in the *after-output-buffer*,
- if its *before-output* component is not empty,
    - the *before-output* is evaluated and stored in the *before-output-buffer*,
    - the *action* specification is stored in the *action-buffer*,
    - the *interpreter-phase* is set to BEFORE-SENDING,
    - *sigma* is set to 0,
- otherwise, the *action* is evaluated immediately,
    - which sets *sigma* and the model *phase* and,
    - the *interpreter-phase* is set to DOING.

The internal transition and output functions dictate what happens if no external events occur in the time interval of length *sigma*:

- if the *interpreter-phase* is BEFORE-SENDING
    - the contents of the *before-output* buffer are sent out,
    - the action in the *action-buffer* is evaluated and,
    - the *interpreter-phase* is set to DOING.

- if the *interpreter-phase* is DOING
    - then if the *after-output-buffer* is not empty,
    - the contents of the *after-output-buffer* are sent out,
    - the *interpreter-phase* is set to TEST-CONDITION,
    - *sigma* is set to 0 and a new cycle is thus initiated.

Rule-Based Specification of Atomic-Models 213

Note that the *before-output* is always produced with zero time delay in response to an external event. If a non-zero delay is desired, such an output must be produced as an after-output. Notice also that the before-output does not violate the atomic-model restriction on generating an output just before internal events. The before-output is always produced in this way after a zero-time internal event but the user need not write the lines in the transition and output functions to make this happen.

```
(define (first-satisfied lst env)
    (let loop (
        (rem lst)
      )
      (cond
((null? rem) '())
((eval (activity-condition (car rem)) env)
 (car rem)
 )
(else (loop  (cdr rem)))
   )
  )
)

(define (ext-for s e x)
  (set! (state-saved-sigma s) (state-sigma s) )
  (case (state-interpreter-phase s)
    ((doing test-condition)     ;;;only phases for receiving input
     (let* (
            (env (eval (state-name s) user-initial-environment))
            (act* (first-satisfied (state-ext-activities s) env))
            (before-output
                 (when act* (eval (activity-before-output act*) env)))
            (after-output (when act* (activity-after-output act*)))
            (action (when act* (activity-action act*)))
           )
       (set! (state-after-output-buffer s) after-output)
       (cond
         ((null? act*)
          (set! (state-interpreter-phase s) 'passive)
          (set! (state-sigma s) 'inf)
         )
         (before-output
          (set! (state-before-output-buffer s) before-output)
          (set! (state-action-buffer s) action)
          (set! (state-interpreter-phase s) 'before-sending)
          (set! (state-sigma s) 0)
         )
         (else
          (set! (state-sigma s) (state-saved-sigma s))
          ;;expect action to set sigma; if not, use saved-sigma
```

Figure 9.3. Functions used in *forward-models* inference engine.

```
                (eval action env)
                (set! (state-interpreter-phase s) 'doing)
                )
      )))
      (else (set! (state-sigma s) (state-saved-sigma s)))
    )
  )

  (define (int-for s)
    (case (state-interpreter-phase s)
      ('before-sending
          (let (
                (env (eval (state-name s) user-initial-environment))
                )
            (set! (state-sigma s) (state-saved-sigma s))
              ;;expect action to set sigma; if not, use saved-sigma
            (eval (state-action-buffer s) env)
            (set! (state-interpreter-phase s) 'doing)
            )
          )
      ('doing
              (set! (state-interpreter-phase s) 'test-condition)
              (set! (state-sigma s) 0)
      )
      ('test-condition
          (let* (
                 (env (eval (state-name s) user-initial-environment))
                 (act* (first-satisfied (state-int-activities s) env))
                 (before-output
                     (when act* (eval (activity-before-output act*) env)))
                 (after-output (when act* (activity-after-output act*)))
                 (action (when act* (activity-action act*)))
                 )
            (set! (state-after-output-buffer s) after-output)
            (cond
              ( (null? act*)
        (set! (state-interpreter-phase s) 'passive)
                (set! (state-sigma s) 'inf)
                )
              ( before-output
                (set! (state-before-output-buffer s) before-output)
                (set! (state-action-buffer s) action)
                (set! (state-interpreter-phase s) 'before-sending)
                (set! (state-sigma s) 0)
                )
              ( else
                (set! (state-sigma s) (state-saved-sigma s))
                 ;;expect action to set sigma; if not, use saved-sigma
        (eval action env)
                (set! (state-interpreter-phase s) 'doing)
                )
      )))
      (else
        (set! (state-interpreter-phase s) 'passive)
        (set! (state-sigma s) 'inf)
        )
  ))
```

Figure 9.3. (continued).

```
(define (out-for s)
  (let (
       (env (eval (state-name s) user-initial-environment))
       )
    (case (state-interpreter-phase s)
      ('before-sending (state-before-output-buffer s))
      ('doing (cond ((eval (state-after-output-buffer s) env))
                    (else (make-content))))
      (else (make-content))
      )
    ))
```

Figure 9.3. (continued).

9.2.1 Expressive Power of Forward-Models *vis-a-vis* Atomic-Models

The above realization shows that any model expressed as a forward model can also be expressed as an atomic model. Thus, *forward-models* is a sub-class of *atomic-models*. What about the converse? Are there atomic models that cannot be expressed as forward models? If so, then the *forward-models* class would offer convenience at the price of expressive power. Fortunately, this is not so. Indeed, we can show that every atomic model can be simulated by a forward model in the sense of there existing a structure preserving homomorphism from the latter to the former (Zeigler, 1984). The proof is straightforward: given *ext-m, int-m,* and *out-m* of an atomic model M, we define a forward model representative, F as follows:

(make-pair forward-models 'f)

(send f def-state (send m get-ind-vars))

(send f set-ext-activities
    (list (make-activity 'condition '#t
                     'action '(ext-m s e x))))

(send f set-int-activities
    (list (make-activity 'condition '#t
                     'before-output '(out-m s)
                     'action '(int-m s))))

Now, let F and M be started in corresponding states, i.e., F is started with *interpreter-phase* set to TEST-CONDITION and has all of its additional state variables set to values equal to the respective state variables of M. The reader may verify that F and M will continue to transit to corresponding states and to produce the same outputs as the same times. Thus F can be shown to simulate M in a homomorphic fashion (the morphism is not an isomorphism since F has many more states than does M).

The foregoing shows that we can express any atomic model in *forward-models* form. Consequently, there is no loss of expressive power within the *forward-models* class. Note however, that the proof does **not** offer a practical means to do this! Generally, we do not have available the functions we wish to represent. We turn to *forward-models* when it is easier to develop these functions in the rule oriented style of thinking or when the we desire the additional advantages arising from granularity to be discussed next.

9.3 Inheritance and Specialization

As we have seen, rule-based model specification in class *forward-models* exemplifies the knowledge-chunk modularity often claimed for rule based systems. However, placing rules together in a set is reminiscent of superposition of inputs in dynamic systems: the system must be linear for the output to be the superposition of the individual outputs. This means that juxtaposed behaviors must either be completely non-interacting or it must be possible to determine and control the effects of their interaction. As we shall now show, inheritance and system entity structuring can be employed to exert such control. However, the user is still responsible for properly testing models so that the desired behavior results from the "superposition" of inherited behaviors.

9.3.1 Inheritance in Forward-models

Rule juxtaposition implemented in class *forward-models* makes it possible to further extend the use of inheritance to construct atomic models. Using SCOOPS, specialized classes of *atomic-models* can

Rule-Based Specification of Atomic-Models 217

be defined. However, such definitions are of limited utility since essential parts of model structure, the transition and output functions, have to inherited, or overridden, as a whole — they can not be partially modified by the inheriting class. As we have now seen, *forward-models* provides a means for transmitting model structure in the form of more heritable quantities: rules. To define meaningful model structure rules inherited from a parent class must be combinable with more specialized rules provided by the child class. Such combination must involve an analog of the ability of local methods to override inherited methods with the same name. In the case of inherited rules, one can give locally supplied rules greater priority in conflict resolution mechanisms so that such rules override inherited ones. In other words, if a local rule and an inherited rule are both triggered (have their conditions satisfied), then the local rule should fire. Since the inference engine underlying forward models always scans the external and internal activities lists in head-to-tail order, placing inherited rules at the tail of respective lists will achieve the desired priority ordering.

The method *inherit-from* of *forward-models* carries out concatenation of rules following the above lines. Let M and M' both be forward models. The message:

(send m inherit-from m')

- extends the state-variables of M to include any new ones employed by M' (the method *def-state* will do this nicely),

- adds the internal-activities of M' to the tail of the internal-activities list of M,

- adds the external-activities of M' to the tail of the external-activities list of M.

Figure 9.4a shows a generator, EXP which produces outputs at exponentially distributed inter-arrival times (the output segment is said to be a poisson process). Now consider inheriting the rules of the "demon" in Figure 9.4b. The demon, LOW-MEAN watches to see that the value for the *mean* parameter is a predetermined constant,

```
(make-pair forward-models 'exp)

(send  exp def-state '(mean stream interarrival-time))

(send  exp set-display)

(send  exp set-s (make-state 'interpreter-phase 'test-condition
                             'phase 'active
                             'sigma 0
                             'stream 1
                             'mean 10
                             )
)

(send exp add-int-activities
    (list
          (make-activity
                'condition '(and (equal? (state-phase s) 'active)
                                 (state-stream s)(state-mean s))
                'before-output
                   '(make-content 'port 'out 'value (gensym))
                'action      '(begin
                                (set! (state-interarrival-time s)
                                   (expon (state-mean s)
                                          (state-stream s)))
                                (hold-in 'active
                                   (state-interarrival-time s)))
          )
    )
)
```

Figure 9.4a. Forward model of exponential generator.

```
(make-pair forward-models ' low-mean)

(send  low-mean def-state '(mean))

(send  low-mean set-display)

(send  low-mean set-s (make-state 'interpreter-phase 'test-condition
                                  'sigma 0
                                  'mean 1
                                  )
)

(send low-mean add-int-activities
    (list
          (make-activity
                'condition '(or (null? (state-mean s))
                                (not (equal? (state-mean s) 1)))
                'action   '(begin (set! (state-mean s) 1)
                                  (set! (state-sigma s) 0))
          )
    )
)
```

Figure 9.4b. Forward model of mean setting "demon".

say 1; if not it sets it to that value. Combining the two sets of state-variables and lists of activities results in a model that will first set the mean to 1 and then start generating successive outputs. In this case, the order in which the two internal activities, one each from EXP and LOW-MEAN, appear in the list affects the resulting behavior. The demon activity should come first to assure proper generation right from the start.

The proper order arises if we use:

(send low-mean inherit-from exp)

Then LOW-MEAN inherits the state-variable *stream* from EXP. The internal activity of EXP will be appended at the end of the list of internal activities of LOW-MEAN. In general, the concatenated rule sets must be checked for consistency so that their juxtaposition make sense. The system entity structure can greatly assist in assuring such consistency as we shall now show.

9.3.2 Specialization

The power afforded by inheritance shows up clearly at the knowledge representation level, namely in the system entity structure. Recall that the specialization relation allowed us to conveniently express alternatives for model structure. Having pruned an entity structure and removed all specializations, the *transform* operator synthesizes a model from the resulting pruned entity structure. The *transform* operator must call upon inheritance to synthesize models corresponding to the chosen specialized entities. Without inheritance the models named by all the specialized entities would have to be resident in the model base.

To show how specialization is related to inheritance, consider the following SES fragment:

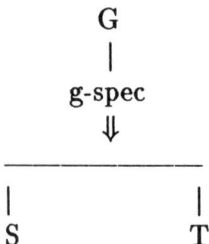

In pruning, we select a specialized entity, S or T, to replace the general entity G. If S is chosen for example, the result will be the pruned entity structure:

S_G

i.e., a single specialized entity which may be called "S specialization of G". The order, in which the specialization choice comes first, is natural. Think of adjectives corresponding to specialization choices and nouns corresponding to general entities. For example, let G be "dog" and S be "small", then "S specialization of G", corresponds to "small_dog".

The specialized entity S_G is transformed using the following rules:

- *transform* S into a model of the same name
- (rule 1) if both S and G are instances of *forward-models* (or its subclasses) then
  - *transform* G into a model of the same name
  - the *transform* of S_G is the result of telling a copy of S to inherit-from G.
- (rule 2) otherwise, the *transform* of S_G is a copy of S.

The first rule expresses the means by which a specialized entity S_G is synthesized through inheriting the structure of the general entity G to the specialized choice S. The second rule by-passes such inheritance and returns a copy of S as the result of transforming S_G. The rationale is that both S and G must be forward models for inheritance to be possible; if not, S must itself give rise to the specialized entity S_G.

Consider the SES of Figure 9.5a which offers a family of choices for generators. Some of the models referred to are shown in Figure 9.5b. Starting the pruning from GEN, we might choose to have a random generator, RND and then select EXP as the desired inter-arrival distribution (rather than NORM for a normally distributed inter-arrivals). This leaves the choices of stream (initial random number seed) and mean to be made in arbitrary order. The result of pruning might thus be the PES with root, LOW-MEAN_STRM-ONE_EXP_RND_GEN. When transformed this results in a model with activities inherited from LOW-MEAN, STRM-ONE, EXP, RND and GEN in the order placing the more specialized activities ahead of more generalized ones. In particular, the "demon" rules appear before the generator rules. We thus see how the SES can be used not only to structure a family of models but also to ensure that the order in which inheritance is performed is as required. A second example of such structuring will be discussed in a moment.

9.3.3 Constraints

As just seen, when pruned, a system entity structure forces certain choices to be made before others. It also eliminates certain possibilities once certain selections are made. For example, once EXP is selected in Figure 9.5a, there is no choice for the standard deviation parameter, STD-SPEC which is appropriate only for the selection of NORM.

However, there remain forms of constraints that cannot be specified in this manner. For example, consider a constraint that requires the mean and standard deviation parameters for NORM to be related, e.g., both small or both large. This form of constraint can be specified with an entity structure command, *add-constraints*. For example,

(add-constraints e:gen '(low-sd sd-spec select low-mean mean-spec))

specifies that if LOW-SD is selected from the SD-SPEC specialization

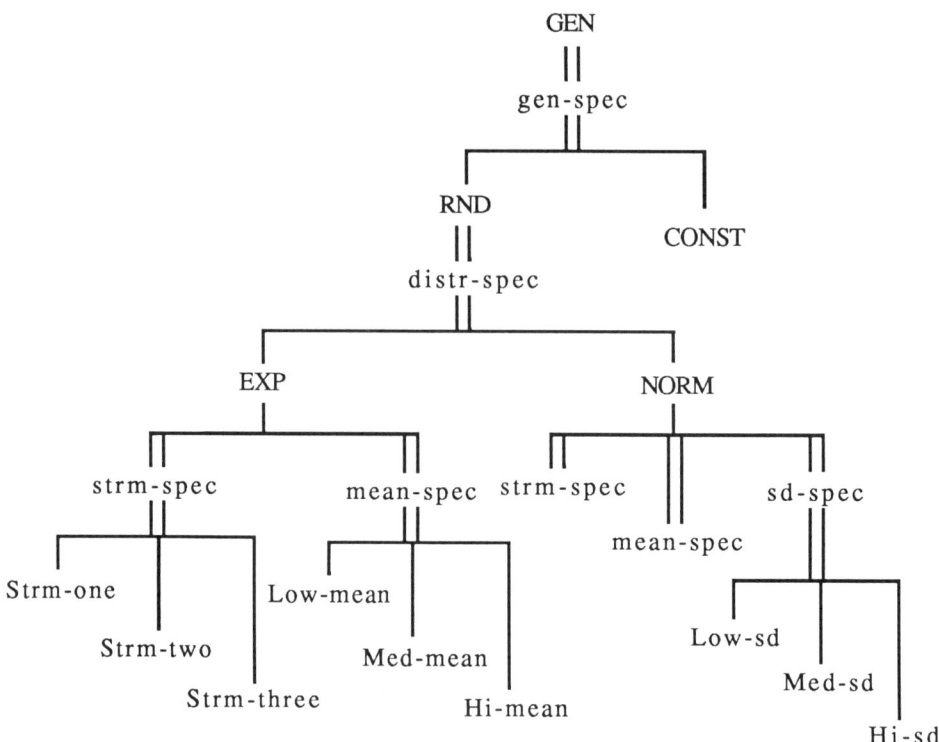

Figure 9.5a. Family of generator models.

Rule-Based Specification of Atomic-Models

```
(make-pair forward-models 'gen)
(send gen def-state '(interarrival-time))
(send gen set-display)
(send gen set-s (make-state    'interpreter-phase 'test-condition
                               'phase 'active
                               'sigma 0
                         )
)

(send gen add-ext-activities
      (list
            (make-activity
              'condition   '(and (equal? (state-phase s) 'active)
                                 (equal? (content-port x) 'stop))
              'action      '(passivate)
            )
      )
)


;;;;;;;;;;;;;
(make-pair forward-models 'norm)
(send norm def-state '(stream mean sd interarrival-time))
(send norm set-display)
(send norm set-s (make-state 'interpreter-phase 'test-condition
                             'phase 'active
                             'sigma 0
                             'stream 2
                             'mean 10
                             'sd 2
                       ) )

(send norm add-int-activities
   (list
      (make-activity
          'condition   '(and (equal? (state-phase s) 'active)
                             (state-stream s)(state-mean s) (state-sd s))
          'before-output '(make-content 'port 'out 'value (gensym))

          'action      '(begin
                           (set! (state-interarrival-time s)
                                 (normal (state-mean s)(state-sd s)
                                         (state-stream s)))
                           (hold-in 'active (state-interarrival-time s)))
          ) )
)
```

Figure 9.5b. Generator forward model specifications.

```
(make-pair forward-models ' strm-one)  ;;don't use numbers or hyphen
(send  strm-one def-state '(stream))
(send  strm-one set-display)
(send  strm-one set-s (make-state 'interpreter-phase 'test-condition
                                  'sigma 0
                                  'stream 1
                      )
)

(send strm-one add-int-activities
    (list
          (make-activity
              'condition '(or (null? (state-stream s))
                              (not (equal? (state-stream s) 1)))
              'action  '(begin (set! (state-stream s) 1)
                               (set! (state-sigma s) 0))
          )
    )
)

;;;;;;;;;;;;;

(make-pair forward-models ' hi-mean)
(send  hi-mean def-state '(mean))
(send  hi-mean set-display)
(send  hi-mean set-s (make-state 'interpreter-phase 'test-condition
                                 'sigma 0
                                 'mean 10
                     )
)


(send hi-mean add-int-activities
    (list
          (make-activity
              'condition '(or (null? (state-mean s))
                              (not (equal? (state-mean s) 10)))
              'action  '(begin (set! (state-mean s) 10)
                               (set! (state-sigma s) 0))
          )
    )
)
```

Figure 9.5b. (continued).

Rule-Based Specification of Atomic-Models 225

then LOW-MEAN must be selected from the MEAN-SPEC specialization. The converse constraint is specified by:

(add-constraints e:gen '(low-mean mean-spec select low-sd sd-spec))

A second form of constraint is exemplified by the following:

(add-constraints e:gen '(low-mean mean-spec deselect hi-sd std-spec))

Here, selecting LOW-MEAN from MEANS-SPEC disqualifies HI-STD as a selection from STD-SPEC. Thus a low mean and a high standard deviation are disallowed. However, the combinations of low-mean/med-sd and low-mean/low-sd are still viable.

Such constraints are automatically enforced in the pruning process by a kind of miniature forward chaining inference engine. To assure that only desired combinations are permitted, the user must specify the full set of constraints in the pairwise fashion indicated above. A more powerful constraint specification language would, of course, be desirable.

9.3.4 A Robot Co-ordination Model

To further demonstrate the power of rule set inheritance, consider modelling a small robot-managed laundry. The SES in Figure 9.6a can be pruned so as to select a robot capable of handling a drier, a washer, or both together. Constraints ensure that a limited capability robot is not put into an environment it can't handle!

A general part of the robot's behavior is specified in the forward-model of Figure 9.6b. This is a set of activities for co-ordinating the handling of tasks whether they be connected with washing, drying, or both. Recall that these activities will be appended to the end of the more specific ones needed to do the actual laundry tasks. Therefore, some of them serve as defaults to be overridden. Others serve as organizers to be executed after specialized tasks have been performed and a new cycle of activity started. While the robot is performing its specialized tasks, it does not allow itself to be disturbed. Rather it stores all incoming messages (such as buzz from the washer when it finished) in "short term memory" (otherwise called a mail-box) and returns to examine them after completing current tasks.

(I)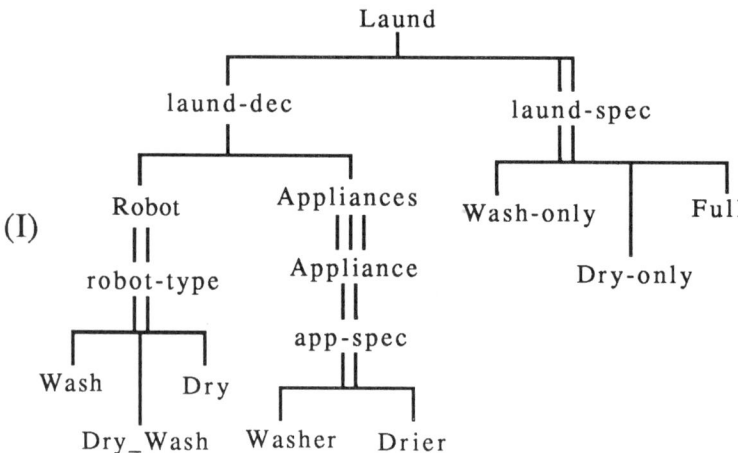

(II)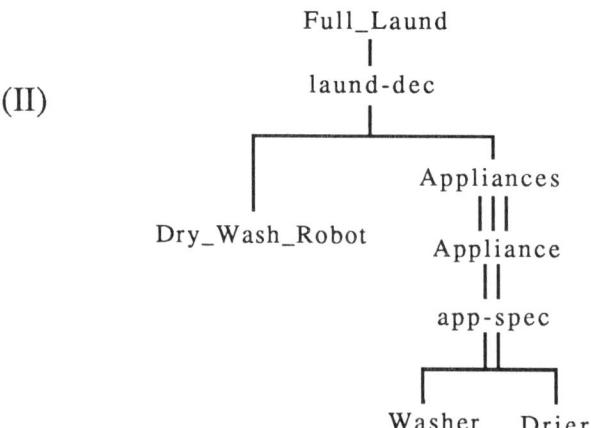

Figure 9.6a. Robot laundry management model: (I) SES, (II) PES.

```
(make-pair forward-models 'robot)
(send robot def-state '(stm influencees))
(send robot set-s (make-state   'interpreter-phase 'test-condition
                                'phase 'recall
                                'sigma 0))

(send robot set-display)

(send robot set-ext-activities
    (list
       (make-activity
          'condition #t
          'action '(begin (set! (state-stm s)
                          (append (state-stm s)(list (content-port x))))
                          (continue))
       )
 ))

(send robot set-int-activities
     (list
       (make-activity
          'condition       '(equal? (state-phase s) 'start)
          'action          '(passivate)
       )
       (make-activity
           'condition    '(and (equal? (state-phase s) 'recall)
                               (state-stm s))
           'before-output '(make-content 'port 'error
                                         'value '(illegal input))
           'action       '(begin (set! (state-stm s) (cdr (state-stm s)))
                                 (hold-in 'recall 1))
       )
       (make-activity
          'condition       '(equal? (state-phase s) 'recall)
          'action          '(hold-in 'start 1)
       )
     )
)

;;;;;;;;;;;;;;;;;;;

(make-pair forward-models 'wash)

(send wash def-state '(dirty-clothes washer-full  washed-clothes stm))

(send wash set-s (make-state 'interpreter-phase 'test-condition
                             'name 'wash
                             'phase 'start
                             'sigma 0
                             'dirty-clothes 2
                             'washed-clothes 0
                    )
)

(send wash set-display)
```

Figure 9.6b. Forward model laundry robot specification.

```
(send wash set-int-activities
   (list
      (make-activity
         'condition    '(and (equal? (state-phase s) 'start)
                             (> (state-dirty-clothes s) 0)
                             (not (state-washer-full s)) )
         'action       '(hold-in 'fill-washer 10)
      )

      (make-activity
         'condition     '(equal? (state-phase s) 'fill-washer)
         'before-output '(make-content 'port 'start-washer)
         'action        '(begin (set! (state-dirty-clothes s)
                                      (- (state-dirty-clothes s) 1))
                                (set! (state-washer-full s) #t)
                                (hold-in 'recall 1))
      )
   )
)

(send wash set-ext-activities
   (list
      (make-activity
         'condition    '(and (equal? (state-phase s) 'passive)
                             (equal? (content-port x) 'washer-buzz)
                             (state-washer-full s))
         'action        '(hold-in 'empty-washer 10)
         'after-output  '(make-content 'port 'out
                              'value '(washing-cycle completed))
      )
   )
)

(send wash add-int-activities
   (list
      (make-activity
         'condition    '(equal? (state-phase s) 'empty-washer)
         'action       '(begin (set! (state-washed-clothes s)
                                     (+ (state-washed-clothes s) 1))
                               (set! (state-washer-full s) #f)
                               (hold-in 'recall 1))
      )
      (make-activity
         'condition    '(and (equal? (state-phase s) 'recall)
                             (equal? (car (state-stm s)) 'washer-buzz)
                             (state-washer-full s))
         'action        '(begin (set!(state-stm s)(cdr (state-stm s)))
                                (hold-in 'empty-washer 10))
         'after-output  '(make-content 'port 'out
                              'value '(washing-cycle completed))
      )
   )
)
```

Figure 9.6b. (continued).

Rule-Based Specification of Atomic-Models

```
(make-pair atomic-models 'washer)
(send washer def-state '(wash-time))
(send washer set-s (make-state   'phase 'passive
                                 'sigma 'inf
                                 'wash-time 100))

(send washer set-ext-transfn (lambda(s e x)
  (case (content-port x)
      ('start-washer
           (if (equal? (state-phase s) 'passive)
               (hold-in 'washing (state-wash-time s))
               (continue)
           )
      )
      (else (continue))
)))
(send washer set-int-transfn (lambda(s)(passivate)))
(send washer set-outputfn (lambda(s)
       (make-content 'port 'washer-buzz)))
```

Figure 9.6b. (continued).

Specific rules for managing washer and drier appliances, as well as simple models for these devices, are shown in Figure 9.6b. Only the washer-related models are shown since the drier models are **isomorphic** to corresponding washer ones. That is, essentially the same approach is taken to modelling the appliances as is the behavior necessary to control them. The SES of Figure 9.6a can be pruned so as to combine these behaviors separately, or jointly, with the co-ordination/default rules. Consider pruning starting from the robot so that full capability is selected. The result will be a PES, P:DRY_WASH_ROBOT. When transformed, this will place activities for drying ahead of those for washing and the co-ordination/default ones. This means that drier activities will have first crack at being triggered and therefore higher priority than washer activities. This is appropriate, since the washer/drier combination form a pipeline (of the sort exemplified in Chapter 5) and downstream processes should be serviced first to avoid unnecessary queuing.

9.4 Specialization and Multiple Entities

Specialization in entity structures containing multiple entities offers an especially powerful means to generate models. In this case, pruning may result in the inclusion of not just one, but of many, selected components in the model.

As an example, consider SES for the laundry in Figure 9.6a. Pruning from LAUND and selecting the full capability option, we obtain P:LAUND@FULL, shown in Figure 9.6c. As we have seen, this PES transforms into a controlled-model corresponding to the multiple entity APPLIANCES. Until now, components of such a kernel-model were isomorphic copies of APPLIANCE, the kernel, which would be generated under the user's control at simulation time (i.e., during the restart process).

Another possibility is now evident. When pruning a multiple entity such as APPLIANCES the subtree below the single entity, APPLIANCE, can be placed into the kernel model and used, at simulation time, to generate any number of desired alternatives for the kernel. Consider for example, pruning E:LAUND. During such pruning, we choose *controlled-models* as the desired subclass of *kernel-models*, as before. However, when pruning arrives at the single entity, APPLIANCE, we will be asked whether we wish the entity structure to be cut at this point. An affirmative answer will result in two actions:

- the PES E:LAUND will have the subtree below APPLIANCE removed, and

- a new entity structure, E:APPLIANCE consisting of APPLIANCE and its substructure is created:

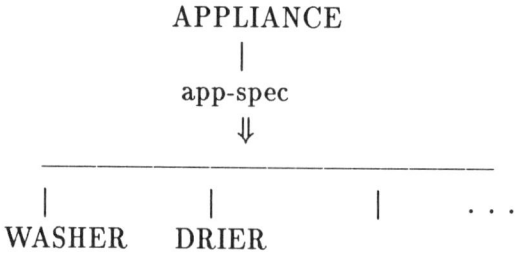

Now, when transforming P:LAUND@FULL, the user can choose whether to have the entity structure E:APPLIANCE replace the model APPLIANCE as the progenitor of components for |co-APPLIANCES|, the resulting kernel model. At simulation time, (during restart), the init-new method will check for the presence of an entity structure rather than a model. If present, this entity structure, E:APPLIANCE, can be used to generate any number of any of the possible prunings of the structure. Thus, for E:APPLIANCE we can have any desired number of copies of WASHER and DRIER, as components for |co-APPLIANCES|. Our robot model is not set up to handle more than one of each but it can readily extended to do so.

The process just described is one means of realizing the semantics of multiple entities with specialization. It delays, until runtime, the choice and construction of components for *kernel-models*. This has the advantage of runtime flexibility, but the disadvantage of having to respecify the same choices each time one wants to repeat the construction of particular configuration. In big entity structures, this can be a tedious and time consuming process. An other approach, which operates entirely at the entity structure level, has been implemented in DEVS-Scheme along the lines described in (Zhang and Zeigler, 1989). In this case, the choices are all encoded in the resulting pruned entity structure which can be reloaded as desired. Reusability is thus enhanced.

9.5 DEVS-Scheme Methodology Reviewed

Let us review the methodology presented here. To develop a family of models for investigating alternatives for a model domain, (life support systems, computer architectures, robot-managed laboratories, etc.) the following steps are executed:

1. A system entity structure (SES) is constructed. The atomic entities (i.e., leaves in the entity structure) must have corresponding models in the model base. Other entities in the structure represent systems, subsystems or components, that can be automatically synthesized from models of atomic entities.

2. The system entity structure is pruned to study the particular alternative of interest at the time. Pruning may begin with any entity in the structure. The resulting pruned entity structure (PES) represents a particular design alternative for the system, subsystem or component represented by that entity.

3. A pruned entity structure directs the synthesis of a hierarchical simulation model under the *transform* procedure. Models of the atomic entities in the model base are replicated and coupled together in a hierarchical fashion to form successive levels of components and finally, the overall coupled model. (When the same entity occurs more than one once its model is replicated to produce isomorphic copies for each occurrence.)

4. Once transformed, the simulation model is ready for simulation experiments to test its performance in meeting the objectives at hand.

5. The above steps are repeated to study different alternatives. Once a pruned entity structure has been created and saved, it is detectable by the pruning process and can be re-employed, without repruning, whenever the entity at its root is required. Thus as a study progresses, the reusable stock of coupled models grows. More of this in Chapter 13.

The system entity structure, and the underlying object-oriented environment for hierarchical, modular model synthesis, provide a powerful medium for generating and studying alternatives for richly structured modelling domains. In the ensuing part of the book, we present examples of such domains involving intelligent agents.

Chapter 10

A ROBOT-MANAGED LABORATORY OF THE FUTURE

Intelligent agents make and use models. Realistic modelling of such agents and their societies requires that we represent such model-based activity to a degree of fidelity not possible with conventional simulation tools. To set the context for this discussion, we first demonstrate how the DEVS-Scheme environment implements a model base for robot management of space-borne laboratories. The models show how the classes *controlled-models* and *forward-models* combine to help specify multi-level organizations of autonomous, mobile agents.

We consider the design of a simulation environment for the study of semi-autonomous robot architectures that manage chemical, or similar, laboratories aboard a Space Station. Laboratory management includes servicing and calibration of equipment, set-up of experiments to external specifications, monitoring and control of experiments in progress, measurement of results, and finally recording and analyzing of data.

The environment should:

- support development of robot cognitive systems and strategies for effective multi-robot management of laboratory experiments,

- support study of the trade-off in partitioning tasks between hard and soft forms of automation, i.e., we could have robot-free laboratory containing a large number of special purpose "intelligent" instruments capable of almost complete self-control or a small number of very flexible robots that can be manage a small number of general purpose instruments,

- enable assessing the nature of human supervision initially required, and development of workable human-robot co-operation protocols.

It is timely to begin exploration of advanced robot-controlled instrumentation. For example, handling fluids in orbit will be essential to many of the experiments being planned in manufacturing and biotechnology. However, the microgravity conditions of space necessitate radically different approaches to fluid handling than common on earth. As experience in space accumulates, approaches and instrumentation will likely undergo continual modification, enhancement, and replacement. Thus, robots for managing such equipment must be sufficiently intelligent and flexible so that constantly changing environments can be accommodated.

In designing the robot models, we assume that necessary mobility, manipulative and sensory capabilities exist so that we can focus on task-related cognitive requirements. Such capacities, the focus of much current robot research, are treated at a high level of abstraction obviating the need to solve current technological problems. Organizational issues are introduced from the beginning since individual robot capabilities may be much influenced by co-operative requirements.

Let us first focus on representing the organizational aspects of the multi-robot system. This requires representing how robots can communicate and co-ordinate their activities. One problem to be tackled is how to model communication and other interaction among moving robots and objects. In an object-oriented, modular modelling paradigm, there can be no direct sharing of positional information (recall Section 1.7). Thus we need to include some object — possibly fictitious — that is aware of the locations and orientations of all other objects at all times. An elegant solution is possible by using the *controlled-models* class as we now show.

10.1 Multilevel Hierarchical Robot Model

A system entity structure (SES) for the ROBOT-SYSTEM is shown in Figure 10.1. After pruning, the entity structure is transformed into is a hierarchical model containing controlled models at two levels (Figure 10.2). At the top level, the ROBOT-SYSTEM is a controlled model containing a SPACE-MANAGER (the omniscient object) as controller, and ROBOTS as components. Each ROBOT is decomposed into MOTION-SYSTEM, SENSORY-SYSTEM, and COGNITION-SYSTEM. The MOTION-SYSTEM keeps track of ROBOT's motion information such as position, direction, speed, etc.. It accepts such motion commands as move, change-speed, etc. from the COGNITION-SYSTEM . When a robot changes its position, the MOTION-SYSTEM sends its new location and direction to the SPACE-MANAGER.

A ROBOT receives and sends messages via its SENSORY-SYSTEM. The messages are sent on ports 'send and 'receive. A slot, called a *channel*, is used to distinguish the transmission medium in the communication between ROBOTS and SPACE-MANAGER. The SENSORY-SYSTEM places an outgoing message on port 'send, specifies the outgoing channel and places the message's output port in a second slot. On the receiving end, the reverse "decoding" takes place. The SENSORY-SYSTEM reacts appropriately to incoming channel; it also uses the output port to route the incoming message to destinations within the robot using the usual external input coupling. Messages on certain channels, such as touch, are reflected

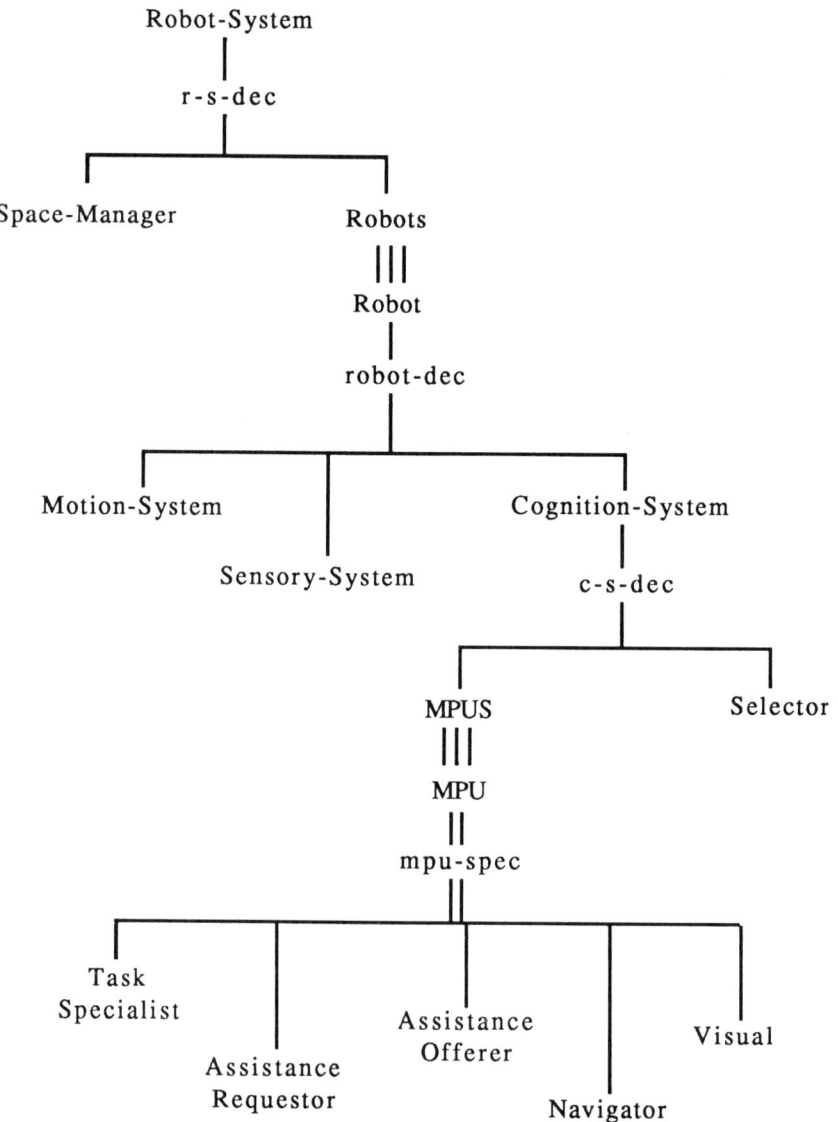

Figure 10.1. SES for the robot system.

back to the SPACE-MANAGER by SENSORY-SYSTEMs upon receipt, as well as being transmitted to the COGNITION-SYSTEM. Such echo messages are used by the original sender to ascertain its spatial relationship to the receiving ROBOT.

The COGNITION-SYSTEM is itself a controlled model consisting of a SELECTOR as controller, and MPUs (Model-Plan Units) as components. MPUs are task specialists that are designed by employing models of intended tasks and plans of action based on such models. This is the major topic of subsequent chapters.

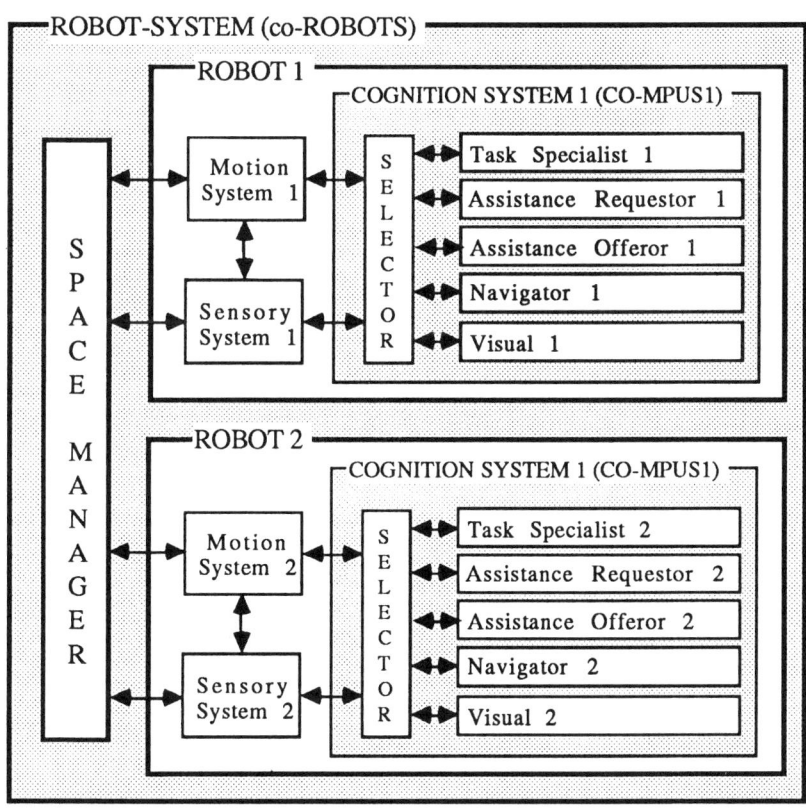

Figure 10.2. Minimal robot system organization.

10.2 Space Management for Mobile Components

The SPACE-MANAGER is the controller in the ROBOT-SYSTEM controlled model. It is a modelling artifact – necessitated by the object-oriented, modular modelling paradigm – to conveniently represent knowledge of where objects are and with whom they can communicate and interact. Motion and communication of ROBOTS are managed by the SPACE-MANAGER. When a ROBOT moves around, its MOTION-SYSTEM sends its new location and direction to the SPACE-MANAGER which keeps track of the ROBOTS' positions and directions. When a ROBOT wishes to communicate with other ROBOTS, it sends message via its SENSORY-SYSTEM to the SPACE-MANAGER which relays the message only to those ROBOTS within the range of the sender. The range is determined by the channel on which the message is sent. Thus different transmission media and sensory modalities can be modeled, such as light and vision, sound and hearing, pressure and touch, etc. To implement robot vision, the seeing ROBOT sends its "want-to-see" message via the LIGHT channel to the SPACE-MANAGER. The SPACE-MANAGER decides which ROBOTS are located within the line of sight of the viewer. The ROBOT that is closest to the viewer is chosen as target. Since the SPACE-MANAGER has complete knowledge of locations and directions, it can easily compute the viewing distance and perspective, and attaches these two pieces of viewing data to the light message before routing it to the target. Upon receiving the light message, the target compute its reflected image according to the viewing distance and perspective given it (details are in (Luh 1989)).

Since the SPACE-MANAGER has complete knowledge of locations, it can detect collisions between ROBOTS. Space is viewed as a kind of resource shared by its occupants so that collisions represent attempts to occupy the same space more than once at the same time. The SPACE-MANAGER can report such an event but do nothing to prevent it. However, the SPACE-MANAGER may be given greater intelligence to co-ordinate the ROBOTS, for example to prevent collisions, and to do other space resource management. In this case, it becomes "actual", at least in part.

10.3 Robot Cognition System

As indicated, each ROBOT's COGNITION-SYSTEM is also a controlled model containing a SELECTOR as controller, and MPUs (model-plan units) as components. The SELECTOR is essentially a bi-state device whose state is determined by the MPUs' responses. In the *open* state, all incoming sensory inputs are broadcast to MPUs. The first one to respond will become the activated MPU. Once a MPU activation has occurred, the SELECTOR is switched to the *closed* state in which it passes on the incoming sensory inputs to the activated MPU. The latter pays attention only to those inputs which matter to achieve its goals. Moreover, the "action-by-exception" control ensures that an MPU, once initiated, retains activation until its plan is successfully executed, or until a significant discrepancy arises between the actual results of carrying out the plan and the results expected of its model. Thus, upon completion of the activation plans or receiving a discrepancy alert, the SELECTOR is switched back to the *open* state in which MPUs will compete for activation again. In such a way, we can minimize the sensory inputs the system must attend to at one time.

The MPUs comprising the robot's brain are of two kinds: those specialized for carrying out specific tasks and those specialized for more general tasks involving communication, motion, vision, co-operation, etc. A prototype minimal configuration illustrated in Figure 10.2 contains two robots each with the following MPUs.

TASK-SPECIALIST: a MPU specialized for executing a particular task (i.e., is further specialized in the SES). When help or visual identification of an object is needed in performing this task, it relinquishes control to the ASSISTANCE-REQUESTOR or VISION-EXPERT, respectively.

ASSISTANCE-REQUESTOR: a MPU specialized for the task of requesting help from other robots. When it is activated, it initiates a protocol which tries to make contact with ROBOTS within its range and to engage one which can provide the needed assistance. (Figure 10.3)

ASSISTANCE-OFFEROR: a MPU specialized for the task of dealing with incoming requests for help emitted from ASSISTANCE-REQUESTORs of other ROBOTs. When activated, it decides if help can be offered, and if so, engages in a dialogue with the ASSISTANCE-REQUESTOR of the help-seeking ROBOT and sets up a rendezvous. It relinquishes control to the NAVIGATOR to bring the ROBOT to the requestor's work site.

NAVIGATOR: a MPU specialized for directing the motion subsystem to bring the ROBOT to a given destination. It requests the current motion state from the MOTION component, and sends it new parameters (direction, speed, and time-step) for traveling to the vicinity of the destination. Once there, it directs the MOTION component in physically contacting the object or ROBOT at the destination. The touch channel is used for judging when contact has been made.

VISION-EXPERT: a MPU specialized for the task of visual identification of objects. It relinquishes control to NAVIGATOR to bring the ROBOT to new locations when different viewing distances and perspectives are needed. Once there, it resumes control to accept a visual image and to identify objects by consulting its built-in recognition system (Luh, 1989).

As shown in Figure 10.1, the MPUS are defined as a multiple entity in the system entity structure. As discussed earlier, we can specialize such a multiple entity to generate any number of desired alternatives. Thus, we can have any desired copies of TASK or its variants, ASSISTANCE-REQUESTOR, VISION-EXPERT, etc., as components for a ROBOT's brain depending on the real application requirements. For example, a simple mobile, seeing ROBOT might contain a simple TASK, one VISION-EXPERT, and one NAVIGATOR as its MPU suite.

```
(make-pair forward-models 'assis)

(send assis def-state '(name need-help position))

;;;;;;; respond to command to start request-help protocol

(send assis add-ext-activities
    (list
        (make-activity
            'condition '(and (equal? (state-phase s) 'passive)
                             (equal? (content-port x) 'ready-help)
                        )
            'before-output '(make-content 'port 'respond 'source
                                          (state-name s))
            'action '(passivate-in 'active)
        )
        (make-activity
            'condition '(and (equal? (state-phase s) 'active)
                             (equal? (content-port x) 'start-help)
                        )
            'action '(hold-in 'get-info 0)
        )
    )
)

;;;;start help protocol

(send assis set-int-activities
    (list
        (make-activity
            'condition '(equal? (state-phase s) 'get-info)

            'before-output '(make-content 'port 'info?
                                          'source (state-name s))
            'action '(passivate-in 'wait-for-info)
        )
    )
)

(send assis add-ext-activities
    (list
        (make-activity
            'condition '(and
                            (equal? (content-port x) 'motion-info)
                            (equal? (state-phase s) 'wait-for-info)
                        )
            'action '(begin
                        (set! (state-position s)
                            (car (content-value x)))
                        (hold-in 'active 1)
                     )
        )
    )
)
```

Figure 10.3. Forward model specification of ASSISTANCE-REQUESTOR.

```
(send assis add-int-activities
    (list
        (make-activity
            'condition '(and (equal? (state-phase s) 'active)
                             (state-need-help s))
            'before-output '(make-content 'port 'ask-for-help
                                          'source (state-name s)
                                          'value (state-position s))
            'action '(passivate-in 'wait-for-help)
        )
    )
)

(send assis add-ext-activities
    (list
        (make-activity
            'condition '(and (equal? (content-port x) 'help-offered)
                             (equal? (state-phase s) 'wait-for-help)
                        )
            'before-output '(make-content 'port 'ask-for-help
                                          'source (state-name s)
                                          'value 'ok)
            'action '(passivate-in 'accept-help)
        )
        (make-activity
            'condition '(and (equal? (content-port x) 'help-offered)
                             (equal?  (content-value x) 'ready)
                             (equal? (state-phase s) 'accept-help)
                        )
            'action '(hold-in 'working 10)
            'after-output '(make-content 'port 'finished
                                         'source (state-name s))
        )
    )
)

;;;;;no help needed

(send assis add-int-activities
    (list
        (make-activity
            'condition '(equal? (state-phase s) 'active)
            'before-output '(make-content 'port 'starting)
            'action '(hold-in 'working 100)
            'after-output '(make-content 'port 'finished)
        )
        (make-activity
            'condition '(equal? (state-phase s) 'working)
            'action ' (passivate)
        )
    )
)
```

Figure 10.3. (continued).

The MPUs are developed in the class *forward-models* of DEVS-Scheme as discussed earlier. Inheritance and specialization are used to organize MPUs' capabilities. For example, the generic MPU (Figure 10.4) has a rule for self-identification and a default rule for normal continuation when no other rules applies for an external event.

```
(make-pair forward-models 'mpu)

(send mpu def-state '(name))

;;;;;;identification protocol

(send mpu set-ext-activities
    (list
        (make-activity
            'condition '(and (equal? (state-phase s) 'passive)
                             (equal? (content-port x) 'request-id)
                         )
            'before-output '(make-content 'port 'respond
                                          'source (state-name s))
            'action '(passivate)
        )
    )
)

;;;;;;;;default continuation

(send mpu add-ext-activities
    (list
        (make-activity
            'condition '#t
            'action '(continue)
        )
    )
)
```

Figure 10.4. Forward model specification of general MPU.

The MPU which specializes in visual identification of objects has additional rules for visual data acquisition and identification process. When pruning for a particular MPU, inheritance will cause the two external activities of the general MPU to be appended at the end of the list of existing external activities. Thus, the inheritance mechanism ensures that all specialized MPUs, such as ASSISTANCE-REQUESTOR, NAVIGATOR, etc., also have the ability to identify themselves. In the same way, a generic TASK MPU (Figure 10.5) has rules to request help, to call the NAVIGATOR, to call in

VISION-EXPERT, etc., under specific conditions. Thus, in addition to performing particular task, each task specialist also has ability to communicate and cooperate with other MPUs.

```
;;;;;;; GENERIC TASK ;;;;;;;

(make-pair forward-models 'task)

(send task def-state '(
                ;; call visual
                    position
                    direction
                    object-class
                    object-name
                    object-position
                ;; call navig
                    navig-destination
                    echo-status
                   )
)

(send task set-s (make-state         'interpreter-phase 'test-condition
                                     'ext-activities '()
                                     'int-activities '()
                                     'before-output-buffer '()
                                     'after-output-buffer '()
                                     'action-buffer '()
                                     'sigma 'inf
                                     'phase 'passive
                                     'name 'task
                                 )
)

;;;;;;;identification protocol

(send task set-ext-activities
    (list
        (make-activity
            'condition ' (equal? (content-port x) 'request-id)

            'before-output '(make-content 'port 'respond
                                          'source (state-name s))
            'action '(continue)
        )
    )
)
```

Figure 10.5. Forward model specification of generic TASK.

```
;;;;;;; request-help protocol ;;;;;;;
;;;;send request for help to assis
(send task add-int-activities
    (list
        (make-activity
            'condition '(equal? (state-phase s) 'send-need-help)
            'before-output '(make-content 'channel 'ready-help
                                            ;;to simulate external input
                                            'port 'in)
            'action '(hold-in 'send-start-help 1)
        )
        (make-activity
            'condition '(equal? (state-phase s) 'send-start-help)
            'before-output '(make-content 'channel 'start-help
                                            'port 'in)
            'action '(passivate)
        )
    )
)
;;;;; help-offered & resume working, called by ASSIS or OFFER
(send task add-ext-activities
    (list
        (make-activity
            'condition '(and (equal? (state-phase s) 'passive)
                             (equal? (content-port x) 'start-working)
                        )
            'before-output '(make-content 'port 'respond
                                           'source (state-name s))
            'action '(hold-in 'resume-working 1)
        )
    )
)
;;;;;;; vision protocol ;;;;;;;
;;;;;;; call visual
(send task add-int-activities
    (list
        (make-activity
            'condition '(equal? (state-phase s) 'send-start-visual)

            'before-output '(make-content 'port 'in
                                           'value (list (state-position s)
                                                        (state-direction s))
                                           'channel 'start-visualization)
            'action '(passivate-in 'wait-for-object-data)
        )
    )
)
```

Figure 10.5. (continued).

```
;;;; object-identify result

(send task add-ext-activities
    (list
        (make-activity
            'condition '(and
                         (equal? (state-phase s) 'wait-for-object-data)
                         (equal? (content-port x) 'object-identify)
                         (equal? (state-object-class s)
                                 (car (content-value x))))
            'before-output '(make-content 'port 'respond
                                          'source (state-name s))
            'action '(begin
                       (set! (state-object-position s)
                             (cadr (content-value x)))
                       (set! (state-object-name s)
                             (caddr (content-value x)))
                       (hold-in 'object-expected 0))
        )
        (make-activity
            'condition '(and
                         (equal? (state-phase s) 'wait-for-object-data)
                         (equal? (content-port x) 'object-identify))
            'before-output '(make-content 'port 'respond
                                          'source (state-name s))
            'action '(hold-in 'no-object-expected 1)
        )
    )
)

;;;;;;; navigation protocol ;;;;;;;;

;;;;;;; call navig

(send task add-int-activities
    (list
        (make-activity
            'condition    '(equal? (state-phase s) 'send-start-navig)
            'before-output '(make-content 'port 'in
                                          'value (state-navig-destination s)
                                          'echo-status (state-echo-status s)
                                          'channel 'start-navigation)
            'action '(passivate-in 'moving)
        )
    )
)

;;;; arrived

(send task add-ext-activities
    (list
        (make-activity
            'condition '(and (equal? (state-phase s) 'moving)
                             (equal? (content-port x) 'arrived))
            'before-output '(make-content 'port 'respond
                                          'source (state-name s))
```

Figure 10.5. (continued).

```
                'action '(hold-in 'arrived 0)
            )
        )
    )
    ;;;;; finished ;;;;;
    (send task add-int-activities
        (list
            (make-activity
                'condition '(equal? (state-phase s) 'finished)
                'action '(passivate)
            )
        )
    )
    ;;;;; default ;;;;;
    (send task add-ext-activities
        (list
            (make-activity
                'condition '#t
                'action '(continue)
            )
        )
    )
```

Figure 10.5. (continued).

10.4 Robot-Managed Laboratory Model

A system entity structure for the SPACE-STATION LAB is shown in Figure 10.6. After pruning, the entity structure is transformed into a controlled model containing a SPACE-MANAGER as controller, and OBJECTS as components. Each OBJECT is specialized into ROBOT and EQUIP. Each ROBOT is decomposed into MOTION-SYSTEM, SENSORY-SYSTEM, REFLECTOR-SYSTEM and COGNITION-SYSTEM. The REFLECTOR-SYSTEM is employed to generate an OBJECT's image upon receiving a LIGHT signal. The EQUIP is a generic entity for laboratory equipment which is modeled much the same as the ROBOT. However, EQUIP has no BRAIN and its MOTION, SENSORY and REFLECTOR subsystems are always passive. Note that OBJECTS are also defined as a multiple entity, and with the pruning discussed earlier, we can have any desired number of ROBOTs and EQUIPs in the laboratory.

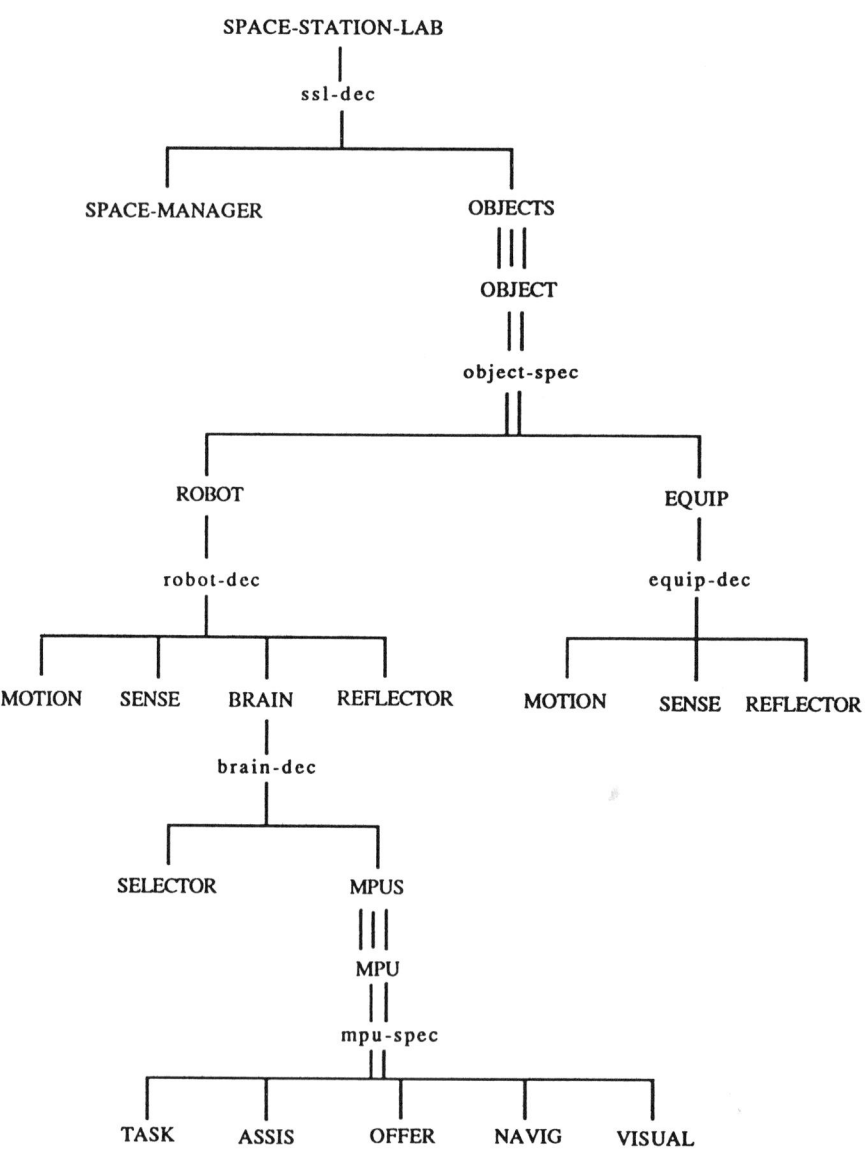

Figure 10.6. System entity structure for SPACE-STATION LAB.

Chapter 11

ENDOMORPHY: MODELS WITHIN INTELLIGENT AGENTS

To achieve realism, models of intelligent agents must be able to represent not only their decision making capabilities but also the models on which such capabilities are based. This rather complex situation is depicted below:

- real world consists of:
  - system being controlled, managed, designed
  - intelligent agent
  - decision making component
  - model of system being controlled

- simulation model consists of:
  - model of system being controlled, etc.
  - model of intelligent agent

– model of decision making component
   – model of model of system being controlled

The point is that in modelling the intelligent agent, the simulation model must represent not only its decision making component, but also the model of the real system this decision making component uses to arrive at its decisions.

As a concrete illustration, consider modelling of air traffic control (Middelton and Zanconato, 1986). The simulation model must contain representations of aircraft being controlled and the radars that detect them as well as of the human air traffic controllers. The latter models contain not only representations of the decision making employed by air traffic controllers but also of the pictures (models) of the world built up from the radar data that the controller uses to generate commands. The latter representation includes the look-ahead use of internal models to answer "what if" questions used in planning such as "what would happen if that aircraft moved there?".

There are three models of the controlled system in such a situation:

- ME = model of system being controlled, external to intelligent agent

- MI = model of system being controlled, internal to intelligent agent

- MMI = model of MI employed in the simulation

Models ME and MMI are components in a simulation model. Let MB be the base model of the system being controlled (the most refined model considered for it (Zeigler, 1976, 1984)). Then the models are related by abstraction, i.e., some form of homomorphic relation, as in Figure 11.1a, where MMI is an abstraction of MI which in turn is an abstraction of MB. The methodological issues concern what form such abstractions take and what should be preserved in the morphic relations.

Before it passes us by, let us note the first manifestation of the concept of endomorphy, introduced in Chapter 1. Our simulation model, SM of the agent and the controlled system now contains a component, MMI (representing the agent's internal model) which is homomorphically related to a second component, ME (representing the controlled system). Therefore SM has an endomorphism from one part of itself to another.

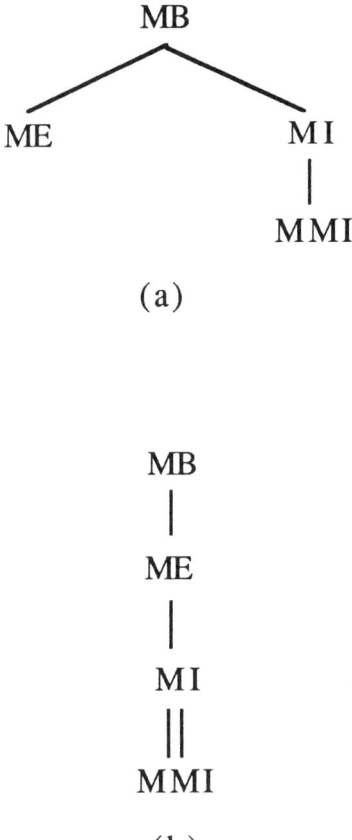

Figure 11.1. Abstraction related models. MB = base model, ME = external model, MI = internal model, MMI = internal model of MI. Single bar (|) denotes homomorphism; double bar (||) is isomorphism.

252   *Object-Oriented Simulation*

We shall discuss a methodology based on a more specialized version of the abstraction relations shown in Figure 11.1b. Here MB is a continuous state model, and ME is a discrete event model derived from it in a manner to be discussed. We shall show how MI, also a discrete event model, is abstracted from ME and how it can actually be used in designs of real robot cognition systems. Each abstraction is governed by an underlying morphism. By transitivity, MI is also a valid abstraction of MB. For simplicity of discussion, we assume that MMI and MI are isomorphic (i.e., that our simulation model of the agent's internal model is identical to it).

11.1 Approach to Endomorphy: Multifacetted Modelling Methodology

In objectives driven modelling methodology (Zeigler, 1984), the modeller's intended use of the model drives the process of model construction. Likewise, the agent's intended use of its internal model is a key consideration. For example, consider designing an intelligent robot to conduct experiments in a laboratory, as in the previous chapter. Each of the distinct types of objects (instruments, materials, etc.) must be represented in the above way. In addition, each object has several different models that relate to different interactions with the robot. These interactions include perception, manipulation, activation, diagnosis, and repair. Each interaction involves a two-way communication involving action and reaction as in:

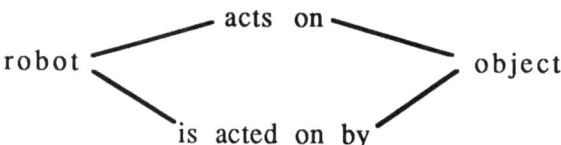

where "acts on" is a member of {perceives, manipulates, activates, diagnoses, repairs} and "is acted on" is a member of {is perceived, is manipulated, is activated, is diagnosed, is repaired}.

Endomorphy: Models within Intelligent Agents

For each type of action, the robot needs a corresponding model of the object to determine the particular action to take. By the simplification just made, a simulation of the robot will use the same model the real robot would use. For each type of reaction, the simulation needs a corresponding model of the object to account for its response. Thus the abstraction hierarchy splits up into several replications associated with each action type as in Figure 11.2.

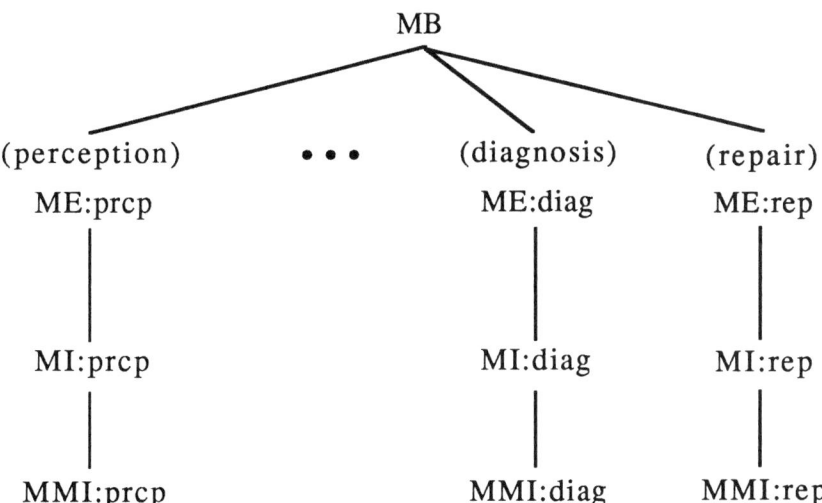

Figure 11.2. Abstraction related models categorized by type of interaction.

Consider the perception interaction: To simulate a robot-managed laboratory, we need a model of each object to account for the perceptual image, ME:prcp, it presents to the perception apparatus of the robot (for example, the visual image it presents to the robot's vision system). Likewise, we need a model of the robot's perceptual decision making apparatus and the the model of the object, MI:prcp, it employs to identify it. By assumption, MMI:prcp, the simulation model of MI:prcp is isomorphic with it.

The same reasoning holds true for each of the other modes of interaction. To illustrate once more, for the case of diagnosis: we need a model ME:diag of the real system being diagnosed which responds to the robots diagnostic probes as the real system would; and we need a model MI:diag (or MMI:diag) of the real system that the robot uses to do the diagnosis.

11.2 Process Laboratory Model

To illustrate the foregoing considerations, we present more detail on the laboratory environment in which we expect our robot models to operate. The laboratory environment is constructed on the basis of object-oriented and hierarchical models of laboratory components within DEVS-Scheme. A more elaborate system entity structure for SPACE STATION LABORATORY decomposes this entity into MATERIALS, INSTRUMENTS, and a WORKSPACE (see Figure 11.3). Each of the latter entities will have one or more classes of objects (models) expressed in DEVS-Scheme to realize it. MATERIALS are specialized by physical state into the classes GAS, LIQUID, and SOLID, and will be further subclassified as needed. ACTIONPLANS consist of four types: TRANSFORMATION (which transforms the state of a single material), COMBINATION (which produces a new material from several input materials, e.g. chemical reactions), TRANSLATION (which changes the physical co-ordinates of a material, e.g. pumping), and SEPARATION (which partitions a material into several components.

UNIT OPERATIONS are carried out with one or more INSTRUMENTS, which may be TRANSPORTERS, TRANSFORMERS (e.g. centrifuges), COMBINERS (e.g. mixers), or SEPARATORS. To illustrate the special nature of space, consider TRANSPORTERS. Since air/liquid interfaces are not permitted under microgravity

Endomorphy: Models within Intelligent Agents

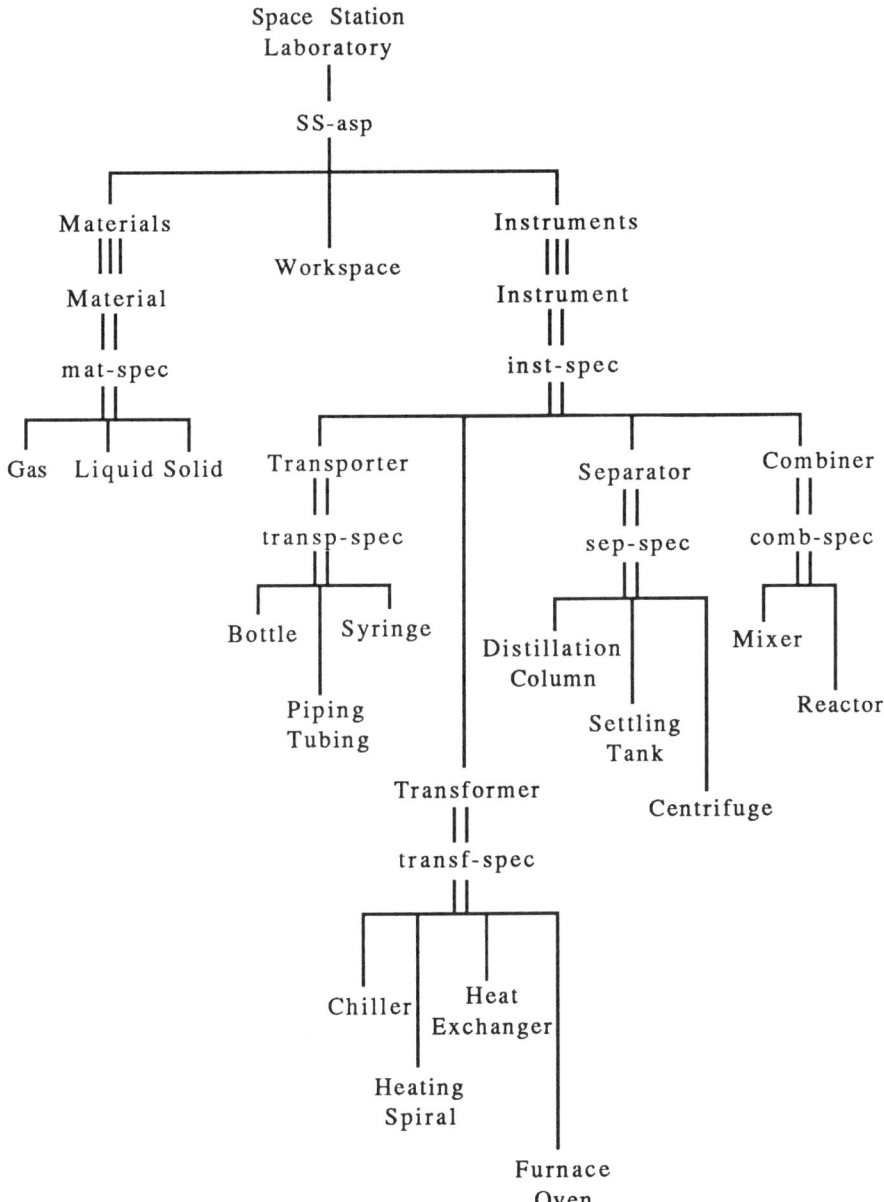

Figure 11.3. SES of Laboratory.

conditions, standard earth-bound containers, such as beakers, cannot be used. A design of a space adapted "beaker" would have an aluminum bottle containing an inflatable bag, which is the actual liquid container; liquid is injected/extracted by means of syringes; air pressure between the outside of the bag and the inside of the bottle wall ensures that the bag remains "full" at all times.

Action plans will be described as sequences of UNIT OPERATIONS with associated MATERIALS and INSTRUMENTS. For example, injecting several liquids into a bottle, placing the bottle in a shaker, and then placing it in a heater is a sequence related to experimentation with chemical reactions.

INSTRUMENTS will have attributes which include operational conditions so that normal and abnormal operating behavior can be studied. UNIT-OPERATIONS will have associated models whose construction will be discussed in the context of the robot Model-Plan Unit (MPU).

To set up a particular laboratory environment, the LABORATORY entity structure is pruned to create a pruned entity structure, and transformed into a laboratory model. Constraints on the possible configurations of components, especially those imposed by microgravity and space environments, are captured by appropriate synthesis and selections rules (Rozenblit and Huang, 1987).

11.3 Robot Models: Designing Model-Plan Units

Recall that the COGNITION-SYSTEM of a robot is a controlled-model consisting of a SELECTOR (controller) and task specialists called MPUs (Model-Plan Units). Each MPU is decomposed into sub-components each containing a decision maker and an internal model oriented toward dealing in a particular interaction with the aspect of the laboratory in which the MPU specializes. For example, the simplified structure used for testing in Figure 11.4, shows a MPU specialized for fluid handling. The MPU is decomposed into an operator for filling and emptying a bottle and a diagnoser for discovering

Endomorphy: Models within Intelligent Agents

the causes of any operational faults. As in the paradigm of Figure 11.2, each sub-component has its model of the bottle. Indeed, there are three such sub-models in the simulation model:

- BTL-E : a model of the bottle external to the mpu, representing the real bottle it operates on (an example of ME)

- BTL-O : an operational model of the bottle used by a controller, CONTRL, to generate its commands and verify the received sensor responses (an example of MMI)

- BTL-D: a classification, or expert-system-like model, employed by the diagnoser inference engine, DIAGN, to determine the probable source of breakdown when it occurs (an example of MMI).

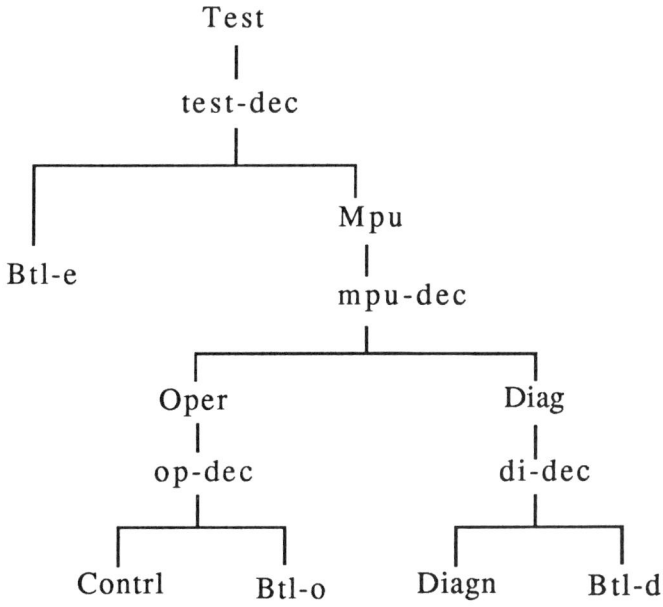

Figure 11.4. SES for testing a bottle handling MPU with operational and diagnostic capabilities.

In this configuration, the external model, BTL-E, is able to respond to both operational commands and diagnostic probes. To agree with Figure 11.2, it should be decomposed into distinct models for each of these aspects. The advantage in folding different submodels into one as we have done, is the straightforward sharing of common parameter and state variables. In contrast, distinct models incur communication overhead required to synchronize such shared variables.

As discussed, the various models of the same system can all be derived from some base model by abstraction processes. Recall that in this methodology, the base model, MB, is assumed to be continuous, while the external, ME, and the internal model, MMI, employed in the simulation are discrete event. Since we have asserted that the internal model, MI, actually employed by an agent is also discrete event, we start with a justification of this possibility.

11.4 DEVS Representation of Dynamic Systems

We return to discuss the methodology associated with Figure 11.2, in which a base model of a system is abstracted into external and internal models for use by an intelligent agent. For concreteness we assume that the system to be controlled is a deterministic continuous system well modelled with conventional differential equation techniques. This constitutes its base model, MB in Figure 11.2. Moreover, we assume that the process receives input stimulations which are piecewise constant time functions (sequences of step functions). With these assumptions we outline an approach to constructing a discrete event abstraction, ME. It serves both as the external model of the controlled system in a simulation, as well as the progenitor of a discrete event model, MI, to be employed in event-based control. (The approach to be discussed however, applies to a much wider class of dynamical systems (Zeigler, 1984). Indeed, the characteristics of a system which permit it to be represented in DEVS formalism throw

Endomorphy: Models within Intelligent Agents

light on the fundamental nature of real systems which are typically viewed as discrete event systems.)

Let Figure 11.5 represent the state space of the continuous base model MB. We assume that its output is a finite set. Indeed, let its output be determined by a conjunction of threshold type sensors discussed above: for each state, some of the sensors will be above threshold, others will not. A finite set of sensors, each with a finite set of states will yield a finite set of combinations of output states (mathematically, the crossproduct of the sensor states). Since the output set is finite, it partitions the state space into a finite set of mutually exclusive blocks as shown in Figure 11.5. Each block is an equivalence class of states, equivalent in the sense that they yield the same output, i.e, the same array of sensor outputs.

We now show how to construct a DEVS model, ME to validly represent MB. Let MB be in some state q residing in some output partition block as shown in Figure 11.5. Let us follow the state trajectory of MB starting from state q. Since by assumption, input to MB is piecewise constant, let the current input value be x. Then there are two next events which can occur: (a) the state reaches, and just crosses, the boundary of the partition block containing q, or (b) the input changes to another constant value, x' before the boundary is reached. The first case (a) is modelled as an internal event in the DEVS model, the second (b) as an external event. We will show that events such as these are sufficient to fully capture the input-output behavior of MB (how its input trajectories are correlated with its output trajectories, not necessarily preserving all of its internal structure).

Let a typical state of the DEVS model, ME be a pair (q, x) which represents the current state of the modelled system, MB, and its current input value. The time advance function $ta(q, x)$ is defined as the smallest time taken to cross the boundary indicated in (a) above. The internal transition function $int(q, x)$ is defined as (q', x), where q' is the state "just over" the boundary, belonging to the newly reached output block, reached by the continuous system in time $ta(q, x)$. The output function $out(q, x)$ is defined as the output of the original system in state q', namely the output value characteristic of the partition block it resides in. Started in state (q, x), the DEVS model will remain in this state for a period $ta(q, x)$, after which it will output the value $out(q, x)$ and transit to state $int(q, x)$ (providing there is no input change in the meantime). The next internal transition from state $(q', x)(int(q', x))$ is determined in exactly the same manner as that from (q, x). Note how this discretely changing behavior parallels that of the original system: at exactly the time points at which the original output changes values, the DEVS model outputs the new value.

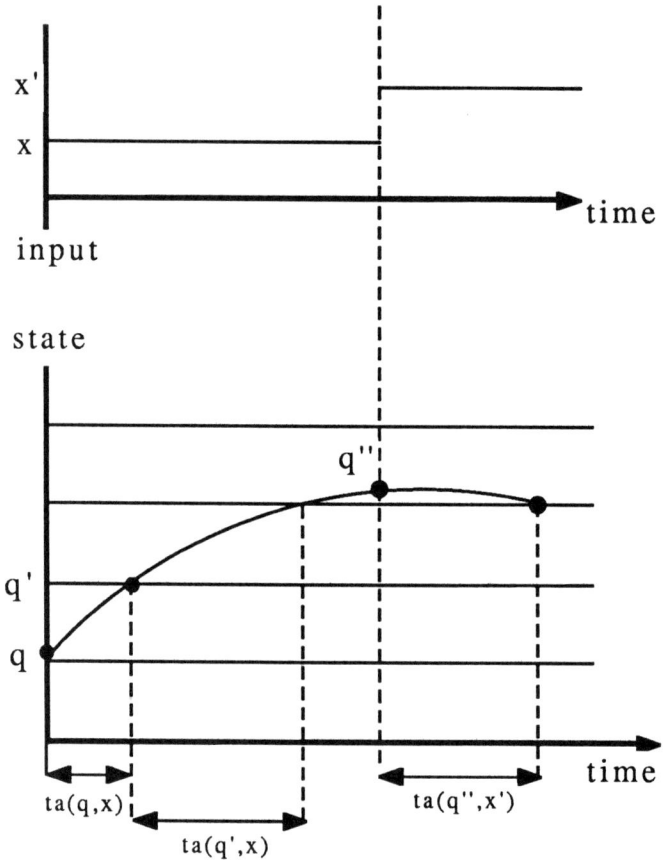

Figure 11.5. State space of continuous base model.

Once more start the DEVS model, ME in a typical state (q, x). However, this time consider case (b), i.e., the input to the system step-changes to a constant value x' after an elapsed time e, where $0 \le e \le ta(q, x)$ (hence, before the next boundary is reached). This change in input is presented to the DEVS model as an external event. Accordingly its external transition function $ext((q, x), e, x')$ is defined as (q'', x') where q'' is the state in which the original system would find itself having received a constant input x for a time e. Note that by assumption, the original system remains in the same output block while the input changes and likewise, the DEVS model does not produce an output at the corresponding external transition. Change in output occurs only when the original system crosses an output partition boundary and is produced, correspondingly, just before the DEVS model makes an internal transition. External events to the DEVS model serve to inform it of input changes, and cause transitions which update its state representation of the original system so as to remain in step with it.

Zeigler (1984) showed that the DEVS model is in a homomorphic relation to the original system called a *system morphism*. In such a morphism, a correspondence between the states of the two systems is preserved under corresponding transition and output operations (recall the discussion in Chapter 1).

It should be clear from the above construction that a discrete event model of a system affords a more efficient simulation than a differential equation model of the same system. The differential equation solution requires a step-by-step generation of successive model states while the discrete event form computes state changes only a event times. To do this the DEVS model employs its time-advance and internal transition function to predict the time and state of next boundary crossing; it also employs its external transition function to update its state when a change in input regime occurs.

11.5 Obtaining the Characteristic Functions of the DEVS Model

We see that to represent validly a continuous system of the type described above by a DEVS model, we need to construct the functions $ta(q,x)$ [time advance function], $int(q,x)$ [internal transition function], and $ext((q,x),e,x)$ [external transition function]. There are several approaches to this depending on our knowledge of the original system:

- The original system is analytically tractable.

  If the original system differential equations have tractable analytic solutions, then we can express the external transition function analytically. Depending on the nature of the output partition, we may also be able to obtain closed form expressions for the time advance function and hence for the internal transition function.

- The original system has a differential equation model which can be simulated in advance.

  If we have a good model of the the system which can be numerically solved, we can obtain tabular approximations of the required functions by performing simulation runs. The number of runs depends on the degree of approximation desired. Such runs yield state trajectories for constant inputs which may then be reduced to the form required by the functions.

- No model exists but we have experimental access to the real system.

  We can obtain data for the required functions by experimenting directly with a real system to be represented by a DEVS model. To do this we outfit the system with its finite state sensors. We can employ the resulting output set as the state space of the model or we may choose a more refined set of sensors to characterize the state. Having chosen the output and state representations, we proceed with experiments just as in the simulation case above.

- The simulation system learns the DEVS model structure on-line.

Rather than simulate a model to build up the required tables in advance, we acquire the information while running. There is a higher level supervisory system which after each event (boundary crossing, or external input change) decides whether enough information exists to schedule the next event (time advance and internal transition known for current state or neighboring state). If so, such scheduling replaces the original step-by-step simulation execution. In this way, all the actually encountered states are learned and the system gradually moves over to discrete event simulation.

The complexity of the problem is greatly reduced if

- the placement of sensors is such that only one (or a small number of) sensor(s) can change state at a time,

- inputs are allowed to change only at boundary crossings, as would be the case for the use of DEVS to event-based control, soon to be discussed,

- the system can only be started in one (or a small number of) state(s),

- the system state trajectories starting from the allowable initial states access a relatively small subset of the possible states, and

- coarse state spaces are employed and probability distributions are used to take care of the resulting uncertainties in timing, transition, and output estimates.

11.6 Robot Fluid Handling MPUs

In microgravity all fluid handling must be done without the creation of liquid-gas interfaces. To transfer fluids, a doubly-contained bottle, in which the inner chamber is under pressure within the outer frame, can be used. The basic idea is that the inner chamber will contain only liquid, never both liquid and gas. When being filled, it expands to adjust to the influx volume; conversely, when emptied, it contracts. Filling and emptying are performed with a syringe injected into the inner chamber. A continuous base model, btl, describes these processes.

As shown in Figure 11.6, we shall construct a DEVS model, BTL-E, to serve as the external model of the bottle in a discrete event simulation. We shall also derive a DEVS model, BTL-O, from BTL-E, which serves as the internal model used by the robot to operate the bottle.

Assume that we have sensors responding to two levels of presure in the outer chamber called HIGH and LOW (Figure 11.7). To fill, a constant flow of liquid enters the inner chamber from the syringe. When the liquid level reaches HIGH, this input is to be turned off. Similarly, to empty the bottle, a constant flow of liquid is extracted from the inner chamber into the syringe. Considering the liquid level l, as the underlying state variable, there are three output partition classes: UNDER-FILLED = $\{l \leq \text{LOW}\}$, BETWEEN = $\{\text{LOW} \leq l \leq \text{HIGH}\}$, and OVER-FILLED = $\{\text{HIGH} \leq l \leq \text{TOP}\}$. Given the fill rate we can easily compute the time required to reach the boundaries of the classes. We consider a change in fill rate (e.g. from 0 to a fixed value) as an external event. Internal transitions occur while the fill rate is constant. Note that the possible transitions are severely constrained when filling since the level can only rise; likewise, when emptying, the level can only fall.

The basic phase transition diagram for BTL-E is shown in Figure 11.8. The transition from EMPTY to FILLING is caused by the external event step-increasing the fill rate from 0 to a non-zero value. The transition from FILLING to OVER-FILLING is an internal event, whose time advance corresponds to the filling time.

Endomorphy: Models within Intelligent Agents

```
btl     = continuous base model
 |
btl-e   = DEVS external model
 |
btl-o   = DEVS internal model
```

Figure 11.6. Abstraction sequence for models of bottle.

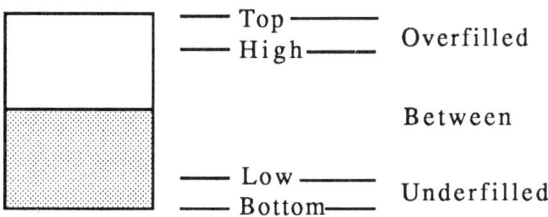

Figure 11.7. Base model of bottle.

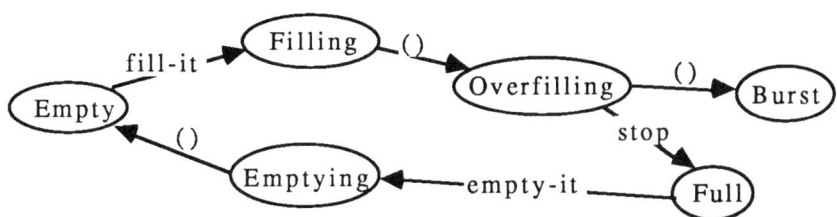

Figure 11.8. Phase transitions for DEVS model of bottle.

The transition from OVER-FILLING to FULL is an external event caused by shutting off the influx. *Mutatis mutandi* for the transitions FULL to EMPTYING to EMPTY.

More formally, each state is a pair (l, x) where l is the liquid level in the inner chamber and x the fill (or empty) rate:

EMPTY $= \{(l,0)|\ l$ in UNDER-FILLED$\}$,

FILLING $= \{(l, x_f)|\ l$ in BETWEEN$\}$,
where x_f a positive constant fill rate,

OVER-FILLING $= \{(l, x_f)|\ l$ in OVER-FILLED$\}$,

FULL $= \{(l,0)|\ l$ in OVER-FILLED$\}$,

BURST $= ($TOP$, x_f)$,

EMPTYING $= \{(l, x_e)|\ l$ in BETWEEN$\}$,
where x_e a negative constant empty rate.

The external event, changing x from 0 to x_f, clearly moves state (LOW,0) in EMPTY to a state (l, x_f) in FILLING. The time-advance for such a state is

$$ta(l, x_f) = \text{time to reach the HIGH boundary.}$$

i.e., the filling time. The internal transition from FILLING to OVER-FILLING occurs when $ta(l, x_f)$ has elapsed. It is of the form

$$int(l, x_f) = (\text{HIGH}, x_f).$$

The external event changing x from x_f to 0 causes the transition from OVER-FILLING to FULL. The transition has the following form:

$$ext((\text{HIGH}, x_f), e, 0) = (l', 0).$$

Endomorphy: Models within Intelligent Agents 267

where l' is a level in OVER-FILLED resulting from the continuation of the non-zero influx during the interval e, before the inflow is turned off.

Assuming no leakage, FULL is a passive state, i.e., $ta(l,0)$ is infinity since the level, l remains fixed.

Note that if the influx is not shut-off, the level continues to increase to reach TOP, where the bottle bursts. This is represented in the internal transition from OVER-FILLING to BURST, i.e.,

$$int(\text{HIGH}, x_f) = (\text{TOP}, x_f).$$

The emptying process follows a somewhat simpler path.

Figure 11.9 shows the part of an implementation of the DEVS model, BTL-E relating to filling. We use the DEVS-Scheme class *forward-models* to conveniently express the transitions and outputs in the form of sensor responses. Also note the use of macros within the rules to compute times and levels needed in the model. Since the macros are evaluated in the environment of the model, they can refer to any of its variables directly. Use of macros in this way helps to make the rule codes more understandable.

The model in Figure 11.9 represents a few of the likely problems that might arise in operation. It allows the syringe tube to be inserted askew, the tube to be blocked and leakage to occur through the inner chamber wall. These anomalous conditions can be imposed on the model by assigning it the appropriate parameter values. The task of the MPU that operates the bottle will be to detect abnormal behavior during operation and diagnose its source as one of these anomalies. We shall return to discuss modelling of anomalous conditions later.

11.7 Table-Models: Deriving Internal Models from External Models

Having derived an external DEVS model of a continuous system, we are in a position to further abstract it for use an an internal model

```
(make-pair forward-models 'btl-e)

(send btl-e def-state '(
        ;structure constants
            nominal-rate
            filled-level      ; = HIGH
            empty-level       ; = LOW
            burst-level       ; = TOP
            tube-angle-range
        ;structure parameters
            tube-angle
            tube-constriction
            leakage-rate
        ; state variables
            level
))

(send btl-e set-s (make-state    'interpreter-phase 'test-condition
                                 'sigma 'inf
                                 'phase 'empty
                                 'nominal-rate 10
                                 'filled-level 100
                                 'empty-level 1
                                 'burst-level  200
                                 'tube-angle-range '(89 91)
                                 'tube-angle 90
                                 'tube-constriction 10
                                 'leakage-rate 0.001
                                 'level 0
))


;;;;;;;;;;;;; macros
(macro fill-rate (lambda(e)
'(let* (
        (angle-effect (* .1 (abs (- (state-tube-angle s) 90))))
        (constriction-effect (* .1 (state-tube-constriction s)))
        (rate (- (state-nominal-rate s) (state-leakage-rate s)
                        angle-effect constriction-effect))
        )
(if (> rate 0) rate .001)
)))
(macro fill-time (lambda(e)
'(let* (
        (fill-amount (- (state-filled-level s)(state-level s)))
        )
 (if (> fill-amount 0)
     (/ fill-amount (fill-rate))
     1
 )
)))
```

Figure 11.9. *Forward-models* specification of BTL-E (partially shown), the external model of the bottle operational behavior for filling.

```
(macro empty->full (lambda(e)   ;to approximate condition along route
'(let* (
        (fill-amount (- (state-filled-level s)(state-level s)))
        )
(/ fill-amount 2)
)))

(macro over-full (lambda(ex)
'(+ (state-level s)( * e (fill-rate)))
))

(macro burst-time (lambda(ex)
'(/ (- (burst-level s) (state-level s)) (fill-rate))
))


;;;;;;;;;;;;;;;;;;;;;;;;;;response to control commands

(send btl-e set-ext-activities
  (list
     (make-activity
         'condition  '(and (equal? (state-phase s) 'empty)
                           (equal? (content-port x) 'command)
                           (equal? (content-value x) 'fill-it)
                      )
         'action     '(begin
                           (hold-in 'filling (fill-time))
                           (set! (state-level s)(empty->full))
                      )
     )
  )
)


(send btl-e set-int-activities
  (list
     (make-activity
         'condition     '(equal? (state-phase s) 'filling)
         'before-output '(make-content 'port 'sense
                                       'value (list 'full-sensor #t))
         'action        '(begin
                             (set! (state-level s) (state-filled-level s))
                             (hold-in 'over-filling (burst-time))
                         )
     )
  )
)

(send btl-e add-ext-activities
  (list
     (make-activity
         'condition  '(and (equal? (state-phase s) 'over-filling)
                           (equal? (content-port x) 'command)
                           (equal? (content-value x) 'stop)
                      )
```

Figure 11.9. (continued).

```
                'action '(begin (set! (state-level s) (over-full))
                                (passivate-in 'full)
                        )
            )
        )
    )

    (send btl-e add-int-activities
        (list
            (make-activity
                'condition  '(equal? (state-phase s) 'over-filling)
                'action     '(begin (set! (state-level s) 0)
                                    (passivate-in 'burst)
                            )
            )
        )
    )
```

Figure 11.9. (continued).

```
(make-pair table-models 'btl-o)
;;;attributes:         state       input    next-state   out       ta   next-ta next-wind
(send btl-o assert '(empty    fill-it  filling      ()        inf  20      3      ))
(send btl-o assert '(filling  ()       over-        full-     20   1000    30     ))
                                       filling      sensor
(send btl-o assert '(over-    ()       burst        ()        1000 inf     ()     ))
                     filling
(send btl-o assert '(over-    stop     full         ()        1000 inf     ()     ))
                     filling
(send btl-o assert '(full     empty-it emptying     ()        inf  20      6      ))
(send btl-o assert '(emptying ()       empty        empty-    20   inf     ()     ))
                                                    sensor
(send btl-o plan  '(empty) 'full)
(send btl-o plan  '(full)  'empty)

(send btl-o add-introspection)
```

Figure 11.10. *Table-models* specification of BTL-O (partially shown), the internal operational model of the bottle used by an MPU.

Endomorphy: Models within Intelligent Agents

within an intelligent agent. For this purpose we introduce yet another means of specifying *atomic-models*, viz., the sub-class *table-models*. Figure 11.10 shows how an internal model of the bottle, BTL-O, is specified as a table model.

The information required to specify the transition and other functions of an atomic model is provided in the form of tuples in a relation, called the *transition table*. For example, the first assertion of such a tuple states that if the current *state* is EMPTY and the *input* is FILL-IT then the *next-state* is FILLING; also the *output* in the current state is nil (*out* = ()) and its time-advance is infinity (*ta* = 'inf). It is convenient also to specify the time-advance of the next-state. This is given in bracketed form, i.e., as an interval in which the time advance is expected to fall. We shall see later that this interval, or *window*, is employed by a suitable event-based controller. The window is given by two fields: *next-ta* gives its lower bound, and *next-wind* gives its width. Thus for example, the minimum time-advance for FILLING is 10 and its window width is 3 (so its maximum is 13). Note that external transitions are distinguished by having a non-null value for the input field, while internal transitions have a null input.

In addition to the inherited variables, *phase* and *sigma* every table-model has state variables for the transition table, a *goal table* (to be discussed later) and a *window*. As with *forward-models*, the internal and external transition, and output functions of *table-models* implement an interpreter of the transition table. Figure 11.11 describes their definitions in pseudo-code.

Consider the approach taken to construct the external and internal operational models such as BTL-E and BTL-O, respectively. We derived BTL-E from the base model, btl, by the abstraction techniques discussed in Section 11.4, which convert continuous models into homomorphically equivalent discrete event models. Having the discrete event model, BTL-E, we can derive the table model, BTL-O suitable for use by a generic controller to be discussed later. BTL-O is intended to be a simplified version of BTL-E which is valid in the region of normal operation of the system. More specifically,

BTL-E and BTL-O are related by an approximate *homomorphism* (Zeigler, 1976), in which corresponding states have the same outputs and transition to corresponding states; only the time advance values of corresponding states may differ. This divergence, however, must lie within definite windows. The window associated with a state, in a table model such as BTL-O, is determined by bracketing the time advance values of all internal transitions associated with the corresponding states in its parent model, BTL-E.

More formally, consider once again an external DEVS model such as BTL-E. Let (q, x) represent a state q which resides on a boundary and an input x which a controller wishes to exert to drive the state to a second boundary. Then the value $ta(q, x)$ returned by the DEVS time-advance function is the time required to reach the desired boundary from state q under input regime x. Since the controller knows the system state only up to its being on the given boundary (i.e., only from the sensor outputs) the time to wait for a sensor response can only be narrowed to lie between the smallest $ta(q, x)$ and the largest $ta(q, x)$ for states q on the boundary. Thus the window given by the DEVS model is the interval:

$$[min\{ta(q,x)\}, max\{ta(q,x)\}],$$

where the min and max operators are taken over states q on the boundary in question.

11.8 Windows in Table-Models: Parameter Sensitivity Analysis

We have stressed that the table model used by the controller is only valid under normal operation. However, what determines normal operation?

To deal with this issue, the discrete event model derived from the continuous base model must include sufficiently many parameters to account for faults in structure and behavior of interest. Such parameters are assigned nominal values corresponding to normal operation in the real system. (Human) knowledge must be used to determine the departures from such nominal values that still constitute normal operation. In a manner akin to parameter sensitivity analysis (Cellier, 1986), the time windows assigned to the table model must bracket the effects on time advance values due to parameter variations within normal limits.

For example, as in Figure 11.9, the model BTL-E contains three, so-called structure parameters, to delineate normal, from abnormal, circumstances. These are tube-angle, tube-constriction, and leakage-rate. Ideally, the syringe tube is perpendicular to the bottle opening, it is not blocked and there is no leakage in the bottle. Abnormal operation may be occasioned by misalignment of the tube, clogging of the influx passage, or leakage through the inner chamber material. Tolerances in the model parameters must reflect answers to such questions as: how much can the tube be bent and still work? how much clogging still permits acceptable flow? How much leakage is characteristic of the wall material? We specify such tolerance ranges as lower and upper extremes. For example, the tube angle tolerance is given as an interval enclosing the nominal value, such as (89 91), while leakage rate tolerance is given by a single upper bound. Let us refer to the set of parameter values characterizing normal operation as the normal box in parameter space. Having specified the normal box, we can use the model to bracket the time advance values.

For example, to determine the window on the time advance for the phase, FILLING, we assign values to structure parameters and note the value returned by the macro fill-time. In the worst case, all points within the normal box defined in parameter space have to be considered. More explicitly, filling the bottle means taking the liquid level from the boundary LOW and the boundary HIGH. Accordingly, the time window required to do the filling is

$$[min\{ta(\text{LOW},p,x_f)\},\ max\{ta(\text{LOW},p,x_f)\}],$$

where the *min* and *max* are taken over all parameter values p in the normal box (the time-advance function is shown as an explicit function of both state q and parameter assignment p).

However, often it is sufficient to examine only the extremal corners of the normal box. For example, in the case of FILLING, the effect of parameter variations is always to increase the filling time. Thus the minimum time is obtained when all parameters are at their nominal settings. The maximum time is obtained by setting the parameters to their extreme values.

We should note the deeper assumptions that justify the foregoing approach to window derivation. These are 1) that the distribution of time advance values associated with the points *within* the normal box lies within an interval (the window) and 2) this interval is not intersected by the distribution of time advance values associated with points *outside* the normal box. A common justification for the separability assumption is that the effect of parameter deviation on time advance is monotonic (increasing or decreasing). Certainly, this approach will not apply where the continuous base model is chaotic (small differences in initial state or parameter values may lead to large difference in state trajectories). While the DEVS external model can still be defined, the time windows needed for control may not exist.

Chapter 12

ENDOMORPHY: MODEL USAGE WITHIN INTELLIGENT AGENTS

We will show how internal models employed by intelligent agents can be well designed in discrete event form. First, we develop the theory of event-based control of systems (Zeigler, 1989). Then we show how to embed such control within robot model cognition systems.

12.1 Event-Based Control

The discrete-event (DEVS) based models of instruments and processes, discussed in the last chapter, can be used to guide robotic manipulation of devices in the execution of typical laboratory procedures such as filling, mixing, heating, etc.

In the conventional approach to control, the controller sends out a command to the data acquisition sub-system to sample the process at regular intervals. When the sampled value returns, it is stored and tested. Depending on the outcome of the test, a corrective control action command is emitted. Testing of the sampled value is performed by determining whether it lies within a window, i.e., a sub-interval of the sensor output range.

The alternate form of control logic, called *event-based*, is described by the DEVS pseudo-coded model in Figure 12.1. Here the model moves through its checkstates in concert with the received input, as long that input arrives in the expected time window. Each checkstate Pi, has associated with it a minimum time, $t_{min}(\text{Pi})$, and a window, $window(\text{Pi})$. The model starts in some assumed checkstate P1 with sigma set to $t_{min}(\text{P1})$. This means that it will stay in phase WAIT P1 for a duration $t_{min}(\text{P1})$. If a sensor input is received during this period, the external transition function recognizes this as an error since it is too early for the expected sensor response. The internal transition function causes the model to transition to phase WINDOW once $t_{min}(\text{P1})$ has elapsed without external interruption. The model is scheduled to stay in this phase for a duration given by $window(\text{P1})$. If a sensor input is received during this period, the external transition function tests it for validity. If the test succeeds, an appropriate control command is issued from a transient phase SEND-COMMAND, checkstate is updated to P2 say, the WAIT phase is entered and the model is scheduled to remain there for the appropriate duration, $t_{min}(\text{P2})$. If the test fails, an error is reported. Finally, the internal transition function causes an error transition if the period, $window(\text{P1})$ has elapsed without receipt of the expected sensor input (any subsequent input would arrive too late).

It should be noted that these forms of control are not mutually exclusive. Indeed, it is straightforward to specify a DEVS model that incorporates both periodic sampling of some sensors and waits for interrupts from the same or other sensors.

Figure 12.2 helps to compare the two forms of logic. The conventional sample data approach requires that the sensor reading be sufficiently precise to be compared with the window requirements. In contrast, event-based logic does not require sensor output precision. Sensors can have threshold-like characteristics. Only two output states are needed although more may be employed. However,

```
initial phase: WAIT
initial sigma: tmin(P1)
initial checkstate: P1


------- external transition -------
when receive value on sensor-port
  case of: phase

    WAIT   : hold-in EARLY 0
    WINDOW: if value = expected (checkstate)
            then hold-in SEND-COMMAND 0
            else hold-in ERROR 0

---------- internal transition -----
case of: phase

    WAIT   : hold-in WINDOW window(checkstate)

    WINDOW: hold-in LATE 0

    SEND-COMMAND: set checkstate = next(checkstate)
                  hold-in WAIT tmin(next(checkstate))

    ERROR: passivate

---------- output function --------
case of: phase

    EARLY: send " input(checkstate) arrived too early" to error-port

    SEND-COMMAND: send  control command(checkstate) to command port

    ERROR:   send " error  in sensor value (checkstate)" to error-port

    LATE: send " input (checkstate) arrived too late" to error-port

    else : send null message
```

Figure 12.1. DEVS description of event-based control.

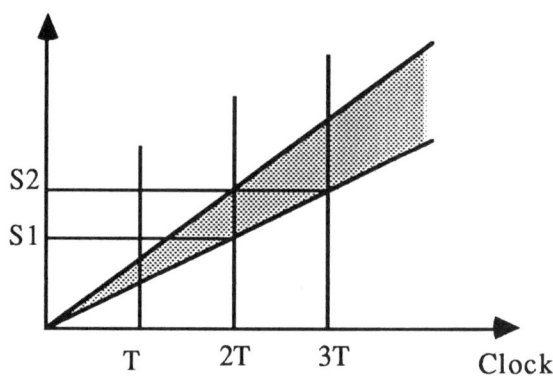

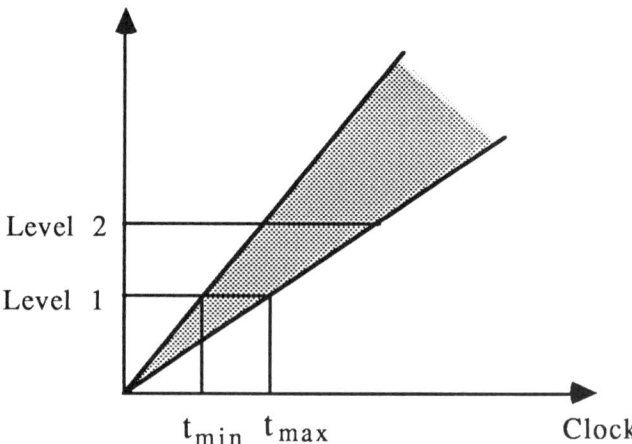

Figure 12.2. Comparison of sampled data and event-based logics.

Endomorphy: Model Usage within Intelligent Agents 279

to generate the time windows the output states of the sensor must be accurately and reliably correlated with values of significant process variables. In an example we shall discuss, a sensor might respond when a container is filled to a fixed level. The level must be known sufficiently accurately for the purposes at hand, but the sensor need only respond reliably when this level has been reached. Since the approach depends on comparison of the clock time with the time windows, the burden of precision is placed on the clock rather than on the sensor.

An essential advantage of event-based control is that the error messages it issues can bear important information for diagnostic purposes. This possibility arises when a DEVS model is developed for the process and used to determine the time windows for sensor feedback. As a side benefit, causes for other than expected responses may also be deduced. We now discuss construction of such models and return to their use for event-based control.

12.2 Using DEVS Models of Processes to Construct Event-Based Control Models

It is quite straightforward to construct DEVS event-based controllers for a system having DEVS model representations. Recall that the system is outfitted with finite-state sensors which divide its state space into a finite output partition. We take the control task as moving the state from an initial position on a given boundary to a succession, possibly cyclic, of boundaries. More concretely, this means we want the system to go through a predetermined sequence of states as reported by sensor readings. Our control logic will, as each boundary crossing is achieved, issue a control action, i.e., send an appropriate input to the system, in order to move it to the next desired boundary. As indicated before, rather than continuously monitor the state trajectory, for each step in the sequence, the controller has a time window in which it expects the appropriate sensor state(s) to change to confirm the expected boundary crossing. The time windows are derived from the DEVS external model of the system. They can be expressed in a table model as we have seen.

Figure 12.3 shows the event-based controller, called *operator*, as consisting of the two components, a *controller*, proper and a DEVS model. As discussed in the last chapter, such an operator is one subcomponent of a MPU (Model-Plan Unit) within a robot cognition model. The controller is a generic engine, similar to an inference engine, which can use the DEVS model, a suitable table model such as BTL-O for the space laboratory bottle. The controller obtains information from the model relating to commands, using its *goal-table*, and expected responses times and windows, using its *state-table*. The controller issues these commands to the controlled device. When proper response signals are received the controller causes the model to advance to the next state corresponding to the one the device is supposed to be in. Thus if the model is valid, and operation proceeds normally, the underlying homomorphic relation is maintained between the model and the controlled device. The controller ceases interacting with the device as soon as any discrepancy occurs in this relationship and calls on a diagnoser to figure out what happened. A planner prepares the *goal-table* of the table model as we shall show.

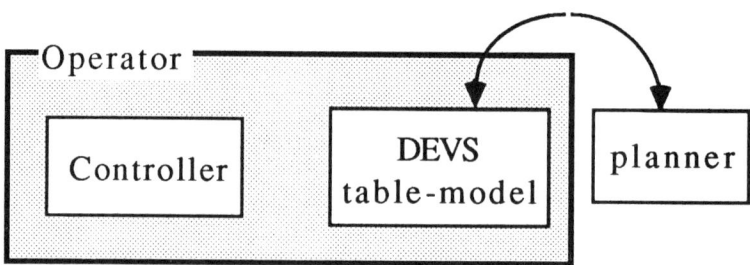

Figure 12.3. Event-based controller design.

A forward model of such a controller is shown in Figure 12.4. The activity rules realize the following algorithm (we use fluid handling as a running example in which the controller uses the bottle model BTL-O):

1. ascertain the phase of the model, which corresponds to the current state of the device, and the goal, i.e., the model phase (and corresponding device state) to be achieved,
   Example: for an empty bottle, the initial model phase is EMPTY. To fill the bottle, the desired goal phase is FULL.

2. passivate the model in the given initial phase,

3. if the current model phase is the goal phase, report success and relinquish control,

4. interrogate the model to find out what input it requires to bring it to the next phase along the goal trajectory and apply that input to it (thus bringing it to the next phase using its external transition function). Get from the model this next phase, its time advance window, and output,
   Example: starting from EMPTY, the input required is FILL-IT, the next phase is FILLING, and the time advance window brackets the normal range of times to fill the bottle. The output expected is from FULL-SENSOR.

5. if required input is a stop command, then issue this command and return to step 3,
   Example: after the filling, the influx must be shut off. This is done without verification from the device,

6. passivate the model in its current phase and issue the input command (obtained from the model in step 4) to the device,
   Example: passivate the model in FILLING and send the command FILL-IT to the bottle to start the fluid inflow.

7. as detailed in the description of event-based control (Section 12.1), wait for a verification response from the device. Issue

appropriate error messages and disengage if the response is too early, or too late, or does not match the model output (according to the information obtained in step 4), and

8. if the device response is valid, cause the model to execute its internal transition function and get the resulting phase from it and return to step 3.

   Example: if a signal from FULL-SENSOR is received in the required time window, then cause the model to carry out its internal transition to OVER-FILLED, thus keeping it in state correspondence with the device. Return to step 3 to test whether the goal phase has been achieved (it hasn't).

```
(make-pair forward-models 'contrl)
(send contrl def-state '(goal initial-phase outport window model-phase))
(send contrl set-s (make-state    'interpreter-phase 'test-condition
                                  'ext-activities '()
                                  'int-activities '()
                                  'sigma 'inf
                                  'phase 'passive
                                  'goal 'full
                                  'initial-phase 'empty
                   )
)

(send contrl set-ext-activities
  (list
    (make-activity
       'condition    '(and (equal? (state-phase s) 'passive)
                           (equal? (content-port x) 'start))
       'action       '(hold-in 'start 0)
    )
))
(send contrl set-int-activities
  (list
    (make-activity
       'condition '(equal? (state-phase s) 'start)
       'before-output '(make-content 'port '%obey% 'value
                         '(passivate-in ',(state-initial-phase s)))
       'action '(begin
                  (set! (state-model-phase s)(state-initial-phase s))
                  (hold-in 'check 0))
    )
)
```

Figure 12.4. Forward-models specification of CONTRL, the generic operational control engine which interrogates an internal model such as BTL-O to formulate control commands.

```
        (make-activity
            'condition   '(and (equal? (state-phase s) 'check)
                               (equal?  (state-goal s)(state-model-phase s))
                         )
            'before-output '(make-content 'port 'finished)
            'action '(passivate)
        )
        (make-activity
            'condition '(equal? (state-phase s) 'check)
            'before-output
                           '(make-content 'port '%interrogate%
                                          'value '(list (input? ',(state-goal s))
                                                        (time-advance?)
                                                        (output?)
                                                        (get-sv 'window)
                                                        (get-sv 'phase) ))
            'action '(passivate-in 'wait-for-info)
        )
))

(send contrl add-ext-activities
  (list
    (make-activity
        'condition '(and (equal? (state-phase s) 'wait-for-info)
                         (equal? (content-port x) '%report%)
                         (equal? (car (content-value x)) 'stop))
        'before-output '(make-content 'port '%obey%
                                      'value '(passivate))
        'action       '(begin
                         (set! (state-model-phase s)
                               (car (cddddr (content-value x))))
                         (hold-in 'check 1))
        'after-output '(make-content 'port 'command
                                     'value (car (content-value x)))
    )              ;;needed here to allow external model to complete
    (make-activity
        'condition '(and (equal? (state-phase s) 'wait-for-info)
                         (equal? (content-port x) '%report%))
        'before-output '(list
                          (make-content 'port '%obey%
                                        'value '(set-sv 'sigma 'inf))
                          (make-content 'port 'command
                                        'value (car (content-value x)))
                        )
        'action    '(begin
                      (set! (state-outport s)
                            (content-port (caddr (content-value x))))
                      (set! (state-window s) (cadddr (content-value x)))
                      (set! (state-model-phase s)
                            (car (cddddr (content-value x))))
                      (hold-in 'wait-for-sensor (cadr (content-value x)))
                    )
    )
```

Figure 12.4. (continued).

```
            (make-activity
                'condition    '(equal? (state-phase s) 'wait-for-sensor)
                'before-output '(make-content 'port 'error
                                      'value (list (content-port x) 'too-early
                                                      (state-model-phase s)))
                'action '(passivate-in 'error)
            )
))

(send contrl add-int-activities
   (list
        (make-activity
            'condition '(equal? (state-phase s) 'wait-for-sensor)
            'action '(hold-in 'window (state-window s))
        )
))

(send contrl add-ext-activities
   (list
        (make-activity
            'condition    ' (and (equal? (state-phase s) 'window)
                                 (equal? (content-port x) 'sense)
                                 (equal? (state-outport s)
                                           (car (content-value x))))
            'before-output '(make-content 'port '%interrogate% 'value
                                      '(begin (int-transition)(get-sv 'phase)))

            'action   '(passivate-in 'wait-for-next-phase)
        )
        (make-activity
            'condition    '(and (equal? (state-phase s) 'wait-for-next-phase)
                                (equal? (content-port x) '%report%))
            'action       '(begin (set! (state-model-phase s)
                                         (content-value x))
                                  (hold-in 'check 0))
        )
        (make-activity
            'condition '(and (equal? (state-phase s) 'window)
                             (equal? (content-port x) 'sense))
            'before-output '(make-content 'port 'error
                                  'value (list 'wrong-sensor
                                                 (car (content-value x))))
            'action '(passivate-in 'error)
        )
))

(send contrl add-int-activities
   (list
        (make-activity
            'condition    '(equal? (state-phase s) 'window)
            'before-output '(make-content 'port 'error
                                  'value (list  (state-outport s)
                                                 'too-late
                                                 (state-model-phase s)))
            'action '(passivate-in 'error)
        )
))
```

Figure 12.4. (continued).

12.3 Introspection and Super-Simulation

In the implementation of Figure 12.4, the controller acts as a kind of super-user (really a "super-simulator") of the table model. Normally, only a simulator can query or direct its assigned atomic model to execute the latter's transition and other functions during the course of simulation. However, we can configure any atomic model (or subclass instance) to be controllable in this manner by other components within the simulation model. Perhaps, somewhat suggestively, we call the ability to be interrogated and super-simulated — *introspection*. The definition for the method, *add-introspection*, which the does the necessary modification is shown in Figure 12.5. This method adds two input ports, '%interrogate% and '%obey%, and one output port, '%report% to an atomic model. The model's external transition function is modified so that it reacts to a message on port '%obey% by evaluating its content-value in the model's environment. Definition and behavior of *add-introspection* is similar to experimental frame instrumentation discussed in Chapter 6.

For example, suppose we add introspection capability to BTL-O:

(send btl-o add-introspection)

Now we can cause it to evaluate its own int-transition method, as in:

(send btl-o inject '%obey% '(int-transition))

Note that the *content-value* sent to BTL-O is '(int-transition), i.e, just the name of the method to apply the internal transition function and its arguments (none in this case). This is sufficient, since within the environment of an object, a method is really a procedure bound to the method name.

Using the '%obey% input port, any other component model can direct the introspecting model to execute any expression which evaluates in the latter's environment. For example, it can be ordered to go through a sequence of internal transitions until a phase 'goal is reached as in:

```
(define-method (atomic-models add-introspection)()
(def-state '(name %temp-phase% %temp-sigma% %result%))
(set-sv 'name name)
(let (
    (old-int int-transfn)
    (old-ext ext-transfn)
    (old-out outputfn)
    )
(set! int-transfn (lambda(s)
   (if (equal? (state-phase s) '%report%)
      (hold-in (state-%temp-phase% s) (state-%temp-sigma% s))
      (old-int s)
   )))
(set! ext-transfn (lambda (s e x)
   (case (content-port x)
      ('%interrogate% (interrogate s e x))
      ('%obey% (obey s e x))
      (else (old-ext s e x))
   )))
(set! outputfn (lambda(s)
(if (equal? (state-phase s) '%report%)
   (make-content 'port '%report% 'value (state-%result% s))
   (old-out s)
   )))
))


(define (interrogate s e x)
(let* (
    (request (content-value x))
    (model (eval (state-name s) user-initial-environment))
    (result (eval request model))
    )
(eval '(begin
    (set-sv '%result% ,result)
    (set-sv '%temp-sigma% (get-sv 'sigma))
    (set-sv '%temp-phase% (get-sv 'phase))
    (hold-in '%report% 0)
    ) model)
))


(define (obey s e x)
(let (
    (request (content-value x))
    (model (eval (state-name s) user-initial-environment))
    )
(eval request model)
(continue)
))
```

Figure 12.5. The method *add-introspection*.

```
(define order '(let loop ()
  (cond
    ((equal? (state-phase s) 'goal) (passivate))
    (else (int-transition) (loop)) )))
(send btl-o inject '%obey% order)
```

Sending a message *content* to the '%interrogate% port similarly causes an evaluation of its *content-value*. Now however, the result of the evaluation is immediately put out on port '%report% where it can be routed to an input port of the interrogator or other components. Thus in several phases, the controller of Figure 12.4 sends an output to port '%interrogate%, then passivates in a waiting phase. When an input is received on its input port '%report%, it knows that this is the answer to its interrogation.

As noted earlier in contrasting the modular systems ,and object-oriented, paradigms (Chapter 1), the *send-wait-receive* protocol implementable through introspection, being entirely modular and time-based, differs substantially from the *send-receive* protocol of the underlying SCOOPS.

12.4 Table-Models: Command Sequence Planning

A table model, such as BTL-O, used as an internal model coupled to the controller, must have a method, *input?*, which returns the next input required to reach a goal from the current state. Another method, *plan*, is required to figure out what this input should be. *Table-models* facilitates writing the *plan* method. All the information needed by such a planner is given explicitly in the *state-table*, rather than implicitly for that would necessitate considerable analysis to elicit. The planner produces a time optimal path from an initial state to a goal state. The result is stored as a relation, the *goal-table*, as in Figure 12.6. This *goal-table* is used by the method, *input?*, mentioned before to determine the input required for continuing toward the goal.

state	goal	input	time-to-reach-goal
empty	full	fill-it	0
filling	full	()	20
over-filled	full	stop	20
full	empty	emtpy-it	0
emptying	empty	()	20

Figure 11.6. *Goal-table* of BTL-O.

The planner works by developing paths backward from the goal until the given initial states (possible starting states of the controlled system) are reached. As each each state is encountered, an entry is made in the *goal table* for it with the *time-to-reach-goal* entered. If a state is encountered again, with a smaller *time-to-reach-goal*, a new entry replaces the existing one; otherwise no change is made. When such a replacement occurs any predecessors of the state in the *goal-table* must have their *time-to-reach-goal* downward adjusted accordingly. This is a form of dynamic programming (Nilsson, 1981) based on the principle that every subpath of an optimal path must itself be optimal. Thus we need to keep track only of the input required to continue an optimal path from any state, not the whole path itself.

For example, in the model of Figure 12.7, we have added the possibility to fill the bottle faster in two stages. This can be done by placing a new boundary between LOW and HIGH and using a higher fill rate. Working backwards from phase full, the planner would first build up the *goal-table* as in Figure 12.6 since the corresponding path is shorter in terms of states. However, branching backwards from OVER-FILLED to FAST-FILLING2, it eventually reaches EMPTY through a quicker route and revises the entry of EMPTY so that the associated input is now FAST-FILL rather than FILL-IT. Since discrete event models embody timing it is natural to base optimal sequencing on predicted execution time. However with appropriate augmentation, other criteria, such as cost, could be included as a basis for planning.

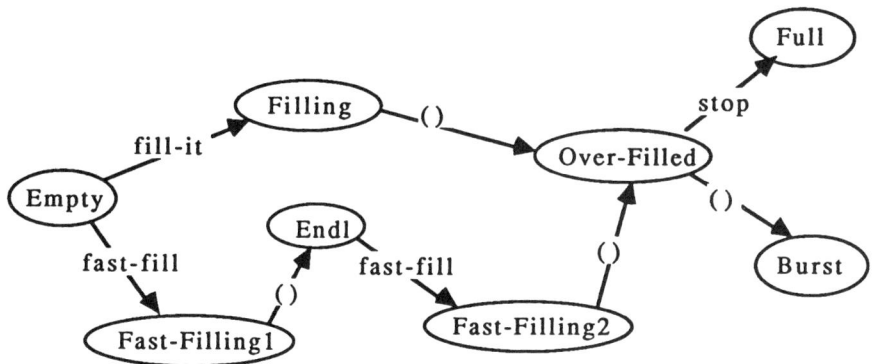

Figure 12.7. Bottle model with two rates of filling.

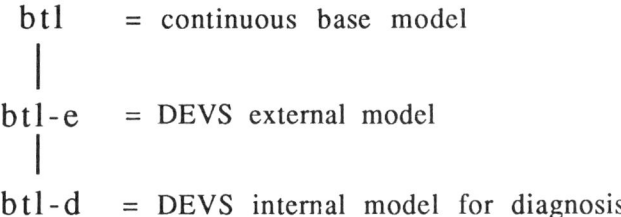

Figure 12.8. Abstraction models of bottle in diagnostic frame.

12.5 Breakdown Diagnosis

Recall that the operator and diagnoser subcomponents of an MPU are coupled so that once the controller has detected a sensor response discrepancy, the diagnoser is activated. Data associated with the discrepancy, such as the phase in which it occurred, and its timing (too early, too late), are also passed on to the diagnoser. From such data, as well as information it can gather from auxiliary sensors, the diagnoser tries to discover the fault that occurred. This diagnosis is passed to a unit that tries to restore the system to normal operation. For example, if the verification from the FULL sensor was too late during FILLING, the diagnoser might determine that the tube was most likely misaligned and the repair unit would then try to correct the alignment. We shall not discuss modeling of the repair process here.

As in the model abstraction paradigm of the previous chapter, there are three related models. Figure 12.8 illustrates for the case of the bottle where the models are the base model, btl, the external model of the bottle which reacts to diagnosis probes, BTL-E, and the internal model used by the diagnoser, BTL-D. Recall that the external model, BTL-E, serves for both operations and diagnostics and is a homomorphic abstraction of the base model, btl. However, the homomorphism must relate to the diagnostic sensor responses — this is a different experimental frame than the one associated with operational behavior. That is, the requirement for validity of BTL-E in the diagnostic frame is that it replicate the responses produced in the base model due to sensor interrogations. Some of the activities modelling diagnostic sensor response of BTL-E are shown in Figure 12.9.

There is much discussion in the literature on the design of diagnostic expert systems. It is not germane to touch on this discussion here except to place such design into our discussion of model abstraction. The diagnostic model, for example, BTL-D, employed by the diagnoser inference engine, is derived from the external model, e.g., BTL-E, but not in a homomorphic fashion. Indeed, the diagnosis is an inversion process going from external effects to underlying

Endomorphy: Model Usage within Intelligent Agents 291

causes. The validity criterion for the diagnostic model is thus the following: the occurrence of every fault representable in the external model, e.g., BTL-E, should be identifiable by the diagnostic model, e.g. BTL-D, under the operation of the diagnosing inference engine. Simulation of the external model, BTL-E can be employed to derive a cause-to-symptom table, which is then inverted in the form of rules for going from symptom to cause.

```
(send btl-e add-ext-activities
  (list
      (make-activity
          'condition   '(equal? (content-port x) 'read-back-up-sensor)
          'action      '  (hold-in 'reading-back-up-sensor 1)
          'after-output '(make-content 'port 'sense
                          'value (list 'back-up-sensor
                            (cond
                              ((> (state-level s)
                                  (state-filled-level s)) 'full)
                              ((< (state-level s)
                                  (state-empty-level s)) 'empty)
                              (else 'in-between)
                              )))
                          )
      )
      (make-activity
          'condition   '(equal? (content-port x) 'read-tube-sensor)
          'action      '(hold-in 'reading-tube-sensor 10)
          'after-output '(make-content 'port 'sense
                          'value (list 'tube-sensor
                            (if
                              (or
                                (> (state-tube-angle s)
                                   (cadr (state-tube-angle-range s)))
                                (< (state-tube-angle s)
                                   (car (state-tube-angle-range s)))
                              ) 'off-angle 'normal)))
      )
      (make-activity
          'condition   '(equal? (content-port x) 'visual-inspect)
          'action      '(hold-in 'visual-inspection 100)
          'after-output '(make-content 'port 'sense
                          'value (list 'vision
                            (list (state-level s)
                                  (state-tube-angle s)
                                  (state-tube-constriction s))))
      )
  ))
```

Figure 12.9. Specification of external model BTL-E activities relating to response to sensor interrogations (partial).

The diagnostic model of the bottle, BTL-D, is implemented in the *forward-models* class in DEVS-Scheme. Some of the diagnostic rules, expressed as activities, are given in Figure 12.10.

The rules of BTL-D are all conditioned upon its being in phase RUN. It is placed in this phase by the inference engine, DIAGN, shown in Figure 12.11. DIAGN implements a basic forward chaining approach in which first all diagnostic sensor readings are requested, and then the diagnostic model is exercised until a diagnosis is made or all rules are fired without a conclusion being reached. Given the availability of the underlying Scheme language, much more sophisticated strategies can be implemented in DEVS-Scheme. However, it is beyond our scope to discuss them here (Sarjoughian, 1989).

12.6 Testing MPU Designs

The proof of the pudding is in the taste. By issuing the *transform* command, an entity structure such as in Figure 11.4, can be transformed into a simulatable test mockup. In this mockup, we can set the external model, BTL-E into an initial state and parameter setting which represents either a normal or abnormal condition. We set the internal operational model, BTL-O, into a corresponding phase, assign a goal phase to the control model, CONTRL, and start simulation. If BTL-E is started in a normal condition, the simulation should run to the point where CONTRL achieves its goal. If started in an abnormal condition, CONTRL should detect this at some point as a window violation and activate the diagnoser which should eventually conclude the responsible fault in agreement with the one introduced at the start of simulation.

12.7 Summary: Methodology for Event-Based Control

The theoretical basis of event-based control has now been developed. A continuous model of a device is developed and abstracted into a

Endomorphy: Model Usage within Intelligent Agents 293

```
(make-pair forward-models 'btl-d)

(send btl-d def-state '(indicator back-up-sensor tube-sensor vision))

(send btl-d set-s (make-state    'interpreter-phase 'test-condition
                                 'ext-activities '()
                                 'int-activities '()
                                 'sigma 'inf
                                 'phase 'passive
                     )
)

(send btl-d add-introspection)
(send btl-d add-int-activities
   (list
      (make-activity
         'condition    '(and (equal? (state-phase s) 'run)
                             (not (equal? (state-back-up-sensor s) 'full))
                             (equal? (car (state-indicator s))
                                     'full-sensor))
         'before-output '(make-content 'port 'diagnosis
                                       'value '(full-sensor is bad))
         'action       '(passivate)
      )
      (make-activity
         'condition    '(and (equal? (state-phase s) 'run)
                             (let* (
                                    (triple (state-vision s))
                                    (tube-angle (cadr triple))
                                   )
                               (or (> tube-angle 91)
                                   (< tube-angle 89)
                               )))
         'before-output '(make-content 'port 'diagnosis
                                       'value '(tube is off-angle))
         'action       '(passivate)
      )
      (make-activity
         'condition    '(and (equal? (state-phase s) 'run)
                             (let* (
                                    (vision-triple (state-vision s))
                                    (level (car vision-triple))
                                    (indicator-triple (state-indicator s))
                                    (sensor (car indicator-triple))
                                    (timing (cadr indicator-triple))
                                    (phase (caddr indicator-triple))
                                   )
                               (and
                                  (equal? sensor 'full-sensor)
                                  (equal? timing 'too-late)
                                  (equal? phase 'filling)
                                  (> level 10)
                               )))
```

Figure 12.10. *Forward-models* specification of BTL-D, the model of the bottle used by the diagnoser (partially shown).

```
                'before-output '(make-content 'port 'diagnosis
                                              'value '(tube is constricted or
                                                       tube is off-angle or
                                                       bottle is leaky))
                'action        '(passivate)
        )
        (make-activity
                'condition  '(and (equal? (state-phase s) 'run)
                                  (let* (
                                         (vision-triple (state-vision s))
                                         (level (car vision-triple))
                                         (indicator-triple (state-indicator s))
                                         (sensor (car indicator-triple))
                                         (timing (cadr indicator-triple))
                                         (phase (caddr indicator-triple))
                                         )
                                    (and
                                         (equal? sensor 'empty-sensor)
                                         (equal? timing 'too-early)
                                         (equal? phase 'emptying)
                                         (< level 1)
                                  )))
                'before-output '(make-content 'port 'diagnosis
                                              'value '(bottle is leaky))
                'action        '(passivate)
        )
))
```

Figure 12.10. (continued).

Endomorphy: Model Usage within Intelligent Agents 295

```
(make-pair forward-models 'diagn)

(send diagn def-state '(sensor-response-pairs))

(send diagn set-s (make-state    'interpreter-phase 'test-condition
                                 'ext-activities '()
                                 'int-activities '()
                                 'sigma 'inf
                                 'phase 'passive
                                 'sensor-response-pairs '()
                  )
)

(send diagn set-ext-activities
  (list
    (make-activity
        'condition    '(and (equal? (state-phase s) 'passive)
                            (equal? (content-port x) 'start))
        'action       '(begin
                         (set! (state-sensor-response-pairs s)
                              (list (list 'indicator (content-value x))))
                         ;;create pair: (indicator (sensor timing phase))
                         ;;make it the only element on s-r-pairs
                         ;; comes from contrl
                         (hold-in 'start 1))
     )
))

(send diagn set-int-activities
  (list
    (make-activity
        'condition    '(equal? (state-phase s) 'start)
        'before-output '(make-content 'port 'read-sensors)
        'action       '(passivate-in 'wait-for-sensors)
     )
))

(send diagn add-ext-activities
  (list
    (make-activity
        'condition    '(and (equal? (state-phase s) 'wait-for-sensors)
                            (equal? (content-port x) 'done))
        'before-output '(make-content 'port '%obey% 'value
                            `(set-pairs ',(state-sensor-response-pairs s)))
        'action '(hold-in 'start-diagnosis 1)
     )
    (make-activity
        'condition    '(and (equal? (state-phase s) 'wait-for-sensors)
                            (equal? (content-port x) 'sense))
        'action       '(set! (state-sensor-response-pairs s)
                          (cons (content-value x)
                               (state-sensor-response-pairs s)))
     )
))
```

Figure 12.11. *Forward-models* specification of DIAGN, a diagnostic inference engine.

```
(send diagn add-int-activities
  (list
    (make-activity
       'condition '(equal? (state-phase s) 'start-diagnosis)
       'before-output (make-content 'port '%obey% 'value
                                    '(hold-in 'run 1))
       'action '(hold-in 'wait-for-diagnosis 100)
    )
))

(send diagn add-ext-activities
  (list
    (make-activity
       'condition   '(and (equal? (state-phase s) 'wait-for-diagnosis)
                          (equal? (content-port x) 'diagnosis))
       'before-output '(make-content 'port 'out
                                     'value  (content-value x))
       'action      '(passivate)
    )                           ;;wait for first true cause
))

(send diagn add-int-activities
  (list
    (make-activity
       'condition '(equal? (state-phase s) 'wait-for-diagnosis)
       'before-output '(make-content 'port 'out 'value 'no-diagnosis)
       'action        '(passivate)
    )
))
```

Figure 12.11. (continued).

DEVS model. The abstraction is based on homomorphic preservation of the device input-output behavior where inputs are operation commands to the device and outputs are responses of finite-state sensors attached to the device to observe its state. Selection of controls and sensors must reflect the operation objectives; the resultant abstraction is tuned to this experimental frame (choice of inputs (commands) and outputs (sensors)). The DEVS model abstracts incremental micro-state transitions from the continuous model and replaces them by nominal times taken for macro-state transitions (which correspond to crossing of sensor thresholds). For each such transition, there is also a window which brackets the nominal time. This window is essential since it allows for normal deviations in the operation of the device; a device transition time falling outside the window means the device is faulty.

We have seen how a generic controller can simulate and interrogate such a DEVS model to issue commands needed to achieve given goals. Note that endomorphy arises once again since simulation of such event-based control incorporates a simulation within itself. The relative simplicity of the DEVS abstraction facilitates planning, i.e., developing plans (*goal-tables*) for achieving goals by analyzing the model transition structure.

Chapter 13

MODEL BASE MANAGEMENT AND ENDOMORPHIC SYSTEMS

An autonomous, intelligent system needs not just one, but many, models on which to base its operation, diagnosis, repair, planning, etc. These models differ in level of abstraction and in formalism. Concepts and tools are need to organize the models into a coherent whole. An organized model base helps the agent to cope with the multiplicity of objects and situations in its environment and to link its high level plans with its actual low level actions. This chapter deals with the management of model bases using system entity structure concepts. We show how the pruning process supports reuse of previously pruned structures. Concepts of context-sensitive pruning and partitioned entity structure bases are introduced to promote model base coherence and evolvability. The chapter closes with a discussion of research issues that arise when such model bases include models of the agent itself.

13.1 Reuse of Pruned Entity Structures

So far we have discussed how to create a *system entity structure (SES)* whose prunings transform into a family of models. The power to generate a large collection of models brings with it the need to archive the collection for *reuse*. Think of the SES as a powerful printing press. If we don't properly catalogue the books rolling of the press, we will have trouble finding existing books that meet our current needs. Then we'll be in the wasteful position of having to reproduce them from scratch. In fact, the library analogy understates the problem. It fails to capture the hierarchical nature of models, i.e., the fact that models once catalogued can be employed as components in new models, which themselves should be catalogued for reuse.

The situation is described in Figure 13.1. A given SES can be pruned to create a number of *pruned entity structures (PES)* which are in turn transformed into simulation models. The SES is our "printing press" and the collection of PES's the "books" to be archived. Recall that a PES uniquely represents a model in that the PES contains all the information needed by the transformation process to synthesize it. We assume that the model base is complete in the sense that it contains models for all the atomic entities referenced in the PES's.

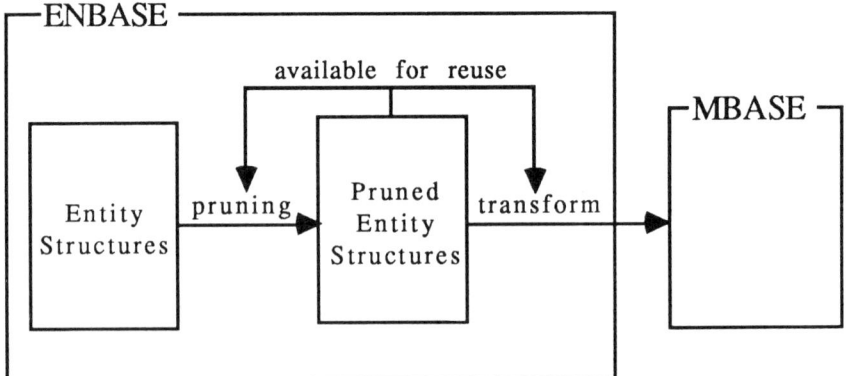

Figure 13.1. Reusability of pruned entity structures.

13.1.1 Basic Cataloguing

The basic requirements of cataloguing are simple to state: a PES should be catalogued in such a way as to facilitate subsequent recognition and retrieval.

Figure 13.2a depicts how these basic requirements are satisfied in the current version of DEVS-Scheme (this is an area in need of further research). Suppose that we have an entity structure E:A with root A. Pruning E:A we can start at any sub-entity B. This normally results in a PES with root B. If the user desires to store this PES, it will be saved under the name P:B@V (i.e., in a file b@v.p as in Section 7.3), where v is a symbolic extension that the user supplies. Extensions can be used to identify different prunings all having the same root and therefore representing different models of the same entity. Employing a time-stamp extension would be reminiscent of software version control. However, in the present context, the extension should summarize the distinguishing characteristics of the PES. In an example related to Section 8.3, P:A@BR-SIP suggests an architecture in which the *kernel-models* subclass has been specified as *broadcast-models* and the kernel is a SIP processor; P:A@HY-PEL might be another pruning of e:a characterized by a hypercube architecture with a PEL processor.

As implied, there is an exception: if B has specializations, the root of the resulting PES will have a name that reflects the sequence of specialized entities selected, with B the last in the series (Section 9.2). However, the archived name is still of the form P:B@V since the result is still a version of B. Note that V can be used to summarize the series if desired. For example, a PES with root, BTL_TASK_MPU might be named P:MPU@BTL to facilitate its retrieval when versions of MPU are being sought.

In a frequently occurring special case, we may save several prunings P:A@V1, P:A@V2, P:A@V3,... of E:A starting from the root A. Subsequently, to display the existing versions of A we can use the query, (*show-versions-of* 'a); the set of versions of A is returned by (*get-versions-of* 'a). To reconstruct a model from version P:A@Vi,

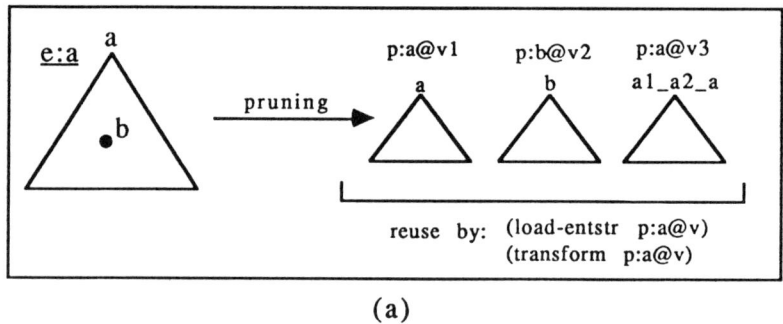

(a)

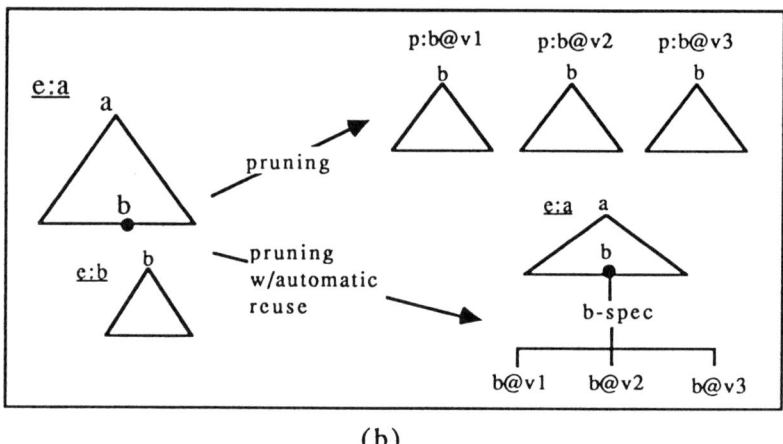

(b)

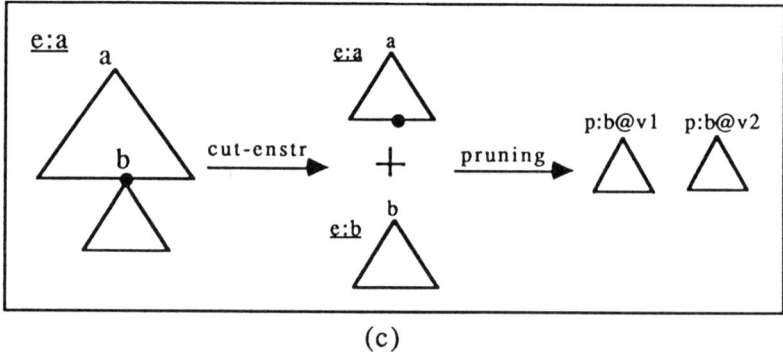

(c)

Figure 13.2. Cataloguing of pruned entity structure for reuse.

Model Base Management and Endomorphic Systems   303

we load it using (*load-entstr p:a@vi*) and then call the *transform* procedure with (*transform p:a@vi*).

13.2 Hierarchical Reuse of PES Versions

Consider Figure 13.2b in which there is an SES e:a having a leaf entity, B. Also, an SES with B as root, E:B exists. We will return to see how this important situation might arise. As shown, suppose that several prunings, P:B@V1, P:B@V2,...of E:B have already been saved. Our next requirement for reusability is that when the leaf entity B is encountered in the pruning procedure, such versions automatically be available for user selection. This captures the hierarchical sense of model reuse mentioned above, since existing versions of B can be "pulled of the shelf" and "plugged in" as components to a more encompassing model A.

To realize such hierarchical retrieval, the pruning procedure uses the following rules when encountering a leaf entity B:

1. if there is a model for B in the model base, skip the next steps,

2. if there is an SES, E:B and (*get-versions-of 'b*) is nil, replace B in E:A by a copy of E:B and allow the user to continue pruning the new substructure copy of E:B,

3. if there is no SES, E:B and (*get-versions-of 'b*) is not nil, then add a new specialization B-SPEC to B whose members are named in one-correspondence with the versions of B. The entity selected by the user from B-SPEC replaces B in the resulting PES. When transforming this PES, transform will encounter the leaf entity selected by the user, say B@Vi. At this point it invokes itself recursively to transform the corresponding PES P:B@Vi. The resulting model for B is employed as a component in the hierarchical model being synthesized, and

4. if both a system, and pruned, entity structures exist for b then allow the user to choose to prune the SES as in rule 2 or to select from existing versions of as in rule 3.

As an example, suppose we have an SES E:BTL and have pruned it to obtain external, operational and diagnostic versions, viz., P:BTL@E, P:BTL@O, and P:BTL@D, respectively. In any SES containing BTL as a leaf entity, we can select from the existing versions of BTL, or prune E:BTL afresh to generate a new version needed in this particular situation.

13.3 Partitioned System Entity Structures

As just suggested, more than one SES may exist in the entity structure base, each one representing a family of models for its root entity. In principle, every entity might have its own SES but this would lead to extreme fragmentation of the encoded knowledge. Reasons for giving an entity its own SES include: the large size of its family of possible prunings, its high likelyhood of being modified, and its occurrence in several places of existing SES's. Thus, factoring an SES into smaller SES's provides a modularity that is in much the same spirit as already discussed for models and rules. Moreover, we shall see that partitioning is crucial to achieving coherence in endomorphic model-bases.

Figure 13.2c shows tools for creating and partitioning SESs. Given an SES, E:A with a leaf entity, B, we can use an operation, *cut-entstr* which:

- removes the substructure of B from E:A,

- reincarnates it in the form an SES, E:B, and then

- allows the user to prune E:B as many times as desired.

As discussed above, the pruning process is capable of "sewing together" pieces of SES's which fit. It does so only as it needs to, i.e., when it arrives at a leaf entity which has an associated SES. In this way, we avoid patching in SES's that might never be reached in the particular pruning being made. If desired, the user can piece together SES's with *add-sub-entstr*.

13.4 Context Sensitive Pruning

Due to the uniformity axiom (Chapter 7), a multiply occurring entity subtends the same substructure where ever it occurs. Pruning however, must be able to break this uniformity so that different prunings can be made in the different occurrences. One way to understand the situation is to consider an SES E:A from which an SES E:B has been extracted (Figure 13.3a). This leaves an entity B which occurs at a number of places in the exterior of the structure (by uniformity, if B is a leaf entity in one occurrence it must be so for all occurrences). When pruning of E:A arrives at B, the user is given the choice of *context sensitive* or *insensitive* pruning. In the latter, E:B is pruned only once; by uniformity of E:A, B receives the selected substructure at each of its occurrences.

In *context sensitive* pruning, copies of E:B are made for each occurrence of B. Each copy is separately pruned, renamed and pasted back in the appropriate context. Recall that due to the valid brothers axiom (Chapter 7) each occurrence of B is reached by a uniquely labelled path from the root. This path (actually the minimal part needed for proper discrimination) provides the context needed by the user for pruning. Each item in a pruned copy of E:B is renamed to be distinct from occurrences in other copies of E:B. In renaming, couplings and priority lists are altered appropriately. Note that E:B may itself have multiple occurrences of entities. Thus context sensitive pruning is a recursive procedure.

A multiple entity, as shown in Figure 13.3b, is pruned in a similar manner. The single entity B is replaced by a set $B_0, B_1, \ldots, B_n$ whose size is determined by the user. (This structure is transformed to a kernel model (Chapter 8)). The resulting SES clearly satisfies the valid brothers axiom. For each such brother B_i, a copy of E:B is pruned, renamed in the context of B_i (plus more of the path extending back to the root, if needed), and attached to B_i. Actually, for convenience, the user is asked to decide on a number of equivalence groups. Elements in the same group are given the same pruning (but different naming). This obviates the need to specify each component

306   Object-Oriented Simulation

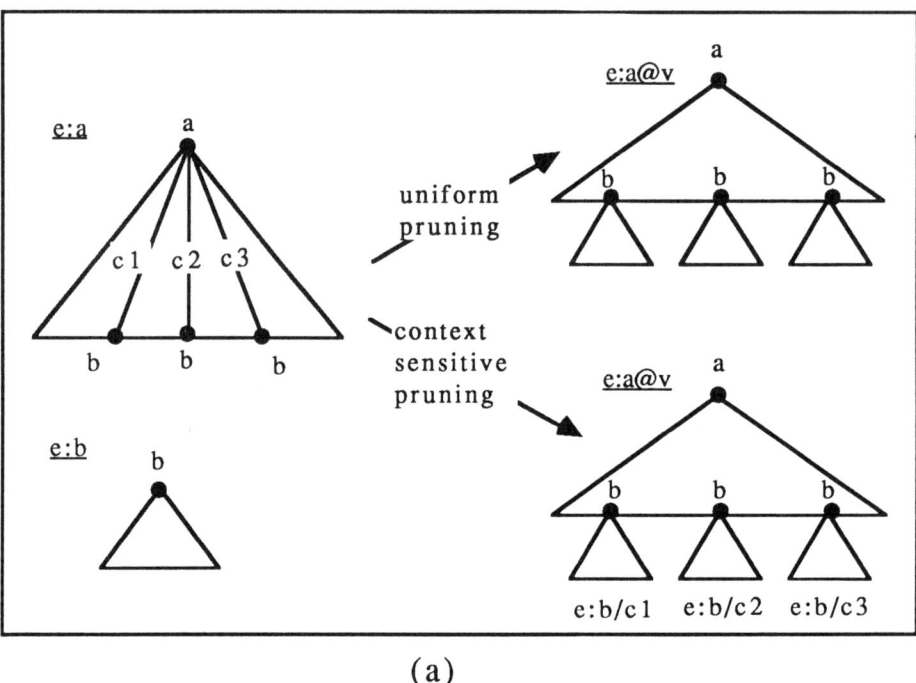

(a)

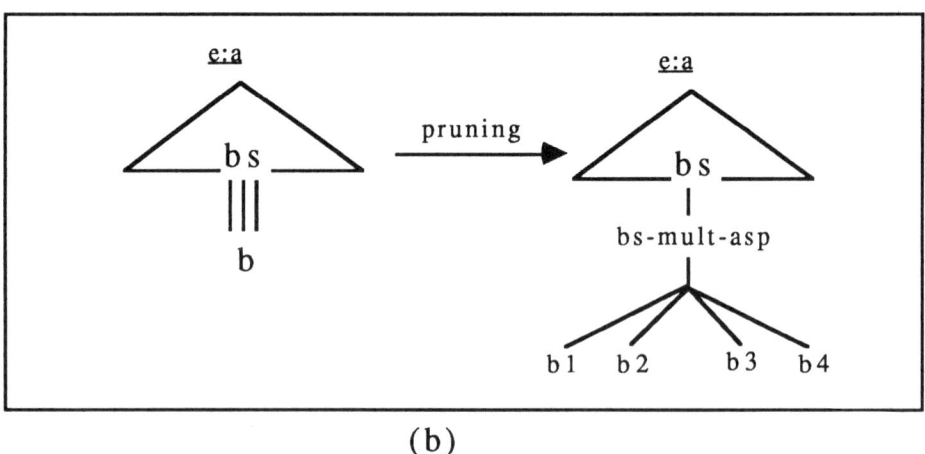

(b)

Figure 13.3. Pruning of multiply occurring entities (a) and of multiple entities (b).

Model Base Management and Endomorphic Systems 307

in a kernel-model separately. In the limiting case of only one group, we have a homogeneous model, where the components are mutually isomorphic.

13.5 Model Coherence and Context Sensitive Constraint Rules

Consider the SES for testing the space adapted bottle reproduced in Figure 13.4. A model of the bottle is referenced in three places but each is labelled differently (BTL-E, BTL-O, BTL-D). In this approach there is no formal way of recognizing that models of the same underlying entity are being referenced. The various models of bottle are dispersed throughout the structure. We can greatly improve coherence by using an SES in which the generic entity BTL replaces each of its special cases and by collecting them together as specializations in an SES, E:BTL, as in Figure 13.4. Organizing models by the entity they model, rather than the context they are used in, facilitates evolvability. Recall that models of an entity may be related by abstraction relationships so that when one is changes others must be amended to retain consistency.

Choosing context-sensitive pruning, we can select the specializations, BTL-E, BTL-O, and BTL-D in the corresponding contexts, TEST-DEC, OP-DEC, and DI-DEC, respectively. This is a slight bit of extra work, but it need only be done once since the resulting PES can be saved for reuse.

The advantage of such coherence is even more evident when we generalize the entity structure base so as to apply to an arbitrary instrument handling MPU. As shown in Figure 13.5, we can choose context insensitive pruning of E:INSTRUMENT to select a specialized entity such as BTL to uniformly replace the general entity INSTRUMENT in E:TEST. After this pruning step, the pruning of E:BTL proceeds as above. Note that the power in this approach is that the same SES E:TEST may be pruned to generate a family of models capable of testing MPUs for handling the various instruments organized in E:INSTRUMENT. Moreover the system is nicely

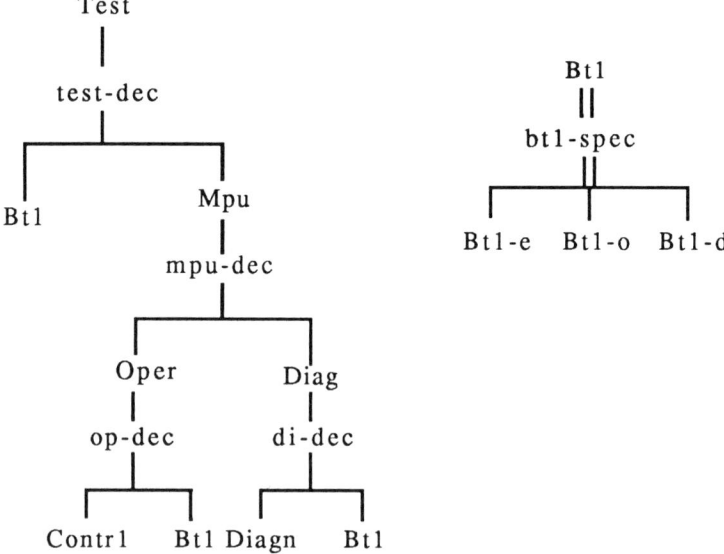

Figure 13.4. Entity structure base for testing a bottle handling MPU with operational and diagnostic capabilities.

Model Base Management and Endomorphic Systems

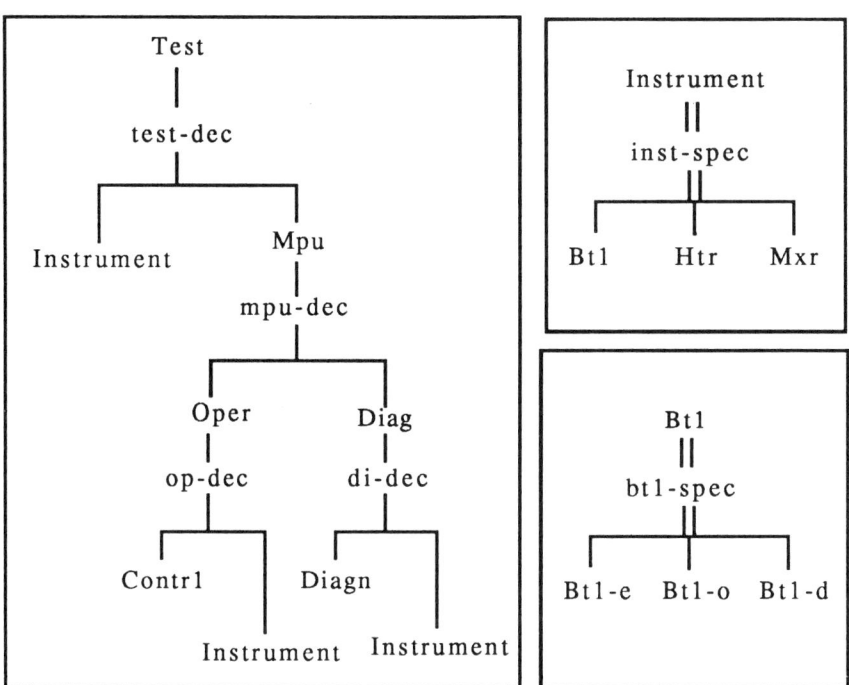

Generalized context sensitive selection rules:

In the context test-dec, select x-e from x-spec
In the contex op-dec, select x-o from x-spec
In the context di-dec, select x-d from x-spec

Figure 13.5. Coherent Entity Structure Base for testing an arbitrary instrument handling MPU with operational and diagnostic capabilities.

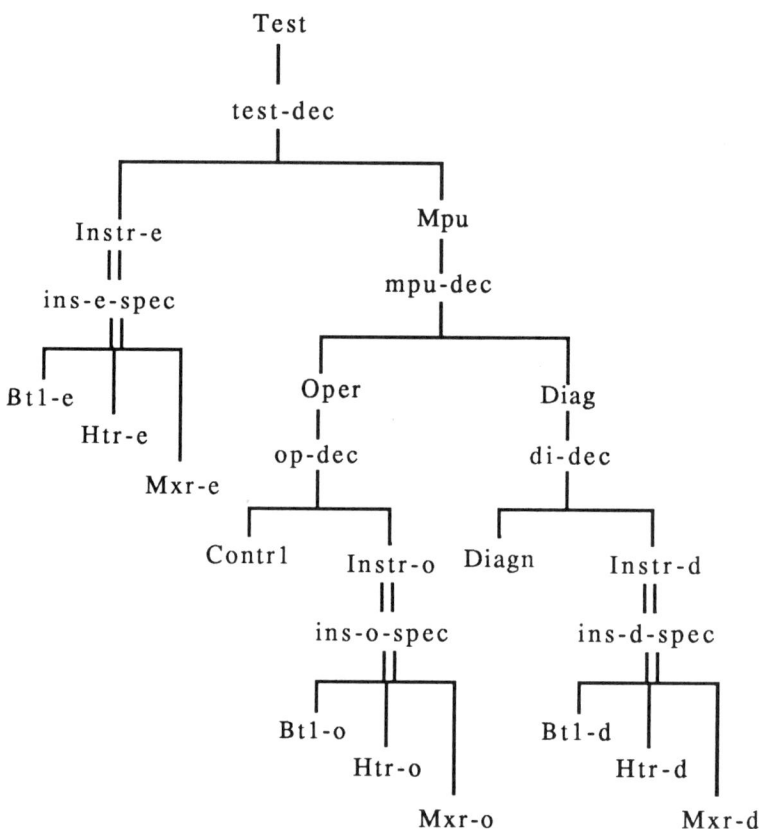

Selection Rules:

    If select Btl-e from Instr-e then select Btl-o from Instr-o
                                       and select Btl-d from Instr-d
    .....

Figure 13.6. Dispersed SES for testing an arbitrary instrument handling MPU with operational and diagnostic capabilities.

evolvable: to add a new instrument, we place its name in E:INSTRUMENT and define a new SES for its models.

Compare the above with an alternative SES in which the models of instruments are distributed into specializations according to context as in Figure 13.6. To add an instrument, we must add the proper specialized version in three different specializations. To generate a test model for a particular instrument, we must consistently select the appropriate representative in each of the specializations. As shown in Figure 13.6, constraint rules, of the form discussed in Chapter 9, can enforce the required consistency. A corresponding class of rules can be defined to assist context sensitive pruning. As shown in Figure 13.4, we can have the selection of an entity from a specialization be governed by context. Moreover as shown in Figure 13.5, imposing syntactic patterns, we can state a generalized rule to replace an indefinite number of special cases of the same form.

13.6 Model Bases in Endomorphic Systems and Intelligent Agents

The approach to entity structure base organization just outlined helps to organize the models employed in an autonomous system such as the robot architecture of Chapter 10. The interesting, and complicating, fact of autonomous systems is their use of internal models. Valid representations of such systems must also represent their internal models. We have argued that such models should be organized according to the entities they concern rather than dispersed among the contexts they are used in. Moreover, as we have seen, simulation models of such systems must incorporate external models of the same parts of reality in order to be able to test how well that modelled agents perform in their environment.

As an example, let us return to the space-borne laboratory environment. A partitioned entity structure base for this system is illustrated in Figure 13.7. Let us enumerate the entities possessing both internal and external models.

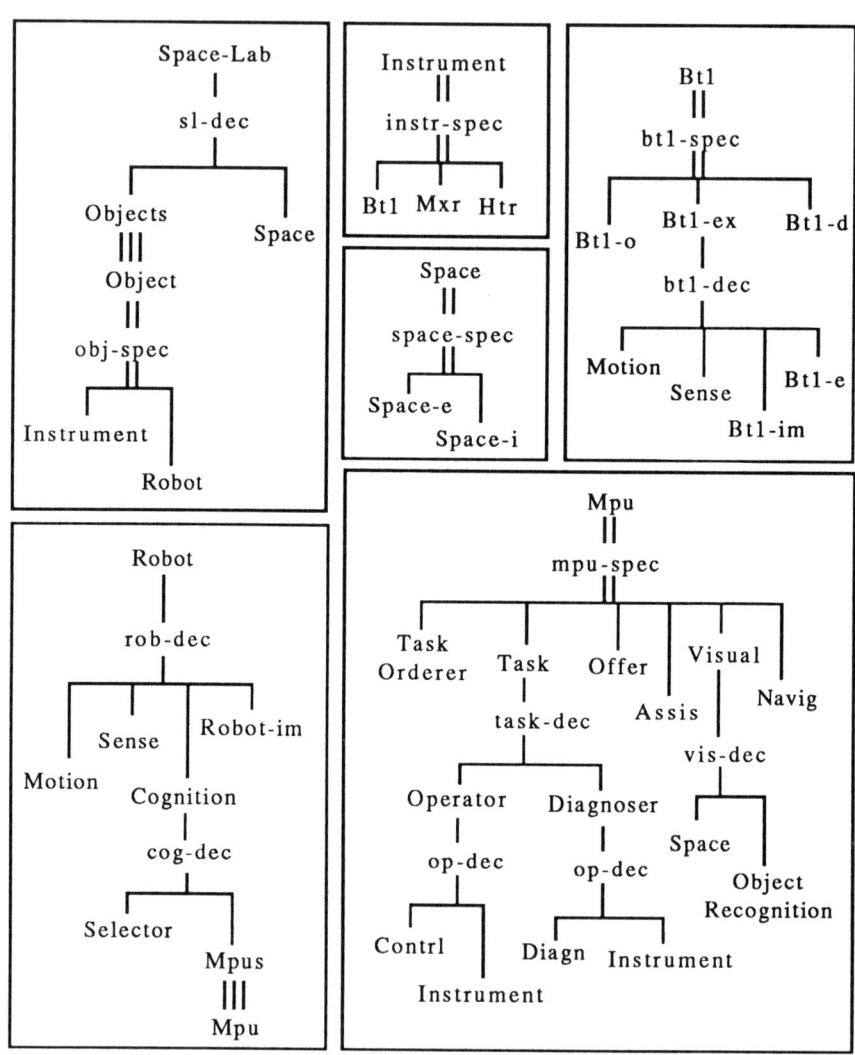

Figure 13.7. Partitioned entity structure base for space-borne laboratory.

- *objects*, including robots and instruments, have external models for perception interactions. Such a model represents how the object generates images in response to interrogations such as robot visual inspection requests. Internal model counterparts to these external models are organized into a classification system used by the robot to identify objects,

- *instruments*: as discussed above, each type of instrument is represented in internal models within an MPU in the brain related to operation and diagnosis; an external model of an instrument is used to respond to robot manipulations and to robot diagnostic probes, and

- *world map*: the locations and orientations of objects are maintained within an external model of space; correspondly, each robot has an internal spatial map to help it determine the locations of objects it wishes to manipulate or avoid. Such a world model also helps to plan the actions needed to carry out an experimentation procedure and to navigate from place to place.

Note that we have a variety of model functional types:

- *static models*, or memoryless models, represent relations in a modelled system that are invariant over time. For example, image generators for objects answer questions concerning how objects look from various points of view, and

- *dynamic models* whose response is history dependent and are also said to have memory; systems theory shows that whether they are intentionally designed that way or not, such models can be given a state representation in which all history captured in a single (perhaps complex) state (Zeigler, 1984).

    Under *dynamic* models we have:
    - *updatable models* can be updated to stay in homomorphic state correspondence with a system being tracked and can

be queried to answer certain questions about the system using the maintained state knowledge. For example, the world map maintains knowledge of spatial locations and can answer questions about proximity relations: what are the objects closest to a given location, for instance. Such models however cannot extrapolate beyond their current state, and

- *state transition models* have state transition and output functions that give them power to extrapolate into the past or future. Accordingly there are:

    * *retrodictive models* have non-deterministic state transitions so that they cannot provide unique predictions about future states. They however be used to account for the occurrence of a state, once it happens, in terms of what state trajectories could precede it. In other words, such models can explain why something happened but there are to many alternatives for it to predict what will happen. The instrument diagnostic models are of this character: they do not predict fault occurrences, but after one has occurred they can be applied to deduce the origin of the fault, and

    * *predictive models* which have deterministic state transitions and hence uniquely predict future states based on present states. Of course, the key question here is the validity of the model, i.e., whether its predictions are reliable or not as a basis for decision making. The instrument operational models are examples as they are used to predict what the next control input should be and what next state should be achieved and in what time window a confirming response is expected.

13.6.1 Endomorphy: Self-Models and Self-Knowledge in Intelligent Agents

We have so far considered knowledge and models from the point of view of the System Entity Structure/Model Base Framework as implemented in DEVS-Scheme. We have also examined how in modelling autonomous, intelligent systems interacting with their environments, we must incorporate, and organize, models which are internal to an intelligent agent and distinguish them from models of the environment. It is time to revisit the claim made at the end of Chapter 1 that future modelling of endomorphic systems will require us to embed in them sophisticated formulations of the principles of modelling and simulation methodology. One sub-theme becomes apparent: modelling by, and of, model-making agents, is inherently a self-referencing process, apt to lead to infinite regress. Methodological principles provide a key to understanding how this regress is averted. Properly conceiving ourselves, and our adversaries, as endomorphic, decision making agents may be crucial to our survival in the nuclear age (Davis, 1989)

Future endomorphic systems will possess representations of their own knowledge processes as well as those of the other social actors with whom they interact (Shaw and Gaines, 1986). Modelling the interaction among such socially aware agents introduces yet a greater degree of complexity, as illustrated in the following:

real world consists of:

>   intelligent agent1
>   decision making component
>   model of intelligent agent2
>   model of self
>
>   intelligent agent2
>   decision making component
>   model of intelligent agent1
>   model of self

Here, we have replaced the system confronting an intelligent agent by another agent. Each agent then has a model the other as well as of itself. This makes intelligent agents endomorphic systems. There is the potential for infinite recursion as agent1's model of agent2 should include agent2's model of agent1, which should include agent1's model of agent2, ... *ad infinitum*. This was pointed out by Davis in his presentation of a knowledge-based simulation war game involving adversaries that represent major nuclear powers (Davis, 1986). Actually, such an infinite recursion is possible in a situation involving a single intelligent agent, if we consider that the agent might consider a part of itself to be in the system to be controlled:

real world consists of:

>system being controlled, managed, designed
>>external to agent
>>internal to agent (self)
>
>intelligent agent
>>decision making component
>>model of system being controlled

Here the agent's model of the system being controlled may include a model of its own internals which may include its model of the system being controlled, ... *ad infinitum*. Clearly, the recursion in such cases must be halted — begging the question as to how this is done in reality and how it can be done in simulation models.

13.7 Minsky's Views on Models and Knowledge

> Model: Any structure that a person can use to simulate or anticipate the behavior of something else.[1]

To gain a cognitive science, as opposed to cognitive engineering, perspective on model making, let us look at Marvin Minsky's "Society of Mind" (Minsky, 1986), perhaps the most comprehensive

---

[1] p.330, Minsky, M., Society of Mind, ©1986 by Simon and Schuster, New York, NY.

Model Base Management and Endomorphic Systems 317

attempt to understand mind and brain. The above is what we find as a definition for "model" in the glossary.

> ...a model is anything that helps a person answer questions ...a person could possess a 'mental model', ...in the form of some machinery or subsociety of agents inside the brain. This provides us with a simple explanation of what we mean by knowledge: Jack's knowledge of A is simply whichever mental models, processes, or agencies Jack's other agencies can use to answer questions about A.[2]

This last definition of model is consistent with Minsky's (1965) earlier concept. The one in the glossary can be reconciled with it if we interpret "simulate the behavior of" and "anticipate the behavior of" to be asking questions about observations of the "something else" that can be made over time, in the past or the future.

For Minsky, a person's model of the world is simply all the models that his mind can use to answer questions about things in the world. Likewise, a person's model of himself is the set of all mental models his mind has of his parts. To answer a general question about oneself necessitates an active introspection to make a "model of (one's) model of oneself".

As for making models of models of models of oneself this leads to an infinite regress which is broken only because we get "confused and lose track of distinctions between each model and the next". Minsky seems to be saying that:

1. knowledge is object-oriented, i.e., it is associated with objects,

2. the knowledge of an object is equivalent to the current set of models of the object,

3. a model is a device for answering questions about an object,

4. knowledge in general is the sum total of knowledge of objects,

---
[2]p.303, Minsky, M., Society of Mind, ©1986 by Simon and Schuster, New York, NY.

5. the only model of a composite object, such as the world, or the self, that exists initially is one that is a disjoint sum of models of its components,

6. to answer certain questions about a composite object may require active processing of its component models to generate a new (summary, abstract) description — this is in effect a model of the existing model of the composite object, and

7. the infinite regress implicit in 6. is halted naturally due to limitations in processing capacity.

Statement 6 reaffirms that intelligent agents are endomorphic systems.

13.7.1 Why Infinite Regress Does Not Occur

Although, the SES/MB framework we have developed agrees in outline with the foregoing set of statements, there are aspects that we have plowed in greater depth and there are others that require much research. Here, we shall limit discussion to statement 7 which we claim is false.

One key point that we have stressed is that the nature of a model is related to its intended use. Thus, to be able to construct valid simulation models of an intelligent agent's model, we must take into account the agent's model making activity. This leads to an extension of the original formulation where we add a model constructor component to the agent:

real world consists of:

        system being controlled, managed, designed
        intelligent agent
            decision making component
            model of system being controlled
            model constructor

Model Base Management and Endomorphic Systems 319

simulation model consists of:

> model of system being controlled, managed, designed
>
> model of intelligent agent
>> model of decision making component
>> model of model of system being controlled
>> model of model constructor

Thus to some extent we must have a model of an intelligent agent's model construction methodology to know how to make models of its models of the real world. Although clearly real intelligent agents need not follow a normative methodology (e.g., multifacetted methodology) such a methodology provides a starting point for considering how to make such internal models.

Taking account of the modelling methodology employed by an intelligent agent helps to understand how model self-embedding does not necessarily lead to infinite regress. Plainly stated, models of models would exist only if (1) the objectives of the modeller require that they be there, and (2) the modeller has the data and competence to build useful ones. Moreover, such models would necessarily be simplified versions of the system in which they are embedded.

To see this, consider Figure 13.8a which presents an SES for the world that distinguishes myself from others and that considers my mind as a coupling of a decision maker and its associated model of the world. An understanding of infinite regress can be had by letting the model of the world be an exact replica of the world. To do so set "model of world" = "world", thus resulting in an SES which does not satisfy the strict hierarchy axiom (Chapter 7) and which therefore unfolds to an infinite structure. Basically, the paradox or vicious circle arises because the model of the world has to fully describe itself in this situation.

Two commonly occurring analogies come to mind. Next time you are trying on clothes in a store try viewing yourself between two almost parallel mirrors. Also on our television screens we often see a news-person in front of a monitor displaying the same

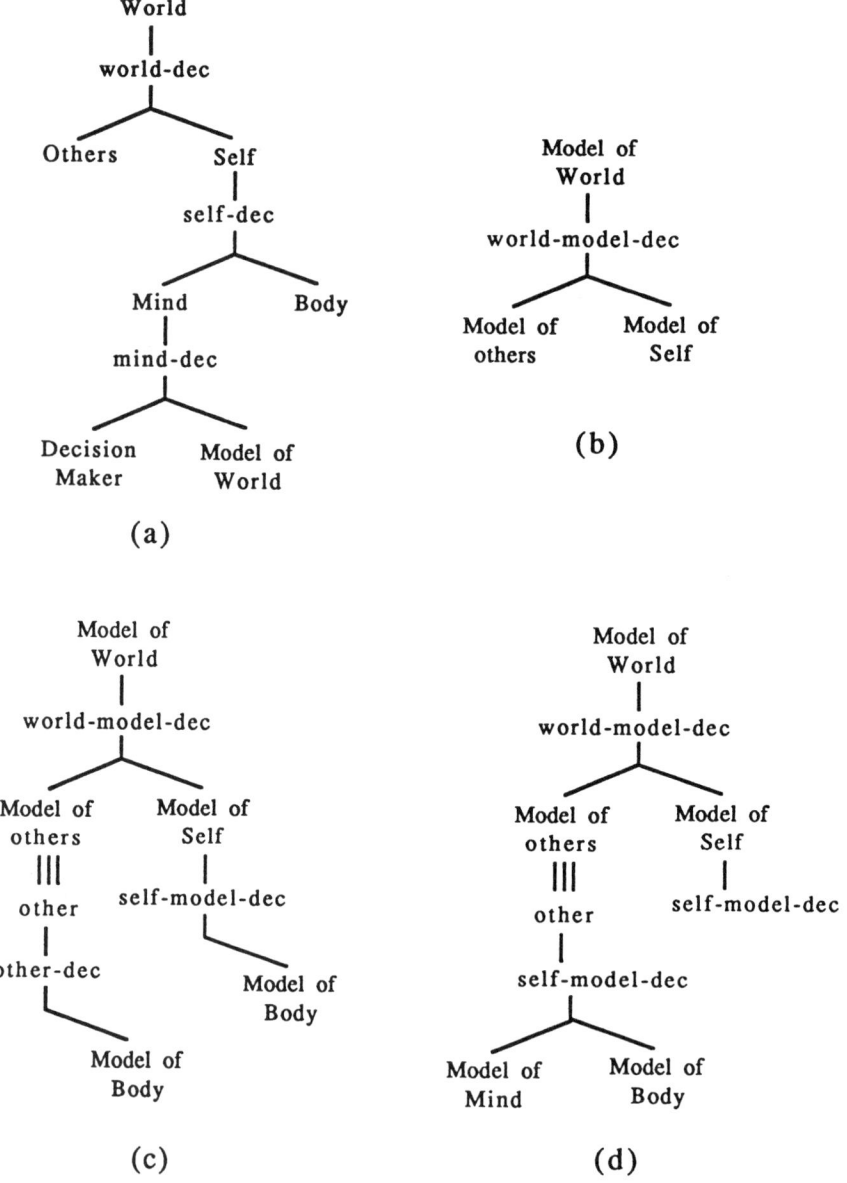

Figure 13.8. Possible entity structures for an endomorphic agent.

image we are looking at (hence, being fed back to video camera). In either case, there results a potentially infinite, inclusive series of replications of the same scene. Such series must terminate in reality due to the limited size and resolution of optical materials. In our analogy, this point is where the model of the world (the video screen display) departs from equality with the world itself (the scene consisting of the announcer and the screen). This tells us that infinite regress is naturally averted when an embedded model is a simplified (aggregated, abstract, fuzzy, qualitative) representation of the enclosing system.[3]

Even if there were no limits to resolution in the self-embedding video, the screen image would take an infinite amount of time to stabilize. Imagine turning on the camera. First it would see the person and a blank screen on the monitor behind her. This scene is transmitted to the monitor after some delay, Δ. The camera now reacts to the new scene, and Δ seconds later, it appears on the monitor behind the person. The camera in turn reacts to this scene, and since each such iteration results in a new image, the process continues indefinitely. At any time there is a well-defined picture on the monitor and viewed by the camera — the record of the previous iterations.[4]

A similar iterative process could happen in a simulation with endomorphic capabilities as exemplified in the Rand Strategy Assessment System (Davis and Hall, 1989). In this, first of its kind, simulation environment, an agent say Red, can call the simulation engine itself, to conduct a lookahead simulation. The lookahead for Red employs versions of models for other agents, i.e., Red's Blue and Red's Green. When the lookahead requires Red's response to their actions, a new lookahead could be initiated. In the absence of some

---

[3] See (Burks, 1986) for a discussion of self-reference in logical systems and the relevance of Von Neuman's demonstration that a system can contain a description of itself in the form of a blueprint for its self-replication: the blueprint does not have to describe itself for this purpose.

[4] Thus, taking time into account also obviates paradoxical self-reference. The latter arises since the time ordered sequence of images is compounded into a single infinite series when Δ vanishes.

termination device, an infinite series of such recursive calls could result. The RAND system apparently limits to recursion to a small number of levels.

13.7.2 Methodological Considerations Limiting Endomorphic Self-models

We have seen that infinite regress occurs when an endomorphic system's world model is as detailed as the real world. However, there is no reason why an agent's world model needs to be so detailed. Indeed, there are good methodological reasons why it should not. Returning to Figure 13.8, my world model can take a multitude of forms according to the my decision making needs, my access to observation of self and others, and my model making capability. For example as in Figure 13.8b, it might only recognize myself and others as physical objects, keeping track of their locations in space. Or it might elaborate the self model to include only a concept of my body. Thus I might recognize only that I have a body but not be aware of having a mind. By symmetry I might recognize some other objects to have bodies like mine (Figure 13.8c). Notice that, as indicated, I may not recognize that others have self-models although I recognize that they have bodies. (Evidence for children having such a body models might be drawn from their ability to imitate body movements of others. This requires an understanding of others' body parts in correspondence with one's own.)

Having models of other's bodies may be useful for navigation, pursuit, predation, etc., but eventually, it would pay to recognize that I and others have decision making capabilities. Think of an airplane with pilot and autopilot. The autopilot has a model of the "body" of the plane not including itself and the pilot. This is necessary and sufficient for certain stabilization actions on the plane. But models of the "bodies" of other airplanes are not sufficient when they are under the control of human pilots. To pursue and attack such an object requires at least some recognition of its pilot's intentions, i.e., a model of its "mind" as well.

Model Base Management and Endomorphic Systems

This leads to a world model as in Figure 13.8d where, by symmetry, both I and others, are recognized as having minds and bodies. A model of mind may be at a high level of aggregation and behavioral in character, such as a table of observed input-output pairs. Perhaps surprisingly, observations necessary to build such a table may be more easily obtainable for others than myself. For example, it is easier to observe others' reactions under stress than one's own.

In any case, the available data and the accuracy of prediction required would determine whether the model of mind might be further elaborated to distinguish the decision making, from the internal, model components. When I get to incorporate a model of my model of the world in my model of self, such a model would be some abstraction of the model of the world in the same way that has been discussed. Therefore, there is nothing inherently paradoxically about having a system contain a self-model. The extent to which it does so depends on methodological considerations.

The difficulty in getting data to construct models at successive levels of refinement probably increases dramatically with each level since finer discriminations must be made in interpreting the observations. This also limits the extent to which models of self can recurse.

Thus, to approach the construction of models employed by intelligent agents, we should start with considerations of the objectives the agent wishes to achieve with such models, aggregation level as related to objectives, and level in the structure and behavior hierarchy at which models can be made. If learning on the part of the agent is considered then we may have to include a fairly detailed model of its modelling methodology, viz., the knowledge discussed in Chapter 1.

We conclude that research on modelling methodology is needed to better understand how to represent models employed by endomorphic agents, as well as how to model the model construction processes employed by such agents.

Chapter 14

DEVS-SCHEME IN THE LARGER SCHEME OF THINGS

This chapter attempts to clarify and evaluate the contribution of DEVS-Scheme to state-of-the-art modelling and simulation. This is done in two ways. First, the "selling point" attributes of DEVS-Scheme are enumerated and briefly described. How DEVS-Scheme can be extended further along these same lines is is also discussed. Second, other properties of simulation environments are considered. Some of these are incompatible with our approach, some can be incorporated fairly readily. The selection of the first list of properties obviously lays out a slanted playing field in favor of DEVS-Scheme relative to other possibilities. Hence, we present the second set, a kind of wish list, gleaned from colleagues and the literature, as a balancing perspective. Together, the properties described should improve our "knowledge base" for designing and evaluating modelling and simulation environments of the future.

14.1 Layers of DEVS-Scheme

The features of DEVS-Scheme can be better understood by organizing them within a set of layers that characterizes its software design structure. In Figure 14.1, Scheme and SCOOPS, the Lisp-based, object-oriented programming system provides the foundation on which the system is built. The properties of this lowest layer make it possible to realize similar properties at the higher layers. For example, the ability to test the behavior of an object in stand-alone fashion is responsible for the same testability property that obtains for model objects on Layer 1. The next layer, which supports systems model construction, acquires many of its properties from both Layer 0 and the systems concepts embodied in the DEVS formalism. Layer 2 relies on Layer 1 to provide the ability to specify models which populate the model base that it organizes. The highest layer, that of systems design, enhances the system entity structure knowledge representation with knowledge related to model-based design.

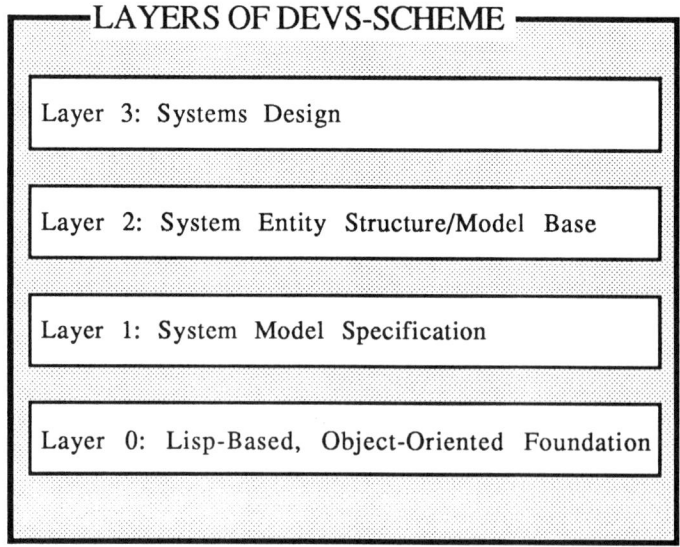

Figure 14.1. Layers of DEVS-Scheme.

14.1.1 Layer 0: Lisp-based, object-oriented foundation

- **Symbolic and Numeric Processing**: Number crunching ability is typically a requirement of traditional models but symbol manipulation capability is essential to knowledge based simulation characterized by intelligent components and/or intelligent model manipulation. In contrast to many artificial intelligence studies, which stay at a high degree of abstraction, knowledge-based simulation, e.g., of robotic systems, must have efficient substrates of both kinds of processing support.

- **Software Design Attributes**: The object concept embodies the fruits of software engineering research: encapsulation (packaging of data and code together), abstraction (the objects behavior as seen through its methods), and information hiding (the structural detail it hides).

- **Environment Development Support**: The symbol manipulation and object-oriented facilities of Scheme make it relatively easy to code complex structures and operations on them. Since Scheme is an interpreted language, it combines levels that would be separated in the translation and execution steps of compiled languages. Thus, like its parent, LISP, Scheme is a "language to develop languages in". In it, an environment can be evolved in which tools are readily developed and integrated. In contrast a compiled language can not as easily support such environment evolution since one must work at both the language and operating system levels to do this.

- **Testability**: an object can be tested against its behavioral requirements specification (e.g., given in axiomatic form) by injecting sequences of messages and comparing the object's response with that expected.

- **Extensibility**: a software system can evolve incrementally by addition of new classes without disturbing previously written code.

- **Replicatability**: since object structures are well defined by their class templates, class specific methods can be written so that objects, no matter how complex, can be easily replicated (copied).

- **Concurrent Implementation**: it is quite natural to extend object behavior so that all objects are simultaneously active; the parallelism in such concurrent object-oriented systems can then be exploited by mapping to multiprocessor architectures.

- **Browsability**: ability of a user to browse easily through the class hierarchy of a system, getting both global and local perspectives. Unfortunately, in contrast to Smalltalk and LOOPS, this is not directly available in SCOOPS.

14.1.2 Layer 1: Systems Model Specification

- **System Theoretic Formal Basis**: the DEVS formalism for discrete event systems is directly implemented as the means of expression in DEVS-Scheme. This provides a sound semantics for discrete event model representation and basis for mathematical and other symbolic processing of model specifications.

- **Model Specification Language**: As a set theoretic construct, the DEVS formalism by itself is not a practical means of specifying models. However, DEVS-Scheme supports the structure of the DEVS-formalism with the underlying expressive power of Scheme, thus offering a combination of the best of both worlds: formal specification with ease of model development.

- **Modularity**: model specifications are self-contained and have input and output ports through which all interaction with the external world must take place. Models, as objects, have the software engineering attributes inherited from Layer 0. In addition, ports provide a level of delayed binding which needs to be resolved only when models are coupled together.

- **Closure under Coupling:** models may be connected together by coupling of input and output ports to create larger, coupled models, having the same interface properties as the components.

- **Hierarchical Construction** follows as a consequence of modularity and closure under coupling; successively more complex models can be built by using as building blocks the coupled models already constructed.

- **Stand-alone and Bottom-up Testability:** due to object encapsulation and input/output modularity, models are independently verifiable at every stage of hierarchical construction. This fosters secure and incremental bottom-up synthesis of complex models.

- **Experimental Frame/Model Separation:** Experimental frames are independently realized as models of special kinds: generators, transducers, acceptors. Having input/output ports, they can be coupled to models to which they are applicable.

- **Isomorphic Replicatability:** copies can easily be made of complex, hierarchical models, with consistent name assignments, as components in kernel-models. Systems isomorphism concepts provide the formal basis for correctness of model replication.

- **Hierarchical Distributed Simulation:** as objects, models can be executed on concurrent object-based processors; however, using the abstract simulator concepts, more advantageous hierarchical multiprocessor systems can be designed and hierarchical models mapped to them so that maximum speed up is obtained. DEVS-Scheme provides timing measurements from the underlying "virtual multiprocessor" simulator to support analysis for optimal multiprocessor mappings. See Appendix A.3.

- **System Manipulations**: derived from the formal structure and system theoretic basis is the ability to implement systems operations such as structure transformations, tests for homomorphism, etc.

- **Model Abstraction and Simplification**: Systems model description, as rendered by the DEVS formalism, facilitates tool development for DEVS representation of continuous systems which can be used for faster simulation and for event-based control. Simplification of DEVS multicomponent models (*coupled-models*) can be obtained by conversion to equivalent *atomic-models*, from which a homomorphic lumped model is constructed. The motivation is not to achieve full validity but to obtain faster running lumped models that can replace a component of a hierarchical model so that its complement can be more efficiently run and tested. See Appendix A.4.

- **System Specification Formalisms within DEVS-Scheme**: The hierarchical, modular modelling and simulation concepts first developed in the DEVS formalism can be implemented in continuous and discrete-time formalisms and combined with DEVS to obtain multi-formalism simulation. See Appendices A.1 and A.2

- **Model Specification Extensibility**: new kinds of model specification formats can be readily added as specialized classes of *atomic-*, and *coupled-*, *models*.

- **Rule-based Modelling**: the specialized class, *forward-models* provides the ability to specify models as sets of activities, which are have a rule-like character and combine symbolic and dynamic model specification.

- **Granularity**: activities within *forward-models* provide the most granular level of specification or knowledge representation in DEVS-Scheme. Sets of activities can be inherited and combined to form larger sets.

DEVS-Scheme in the Larger Scheme of Things

- **Variable Structure Models**: An important capability for studying future high autonomy systems will be to construct models which contain within themselves the ability to alter their own structure. The layers of DEVS-Scheme provided a foundation for developing such capability. See Appendix A.5.

14.1.3   Layer 2: System Entity Structure/Model-Base

- **Axiomatic Specification**: the system entity structure is formally characterized in an axiomatic manner thus facilitating design and verification of the complex operations that are required to support model generation and reuse.

- **Synthesis Constraints**: the system entity structure can be augmented with rules that enforce constraints on selections from specializations. Such constraints can be of a global character where selections in various parts of the SES must be correlated. They also can be sensitive to the context in which the selection is being made. This supports coherence of the entity structure base.

- **Model Synthesis via Pruning**: Hierarchical models can synthesized by creating and transforming pruned entity structures. This requires only that the lowest level atomic-models referenced by the PES reside in the model base.

- **Context-sensitive Pruning**: By uniformity, multiple occurrences of the same entity have isomorphic substructures. However, if desired, this uniformity may be broken in the pruning process so that differently pruned substructures are attached to the same entity in each of its contexts. Similarly, a multiple entity may pruned so as to transform into a heterogeneous kernel-model. The pruned substructures are automatically renamed so as to reveal the context in which they arose.

- **Archivability**: models can be saved on disk in the form of model definition files or as pruned entity structure files. The latter form is preferred both for the convenience of model construction afforded as well as the fact of the automatic cataloguing provided by the environment.

- **Model Base Cataloguing**: Pruned entity structures are given the name of their root entity with a user supplied suffix so that they can be identified as representing alternative models of the root entity.

- **Reusability**: models developed for studying a particular real system, archived in the model base and managed by the system entity structure, are retrievable for use as components in new models. Due to pruned entity naming, hierarchical models expressed in the form of pruned entity structures are just are reusable as those in the model base. This fosters cumulative growth of "off-the-shelf" reusable components.

- **Extensibility with respect to Model Specification Layer**: The code of the pruning and transformation processes is designed so that it does not have to be modified when new sub-classes are added at Layer 1. See Appendix A.6.

14.1.4 Layer 3: Systems Design

The systems design layer supports model-based design. It is implemented by embedding the system entity structure in a richer frame-based knowledge representation scheme called Frames and Rules Associated System Entity Structure (FRASES) (Hu, 1989; Hu and Rozenblit, 1989). For background see also Rozenblit (1985), Rozenblit and Zeigler (1985) and Rozenblit and Huang (1987). This facilitates associating a great amount of information with nodes in the SES which can be used to drive the system design process. The following outlines the kinds of knowledge that can be represented.[1]

---

[1]The structuring capability of the System Entity Structure knowledge representation scheme can be exploited in other application areas besides simulation modelling. Higa (1988) has developed and approach to data base design which controlled experimentation in a classroom setting has shown to be superior to

DEVS-Scheme in the Larger Scheme of Things

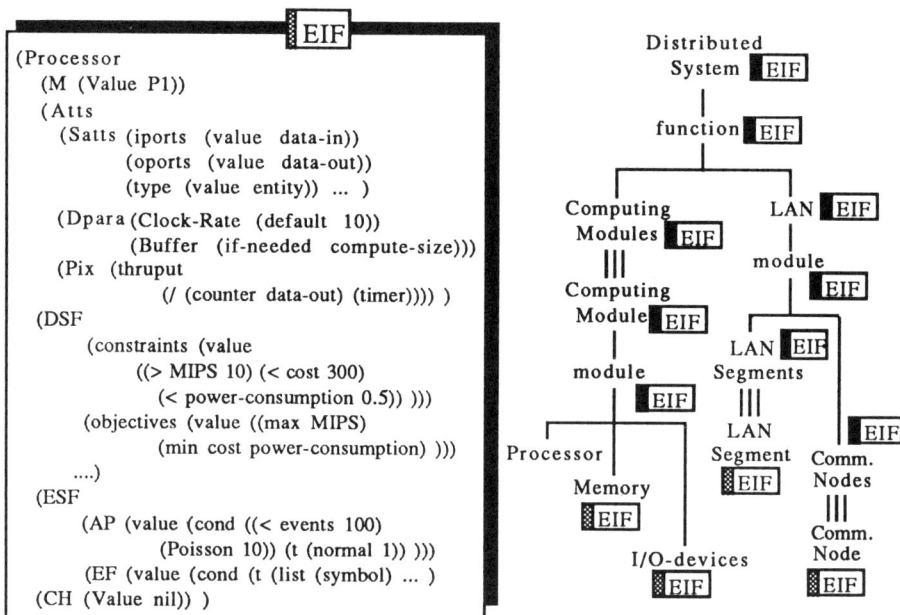

Figure 14.2. FRASES representation of a system entity structure. (EIF = Entity Information Frame)

- **Goal Driven Pruning**: Layer 3 helps users with design model construction by providing guidance in pruning sensitive to their design goals. Rules are attached to FRASES to represent selection and synthesis knowledge. Selection rules attached to specializations specify entity choices in terms of local design criteria. Synthesis rules attached to decompositions constrain the plausible combinations of model components in decompositions. See Figure 14.2 for example.

- **Automated Design Evaluation and Ranking**: Design models synthesized via pruning are automatically subjected

---

conventional schemes. Higa and Sheng (1989) are using this approach to couple knowledge bases and data bases to achieve systems capable of both inference and large data management in an object-oriented framework.

to simulation evaluation in performance-relevant experimental frames and ranked according to multi-criteria decision methods. FRASES attaches slots with nodes for specifications of performance indexes, the system measurements they are based on, the experimental frames that can acquire data for such measurements, and the trade-off criteria for ranking of alternatives.

- **Knowledge Acquisition by Representation (KAR):** The FRASES organization constitutes a set of hypotheses on what it is important for systems design. To the extent that these hypotheses are correct and complete, capturing this knowledge can be facilitated using FRASES as a template for conducting a dialog with a system design expert.

14.2 Other Properties, Other Views

DEVS-Scheme, as it stands, can be viewed as the product of the implementation phase of a software design project that began with the conceptual designs in my earlier books (Zeigler, 1976, 1984). Other simulation software projects continue to wend their way through their own phases. I have attempted to compare and contrast such projects with mine in earlier reports (Chapter 18 of Zeigler, 1984; Zeigler, 1985). Several ongoing research programs, such as those of Ören, Elzas, Nance, and Fishwick are most parallel to mine, in being motivated by methodology rather than application; in other words, dedicated to advancing the state-of-the-art of simulation as an enterprise in general, not just in a particular context. Ören, Nance, and their co-workers, have written extensively not only about their approaches, but also how they fit in within the larger scheme of things (Ören, 1986, 1989b; Nance, 1987; Balci and Nance, 1986). I refer the reader to this literature for extensive discussions of alternatives to the DEVS-based "ideology" presented here. Elzas (1986a,b) and Fishwick (1988, 1989c) are mostly congruent in approach to mine. A second strand of research, that of qualitative and other knowledge representation issues concerning reasoning about physical devices, is becoming intertwined with traditional simulation approaches (see (Widman and Loparo, 1989) for an excellent critical survey). Rather than *precis* this literature (filtered, and doubtlessly, biased), in the following, I shall briefly express my views on issues that these researchers raise.

Development Time and Execution Speed

Two factors enter into the time it takes before a simulation can yield answers: development time and execution speed. Most of the attributes listed above were in the direction enhancing model development hence in reducing development time. Unfortunately, the price paid for the flexibility provided by DEVS-Scheme is execution speed. The speed penalty of Smalltalk with respect to conventional languages has been studied by Thomasma and Ulgen (1988). Likewise, benchmark tests should be carried out to compare DEVS-Scheme development and simulation execution times with compiled language implementations of the DEVS formalism such as DLAB implemented in Modula-2 (Livny, 1988). There are two broad alternatives to improved execution speed. One, DEVS-Scheme can be used to generate model descriptions which can be transferred to other execution environments such as multiprocessor architectures (as described above), or faster compatible environments (Wang, 1989). The second alternative is to exploit faster platforms for executing LISP (Scheme) code as they become available. With the intense interest in applied artificial intelligence and the continuing developments in hardware technology, there is little doubt that such high performance machines will continue to evolve.

Graphics

Visualization and animation through graphics (Melamed, 1987) of complex behavior can be an essential factor in successful use of simulation methodology. Properly presented in graphics, some relationships can be seen to be weird that would be difficult to detect through more information poor displays. On the other hand, some simulation animation displays are mere window dressing while hiding the complexity from the viewer. DEVS-Scheme uses a fairly primitive windowing mechanism to display model component states. Much more can be done to portray hierarchical, modular structures (Chow, 1990).

Help

Help should come in a variety of ways and be tuned to the needs of the user in his current circumstances. Balci (1986) discusses the many possibilities for on-line assistance in a simulation model development environment. More generally a system might be aimed at supporting the beginning modeller (the philosophy behind program generators) or the user who is knowledgeable in his domain but not in simulation methodology (c.f., the variety of discipline oriented packages). DEVS-Scheme is intended for neither: it is unabashedly intended for the user willing to put the necessary effort into learning its general, theory-based concepts.

Other Discrete Event World Views

The three standard formalisms for discrete event model specification (event, activity and process) provide alternative means of model representation, each of which may be advantageous in its own niche domain (Zeigler, 1984; Balci, 1988). The atomic model specification developed in this book is most closely identifiable with the process formalism but endows it with the modularity property that conventional process-based languages do not support. The activities approach supported in *forward-models* is reminiscent of conventional activity scanning (rules and activities superficially look very much alike). However, the flexibility afforded by the *forward-models* paradigm is the basis for granularity, modularity and combinability through inheritance not possible in conventional activity scanning.

Existing object-oriented simulation languages are discussed by Radiya and Sargent (1989). The advantages of non-modular state/time condition constructs of conventional simulation languages are emphasized and shown to be lacking in ROSS (Klahr, 1986). A new approach, ROBS combines such non-modular constructs with object-oriented message passing. In contrast, DEVS-Scheme adheres to a strict modular interaction paradigm. The theory of Chapter 8 in (Zeigler, 1984) can be applied to convert non-modular constructs to modular form (Appendix A.6). We have found however, that with a little practice it becomes natural to think directly in terms of the DEVS modular world-view.

A more history-oriented formalism for discrete event model specification has been recently been proposed (Narain and Rothberg, 1989). This formalism can be understood as residing at a behavioral, rather than the standard structural, level in the system specification hierarchy. The availability of Prolog-like simulation engines make such approaches feasible but many practical and theoretical issues are raised.

Inductive Modelling

George Klir (1985) and others (e.g., Cellier, 1989; Vesantera and Cellier, 1989) have developed a methodology for inducing model structure from behavioral data. Such an approach is strongest in new situations where there is no (or insignificantly little) background knowledge to structure hypothetical models. The problem with current inductive modelling methodology is that it provides no paths for cumulative growth of knowledge, i.e., all models must be derived from scratch with no transfer from existing ones. Cognitive science based discovery programs (Gylmour, 1987; Langely et.al., 1987) might suggest means for integrating inductive and postulational modelling methodologies.

14.2.1 Reasoning from First Principles

Where as inductive modelling may assume too little knowledge is available, qualitative physics may assume too much is available. According to de Kleer (1989) the basic tenet of qualitative physics is that to build machines capable of reasoning about the physical world, we must articulate the tacit knowledge and reasoning strategies of "prephysics." More recent approaches start from a less ambitious and more quantitative foundation (Chiu, 1989). However, there is still a lack of appreciation for the major role of model formalisms in structuring human understanding. The diverse and rich reasoning humans can do needs to be trained in various formalisms and disciplines to work. There is no point in trying to model the dynamics of a spring without using Newton's laws to write the differential equations of motion, and Hooke's law to characterize the elastic force. These were invented because naive physics, common sense, and qualitative reasoning were not adequate to understand the phenomena in question. Thus a computer with all the common sense of humans, and none of humanity's mathematical equipment and modelling methodology developed through the centuries, would have the modelling IQ of kindergarten school child. This is not to say that a computer with *both* common sense and formal modelling knowledge would not be a valuable intelligent assistant. After all, common sense is often what humans find hard hanging onto when they get entangled in complex mathematical or logical reasoning. But the common sense knowledge and qualitative reasoning capability may be more useful in the metalevel, as initial guesses, checks, and boundary conditions, not directly as means to create models and reach conclusions about characteristics of their behavior.

Eventually however, computers should be able to synthesize models from first principles and knowledge of finer granularity than currently possible (Iwasaki, 1989). The level of granularity needs to be matched both to the constraints of feasible computation as well as to the application domain. It does no good to derive a diagnostic model for a fault if the model cannot be created before the consequences of the breakdown are felt. Such synthesis should complement inductive modelling (as discussed above) and be integrated into a full capability modelling and simulation environment (Fishwick, 1989).

Qualitative Modelling

Reasoning from first principles is logically separable from reasoning with models of a qualitative nature. The brunt of development of the latter models in AI has been toward formalisms with greatly reduced state spaces (Kuipers, 1989). It is instructive to compare the DEVS formalism with such approaches.

- Time is an intrinsic element of the DEVS and continuous system formalisms. Both passage of time and state conditions can act as the impetus for transitions. Qualitative models use landmark and other state conditions to generate transitions.

- DEVS models have full expressive power in the sense of being able to simulate any computable model. They also span the range of complexity in the sense that both highly detailed models can be constructed as well as simplified abstractions thereof. Qualitative models are centered at the abstract level of the spectrum.

- the DEVS models resulting from homomorphic abstractions are geared to particular experimental frames determined by the particular control and diagnostic requirements. They are thus efficient from the point of view of behavior generation (simulation) and lead to readily implementable logics for device operation and diagnosis. They are further easily simplified to abstractions that provide a computationally feasible basis for device operation plans. The abstraction process in qualitative models is not well defined in terms of morphisms and is not geared to stated experimental frames.

- Due to their looser specification requirements, qualitative models are non-deterministic. An intractably large space of trajectories may result from feedback-induced branching. This mitigates against costs saved due to relative simplicity. Attempts to reduce ambiguities with additional constraints have met only partial success (Oleyeleye and Kramer, 1989). On the other hand, DEVS models can also be stochastic in nature or have tolerance ranges associated with a set of parameters. Then a set of trajectories may also be sampled to obtain reliable estimates. A well developed statistical theory is available to guide such sampling (Kleinen, 1982).

- It has been claimed that qualitative models are more robust than quantitative models, in the sense that simulation will work even where we don't fully understand underlying mechanisms. Not having to fully specify a model however is dangerous if we wish to rely on its predictions. In the current state of the art, the degree of confidence a modeller can have in his model is proportional to his understanding of the model.

- It has also been claimed that qualitative simulation is cheaper than quantitative simulation presumably because models are less detailed and need not be complete. To be made precise such a claim should be related to the abstraction level of the model, its experimental frame (intended application) and the loss of predictive power it entails. Given these qualifications, it may well be that behavior generation of a simpler qualitative model is much less costly than that of a more detailed simulation model. However, since DEVS models can span a wide range of complexity, the same thing can be said for a simple DEVS model relative to a more complex one.

Natural Language

Ability of a simulation environment to accept model descriptions in the form of natural language (Beck and Fishwick, 1989) and likewise to describe models and their behaviors would be the ultimate in user-friendly interface. In today's technology a significant speed penalty is paid for natural language capability and the universe of discourse is severely limited. Historically, there was a reason for developing other model formalisms besides natural language. They provided quantitative and rigorous means of expressing models and using them effectively to answer questions. Thus, I doubt that natural language can ever replace other means of model specification. However, if a computer were to become both an expert modelling methodologist and could express its knowledge, understanding, and findings in human understandable terms, it would be accepted as a valuable colleague.

Multiple Abstraction Levels in Model-based Diagnosis

Although the need for multiple levels of abstraction has been recognized in mainstream AI (Hamscher and Patil, 1989), there has been little consideration of the importance the morphism concept to this issue. Let us then consider applying the morphism concept to a representative AI diagnosis system that employs levels of abstraction. The ABEL system (Hamscher and Patil, 1989) has two main levels of description: clinical and physiologic (we neglect the intermediate level for simplicity). At each level, there are directed graphs linking nodes (abnormal conditions) by arrows (causal relations). I would extend the representation to add a base model, which is a detailed simulation model of the human being (much of this is unknown, but much is also known).

The clinical and physiologic levels are then represented by experimental frames, the first one very coarse (corresponding to what can be experimentally observed with standard clinical tests) and the second more refined (corresponding to more detailed biochemical experimentation). Experimenting with the base model in these frames, we summarize its dynamical behavior by the causal graphs that ABEL starts with. We should note that many assumptions are needed to do this. When we have an arrow "A causes B" in such a graph, it might mean that when the base model is started in a state characterized by A, after some time, it equilibrates in a state characterized by B. In other words, the causal graphs at the two levels are abstractions of the base model and need to be related to it by a morphic relation to be at all meaningful. This morphism may be quite approximate and one should be careful with it. For example, A may cause B for some states characterized by A but not for all.

Moreover, the two abstractions must themselves be related by a morphism to be consistent with each other. In this case, the morphism is based on the correspondence set up by the developers. This mapping is obtained conceptually as follows: for every base model state, pair up its projections on the clinical and physiologic experimental frames. In other words, look at the base model state with coarse (clinical) glasses and mark down what you see: e.g., METABOLIC ACIDOSIS. Then look at the same state with physiologic glasses and mark down, e.g. HCO_3 LOSS. These images correspond. For the abstractions to be consistent with each other, the correspondence must be a morphism, that is preserve the digraph relations: e.g. if METABOLIC ACIDOSIS causes HYPOKALEMIA then HCO_3 LOSS must cause LOW-SERUM-K. As is evident, a single step at the coarse level may be represented by a whole sequence of steps at the fine level. Morphisms deal with these and other subtleties.

Why have two or more levels of abstraction in the first place? The coarse level is where the symptoms present themselves and where it is easier to understand the causal relations (to the extent that they can be stated there). The finer level can give a better representation of the true dynamics of the system and hence can better account for the causes of an abnormality and the available remedies. The flip side of the coin: the more refined level needs quantitative data and is computationally more expensive.

The system also does not deal effectively with the evolution of diseases over time. This is apparent from the existence of feedback loops in the graph. If A facilitates B and B attenuates A, we have a loop that can equilibrate at high or low levels or oscillate. Only a dynamic simulation model, postulated in the base model, can really predict which will happen. More generally, the approximate character of the causal digraph abstraction in relation to the base model (mentioned above), should warn us not to rely on causal inferences made with it, especially those involving long chains.

The design of ABEL is entirely compatible with the multifacetted modelling framework. How then can this framework help ABEL and other such AI systems?

DEVS-Scheme in the Larger Scheme of Things

- by formalizing the system as above so that a clear understanding of the issues may be had.

- in so doing to see what issues are general in nature and hence amenable to general solutions, and also to see which ones are specific to the domain.

- by applying tools developed based on the multi-facetted framework to deal with the general issues and hence improve the validity and efficiency of the system.

For example, as indicated above, if ABEL were truly model-based, it would have an underlying simulation-type base model which could resolve problems, such as feedback loops, that are unpredictable with non-dynamic causal inference.[2] To be manageable, this would naturally have to be hierarchically decomposed into components. Using the system entity structure we can organize models of the components of a system at the different levels of abstraction. Using morphism concepts we can develop more abstract models from refined models, where possible, and in any case, test models for mutual consistency. The model base as a whole can be kept coherent by the entity structure and by tracing the effects of a modification of a model to all the models morphically related to it. More efficiency might be obtained by directing a diagnostic questions to the least abstract model which can answer it first. Only if a satisfactory answer can't be obtained, then would we go to the next more refined model.

Explanation of Events and Their Causes

Hellman and Bahuguna (1986) enumerated several ways in which explanation as studied by the philosophers could be brought to bear on explaining simulation generated model behaviors. Explanation can take the form of a trace of events which proceeded an event, or led up to a state, of special interest. More difficult is to provide

---

[2] It does employ closed-form analytic equations to resolve some feedback loops.

an analysis of what were the causes, as opposed to accidental circumstances, of the result. But this amounts to abstracting simpler models for the original base model based on observations of its behavior (Reddy *et al.*, 1986; Kosy, 1989) (see the difficulties in inductive modelling). To serve as explanations however, such models must fit human comprehension patterns which skip across arbitrary time and space intervals. Consider, for example: "when the level rises, eventually there will be an overflow". To discover this generalization, we need to mechanically detect and express, the temporal relation, "eventually"? It does little good to re-express the base model in a series of microscopic transition rules when a macroscopic abstraction is what is desired.

Explanation Based on Hierarchical Structure

A mode of explanation suggested by the philosopher Harre, is explanation based on hierarchical structure. Explanation starts by describing the topmost level of components; if the listener is not satisfied, then the components are "opened up" and the next level decomposition revealed. Example:

Child: Why does my tummy hurt?

Parent: You ate too much and your stomach (inside your tummy) is having trouble digesting all the food you ate.

Child: What's my stomach? What's digestion?

Parent: Your stomach is like a jug with lots of acid to break food up into pieces. Digestion is how your body makes use of these pieces to grow. When you eat too much, there isn't enough acid for all the food.

Child: What's acid?

Parent: ...It's time for bed now.

DEVS-Scheme in the Larger Scheme of Things

Explanation obviously stops when the explainee gets tired or when the explainer runs out of knowledge necessary to do the reductive step, or both. Hierarchical, modular model specification, as in DEVS-Scheme, is a good basis for such explanation. But it is far from sufficient. Models must be available at each hierarchical level which can characterize the to-be-explained-behavior at that level without reference to lower levels. Abstraction is needed once again. The system entity structure and a sufficiently rich model base would seem to offer a good basis for tackling this problem.

14.2.2 Quality Assurance

Ören (1987a, 1989) has demonstrated the wide variety of ways in which AI and simulation are error prone, a situation which can be alleviated with a corresponding variety of quality assurance techniques.

To take an example, advanced strong typing can be had by declaring the range of object types that values of model variables may assume. Such knowledge can greatly enhance understandability as well as serve as a basis for powerful model certification and advisory procedures. In contrast, aside from its use of the *content* and *state* structures, DEVS-Scheme does not impose any particular choice of typing of the input, state, and output objects.[5] This enables the implementation to be as general as the DEVS formalism. Of course, strong type checking is then not possible, and it is the user's responsibility to see that objects passed as arguments are in the proper form.

Ören's MAGEST advisor (Ören and Tam, 1988) shows how coupling specifications for GEST can be quality assured. Ören and

---

[5] Scheme (LISP) represents objects as lists built up and decomposed using the *cons*, *car* and *cdr* functions. For such an object, there is no pre-defined type, and hence, there is no need for DEVS-Scheme to pre-specify this type. Scheme, however, does provide special data types such as numbers and strings for convenience as well as structures that can be defined. But, again, variables cannot be declared to be of these types and hence serve merely as undiscriminating memory access locations.

Sheng (1988) show how to achieve "built-in" quality assurance within a modelling and simulation environment using semantic knowledge expressed as rules. Moose and Nance (1988) implement certain kinds of consistency analysis in discrete event specifications.

It would be desirable to extend DEVS-Scheme so that as much quality assurance as possible is done by the system. However, since much of this checking would be done at runtime, the time cost might be prohibitive. As a compromise, it might be feasible to provide two sets of methods for simulation: with, and without, quality assurance apparatus in place.

More broadly viewed, quality assurance concerns any form of augmentation of software so that the chance of error is reduced. The most difficult problems in this regard are in increasing order, syntactic, semantic and pragmatic. A system must know the user's intentions in order to judge whether an (syntactically correct and semantically acceptable) input "adds up." Traditional simulation is notorious for the number of hidden assumptions and mechanisms that could lead to deceptive results. Knowledge-based systems are not likely to be any better in this regard, unless the increased power afforded by AI tools is wisely used.

Chapter 15

EPILOGUE: THE CHALLENGE OF HIGH AUTONOMY SYSTEMS

Our conceptions about how artificial intelligence fits into the world of systems engineering have been evolving rapidly. From expert systems applied in singular contexts, there emerged the concept of intelligent control (Meystel, 1985). Here automatic control researchers attempt to come to grips with the power afforded by AI — that new, unruly, but much sought after, upstart — *vis-a-vis* their own very sophisticated, but increasingly, less applicable, theory. As such application contexts as autonomous land and space vehicles, artificial worlds, telerobotics, and factories of the future multiply, it is becoming clear that autonomy, rather than intelligence, may be the more descriptive characterization of the new systems. In general, autonomy, the power of self-determination, would seem to imply intelligence, given the need to survive in a not-so-benign real world.

As an engineering goal, seeking higher autonomy can be broken down into specific requirements in particular contexts such as: reducing the need for human intervention and supervision in remote, hazardous environments; relieving humans of attending to complex procedures not directly related to their primary objectives; and providing knowledgeable assistance in executing higher level decision making functions. While not minimizing the role of AI techniques, spelling out the engineering goals of higher autonomy might establish a less transient ladder of achievement than specifying the general, and nebulous, goal of building intelligent artifacts. Indeed, perceptions of intelligence are notoriously transient — intelligence always seems to be just beyond the cusp of the well-understood (Ören, 1989a).

Antsaklis *et al.* (1989) propose an architecture for autonomous systems which includes management, co-ordination and execution layers. Such a system needs not just one, but many, models on which to base its operation, diagnosis, repair, planning, etc. These models differ in level of abstraction and in formalism. Those used in planning and diagnosis are typically symbolic and developed with AI tools. Those at the lower levels of abstraction are typically numeric and come from classical control theory. However, both types of models are needed to take a high level plan all the way down to implementation as a series of agent actions. Thus, a key requirement for achieving high autonomy systems is the systematic development and integration of dynamic and symbolic models at the different layers. Knowledge-based simulation offers an ideal environment for designing and testing systems with increased autonomy.

Consider for example, planning and scheduling of resources and processes, a major concern of high autonomy systems. Much AI research has focussed on plan generation without addressing the goodness of the resulting plans (Fox and Smith, 1984). The issue of goodness is especially germane since planners must work on simplified abstractions of complex systems in order to be at all practical. Once plans are derived they should be evaluated in more realistic scenarios before being accepted. An integrated "Planning, Scheduling, Simulation Triumvirate" (Castillo *et al.*, 1989) can combine the capability of AI techniques to generate plans together with the ability of simulation to evaluate them.

In the DEVS-Scheme architecture, a planning and scheduling layer might be developed along side the system design layer. In this approach, the abstractions used in planning and scheduling would be

Epilogue: The Challenge of High Autonomy Systems

integrated through morphic relationships with more detailed simulation models. The rudiments of such an approach were already demonstrated in the design of model-plan units (MPUs) for autonomous robots. As we have seen, higher level planning abstractions are best expressed in symbolical form as opposed to the dynamic models which underlie them. Moreover, the diverse objects and operations require their own abstractions.

Thus, the time is ripe for developing tools for dealing seriously with multifacetted (multi-objective, multi-abstraction, multi-formalism) model/knowledge bases. Such systems should support the maintenance of models in a variety of formalisms and levels of abstraction for a variety of purposes. Building on the basis of the systems entity structure framework, they should provide tools for the systematic derivation of abstractions and the use of morphisms to integrate related models fostering coherence and evolvability. AI needs tools to enable agents to plan, diagnose, and reason effectively with respect to particular objects, but also that organize the various models that support such planning, diagnosis, and reasoning. An organized model base enables the agent to deal with the multiplicity of objects and situations in its environment and to link its high level plans with its actual low level actions. Thus multi-abstraction model bases and morphism concepts should be fundamental concerns of AI research.

Quality assurance is a fundamental and critical issue in high autonomy systems. In his comments on a draft of this book, Ören puts it this way:

"In simple terms, we do not want [high autonomy systems] to (implicitly) emulate human ignorance and stupidity. Their knowledge base and self-assessment of learning processing should prevent them to learn 'the wrong knowledge'. Furthermore, we do not want to give them the freedom of betraying humans, or at least, their masters."

Quality assurance and multi-abstraction concepts are two sides of the same coin. Consistency checking may viewed as the operational means of establishing that appropriate morphisms exist between abstractions of interest. Such checking might have to go all the way up to ascertaining conformity with broadly stated, high level constraints (*a la* Asimov's Three Laws). Here endomorphy appears again. A high autonomy system might have a "conscience", a normative model of world and self, against which planned actions are checked for their moral outcomes (Burks, 1986).

Consistency checking of this sophistication clearly involves a time/space cost and it might be achievable only with unacceptable degradation in system performance. We must then decide whether to omit the system's "conscience" and risk catastrophe or not to deploy the system in the first place. Improved multifacetted model/knowledge base environments, supporting morphy and endomorphy, might lessen the severity of such two-horned dilemmas.

This is a fitting challenge with which to end this treatise.

Appendix A

ADVANCED CONCEPTS AND FACILITIES

A.1 Continuous Model Extensions to DEVS-Scheme

The Discrete Event System Specification formalism (DEVS) was invented to do for discrete event systems what the Discrete Time System (DTSS) and the Differential Equation Specified System (DESS) formalisms already do for continuous systems. Each of these formalisms is closed under coupling. This means one can couple models together so that the resultant again specifies a model in the same formalism. Coupled models can in turn be coupled together which implies ability to construct modular hierarchical models. It is natural therefore to extend DEVS-Scheme so that the more traditional formalisms can be supported and so that models containing components expressed in different formalisms can be developed. Two such extensions have been implemented. Wang (1989) extended DEVS-Scheme to support the construction of hierarchical, modular models of continuous systems. Prahoefer and Zeigler (1989) extended

DEVS-Scheme to support multi-formalism modelling. Wang's extension combines the expressive power of conventional continuous simulation languages with the model organization facilities afforded by the system entity structure. Prahoefer's support of continuous systems modelling is more rudimentary but he demonstrates how an integrated environment can be achieved. (Unfortunately, the two extensions are mutually incompatible in their current form!)

A.1.1 CSSL Extension to DEVS-Scheme

The most widely used *continuous system simulation languages* (CSSL) are not hierarchical or modular in character. Recently, languages supporting hierarchical block diagram models have appeared but as Wang (1989) shows they lack true hierarchical, modular capability. Wang's extension to DEVS-Scheme employs the DYMOLA (Elmqvist, 1978) description language to specify models which are then translated into to DESIRE (Korn, 1989) simulation programs. DYMOLA implements a powerful concept of coupling necessary to achieve true modularity for continuous models. The orientation of such a model, i.e., the choice of input and output variables, is not fixed but is determined by its context. For example, the current into, or the voltage across, a resistor may serve as input variable, depending on whether it is being driven by a current or voltage source. The underlying equations describing the resistor are the same (Ohm's Law) but the form of computation is different depending on the choice of input variable. Model specifications in DYMOLA take a general form which is automatically transformed fit the enclosing context. It is quite straightforward to extend the system entity structure to encode DYMOLA's coupling construct, called the cut. With relatively isolated changes in Layers 1 and 2, the full capability of DEVS-Scheme's entity structure based methodology is then combined with a powerful truly hierarchical, modular CSSL.

A.2 Simulation of Multi-formalism Non-homogeneous Networks

Non-homogeneous networks support the coupling of models expressed in different formalisms. Each of the DESS and DTSS formalisms can employ the same kind of external interface specification (port-value pairs) so we can use the same kind of coupling scheme for non-homogeneous networks as for DEVS models. However, the timing of the values transmitted on the interfaces presents a problem.

Let t be a time instance where the DTSS is scheduled to undertake its state transition. Coupling the DTSS to a DEVS is straightforward. Every output at time t of the DTSS generates an external event sent to the DEVS. In the reverse direction, we can regard an output of a DEVS as held for the period until the next output is generated. Thus the output may serve as a constant input for several simulation steps of the DTSS. Note that an output may be overwritten before being sampled if the inter-output-event time of the DEVS is smaller than the simulation step of the DTSS. Coupling of a DESS to a DEVS brings up similar considerations.

The simulation of non-homogeneous networks can be done in a manner generalizing that for DEVS models. Recall that the abstract simulator for DEVS has a hierarchical structure reflecting the structure of the hierarchical DEVS. Thus a DEVS model can be directly transformed into an executable simulation program using the abstract simulator. Abstract simulators for DTSS and DESS were developed to reflect the hierarchical structure of their respective model. Each of the DTSS and DESS abstract *processors* have their own subclasses — *simulators* and *co-ordinators*. Simulation proceeds by messages passed among the simulators and coordinators. Formalisms differ in the nature of the messages passed and the detailed processing of the co-ordinators and simulators.

Having compatible processors for the different formalisms, the next important step is to provide the appropriate interfaces so that messages passed among them are properly interpreted. The coupling conventions given above were enforced in such interfaces so as to be intrinsic to the simulation process. In this way that the user need not worry about how the inter-formalism couplings are implemented but must only understand the underlying interface conventions.

A.3 Distributed Simulation of DEVS Models

The study of distributed simulation is of increasing interest as commercial multiprocessors become widely available. Hierarchical simulation is a form of distributed simulation in which hierarchical model structure is preserved. With hierarchical simulation, model structure and behavior can be more easily observed and understood in relation to the real system being modelled in a "one-one analogy" (Dekker, 1984).

Several approaches to distributed simulation of discrete event models have been developed and experimental systems implemented (Peakock *etal.*, 1979; Reynolds, 1983). The exploitation of the natural parallelism in distributed simulation must overcome the bottleneck of time-ordered event lists. Commonly, synchronization and inter-communication mechanisms are required in distributed simulations in order to maintain strict synchronization of local and global clocks. Alternatively, rollback mechanisms must exist to compensate for synchronization violations (Jefferson and Sowiqral, 1985). Though some simulation data has been obtained to measure the performance of these mechanisms, little is known about the theoretical limits of speed-up made possible with distributed simulations. Also little has been learned about the relation of these limits to properties of discrete event models.

Theoretical analysis based on the DEVS hierarchical, modular formalism has indicated that significant speed-up, of an exponential nature, is possible by employing hierarchical multiprocessor architectures as opposed to uniprocessor simulation (Concepcion, 1984; Zeigler and Zhang, in press). The DEVS-Scheme environment provides a vehicle to develop methods for collecting simulation execution data, and using this data to evaluate alternative hierarchical

Appendix

architectures for model simulation. Indeed, the simulation strategy employed in DEVS-Scheme actually realizes a "virtual" multiprocessor architecture. Were each of the processor objects realized by a physical processor, the simulation architecture would represent one possible implementation of a DEVS model on a multiprocessor system. This architecture, called the *fully distributed* assignment, is one member of a family of possibilities, representing a one-to-one assignment of model components to processors. Other possibilities exist in which models are mapped to processors in a many-to-one fashion. Such assignments are of interest since theoretical analysis suggests that communication overhead grows linearly with the height of the composition tree in the fully distributed assignment. Thus using a smaller number of processors may result in faster execution time.

Associated with a simulator or co-ordinator object in DEVS-Scheme are instance variables to measure the actual time taken to process the various messages handled by the processor during a simulation run. From these execution times, the times for co-ordination, *co-ord* and table-look up, *tab* taken by co-ordinators estimated. So far an analysis procedure based only on the handling of external events has been implemented. In this analysis, the total accumulated *co-ord* and *tab* for each co-ordinator is calculated by using the following expression:

$$co\text{-}ord + tab = (xtime + ytime) - (\text{sum over children's } xtimes).$$

Here *xtime* is the accumulated time taken by the co-ordinator to handle external event messages (*x-messages*) arriving to it from its parent. These represent inputs arriving to the component from the outside. *ytime* is the accumulated time taken to handle output messages (*y-messages*) arriving to the co-ordinator from its currently imminent child. Such *y-messages* represent outputs generated by the imminent child which are sent by the co-ordinator to its influencees as well as externally. Since the children process such messages as *x-messages*, their *xtime*s must be subtracted from the sum, *xtime* + *ytime* to obtain the actual processing time required by the co-ordinator.

An analysis algorithm, *enclose*, recommends optimal assignments of model components to processors. In the algorithm, a global variable keeps track of the number of processors being used (set to zero initially). The algorithm is invoked with *enclose*(M) where M is the root model in the model structure. *enclose*(M) also returns the expected optimal execution time (for processing external events) made possible with the recommended mapping of models to actual processors. By "enclose a model M" in the algorithm, it is meant that the model M and its children are assigned a single processor (other models may also share this processor), and M is therefore marked *enclosed*. If, for any reason, one child (M_i) of the enclosed model (M) is also marked *enclosed*, the processor assigned to M is then shared by all M's children and M_i's children, and so forth. The algorithm encloses a model with its children in the same processor, if the advantage gained by having them run in parallel is offset by the additional communication time penalty incurred. The communication time parameter, supplied by the user, estimates the time taken for messages to travel over a link (from parent to child or in reverse).

Enclosing a model and its children in a processor can be performed by flattening the model and assigning its parent to a processor (Chapter 7).

A.4 Automated Hierarchical Model Simplification

A suite of tools for supporting simplification of discrete event models was implemented based on the simplification theory developed for DEVS formalism (Zeigler, 1976,1984). The criterion for valid simplification is the homomorphism of DEVS models. In the theory, a DEVS multicomponent model (coupled model) is converted to an equivalent DEVS model (atomic model) for which a homomorphic relationship to a lumped model is sought. In the current approach, rather than attempt to establish such a homomorphism formally, the lumped model is generated from data gathered from simulation runs. Data is gathered in the form of output and transition lists

Appendix 357

which represent the behavior of the equivalent DEVS model as observed through input, state, and output reduction maps provided by the user. The lumped model is generated in such a way that if a homomorphism exists based on the reduction maps the resulting model will be deterministic. Departures from determinism show up in randomly generated transitions and outputs. The goal in providing such simplification is less to provide completely valid (i.e. deterministic) models than to provide faster running lumped models that can replace components of a hierarchical model so that the remainder of the model can be more efficiently run and tested.

The simplification tools are implemented as an extension to the DEVS-Scheme environment. A new class *observers* is further specialized into subclasses: *atomic-model-observers* and *coupled-model-observers*. The observers acquire and store the model behavior at various points in the model structure hierarchy (they are assigned to processors in a manner preserving the parent-child relation defining the hierarchical structure). A code-generator generates the lumped model from the observation data. Details are in Sevinc (1988).

A.4.1 Methodology for Lumped Model Generation and Use

Below we outline the overall procedure in which a lumped model is generated and substituted into the original model for the component model it simplifies.

- a specific model is pruned and transformed into a hierarchical model to be experimented with. Call this the base model,

- the input, state and output reduction maps are defined and assigned to the various components in the model hierarchy for which simplification is desired,

- the simulators and co-ordinators assigned to these models are outfitted with observers,

- the atomic components of the base model are initialized, the simulation is started and the output and transitions lists are acquired by the observers,

- the lumping procedure is invoked to extract a lumped version of the to-be-simplified component,

- The same entity structure is repruned making the entity for the to-be-simplified component a leaf. This component is now to be represented by the atomic-model generated in the preceding step, and

- a transformation process follows to construct a second version of the base model, similar in all respects to the original, except for the replacement of the to-be-simplified component by its lumped counterpart.

Sevinc (1988) reports on experiments with this methodology on a computer network systems which demonstrated its efficacy. Generally, as the number of components lumped together increases the base model simulation time increases exponentially while the lumped model time is approximately constant. Problems in data storage and retrieval, due to large record size, arose when the to-be-simplified component exceeded a certain size. To limit the dimensions of the stored states, further development should give the modeller the ability to group base model states into classes which will act as states for the lumped model (Zeigler, 1984; Sanders and Meyer, 1988; Meyer et. al., 1989).

A.5 Variable Structure Models

Praehofer is also working on an extension to DEVS-Scheme that will allow specification of variable structure models (Zeigler and Praehofer, 1989). The simplest case exhibiting a variable structure occurs when a single component changes from one structure state to another. This is called a *multi-model* by Ören (1989a). As an example we can think of the well known parachute problem where the

Appendix

dynamics change from free fall to retarded fall after opening the parachute. More generally, structure change of this kind involves resetting of parameter values and/or replacement of one component by another. This situation is represented in a system entity structure where one variant of an entity replaces another. In replacing one variant by a second, the values of the common variables have to be transferred as well. For example, the variable representing the height of the falling man has to be transferred from the model of the free fall to that of retarded fall.

A much more complex situation occurs when the problem calls for creation, destruction or modification of components during simulation runs. Modelling of flexible manufacturing systems may require components within a model to be assembled and disassembled. Exchange of components among different sub-networks of a model may be involved. For example, it should be possible to transfer a component representing a resource to a new "place of work" where it is needed more urgently. The modelling of intelligent agents involved in structure changes involves yet more complexity. The model counterpart should have an image (= model) of the prevailing world situation upon which its decisions are based.

The scheme for event-based control discussed in Chapter 11 can be adopted to the problem of controlling the structure state of a variable structure model. Recall that in event-based control, the decisions of the control device are based on the internal model of the system to be controlled. In variable structure modelling, the "internal model" has to represent the possible structure states, and hence the system entity structure, of the variable structure model. In normal simulation, the entity structure is pruned only between distinct simulation runs. This pruning is driven by the objectives of the human modeler. In variable structure simulation this pruning process has to be done by a goal-driven agent and it uses a system entity structure as internal knowledge of possible structure states.

The development of tools to model and simulate such multilevel, endomorphic systems will be a challenge for further development. However, the current DEVS-Scheme simulation environment provides a strong basis on which an environment for variable structure modelling and simulation can be built. A bi-level variable structure architecture can be developed in which each level is a modular, hierarchical DEVS system. The lower level represents the current structure of a model; the upper level is the decision maker directing the structural change. An atomic model on the upper level would have its own system entity structure which represents the possible structure states of the lower level unit it is controlling. Information on state changes occurring at the lower level can be transmitted to the decision layer using observation and introspection methods as in Sections 5.4 and 12.3.

A.6 Using Object-Oriented Concepts to Support Extensibility of Layer 1 with Respect to Layer 2

The code of the *prune* and *transform* processes is designed so that it does not have to be modified when new sub-classes of *models* are added at Layer 1. This requires that all the information required by these processes is accessible by querying SCOOPS or suitably encapsulated into class-specific methods. For example, when pruning arrives at a multiple entity, the user must be offered a choice of *kernel-models* sub-classes to represent it. To do this, the pruner asks SCOOPS to find and report the current sub-classes of *kernel-models*. This obviates the need to independently keep, and revise, a list of sub-classes with every addition (or removal) of a new sub-class. Having been given a choice of sub-class, *prune* must elicit information specific to this sub-class and *transform* must make consistent use of this information to create the user's desired instance of the class. Embedding such class-specific data in *prune* and *transform* would require us to revise these procedures with every addition (or removal) of a *kernel-models* sub-class. Instead, once the class is known, the *prune* and *transform* procedures let the sub-class itself perform those operations which are specific to it.

Appendix 361

A.7 Converting Non-modular to Modular Form

Object-oriented simulation languages typically employ two forms of message passing: *tell* and *ask*, for operations and queries, respectively. (*Tell* and *ask* are specialized forms of *send* used in SCOOPS.) For example, consider a customer in a barbershop. The CUSTOMER object may send a message to the BARBER using its *ready* method:

(tell barber ready myname shave&haircut)

To convert such models to DEVS-Scheme modular form the output function of CUSTOMER would look have the following:

(make-content 'port 'ready 'value '(myname shave&haircut))

In the external transition function of BARBER, we have:

(case (content-port x)

...

('ready (code of method named ready which takes (content-value x) as argument ...)

...

This uncouples CUSTOMER and BARBER. Each may now be loaded independently and tested or used as components in other models. To couple them together in the same model, we create a coupled model with barber and customer as components. For example, a digraph model, BARBERSHOP would be specified by the SES:

(make-entstr 'barbershop) ...

(add-coupling customer barber 'ready 'ready)

...

More likely, there will be many customers so that a multiple entity mapping to a kernel model would be used. The coupling would then be specified in the *out-in coup* but the principle remains the same.

Reformulation of queries such as:

(send barber ask how-much?)

is handled similarly, except that we need an additional port pair for sending the response of the barber back to the customer. The discussion of introspection in Chapter 13 shows how this is done.

Appendix B

DEVS AND GSMP: SOME RELATIONS

This appendix examines the relationship of the DEVS formalism to a mathematically oriented formalism intended to represent the stochastic nature of discrete event models. The formalism, GSMP (Generalized Semi-Markov Process) generalizes the standard Markov process description. Since it is at the state description level, it is similar to DEVS.[1] To enable tractable analytic solutions the GSMP state space must be discrete i.e., a countable set. In the following, we show that very simple DEVS behaviors require an infinite state space and hence cannot be expressed by tractable GSMPs. Indeed, merely having a component keep its scheduled event time despite interruption is impossible without a continuous state set. After showing the limitations of GSMP, we show it can be represented within DEVS. We conclude that DEVS is the more expressive formalism, trading expressiveness for mathematical tractability.

---

[1] However, GSMP does not deal with external events and hence with modular structures.

B.1 Some Simple Behaviors of DEVS

We begin with a review of the set theoretic formulation of the DEVS formalism.

A DEVS (Discrete Event System Specification) is a structure:

$M = \langle X, S, Y, \delta_{int}, \delta_{ext}, \lambda, ta \rangle$
X is the set of external (input) event types
S is the sequential state set
Y is the output set
$\delta_{int} : S \rightarrow S$, the internal transition function
$\delta_{ext} : Q \times S \rightarrow S$, the external transition function
where Q is the total state set $= (s,e) | s \in S, 0 <= e <= ta(s)$
$ta : S \rightarrow R_{+,0,inf}$, the time advance function
$\lambda : S \rightarrow Y$, the output function

Now consider definitions of several simple behaviors. The following are universally quantified over all free variables:

A DEVS M is *time-left preserving* if $ta(\delta_{ext}(s,e,x)) = ta(s) - e$.

This means that the time of the next internal event is unaffected by the occurrence of any input event x. To see this consider M where it has just entered state s. The next internal event is then scheduled to occur in time $ta(s)$. When M receives input x after an elapsed time e has occurred, it transits to state $s' = \delta_{ext}(s,e,x)$. If we wish to have the scheduled time for the subsequent occurrence of the next internal event be unaffected, the time advance for s' should be that for s reduced by the time, e which has already elapsed.

A DEVS M can *assume arbitrary time-advances* if $ta(\delta_{ext}(s,e,x)) = x$, where $x \in R_{+,0}$.

Here we are requiring that the time advance of M be set by its last input which is allowed to be any non-negative real.

A DEVS M is *periodic* if $ta(\delta_{int}(s)) = ta(s)$.

Here we require that the internal events of M occur with constant inter-event spacing, i.e., the time advance value does not change with

Appendix 365

any internal transition. (Of course, an external event could alter the fixed time advance to another value.)

B.2 Proof that the DEVS Behaviors Require Uncountable State Sets

In the normal form of DEVS, the time advance is represented explicitly within the sequential state in the component σ. Thus ta just reads σ to get the time value:

$S = \{s \mid s = (phase, \sigma, ...)\}$.

where $ta(phase, \sigma, ...) = \sigma$.

It is easy to exhibit models that satisfy the above definitions using normal form DEVS.

The DEVS M_1 is time-left preserving where

$\delta_{ext,1}(\sigma, e, x)) = \sigma - e$.

(In DEVS-Scheme, (define (ext1 s e x) (continue)))

The DEVS M_2 can assume arbitrary time-advances if

$\delta_{ext}(\sigma, e, x)) = x$.

(In DEVS-Scheme,
  (define (ext2 s e x)(set! (state-sigma s) (content-value x))))

The DEVS M_3 is periodic where $\delta_{int,3}(\sigma, T) = (T, T)$.

(In DEVS-Scheme,
  (define (int3 s)(set! (state-sigma s) (state-period s))))

An example demonstrating that all three properties can be easily satisfied at once is:

(define (ext s e x)
(set! (state-period s) (content-value x))
(continue))
(define (int s) (set! (state-sigma s) (state-period s)))

Here an external event sets the period to a desired value, but leaves the time to next internal event untouched. At the next internal event, the saved period takes effect.

We see that a normal form DEVS must have an uncountable sequential state set due to the presence of σ. We now show that this is true for arbitrary DEVS which are required to have reasonable time handling properties.

Theorem: If M is either time-left preserving or can assume arbitrary time-advances then M has an uncountable sequential state set.

Proof: Let M be time-left preserving.

Assume that S is countable. Then since $[0, ta(s)]$ is uncountable, there is a pair of unequal elapsed times, e and e', belonging to it such that

$$\delta_{ext}(s,e,x) = \delta_{ext}(s,e',x).$$

(Otherwise, S would have a subset which was in one-to-one correspondence with $[0, ta(s)]$ and would be uncountable.) Since M is time-left preserving, it is easy to show that

$$ta(\delta_{ext}(s,e,x)) - ta(\delta_{ext}(s,e',x)) = e' - e.$$

This is a contradiction since the left hand side vanishes while the right hand side does not. Thus, contrary to assumption, S is uncountable. The proof for the case of arbitrary time-advances is similar albeit more direct.

As a corollary of the theorem, we can show that GSMP is severely limited in expressive power.

Corollary: GSMP as defined by Glynn (1989) cannot express DEVS models which are time-left preserving or can assume arbitrary time-advances.

B.3 Expressing GSMP within DEVS

We now give a DEVS representation of discrete event systems (DES) as formulated by C.G. Cassandras and S.G. Strickland (1989). A DES is a structure:

Appendix

$$DES = (S_d, E, \delta, F)$$

where

S_d is a countable set of states
E is a countable set of events
δ is a transition function
F is a distribution function that can be sampled for event lifetimes.

To realize an equivalent DEVS, we represent each event as having its own DEVS component.

For each i in E, M_i is a normal form DEVS that has external event set $X_i = E$, phase set $= S_d$, whose state as determined by δ, is set by the incoming (imminent) event type:

$$\delta_{ext}(s_d,\sigma,e,x)) = (\delta(s_d,x),\sigma')$$

or by itself, if this is the imminent event

$$\delta_{int}(s_d,\sigma) = (\delta(s_d,x),\sigma'))$$

where

σ' is sampled from F_i if i is imminent or to be rescheduled, and σ - e, otherwise

The output function reports the event type of the imminent event to the others:

$$\lambda(s_d,\sigma) = i \text{ (where } i \text{ is the index of } M_i).$$

In the above we allow the lifetime random variable F_i to return a non-negative real or the symbol 'inf. Recall that 'inf is treated in the DEVS formalism in a manner consistent with its meaning as infinity. Thus if $\sigma' = $ 'inf, then M_i will be passivated, or as can be said, the event type it represents will be come *infeasible*. The feasibility status of event in this approach is automatically carried in the time-left (also called residual time) variable. Other formalisms do not extend the reals with an infinity value and greatly complicate the description of state transitions.

A separate decision is whether an event should be rescheduled. As should be clear in the above definition, this means that a decision whether σ' should be given a newly sampled lifetime or just updated with the new elapsed time. Once again note that by extending the lifetime range to include 'inf, we automatically capture the four combinations of feasibility:

	σ	σ'
feasible $\to$ infeasible	real	'inf
infeasible $\to$ infeasible	'inf	'inf
infeasible $\to$ feasible	'inf	real
feasible $\to$ feasible	real	real'

where real' denotes an updated or new real value as result of a rescheduling decision.

Note that an imminent event must always be given a new lifetime.

When the component DEVSs are coupled together in a broadcast fashion, and all started in the same phase, s_d, the resulting DEVS will be isomorphic to the timed DES defined by C.G. Cassandras and S.G. Strickland (1989). As acknowledged by the latter, this state space has real variable components so is not countable. Since they are also refer to their model as a GSMP they contradict Glynn's (1989) definition of a GSMP.

Bibliography

Adelsberger, H.H. et al. (1986), "Rule Based Object Oriented Simulation Systems", In: *Intelligent Simulation Environments*, (eds.: P.A. Luker & H.H. Adelsberger), Simulation Series, Vol. 17, SCS, San Diego, CA.

Allen, J.F. (1984), "Towards a General Theory of Action and Time", *Artificial Intelligence*, Vol. 23, pp. 123–134.

Allen, P.D. and B.A. Wilson (1988), "Modeling Qualitative Issues in Military Simulations with the RAND-ABEL Language", *Proc. 1988 Winter Sim. Conf.*, San Diego, CA. pp. 372–380.

Antsaklis, P.J., K.M. Passino and S.J. Wang (1989), "Towards Intelligent Autonomous Control Systems: Architecture and Fundamental Issues", *J. Intelligent and Robotic Systems*, Vol. 1, No. 4, pp. 315–342.

Balci, O. (1988), "The Implementation of Four Conceptual Framework for Simulation Modeling in High-level Languages", *Proc. Winter Sim. Conf.*, SCS Publications, San Diego, CA.

Balci, O. and R.E. Nance (1986), *Simulation Model Development: The Multidimensionality of the Computing Technology Pull*, Tech. Rep. SRC-86-012, Systems Research Center, Virginia Tech, Blacksburg, VA.

Beck, H.W. and P. A. Fishwick (1989), "Incorporating Natural Language Description into Modeling and Simulation, *Simulation J.*, Vol 52, pp. 102–109.

Bobrow, D.G. (1985), *Qualitative Reasoning about Physical Systems*, MIT Press, Cambridge, MA.

Bobrow, D.G. (1976), "Dimensions of Representation", In: *Representation and Understanding: Studies in Cognitive Science*, (eds.: D.G. Bobrow & A. Collins), Academic Press, NY.

Bobrow, D.G. and M.J. Stefik (1983), *The LOOPS Manual*, Xerox Corporation, Palo Alto, CA.

Boulding, K.E. (1956), *The Image: Knowledge in Life and Society*, University of Michigan Press, Ann Arbor, MI.

Buchanan, B.G. and E.H. Shortliffe, *Rule-Based Expert Systems*, Addison-Wesley, CA, 1984.

Burks, A.W. (1986), *Robots and Free Minds*, University of Michigan Press, Ann Arbor, MI.

Burks, A.W. (1963), *Cause, Chance and Reason*, University of Chicago Press, Chicago, IL.

Cassandras, C.G. and S.G. Strickland (1989), "Sample Path Properties of Timed Discrete Event Systems", *Proceedings of the IEEE*, Vol. 77, No. 1, January, pp. 59–71.

Castillo, D., S. Green, D. Davis, and M. McRoberts (1989), "The Role of Simulation in Planning, Scheduling, and Simulation Triumvirate", *Proceedings of Fourth AAAI Workshop on AI and Simulation*, pp. 15–22.

Cellier, F. E. (1986), "Enhanced Run-Time Experiments for Continuous System Simulation Languages". *Proceedings of the SCS Multiconference on Languages for Continuous System Simulation*, (ed.: F.E. Cellier), SCS Publications, San Diego, CA, pp. 78–83.

Cellier, F.E. (1989), "General System Problem Solving Paradigm for Qualitative Modeling", In: *Qualitative Simulation, Modeling, and Analysis*, (eds.: P.A. Fishwick and P.A. Luker), Springer Verlag, Berlin (in press).

Chandy, K.M. and J. Misra (1981), "Asynchronous Distributed Simulation via a Sequence of Parallel Computations", *Communications of the ACM*, April 1981, Vol 24, No. 11, pp. 198–206.

Chiu, C. (1989), "Constructing Qualitative Domain Maps from Quantitative Simulation Models", In: *Artificial Intelligence, Simulation and Modelling* (eds.: L.A. Widman, K.A. Loparo, and N. Nielsen), J. Wiley, NY. pp. 275–299.

Chow, C. (1990), *Design of Interfaces for Hierarchical, Knowledge-Based Simulation and Control*, Doctoral Thesis, Dept. of Electrical and Computer Engineering, University of Arizona, Tucson, AZ. (in press)

Concepcion, A.I. (1985), " Mapping Distributed Simulators onto the Hierarchical multibus Multiprocessor Architecture", In: *Distributed Simulation 1985*, (ed.: P. Reynolds), Society of Computer Simulation, San Diego, California.

Concepcion, A.I. and B.P. Zeigler (1988), "DEVS formalism: A Framework for Hierarchical Model Development", *IEEE Transactions on Software Engineering*, Vol. 14, No. 2, Feb., pp. 228–241.

Dahl, O.J. and K. Nygaard (1966), "Simula: An Algol-based Simulation Language", *CACM 9*, pp. 671–688.

Davis, P.K. (1986), "Applying Artificial Intelligence Techniques to Strategic-Level Gaming and Simulation", In: *Modelling and Simulation Methodology in the Artificial Intelligence Era*, M.S. Elzas, T.I. Ören, B.P. Zeigler (Eds.). North Holland, Amsterdam.

Davis, P.K. (1989), *Studying First-Strike Stability with Knowledge-Based Models of Human Decision Making*, RAND Note, R-3689-CC, The RAND Corporation, Santa Monica, CA.

Davis, P.K. and H. E. Hall (1988), *Overview of System Software in the RAND Strategy Assessment System*, RAND Note, N-2755-NA, The RAND Corporation, Santa Monica, CA.

Davis. R. and R. G. Smith (1983), "Negotiation as a Metaphor for Distributed Problem Solving", *Artificial Intelligence*, Vol. 20, No. 1, pp. 63–109.

De Kleer, Y. (1989) "Qualitative Physics, A Personal View", In: *Readings in Qualitative Physics*, (eds.: D. Weld and Y. de Kleer), Morgan Kaufman, Palo Alto.

Delaney, W. and E. Vaccari (1989), *Dynamic Models and Discrete Event Simulation*, Marcel Dekker, NY.

Dekker, L. (1984), "Concepts for an Advanced Parallel Simulation Architecture", In: *Simulation and Model-Based Methodologies: An Integrative View* (eds.: T.I. Ören, M.S. Elzas, and B.P. Zeigler), Springer-Verlag, NY. pp. 235–280.

Dreyfus, H and S. Dreyfus (1986), *Mind over Machine*, MacMillan, NY.

Ehr, W. and A. Wnuk (1985), "Discrete Event Simulation of a Model Family with Boris", *Proc. 11 IMACS World Congress*, Oslo, Norway.

Eisenberg, M. (1989), *Programming in Scheme*, The Scientific Press, Redwood City, CA.

Elmqvist, H. (1978), *A Structured Model Language for Large Continuous Systems*. Doctoral Dissertation, Dept. of Automatic Control, Lund Institute of Technology, Lund, Sweden.

Elzas, M.S. (1986a), "The Applicability of Artificial Intelligence Techniques to Knowledge Representation in Modelling and Simulation", In: *Modelling and Simulation Methodology in the Artificial Intelligence Era*, (eds.: M.S. Elzas, T.I. Ören, B.P. Zeigler). North Holland, Amsterdam, pp. 19–40.

Elzas, M.S. (1986b), "Relations Between Artificial Intelligence Environments and Modelling & Simulation Support Systems", In: *Modelling and Simulation Methodology in the Artificial Intelligence Era*, (eds.: M.S. Elzas, T.I. Ören, B.P. Zeigler). North Holland, Amsterdam, pp. 61-78.

Elbert, J.L. and R.M. Salter (1986), "Modeling Neural Networks in Scheme", *Simulation J.*, 46:5, pp. 193-199.

Fishwick, P.A. (1987), "A Taxonomy for Process Abstraction in Simulation Modelling", *IEEE Int. Conf. Sys. Man & Cyb.*, Vol. 1, pp. 144-151.

Fishwick, P.A. (1988), "The Role of Process Abstraction in Simulation", *IEEE Trans. Sys. Man & Cyb.*, Vol. 18, No. 1, pp. 18-39.

Fishwick, P.A. (1989a), "A Study of Terminology and Issues in Qualitative Simulation", *Simulation J.*, Vol. 51, No. 7, pp. 5-9.

Fishwick, P.A. (1989b), "Qualitative Methodology in Simulation Model Engineering", *Simulation J.*, Vol. 52, No. 3, pp. 95-101.

Fishwick, P.A. (1989c), "Abstraction Level Traversal in Hierarchical Modelling", In: *Modelling and Simulation Methodology: Knowledge Systems Paradigms* (eds.: M.S. Elzas, T.I. Ören, B.P. Zeigler), North Holland Pub. Co., Amsterdam pp. 393-430.

Fishwick, P.A. and P.A. Luker (1990), *Qualitative Simulation Modeling and Analysis*, Springer-Verlag, Berlin (to appear).

Fox, M.S., and S.F. Smith (1984), "ISIS: A Knowledge Based System for Factory Scheduling", *Expert Systems*, Vol. 1, pp. 25-49.

Friedland, P. and M. Zweben, *1989-90 Progress Report and Plan*, AI Research Branch, TR RIA-89-04-03-08, NASA Ames Research Center, .

Futo, I (1985), "Combined Discrete/Continuous Modeling and Problem Solving", *AI, Graphics and Simulation*, (ed.: G. Birtwistle), SCS Pub., San Diego, CA.

Garzia, R.F., M.R. Garzia, and B.P. Zeigler (1986), "Discrete Event Simulation", *IEEE Spectrum*, December, pp. 32-36.

Genesereth, M.R. and N.H. Nilsson (1987), *Logical Foundations of Artificial Intelligence*, Margan Kaufmann, Palo Alto, CA.

Goldberg, A. and R. David (1983), *Smalltalk-80: The Language and its Application*, Addison-Wesley, Reading, MA.

Glynn, P. W. (1989), "A GSMP Formalism for Discrete Event Systems", *Proceedings of the IEEE*, Vol. 77, No. 1, January, 14–23.

Gylmour, C., R. Scheines, P. Spirtes, and K. Kelly (1987), *Discovering Causal Structure*, Academic Press, NY.

Hamscher, W. and Patil, R. (1989), "Tutorial on Model-Based Diagnosis", *Proc. of Eleventh IJCAI*, AAAI Press, Palo Alto.

Harmon, P. and D. King, *Expert Systems: Artificial Intelligence in Business*, Prentice Hall, 1985

Hardt, S. H. (1989), "Aspects of Qualitative Reasoning and Simulation for Knowledge Intensive Problem Solving", In: *Modelling and Simulation Methodology: Knowledge Systems*, M.S. Elzas, T.I. Ören, B.P. Zeigler (Eds.). North Holland, Amsterdam.

Hayes, N. (1989), "Biosphere II — A Prototype for the Future", *IEEE Computer*, Vol. 22, No. 5 (May), pp. 11.

Hayes, P.J. (1981) "The Logic of Frames", In: *Readings in Artificial Intelligence*, (eds.: Webber, B.L. and N.J. Nilsson), pp 451–458.

Hellman, D.H. and A. Bahugana (1986), "Explanation Systems in Computer Simulation", *Proc. Winter Simulation Conf.*, SCS Publications, pp. 90–114.

Higa, K.H. (1988), *End-user Logical Database Design: The Structure Entity Model Approach*, Doctoral Dissertation, MIS Dept., University of Arizona.

Higa, K.H. and O.R. Liu Sheng (1989), *An Object-Oriented Methodology for Database/Knowledgebase Coupling: An Implementation of the Structured Entity Model in Nexpert System*, Working Paper, MIS Dept., University of Arizona.

Ho, Y. (1989), "Editors Introduction", *Special Issue on Dynamics of Discrete Event Systems, Proceedings of the IEEE*, Vol. 77, No. 1.

Hogeweg, P. and B. Hesper (1986), "Knowledge Seeking in Variable Structure Models", In: *Modelling and Simulation in the Artificial Intelligence Era*, (eds.: M.S. Elzas, T.I. Ören, B.P. Zeigler), North Holland Pub. Co., Amsterdam, pp. 227-244.

Hogrefe, D. (1985), "Tool support for Model Description with SDL and Simulation", In: *Cybernetics and Systems*, (ed.: R. Trappl), D. Reidel Pub. Co.

Holland, J.H. (1986), "Escaping Brittleness: the possibilities of general-purpose learning algorithms applied to parallel rule-based systems", In: *Machine Learning: an Artificial Intelligence Approach*, Volume II, R.S. Michalski, J.G. Carbonell, and T.M. Mitchel (Eds.), Morgan-Kaufmann Pub. Co., Los Altos, CA.

Hu, J. (1989), *Towards A Knowledge-Based Design Support Environment For Design Automation and Performance Evaluation*, Doctoral Dissertation, University of Arizona, Tucson, AZ.

Hu, J and J.W. Rozenblit (1989), "Knowledge Acquisition Based on Representation for Design Model Development", In: *Knowledge-Based Simulation: Methodology and Applications* (eds.: P.A. Fishwick and R.D. Modjeski), Springer Verlag, Berlin.

Iwasaki, Y. (1989), "An Integrated Scheme for Using First-Principle Physical Knowledge for Knowledge-based Simulation", *Proceedings of Fourth AAAI Workshop on AI and Simulation*, pp. 57-59.

Jefferson, D. and H. Sowizral (1985),"Fast concurrent simulation using the time warp mechanism", In: *Distributed Simulation 1985*, (ed.: Paul Reynolds), Society of Computer Simulation, San Diego, California.

Karp, P.D. and P. Friedland (1989), "Coordinating the Use of Qualitative and Quantitative Knowledge in Declarative Device Modeling", In: *Artificial Intelligence, Simulation and Modelling* (eds.:

L.A. Widman, K.A. Loparo, and N. Nielsen), J. Wiley, NY. pp. 189–206.

Keene, S.E. (1988), *Programming in Common Lisp Object-Oriented System*, Addison-Wesley, Ma.

Kelly, M. (1989), *System Entity Structure Representation of Life Sciences Laboratory on the Space Station*, Masters Thesis, Dept. of Electrical and Computer Engineering, University of Arizona, Tucson, AZ.

Kerckhoffs, E.J.H. and G.C.Vansteenkiste (1986), "The Impact of Advanced Information Processing on Simulation – an Illustrative Review", *Simulation J.*, 46:1, pp. 17–26.

Kerckhoffs, E.J.H., Koppelaar, H., and H.J. Van Den Herik, "Towards Parallel Intelligent Simulation", In: *Artificial Intelligence, Simulation and Modelling* (eds.: L.A. Widman, K.A. Loparo, and N. Nielsen), J. Wiley, NY. pp. 207–230.

Kim, T., (1988), *A Knowledge-Based Environment for Hierarchical Modelling and Simulation*, Doctoral Dissertation, University of Arizona, Tucson.

Kim, T., G. Zhang, B.P. Zeigler (1988), "Entity Structure Management of Continuous Simulation Models", *Proc. Summer Sim. Conf.*, Seattle.

Kim, T., and B.P. Zeigler (1989), "ESP-Scheme: A Realization of System Entity Structure in a LISP Environment", *Proc. AI and Simulation Multiconference*, SCS Publications, San Diego, CA.

Klahr, P. (1986), "Expressibility in ROSS, an Object-Oriented Simulation System", In: *Artificial Intelligence in Simulation* (eds.: G. C. Vansteenkiste, E.J.H. Kerckhoffs & B.P. Zeigler), SCS Publications, San Diego, CA.

Kleijnen, J. P.C. (1982), Experimentation with Models: Statistical Design and Analysis Techniques. In: *Progress in Modelling and*

Simulation, (ed.: F.E. Cellier), Academic Press, London, pp. 173–185.

Klir (1985), *Architecture of Systems Problem Solving*, Plenum Press, New York.

Korn, Granino A. (1989), *Interactive Dynamic System Simulation*. McGraw-Hill, New York.

Kosy, D.W., "Applications of Explanation in Financial Modeling", In: *Artificial Intelligence, Simulation and Modelling* (eds.: L.A. Widman, K.A. Loparo, and N. Nielsen), J. Wiley, NY. pp. 487–509.

Kuipers, B. J., "Qualitative Simulation", *Artificial Intelligence*, pp. 289–338.

Kuipers, B. J., "Qualitative Reasoning with Causal Models in Diagnosis of Complex Systems", In: *Artificial Intelligence, Simulation and Modelling* (eds.: L.A. Widman, K.A. Loparo, and N. Nielsen), J. Wiley, NY. pp. 257–274.

Langely, P., H.A. Simon, G.L. Bradshaw, and J.M. Zytkow (1987), *Scientific Discovery*, MIT Press, Cambridge.

Livny, M. (1987), "DELab – A Simulation Laboratory", *Proc. of Winter Simulation Conf., Atlanta, GA*, SCS Publications, San Diego, CA.

Luh, C.J. (1989), *Hierarchical Modelling of Mobile, Seeing Robots*, Masters Thesis, Dept. of Electrical and Computer Engineering, University of Arizona, Tucson, AZ.

Manivannan, S. (1989), "Just-in-time Simulation using Artificial Intelligence", *Proc. Winter Simulation Conf.*, SCS Publications, San Diego, CA.

Mesarovic, M.D., D. Macko, and Y. Takahara (1970), *Theory of Hierarchical, Multilevel Systems* Academic Press, NY.

Mesarovic, M.D. and Y. Takahara (1975), *General Systems Theory: Mathematical Foundations*, Academic Press, NY.

Melamed, B. and R.J.T. Morris, (1985), "Visualization Simulation: Performance Analysis Workstation", *IEEE Computer*, Vol. 18, pp. 87-94.

Meyer, J.F., A. Movaghar, and W.H. Sanders (1985), "Stochastic Activity Networks: Structure, Behavior and Application", *Proc. Int. Workshop on Timed Petri Nets*, Torino Italy, pp. 106-115.

Meystel, A. and J.Y.S. Luh (1985), *IEEE International Symposium on Intelligent Control*, IEEE Press, Philadelphia, Pa.

Middleton, S. and R. Zanconato (1986), "BLOBS: An Object-oriented Language for Simulation and Reasoning", In: *Artificial Intelligence in Simulation* (eds.: G.C. Vansteenkiste, E.J.H. Kerckhoffs & B.P. Zeigler), SCS Publications, San Diego, CA, pp. 130-135.

Minsky, M. (1985), "Models, Minds, Machines", *Proc. IFIPS*, AFIPS Press, Montvale, NJ, pp. 45-39.

Minsky, M. (1986), *Society of the Mind*, Simon and Schuster, New York.

Moose, R.L. and R.E. Nance, *The Design and Development of an Analyser for Discrete Event Model Specifications*, Tech. Rep. SRC-87-010, Systems Research Center, Virginia Tech, Blacksburg, VA.

Nilsson, N.J. (1981), *Principles of Artificial Intelligence*, Tioga Pub. Co., Palo Alto, CA.

Nance, R.E. (1987), "A Conical Methodology: A Framework for Simulation Model Development", *Proc. Conf. on Methodology and Validation*, SCS Pubs. SAn Diego, pp. 38-43.

Narain, S. and J. Rothenberg (1989), "A History-Oriented Calculus for Simulating Dynamic Systems", *Proceedings of Fourth AAAI Workshop on AI and Simulation*, pp. 78-81.

O'Keefe, R. (1986), "Simulation and Expert Systems- A Taxonomy and Some Examples", *Simulation*, 46:1, pp. 10–16.

Oleyeleye, O.O. and M.A. Kramer (1989), "The Role of Causal and Noncausal Constraints in Steady-State Qualitative Modelling", In: *Artificial Intelligence, Simulation and Modelling*, (eds.: L.A. Widman, K.A. Loparo, and N. Nielsen). J. Wiley, NY. pp. 257–274.

Ören, T.I. (1975), "Simulation of Time-Varying Systems", In: *Advances in Cybernetics and Systems*, (ed.: J. Rose), Gordon and Beach Science Pub.. England, pp. 1229–1238.

Ören, T.I. (1980), "Design of SEMA: A Software System for Computer-Aided Modelling and Simulation of Sequential Machines", *Proc. Winter Simulation Conference*, IEEE Press, NY, pp 113–123.

Ören, T.I. (1984), "GEST – A Modelling and Simulation Language Based on System Theoretic Concepts", In: *Simulation and Model-Based Methodologies: An Integrative View*, (eds.: T.I. Ören, B.P. Zeigler, and M.S. Elzas), North-Holland Pub. Co., Amsterdam, pp. 3–40.

Ören, T.I. (1986), "Artificial Intelligence and Simulation", In: *Artificial Intelligence in Simulation* (eds.: G.C. Vansteenkiste, E.J.H. Kerckhoffs & B.P. Zeigler), SCS Publications, San Diego, CA. pp. 3–8.

Ören, T.I. (1987a), "Artificial Intelligence and Simulation: From Cognitive Simulation toward Cognizant Simulation", *Simulation*, Vol 48., No. 4, pp. 129–130.

Ören, T.I. (1987b), "Quality Assurance Paradigms for Artificial Intelligence in Modelling and Simulation", *Simulation*, Vol 48., No. 4, pp. 149–151.

Ören, T.I. (1987c), "Taxonomy of Simulation Model Processing", In: *Encyclopedia of Systems and Control* (ed.: M. Singh), Pergamon Press.

Ören, T.I. (1989a), "A Paradigm for Artificial Intelligence in Software Engineering", In: *Advances in Artificial Intelligence in Software Engineering* (ed.: T.I. Ören), Vol. 1, JAI Press, Greenwich, CN (in press).

Ören, T.I. (1989b), "Bases for Advanced Simulation: Paradigms for the Future", In: *Modelling and Simulation Methodology: Knowledge Systems Paradigms* (eds.: M.S. Elzas, T.I. Ören, B.P. Zeigler), North Holland Pub. Co., Amsterdam, pp. 29-44

Ören, T.I. (1989c), "Artificial Intelligence and Quality Assurance in Computer-Aided System Theory", In: *CAST–Computer-Aided Systems Theory, Lecture Notes*, Springer-Verlag, Berlin (in press).

Ören, T.I. and G. Sheng, (1988), "Semantic Rules and Facts for an Expert Modelling and Simulation System", *Proc. 12th IMACS World Congress, Paris*, Balzter Pub. Co., Switzerland.

Ören, T.I. and J.C. Tam, (1988), "An Expert Modelling and Simulation System on Sun Workstation, *Proc. European Simulation Multiconference*, Nice, pp. 255-260.

Ören, T.I. and B.P. Zeigler (1979), "Concepts for Advanced Simulation Methodologies", *Simulation J.*, Vol. 32, No. 3, pp. 69-82.

Overstreet, C.M. and R.E. Nance (1986), "World View Based Discrete Event Model Simplification", In: *Modelling and Simulation Methodology in the AI Era*, (eds.: M.S. Elzas, T.I. Ören, and B.P. Zeigler) North Holland Pub., pp. 165-170.

Padulo, L. and M.A. Arbib (1974), *System Theory*, Saunders, Philadelphia, Pa.

Pedgen, C.D. (1983), "Introduction to SIMAN", *Proc. Winter Simulation Conf.*, SCS Press.

Peterson, J.L. (1981), *Petri Net Theory and Modeling of Systems*, Prentice Hall, Englewood Cliffs, NJ.

Pichler, F. (1984), "Symbolic Manipulation of Systems Models", In: *Simulation and Model-Based Methodologies: An Integrative View* (eds.: T.I. Ören, M.S. Elzas, and B.P. Zeigler), Springer-Verlag, NY, 1984, pp. 217–234..

Praehofer, H. and B.P. Zeigler (1989), "Modelling and Simulation of Non-Homogeneous Models", In: *CAST–Computer-Aided Systems Theory, Lecture Notes*, Springer-Verlag, Berlin (in press).

Radiya, A. and R. Sargent (1989), "ROBS: Rules and Objects Based Simulation", In: *Modelling and Simulation Methodology: Knowledge System Paradigms*, (eds.: M.S. Elzas, B.P. Zeigler, and T.I. Ören), North Holland Pub., Amsterdam, pp. 241–256.

Rajagopalan, R. (1986), "The Role of Qualitative Reasoning in Simulation", In: *Artificial Intelligence in Simulation* (eds.: G.C. Vansteenkiste, E.J.H. Kerckhoffs & B.P. Zeigler), SCS Publications, San Diego, CA.

Reddy, Y.V., M.S. Fox and N. Husain (1985), "Automating the Analysis of Simulations in KBS", *Proc. SCS Multiconference*, San Diego, CA.

Reddy, Y.V., M.S. Fox, N. Husain, and M. McRoberts (1986), "The Knowledge-Based Simulation System", *IEEE Software*, March, pp. 26–37.

Robertson, P. (1986), "A Rule Based Expert Simulation Environment", In: *Intelligent Simulation Environments*, (eds.: P.A. Luker & H.H. Adelsberger), Simulation Series, Vol. 17, SCS, San Diego, CA.

Rozenblit, J.W. (1985), *A Conceptual Basis for Model-Based System Design*, Doctoral Dissertation, Dept. of Computer Science, Wayne State University, Detroit, MI.

Rozenblit, J.W., J. Hu and Y. Huang (1989) "An Integrated, Entity-Based Knowledge Representation Scheme for System Design", *Engineering Design Journal*, (in press).

Rozenblit, J.W. and Y. Huang (1987), "Constraint-Driven Generation of Model Structures", *Proc. of Winter Simulation Conf.*, SCS Publications, San Diego, CA.

Rozenblit, J.W. and Y. Huang (1989), "Rule-Based Generation of Model Structures in Multifacetted System Modelling and System Design", *ORSA J. on Computing* (in press).

Rozenblit, J.W. and Zeigler, B.P. (1985), "Concepts for Knowledge-Based System Design Environments", *Proc. Winter Simulation Conference*, SCS Publications, San Diego, CA. pp. 223–231.

Rozenblit, J.W. and B.P. Zeigler (1986), "Entity-based Structures for Modelling and Experimental Frame Construction", In: *Modelling and Simulation Methodology in the Artificial Intelligence Era* (eds.: M.S. Elzas, T.I. Ören, B.P. Zeigler), North Holland Pub. Co., Amsterdam, pp. 195–210.

Rozenblit, J.W., S. Sevinc, and B.P. Zeigler (1986), "Knowledge-based Design of LANs Using System Entity Structure Concepts", *Proc. Winter Simulation Conf.*, Washington, D.C., pp. 885–865.

Ruiz-Mier, S. and J. Talavage. "A Hybrid Paradigm for Modeling of Complex Systems", In: *Artificial Intelligence, Simulation and Modelling* (eds.: L.A. Widman, K.A. Loparo, and N. Nielsen), J. Wiley, NY, pp. 381–395.

Sanders, W.H. (1988), *Construction and Solution of Performability Models based on Stochastic Activity Networks*, Doctoral Diss., University of Michigan, Ann Arbor.

Sanders, W.H. and J.F. Meyer (1989), "Reduced Base Model Construction Methods for Stochastic Activity Networks", *Proc. Third Int. Workshop on Petri Nets and Performance Models*, Kyoto Japan.

Sampson, J.R. (1984), *Biological Information Processing: Current Theory and Computer Simulation*, Wiley, NY.

Sarjoughian, H. (1989), *Diagnosis of Laboratory Device Operation Faults in Event-based Control*, Masters Thesis, Dept. of Electrical and Computer Engineering, University of Arizona, Tucson, AZ.

Sauer, C.H. and K. M. Chandy (1980), *Computer Systems Performance Modelling*, Prentice Hall, Englewood Cliffs, NJ.

Sevinc, S. (1988), *Automatic Simplification of Models in a Hierarchical Modular Simulation Environment*, Doctoral Dissertation, University of Arizona, Tucson.

Sevinc, S. and B.P. Zeigler (1988), "Entity Structure Based Design Methodology: A LAN Protocol Example", *IEEE Transactions on Software Engineering*, Vol. 14, No. 3, March, pp. 375–383.

Shaw, M. and B.R. Gaines (1986), "The Communal Scientist", In: *Intelligent Simulation Environments* (eds.: P.A. Luker and H.H. Adelsburger), SCS Publications, San Diego CA.

Simon, H.A. (1969), *The Sciences of the Artificial*, MIT Press, Cambridge, MA.

Smith, J.D. (1989), *An Introduction to Scheme*, Prentice Hall, Englewood Cliffs, NJ.

Stroustrup, B. (1986), *The C++ Programming Language*, Addison-Wesley, Reading, MA.

Texas Instruments (1986), *PC-Scheme Users Manual*, Science Applications Press.

Thomasma, T. and Ulgen, O. M. (1988), "Hierarchical, Modular Simulation Modelling in Icon-based Simulation Program Generators for Manufacturing", *Proc. Winter Simulation Conf.*, San Diego, pp. 254–262.

Vesantera, P.J. and F.E. Cellier (1989), "Building Intelligence into an Autopilot – Using Qualitative Simulation to Support Global Decision Making", *Simulation*, 52(3), pp. 111–121.

Wang, Q. (1989), *Management of Continuous Models in DEVS-Scheme: Time Windows for Event-Based Control*, Masters Thesis, Dept. of Electrical and Computer Engineering, University of Arizona, Tucson, AZ.

Waterman, D.A. *A Guide to Expert Systems*, Addison-Wesley Publishing Co., 1985.

Weinreb, D., D. Moon, and R. Stallman (1983), *Lisp Machine Manual*, MIT, Cambridge, MA.

Widman, L.E., "Semi-Quantitative "Close-Enough" Dynamic Systems Models: An Alternative to Qualitative Simulation", In: *Artificial Intelligence, Simulation and Modelling* (eds.: L.A. Widman, K.A. Loparo, and N. Nielsen), J. Wiley, NY, pp. 159–188.

Wilkins, D. E. (1988), *Practical Planning: Extending the Classical AI Planning Paradigm*, Morgan Kaufmann, Palo Alto, CA.

Winograd, T. (1976), "Frame Representations and the Declarative/Procedural Controversy", In: *Representation and Understanding: Studies in Cognitive Science*, (eds.: D.G. Bobrow & A. Collins), Academic Press, NY.

Wymore, A.W. (1967), *A Mathematical Theory of Systems Engineering: The Elements*, Wiley, NY.

Yonezawa, A. and M. Tokoro (1987), *Object-Oriented Concurrent Programming*, MIT Press, Cambridge, MA.

Zadeh, L.A. and C.A. Desoer (1963) *Linear System Theory, The State Space Approach*, McGraw Hill, NY.

Zeigler, B.P. (1976), *Theory of Modelling and Simulation*, Wiley, NY. (Reissued by Krieger Pub. Co., Malabar, FL. 1985).

Zeigler, B.P. (1984), *Multifacetted Modelling and Discrete Event Simulation*, Academic Press, London and Orlando, FL.

Zeigler, B.P. (1985), "System-theoretic Representation of Simulation Models", *IIE Transactions*, 16:1, pp. 19–34.

Zeigler, B.P. (1986a), "System Knowledge: A Definition and its Implications", In: *Modelling and Simulation Methodology in the Artificial Intelligence Era* (eds.: M.S. Elzas, T.I. Ören, B.P. Zeigler), North Holland Pub. Co., Amsterdam, pp. 15–17.

Zeigler, B.P. (1986b), "Toward a Simulation Methodology for Variable Structure Modelling", In: *Modelling and Simulation Methodology in the Artificial Intelligence Era* (eds.: M.S. Elzas, T.I. Ören, B.P. Zeigler), North Holland Pub. Co., Amsterdam, pp. 195–210.

Zeigler, B.P. (1987a), "Knowledge Representation from Minsky to Newton and Beyond", *Applied Artificial Intelligence*, Vol. 1, pp. 87–107.

Zeigler, B.P. (1987b), "Hierarchical, Modular Discrete Event Modelling in an Object Oriented Environment", *Simulation J.*, Vol. 49:5, pp. 219–230.

Zeigler, B.P. (1989a), "The DEVS Formalism: Event-based Control for Intelligent Systems", *Proceedings of IEEE*, Vol. 77, No. 1, pp. 27–80.

Zeigler, B.P. (1989b), "Concepts for Distributed Knowledge Maintenance in Variable Structure Models", In: *Modelling and Simulation Methodology: Knowledge System Paradigms*, (eds.: M.S. Elzas, B.P. Zeigler, and T.I. Ören), North Holland Pub., Amsterdam, pp. 45–54.

Zeigler, B.P., F.E. Cellier, and J.W. Rozenblit (1988), "Design of a Simulation Environment for Laboratory Management by Robot Organizations", *J. Intelligent and Robotic Systems*, Vol. 1, pp. 299–309.

Zeigler, B.P. and T.G. Kim (1989), "The DEVS-Scheme Modelling and Simulation Environment", In: *Knowledge-Based Simulation: Methodology and Applications*, (eds.: P. Fishwick and R. Modjeski), Springer Verlag (to appear).

Zeigler, B.P. and H. Praehofer (1989), "System Theory Challenges in the Simulation of Variable Structure and Intelligent Systems", In: *CAST–Computer-Aided Systems Theory, Lecture Notes*, Springer-Verlag, Berlin (in press).

Zeigler, B.P. and G. Zhang (1989), "Mapping Hierarchical Discrete Event Models to Multiprocessor Systems: Algorithm, Analysis, and Simulation", *J. Parallel and Distributed Computers*, (in press).

Zeigler, B.P., T.Kim, S. Sevinc and G. Zhang, (1989), "Implementing Methodology-based Tools in DEVS-Scheme", In: *Modelling and Simulation Methodology: Knowledge System Paradigms*, (eds.: M.S. Elzas, B.P. Zeigler, and T.I. Ören), North Holland Pub., Amsterdam, pp. 431–450.

Zhang, G. and B.P. Zeigler (1989), "The System Entity Structure: Knowledge Representation for Simulation Modeling and Design", In: *Artificial Intelligence, Simulation and Modelling* (eds.: L.A. Widman, K.A. Loparo, and N. Nielsen), J. Wiley, NY, pp. 47–73.

Index

– A –

ABEL, morphism analysis of, 341
abstraction, 21, 251, 292, 321, 330, 341, 349, 356
acceptor, 184
acquaintances, 8
active values, 5
activities as rules, 205
add-couple, 151, 194
add-introspection, 285
add-item, 151
add-mult, 194
add-mult-mult, 202
add-port-pair, 181, 182
aggregation, 321
applicability of frames to models, 112
architecture
    broadcast, 183
    clustered, 200
    divide and conquer, 69
    hierarchical, 200
    multilayered, 200
    multiserver, 69
    pipeline, 69
    pseudo-code, 72

architecture, using controlled-models, 196
architectures
    multiprocessor, 117, 157
    system entity structure, 157
archivability, 331
artificial intelligence, 347
Asimov's Three Laws, 350
aspect, in SES, 10, 34, 36, 147
atomic-models, 52, 59, 75, 81, 91, 170, 215
    normal form, 75
    simulator, 79
autonomous system, 233, 315, 316, 347
axiomatic specification, 331

– B –

broadcast-models, 181, 183, 188
browsability, 328

– C –

cataloguing, of PESs, 301
causality, 8
cellular-models, 182

class definition,
    object-oriented, 4, 24
closure under coupling, 328
co-ordinators, 62
coherence, of model base, 307
communication protocol, 9
composition tree, 11, 31
concurrent computing, 328
conscience, as an internal
    model, 350
consistency checking, 346
constraints, 221
content-structure, 52
context sensitive pruning, 305
continuous simulation, 330
controlled-models, 182, 196, 233
converting non-modular to
    modular form, 361
coupled-models, 59
    co-ordinator, 105
    digraph-models, 61
    kernel-models, 61
coupling, 7, 29
coupling knowledge, 146
CSSL, extension of
    DEVS-Scheme, 352
current-item, 151

– D –

declarative knowledge, 3, 4
decomposition, 7
decomposition knowledge, 145
DEDS, 41
deepening, 165
delayed binding, 9

demons, 5, 217
design evaluation, 333
DESIRE, 352
DESS formalisms, 351
development time, 335
DEVS formalism, 42, 75, 258, 328, 351, 364
    basic models, 48
    coupled models, 55
    definition, 364
    elapsed time, 366
    relationship to GSMP, 44, 363, 366
    review of, 44
DEVS models for diagnosis, 290
DEVS models for event-based control, 279
DEVS models for planning, 287
DEVS relative to GSMP, 364
DEVS representation of
    dynamic systems, 258
DEVS vs qualitative models, 339
DEVS-formalism, 328
DEVS-Scheme, 41, 43, 69, 75, 77, 231, 326, 351
    atomic-models, 52, 59
    forward-models, 205, 210
    table-models, 267, 287
    broadcast-models, 188
    classes, 59
    co-ordinators, 62

INDEX

controlled-models, 196
coupled-models, 59
  digraph-models, 61
  kernel-models, 61, 180
deep-devs, 165
distributed simulation, 354
flat-devs, 165
forward-models, 205, 210
introspection in, 285
kernel-models
  broadcast-models, 180, 181
  cellular-models, 182
  controlled-models, 182
  hypercube-models, 181
language, 58
layer 0, 327
layer 1, 328
layer 2, 331
layer 3, 332
layers, 326
methodology, 231
processors, 62
  co-ordinators, 62
  root-co-ordinators, 62
  simulators, 62
prune, 39, 160
restart, 154
retrieve, 39
root-co-ordinators, 62
simplification, 356
simulation, 105
simulation modes, 66
simulation process, 62

simulators, 62
system entity structure, 149
table-models, 267, 287
timing measurements, 355
transform, 39, 154, 156
diagnosis, 290
differential equations models, 258
digraph-models, 61, 94, 99, 103, 280
Discrete Event Dynamic Systems, 41
discrete event world views, 336
discrete-event simulation, 88
discrete-time simulation, 330
distributed simulation, 329
  DEVS, 354
    optimal model/processor mapping, 356
distributed simulation, speed-up, 354
divide and conquer architecture, 133
divide and conquer, 117
DYMOLA, 352
dynamic model, 313
dynamic programming, 288
dynamic systems formalisms, 5
dynamic systems, DEVS representation of, 258

– E –

elapsed time, use of, 170
empirical, 8
endomorphic agent, 16, 250
endomorphic simulation model, 16
endomorphic simulators, 16
endomorphic system, 250, 349, 359
endomorphism, 251
endomorphism, in war game, 316, 321
endomorphy, 15, 250, 252, 315
entities, 10
entity, in SES, 34, 36, 147
environments in Scheme, 113
event-based control, 275
event-based controller, 280
evolvability, 20, 28
execution speed, 335
experimental frame, 31, 45, 90, 184
    acceptor, 184
    digraph model, 99
    distributed, 202
    generator, 91, 184
    transducer, 91, 184
experimental frame/model separation, 329
expert system, 11
explanation, 343
extensibility, 21, 28, 327, 330, 332, 360

extensions to DEVS-Scheme, continuous model, 351
external event observation, 113
external models, 250, 267, 313

– F –

flattening, 165
fluid handling systems, 234
formalism, 3
    DESS, 351
    DEVS, 351
    DTSS, 351
    modular vs non-modular, 336
    non-modular vs modular, 361
forward-models, 205, 210, 233, 280, 290, 336
    expressive power, 215
FRASES, 332
fuzzy model, 321

– G –

Generalized Semi-Markov Process, 363
generative, 10
generator, 91, 184
get-children, 181, 182
get-influencees, 181, 182
get-receivers, 181, 182
get-versions-of, 303
goal driven pruning, 332
goal-table, in table-models, 271

INDEX

granularity, 330
graphics, 335
GSMP, 44, 363, 364, 366

- H -

help facilities, 336
hierarchical construction, 329
hierarchical model, 31
hierarchical robot model, 235
hierarchical structure, 8
hierarchical synthesis, 28
hierarchy of levels, 14
homomorphism, 5, 251, 261
hypercube-models, 181

- I -

inductive modelling, 337
infinite regress, in
    endomorphic systems,
    318, 319, 322
inheritance, 5, 216
    system entity structure,
    146, 148
inheritance, in
    forward-models, 216
inheritance, multiple, 28
inheritance, object-oriented, 27
initialization, 141
instrumentation, of models, 112
intelligent agent, 250, 315, 316
internal event observation, 113
internal models, 16, 250, 267, 313

internal state, 8
introspection, in
    DEVS-Scheme, 285
introspection, in war game, 316, 321
isomorphic replicatability, 329

- K -

KAR, 334
kernel-models, 61, 180
    broadcast-models, 181
    cellular-models, 182
    controlled-models, 182
    hypercube-models, 181
knowability, 6
knowledge, 11, 81
knowledge acquisition, 334
knowledge representation
    system entity structure, 145
knowledge, of self, 315, 316
knowledge-based simulation
    systems, 1
knowledge-based system, 4

- L -

laboratory model, 254
laboratory robot model, 233
laboratory, automated, 247
laboratory, space-borne, 247
laundry robot model, 225
life support system, 36
load-entstr, 151
lookahead, in endomorphic
    systems, 321

– M –

make-entstr, 151
mathematical systems theory, 7
message passing, 5
methodology, DEVS-Scheme, 231
methodology, distributed simulation, 355
methodology, endomorphic systems, 318, 319, 322
methodology, for event-based control, 258, 279, 292
methodology, in intelligent agents, 319, 322
methodology, multifacetted, 252, 322
methodology, simplification, 357
methods, 5, 20, 21, 75, 83, 84
    add-ext-activities, 208
    add-ext-event-observation, 113
    add-int-activities, 208
    add-int-event-observation, 113
    add-introspection, 285
    add-port-pair, 61, 181, 182
    def-state, 77
    ext-transition, 61, 81
    get-children, 61, 181, 182
    get-influencees, 61, 181, 182
    get-receivers, 61, 181, 182
    get-sv, 84
    inherit-from, 217
    inject, 83, 142
    int-transition, 61, 80
    make-class, 190
    make-members, 180
    make-new, 190
    output?, 61
    plan, 287
    set-sv, 84
    time-advance?, 61
    translate, 61, 181, 182
mobile components, space management, 238
model, 69, 364
    dynamic
        state-transition, 313
        updatable, 313
    event-based control, 276
    external, 250, 267
    functional types, 313
        dynamic, 313
        static, 313
    fuzzy, 321
    internal, 250, 267
    qualitative, 321
    self, 315, 316
    state-transition
        predictive, 314
        retrodictive, 314
    variable structure, 330, 358
    war game, 316, 321
model base, 10, 33

INDEX

model base cataloguing, 332
model base, coherence, 307
model instrumentation, 112
model specification, 328
model synthesis via pruning, 331
model, self-embedding, 319
model base organization, 155
model-based diagnosis, 341
model-plan unit, 256, 264, 292

model/experimental frame pairs, 103, 184
modelling, 45, 59, 170, 183, 238, 239, 243, 250, 258, 276, 337
model, 11
modular system models, 8
modularity, 29, 328
MPU, 256
multi-component models, 55
multi-abstraction model base, 341, 349
multi-formalism simulation, 330
multiserver, 117
multifacetted methodology, 252
multifacetted modelling methodology, 13
multilevel robot model, 235
multiple entity, in SES, 34, 149, 192, 229, 240
multiplicity of objectives, 12
multiserver architecture, 118

– N –

natural language, 340
non-modular conversion, 361

– O –

object-oriented concepts, 81
object-oriented programming, 19, 327, 360
object-oriented programming languages, 4
objects, 4, 20
optimal model/processor mapping, 356

– P –

partitioned system entity structure, 304, 311
PES, 39, 300
phase variable, use of, 170
pipeline, 117
pipeline architecture, 128
planning, 287
probability distribution, 88
processor
    interruptable, 170
    multi-, 69, 70, 183, 200
    selective, 173
    simple, 69, 72, 75, 88
processors, 118, 128, 133
prune, 39
pruned entity structure, 39, 160, 229, 231, 300
pruning, 39, 160, 220, 231
pruning operations, 11
pruning, context sensitive, 305, 331

pruning, goal driven, 332
pseudo-code, 72, 120, 276

– Q –

qualitative model, 321
qualitative modelling , 339
qualitative models vs DEVS, 339
qualitative physics, 337
quality assurance, 345, 349
queuing, approach to, 88

– R –

Rand Strategy Assessment model, 321
reasoning from first principles, 337
replicatability, 327
representation scheme, 2
resolution level, 321
restart, 154
retrieve, 39
reusability, 28, 332
reuse, of pruned entity structures, 300, 303
robot cognition system, 239
robot model, hierarchical, 235
robot models, 225, 233
    task co-ordination, 225
robot models laboratory, 233
robot, fluid handling, 264
root-co-ordinators, 62
rule-based model formalism, 205
    advantages of, 209

rule-based modelling, 330
rules, activities, 205

– S –

Scheme, 27
Scheme environment, 113
Scheme programming language, 24
SCOOPS, 24, 27
search, 288
select function, 105
selectfn, 105
self-knowledge, 315
self-knowledge, Minsky's views, 316
self-models, 315
self-models, Minsky's views, 316
self-reference, 319
SES, 33, 145, 192, 229, 235, 247, 254, 319
SES/MB, 28, 155, 331
simplification, 330, 356
simulation, 45, 62, 105, 110, 133
simulation environment, 327
simulation languages, 31
simulation, history of, 42
simulation, of coupled-models, 105
simulator of atomic models, 79
simulators, 62
slots, 5
software design attributes, 327

INDEX

space management, mobile components, 238
space-borne laboratory, 247, 311
specialization, in SES, 34, 36, 147, 216, 219, 229
specializations, 10
speed-up, in hierarchical simulation, 354
state trajectories, 122
state-structure, 75
state-table, in table-models, 271
static model, 313
super-simulation, in DEVS-Scheme, 285
symbolic/numeric processing, 327
synthesis constraints, 331
system entity structure, 33, 145, 192, 202, 229, 235, 247, 254, 311, 319
  axioms, 146
  coherence, 307
  commands
    add-constraints, 221
    add-couple, 151, 194
    add-item, 151
    add-mult, 194
    add-mult-mult, 202
    add-priority, 151
    load-entstr, 151
    make-entstr, 151
    partitioned, 304
    prune, 160, 220, 231
    set-current-item, 151
  constraints, 221
  model base, 155
system entity structure, within model, 359
System Entity Structure/Model Base, 10, 28, 331
system manipulations, 329
system theory, 328

– T –

table-models, 267, 287
  goal-table, 271
  state-table, 271
  time windows, 271, 272
taxonomic knowledge, 145
taxonomical hierarchy, 5
testing, 29, 141, 292, 327, 329
  atomic-models, 82
time base, 8
time windows, in table-models, 271, 272
time windows, in event-based control, 276
transducer, 91, 184
transform, 39, 154, 156, 231
translate, 181, 182

– V –

variable structure modelling, 358
variable structure models, 330
vision, modelling of, 243